Lecture Notes in Computer Science 8376

Commenced Publication in 1973
Founding and Former Series Editors:
Gerhard Goos, Juris Hartmanis, and Jan van Leeuwen

Kai Fischbach   Udo R. Krieger (Eds.)

Measurement, Modelling, and Evaluation of Computing Systems and Dependability and Fault-Tolerance

17th International GI/ITG Conference, MMB & DFT 2014
Bamberg, Germany, March 17-19, 2014
Proceedings

Springer

Volume Editors

Kai Fischbach
Udo R. Krieger
University of Bamberg
Faculty of Information Systems and Applied Computer Sciences
An der Weberei 5, 96047 Bamberg, Germany
E-mail:{kai.fischbach, udo.krieger}@uni-bamberg.de

ISSN 0302-9743   e-ISSN 1611-3349
ISBN 978-3-319-05358-5   e-ISBN 978-3-319-05359-2
DOI 10.1007/978-3-319-05359-2
Springer Cham Heidelberg New York Dordrecht London

Library of Congress Control Number: 2014932291

LNCS Sublibrary: SL 2 – Programming and Software Engineering

Typesetting: Camera-ready by author, data conversion by Scientific Publishing Services, Chennai, India

Printed on acid-free paper

Springer is part of Springer Science+Business Media (www.springer.com)

Preface

As conference chairs, it is our pleasure to present this LNCS volume with its contributions on performance and dependability evaluation techniques for advanced distributed systems, computer and software architectures, and communication networks. The papers it contains were presented at the 17th International GI/ITG Conference on "Measurement, Modelling and Evaluation of Computing Systems" and "Dependability and Fault-Tolerance" (MMB and DFT 2014), held during March 17–19, 2014, at Otto-Friedrich-University Bamberg in Germany.

Since the start of the biennial MMB conference series in the early 1980s, we have seen substantial changes in the field of performance evaluation, dependability, and fault-tolerance of computer and communication systems. Modelling and simulation of isolated computer systems and the analysis of their performance and dependability metrics by standard queueing or stochastic Petri net models have been enhanced with more advanced or new methodologies, such as stochastic process algebras or stochastic network calculus, and new areas of application have entered the realm of this research.

Today, we cope with the scientific challenges of very complex, interconnected system architectures that comprise a multitude of hardware and software components. In recent years, measurement, mathematical modelling, and analysis techniques related to these advanced interconnected systems and complex networks have also been expanding into new vital application areas, including energy networks, energy-efficient systems, and social networks among others. Thus, the Program Committee of MMB and DFT 2014 organized three satellite workshops covering corresponding research topics in these fast-evolving areas:

- The International Workshop on Demand Modeling and Quantitative Analysis of Future Generation Energy Networks and Energy-Efficient Systems (FGENET 2014)
- The International Workshop on Modeling, Analysis and Management of Social Networks and their Applications (SOCNET 2014)
- The Second Workshop on Network Calculus (WoNeCa 2014)

Following a thorough review procedure by at least three reviewers and after a careful selection process, the Program Committee of MMB and DFT 2014 conference compiled an interesting scientific program that included 16 regular papers and three tool presentations. In addition, the MMB and DFT 2014 program was fortunate to have two distinguished keynote speeches:

1. "Probabilistic Analysis of the RESTART Protocol and Checkpointing in Computer Reliability" by distinguished Professor Dr. Dr.h.c. Søren Asmussen, Aarhus University, Denmark, whose scientific achievements were honored by the John von Neumann Theory Prize 2010 and the Gold Medal for Great Contributions in Mathematics, awarded by the Sobolev Institute of Mathematics of the Siberian Branch of the Russian Academy of Sciences in 2011

2. "On the Performance of Caching in Information-Centric Networks" by Dr. James W. Roberts, IRT-SystemX, France, who has been honored with the Arne Jensen Lifetime Achievement Award from the International Teletraffic Congress (ITC)

As conference chairs, we express our gratitude to all members of the Program Committee and all external reviewers for their dedicated service, maintaining the quality objectives of the conference, and for the timely provision of their valuable reviews.

We express our sincere appreciation to Otto-Friedrich-University Bamberg as the conference host, as well as to all the members of the local Organizing Committee of MMB and DFT 2014 for their great efforts devoted to the success of the conference.

We thank all the authors for their submitted contributions, all the speakers for their lively presentations, and all the participants for their contributions to interesting discussions.

We acknowledge the support of the EasyChair conference system and express our gratitude to its management team for the commitment to serve the scientific community in an altruistic manner.

Further, we thank Springer, in particular Alfred Hofmann, Vice-President Publishing Computer Science, for unceasing support and excellent management of the LNCS publishing project.

Finally, it is our hope that readers will find these MMB and DFT 2014 proceedings informative and useful for their future research on measurement, modelling, analysis, and performance evaluation of advanced distributed, dependable, or fault-tolerant systems.

March 2014   Kai Fischbach
                                                   Udo R. Krieger

Organization

MMB and DFT 2014 was jointly organized by the German "Gesellschaft für Informatik (GI)" and "Informationstechnische Gesellschaft im VDE (ITG)," Technical Committees on "Measurement, Modelling and Evaluation of Computing Systems (MMB)" and "Dependability and Fault-Tolerance (DFT)," in cooperation with the Faculty of Information Systems and Applied Computer Science, Professorship of Computer Science, on behalf of Otto-Friedrich-University Bamberg, Germany.

Executive Committee

Conference Chairs

Kai Fischbach   Udo R. Krieger

Local Organization Chairs

Cornelia Schecher   Marcel Großmann

Tools Chair

Philipp Eittenberger

Publication Chairs

Philipp Eittenberger   Marcel Großmann

Web Chairs

Andreas Keiper   Klaus Schneider

Program Committee

Lothar Breuer	University of Kent, UK
Peter Buchholz	TU Dortmund, Germany
Hans Daduna	Universität Hamburg, Germany
Hermann de Meer	Universität Passau, Germany
Klaus Echtle	Universität Duisburg-Essen, Germany
Bernhard Fechner	Universität Augsburg, Germany
Markus Fidler	Leibniz Universität Hannover, Germany
Kai Fischbach	Otto-Friedrich-Universität Bamberg, Germany
Reinhard German	Universität Erlangen-Nürnberg, Germany
Boudewijn Haverkort	University of Twente, The Netherlands

Gerhard Haßlinger	Deutsche Telekom, Germany
Holger Hermanns	Universität des Saarlands, Germany
Joost-Pieter Katoen	RWTH Aachen, Germany
Jörg Keller	FernUniversität in Hagen, Germany
Peter Kemper	The College of William and Mary, USA
Udo R. Krieger	Otto-Friedrich-Universität Bamberg, Germany
Wolfram Lautenschläger	Alcatel-Lucent Stuttgart, Germany
Axel Lehmann	Universität der Bundeswehr München, Germany
Ralf Lehnert	TU Dresden, Germany
Erik Maehle	Universität zu Lübeck, Germany
Michael Menth	Universität Tübingen, Germany
Peter Reichl	Universität Wien, Austria
Johannes Riedl	Siemens AG, Germany
Francesca Saglietti	Universität Erlangen-Nürnberg, Germany
Jens Schmitt	TU Kaiserslautern, Germany
Markus Siegle	Universität der Bundeswehr München, Germany
Peter Sobe	HTW Dresden, Germany
Helena Szczerbicka	Leibniz Universität Hannover, Germany
Kurt Tutschku	BTH Karlskrona, Sweden
Oliver Waldhorst	Karlsruher Institut für Technologie, Germany
Max Walter	Siemens AG, Germany
Verena Wolf	Universität des Saarlands, Germany
Bernd Wolfinger	Universität Hamburg, Germany
Katinka Wolter	Freie Universität Berlin, Germany
Armin Zimmermann	TU Ilmenau, Germany

Additional Reviewers

Andreas Berl	Universität Passau, Germany
Steffen Bondorf	TU Kaiserslautern, Germany
Desheng Fu	Leibniz Universität Hannover, Germany
Marcel Großmann	Otto-Friedrich-Universität Bamberg, Germany
Florian Heimgärtner	Universität Tübingen, Germany
Kai-Steffen Hielscher	Universität Erlangen-Nürnberg, Germany
Andrey Kolesnikov	Universität Hamburg, Germany
Stanislav Mudriievskyi	TU Dresden, Germany
Martin Riedl	Universität der Bundeswehr München, Germany
Mark Schmidt	Universität Tübingen, Germany
Bharath Siva Kumar Tati	Universität der Bundeswehr München, Germany
Patrick Wüchner	Universität Passau, Germany

Abstracts of Invited Talks

Probabilistic Analysis of the RESTART Protocol and Checkpointing in Computer Reliability

Søren Asmussen

Department of Mathematical Sciences
Aarhus University
Ny Munkegade
DK-8000 Aarhus C, Denmark
`asmus@imf.au.dk`

Abstract. A task like the execution of a computer program or the transmission of a packet on a communication line may fail. There are various protocols for how the system will deal with this. We consider here RESTART where the task needs to be restarted from scratch, with the aim of assessing probabilities of large delays (in contrast to other protocols like RESUME, this was long an open problem). The result is, somewhat surprisingly, that unless the task time is a bounded random variable, the delay time is always heavy-tailed (for example, with a power tail). We further consider the effects of inserting checkpoints in the task, such that upon failure restarting needs only be done from the last checkpoint.

This is joint work with Lester Lipsky, Pierre Fiorini, Robert Sheahan and Tomasz Rolski.

On the Performance of Caching in Information-Centric Networks

James Roberts

Institut de Recherche Technologique SystemX
8 Avenue de la Vauve BP 30012
91120 Palaiseau, France
james.roberts@irt-systemx.fr

Abstract. Whether the architecture of the future Internet is an incremental evolution of IP or a clean slate design like CCN, it is clear that caching will be increasingly used to reduce the amount of content traffic the network has to carry. It is important to understand the performance of caching in order to quantify its impact on traffic flows and to draw correct conclusions regarding the optimal network structure. We discuss recent work on modelling cache performance, identifying the crucial importance of how user requests are distributed over the vast catalogue of available content and stressing the difficulty in estimating this popularity distribution. Lastly, we consider the memory-bandwidth tradeoff that determines the potential cost advantage of investing in storage capacity rather than in the infrastructure that would otherwise be necessary to transport content across the network. Our evaluations suggest large caches at the network edge are preferable to equipping routers with limited capacity content stores, as envisaged in some proposed architectures.

Table of Contents

Full Papers

Tool Papers

PH and MAP Fitting
with Aggregated Traffic Traces

Jan Kriege and Peter Buchholz

Department of Computer Science, TU Dortmund,
44221 Dortmund, Germany
{jan.kriege,peter.buchholz}@udo.edu

Abstract. *Phase Type Distributions* (PHDs) and *Markovian Arrival Processes* (MAPs) are versatile models for the modeling of timing behavior in stochastic models. The parameterization of the models according to measured traces is often done using *Expectation Maximization* (EM) algorithms, which have long runtimes when applied to realistic datasets. In this paper, new versions of EM algorithms are presented that use only an aggregated version of the trace. Experiments show that these realizations of EM algorithms are much more efficient than available EM algorithms working on the complete trace and the fitting quality remains more or less the same.

Keywords: Phase-type distributions, Markovian Arrival Processes, Expectation Maximization Algorithm, Trace Aggregation.

1 Introduction

An adequate representation of inter-event times, let it be inter-arrival times of packets in a computer network, time between failure in dependable systems, or service times in computer systems, is a fundamental requirement in stochastic modeling. For models that are solved using analytical or numerical techniques and often also for simulation models inter-event times are described by Markov models. Based on the work of Marcel Neuts [20,21], *Phase Type Distributions* (PHDs) and *Markovian Arrival Processes* (MAPs) have been defined and are nowadays widely used in stochastic modeling. PHDs and MAPs are quite general classes of stochastic models that allow one to approximate many distributions and stochastic processes arbitrarily closely [22,11]. However, the parameterization of the models to match some observed behavior is a complex non-linear optimization problem. The general problem is to find the parameters of a PHD or MAP of a given order with respect to an observed sequence of inter-event times such that it is likely that the observed sequence is generated from the PHD or MAP, respectively. This is commonly denoted as parameter fitting. In some application areas, like computer networks, traces can be huge and contain more than a million entries. Methods for parameter fitting of PHDs are a research topic for more than 30 years. Parameter fitting for MAPs is much harder such that most available methods have been developed in the last 10 years.

K. Fischbach and U.R. Krieger (Eds.): MMB & DFT 2014, LNCS 8376, pp. 1–15, 2014.

The number of available papers on parameter fitting of PHDs or MAPs is much too large to mention only a significant portion of them here. Therefore we present only the most important results for the algorithms that are developed in this paper. Overviews on available fitting methods can be found in [1,5,10].

Parameter fitting for PHDs can be made according to the whole sequence of measured data or based on some derived measures, like some moments. Moment based fitting methods can be found for example in [7,12,14]. Moment based fitting is often efficient and almost independent of the number of elements in the trace because only the empirical moments have to be computed from the trace. Fitting based on the first two or three moments is fairly easy. However, when increasing the number of moments usually two problems arise. First, it is sometimes hard to match all moments together with a PHD of given order, such that approximation methods have to be applied [6]. Additionally, estimators for higher order moments are unreliable. As shown in [17], confidence intervals for the moments derived from network traces with more than a million entries are extremely wide if the order of the moments is beyond 3 or 4. This implies that moment based parameter fitting usually has a limited accuracy since the shape of the density is not adequately described by lower order moments. Moment based fitting can be extended to MAPs [6,8,13] by using joint moments or some lags of the coefficient of autocorrelation. However, the problems of the approach are similar to those of moment based fitting approaches for PHDs. Higher order joint moments are hard to approximate and lower order joint moments do not adequately capture the correlation structure. Based on the complete trace data, parameters of a PHD or MAP can be fitted to approximate the empirical density. Most adequate for this purpose are *Expectation Maximization* (EM) algorithms. The first EM algorithm for PHDs has been proposed by Asmussen and his coworkers [2]. Later extensions of the approach improve the runtimes significantly by using more efficient computations and by restricting the classes of PHDs to acyclic structures [9,15,24,29]. The use of acyclic PHDs usually does not reduce the fitting quality. EM algorithms outperform moment based fitting approaches for multimodal densities. EM algorithms are iterative algorithms which are guaranteed to find local optima. However, convergence can be very slow and the time per iteration depends linearly on the number of elements in the trace, the number of parameters (i.e., the order of the PHD) and the difference between small and large elements in the trace. Especially for large network traces fitting times can be prohibitive. In [26] methods are introduced to aggregate the values in a trace and apply afterwards the EM algorithm for the aggregated trace. Examples show that the aggregation step often reduces the fitting times by orders of a magnitude and results in a similar likelihood value, which is a measurement for the fitting quality.

EM algorithms for parameter fitting of MAPs have also been published [3,4,16]. The algorithms work well for small traces, in particular, if these traces have been generated from MAPs of a lower order. If the algorithms are applied to huge network traces, then the convergence is slow and fitting times are often extremely long [17]. This seriously restricts the usability of EM algorithms for MAP fitting of many real problems in modeling computer networks.

In this paper we improve EM algorithms for PHD and MAP fitting. This is done by some slight modifications in the basic EM algorithms and more important by extending the trace aggregation of [26] from PHDs to MAPs. The original approach cannot be used for MAPs because after aggregation, dependencies between elements in the trace are no longer available. Here we extend the approach by keeping some of the information on dependencies in the aggregated trace and use this in the EM algorithm to fit the MAP matrices. Examples show that the aggregated information is sufficient to describe the dependencies in the trace and that the likelihood value of a MAP resulting from an aggregated trace is as good as the likelihood value of a MAP that has been fitted using the original trace. However, fitting based on the aggregated trace is often orders of magnitude faster than the use of standard EM algorithms for the complete trace.

The paper is structured as follows. In the next section the definitions and notations are introduced and the basic EM algorithms for PHD and MAP fitting are presented. Section 3 introduces an aggregation of traces that keeps dependencies partially in the aggregated trace and the extension of EM algorithms for aggregated traces. Afterwards, in Section 4, the new algorithms are applied to one synthetic and two real traces. The paper ends with the conclusions.

2   Basic Definitions

We present the basic notations and definitions which are used in the paper. For further details on PHDs and MAPs we refer to the literature [5]. Furthermore, we introduce a basic EM algorithm which is derived from the EM algorithms proposed in the literature [3,4,16,24].

2.1   Input Modeling

Input modeling is one of the major steps when building stochastic models for real world systems. It is used to define the parameters of a stochastic model, in particular to define the duration of events or the time between events. Usually this modeling is based on some measurements taken from a real world system. These measurements will be denoted as a trace $\mathcal{T} = (t_1, \ldots, t_m)$ where $t_i \geq 0$ describes the ith observation. Observations can be times between events (e.g., the arrival of packets in a computer networks, the occurrence of failures) or the size or duration of an event (e.g., the packet size in computer networks, the duration of a repair operation, the service time at server). We usually use the term interevent times, even if this does not completely capture all situations. m is the order of the trace which can be large, in particular if it results from some automated measurement as used for example in computer networks. From a trace, standard measures like the moments, joint moments, the empirical density or empirical distribution function can be derived using standard means [5]. The goal is to find a stochastic model such that it is likely that the trace has been generated as an output of the model. As model types we consider PHDs for uncorrelated data and MAPs for correlated data. Both model types are introduced in the following paragraphs.

2.2   Phase-Type Distributions

A phase type distribution (PHD) can be interpreted as an absorbing Markov chain with n transient and 1 absorbing state and generator

$$Q = \begin{pmatrix} D_0 & t \\ 0 & 0 \end{pmatrix}$$

where $t = -D_0 \mathbb{1}$ and D_0 is a non-singular $n \times n$ matrix with non-negative non-diagonal elements and row sums smaller or equal to 0. We assume that the initial vector of the PHD equals $(\pi, 0)$ which means that the distribution has no point mass at zero. Then the PHD can be characterized by (π, D_0). Moments, density and distribution function can be computed from this representation using standard means [5,17]. If the parameters of a PHD have been computed to match the values of some trace $\mathcal{T}$, then the fitting quality can be measured in terms of the likelihood or log likelihood value which is computed as follows.

$$\mathcal{L} = \prod_{i=1}^{m} \pi e^{D_0 t_i} t \text{ or } \log \mathcal{L} = \sum_{i=1}^{m} \log \left(\pi e^{D_0 t_i} t \right). \tag{1}$$

The better the likelihood value, the better the fitting quality, but for a given trace it is not clear which likelihood value can be or should be achieved.

2.3   Markovian Arrival Processes

PHDs can be used to describe identically and independently distributed values. In many real applications, for example the inter-arrival times at a router in a computer network, times are strongly correlated such that the modeling with PHDs is not adequate. For this purpose MAPs have been defined [20]. A MAP is defined by a pair of matrices (D_0, D_1) such that $Q = D_0 + D_1$ is an irreducible generator matrix, D_1 is non-negative and D_0 has negative diagonal and non-negative non-diagonal entries. We furthermore assume that D_0 is non-singular to avoid degenerated inter-event time distributions. The behavior of a MAP is as follows. The process behaves like a Markov chain with generator matrix Q and whenever a transition from D_1 occurs, an event is generated. Every PHD (π, D_0) can be represented as an equivalent MAP $(D_0, (-D_0 \mathbb{1})\pi)$. MAPs allow one to model correlated inter-event times. For the computation of basic quantities like moments, joint moments or (joint) densities we refer again to the literature [5,17].

   The likelihood and log likelihood for a MAP according to a trace $\mathcal{T}$ are defined as

$$\mathcal{L} = \pi \prod_{i=1}^{m} \left(e^{D_0 t_i} D_1 \right) \mathbb{1} \text{ and } \log \mathcal{L} = \sum_{i=1}^{m} \log \left(\pi^i e^{D_0 t_i} D_1 \mathbb{1} \right) \tag{2}$$

where $\pi^i = \pi \prod_{j=1}^{i-1} \left(e^{D_0 t_i} D_1 \right)$ and π is an appropriately chosen initial vector. Often the embedded stationary distribution after an event, that is given by the solution of $\pi \left(D_0 \right)^{-1} D_1 = \pi$ subject to $\pi \mathbb{1} = 1$, is used as initial vector.

2.4   EM Algorithms for PH and MAP Fitting

EM algorithms are local optimization algorithms that compute the parameters of some stochastic model from incomplete data. They are nowadays very popular in several branches of computer science and statistics. For the general idea behind the algorithms we refer to the literature [19]. Here we concentrate on specific realizations of EM algorithms for PHDs and MAPs.

An EM algorithm consists of an E-step that determines the expectation of some flows under the current parameter setting and an M-step that changes the parameter in such a way that the flows are maximized assuming the behavior that has been analyzed in the E-step. It can be shown that the combination of the two steps results in a non-decreasing sequence of flows and the flows determine the value of the likelihood function (Eqs. 1 or 2). In this way, a local optimizer is defined that computes the parameters of a PHD or MAP with a locally optimal value of the likelihood function.

We begin with the EM algorithm for PHDs and define the following vectors and matrix.

$$f_{(\pi,D_0),t} = \pi e^{D_0 t}, \quad b_{(\pi,D_0),t} = e^{D_0 t} t, \tag{3}$$

$$F_{(\pi,D_0),t} = \int_0^t \left(f_{(\pi,D_0),t-u} \right)^T \left(b_{(\pi,D_0),u} \right)^T du.$$

Matrix $F_{(\pi,D_0),t}$ contains the flow between two states for the given PHD. The vectors in matrix from (3) can be computed using uniformization [28]. Let $\alpha \geq \max_i |D_0(i,i)|$ and $P_0 = D_0/\alpha + I$. We can define the following two sequences of vectors

$$v^{(0)} = \pi \text{ and } v^{(k+1)} = v^{(k)} P_0, \quad w^{(0)} = t \text{ and } w^{(k+1)} = P_0 w^{(k)} \tag{4}$$

for $k = 0, 1, 2, \ldots$ such that

$$f_{(\pi,D_0),t} = \sum_{k=0}^{\infty} \beta(\alpha t, k) v^{(k)}, \quad b_{(\pi,D_0),t} = \sum_{k=0}^{\infty} \beta(\alpha t, k) w^{(k)}$$
$$F_{(\pi,D_0),t} = \frac{1}{\alpha} \sum_{k=0}^{\infty} \beta(\alpha t, k+1) \sum_{l=0}^{k} \left(v^{(l)} \right)^T \left(w^{(k-l)} \right)^T, \tag{5}$$

where $\beta(\alpha t, k)$ is the probability of k events of a Poisson process with rate α in the interval $(0, t]$. For practical computations, the infinite summations have to be truncated which can be done such that predefined error bounds for the results are observed [28].

We now define some random variables. B_i is the number of times the PHD starts in state i, N_{ij} the number of times the PHD goes from transient state i

to j, N_{in+1} the number of times an event is generated from state i and Z_i the total time spent in state i. All values are computed according to a given trace $\mathcal{T}$.

$$
\begin{aligned}
E_{(\pi,D_0),\mathcal{T}}[B_i] &= \sum_{k=1}^{m} \frac{\pi(i)b_{(\pi,D_0),t_k}(i)}{\pi b_{(\pi,D_0),t_k}}, & E_{(\pi,D_0),\mathcal{T}}[Z_i] &= \sum_{k=1}^{m} \frac{F_{(\pi,D_0),t_k}(i,i)}{\pi b_{(\pi,D_0),t_k}}, \\
E_{(\pi,D_0),\mathcal{T}}[N_{ij}] &= \sum_{k=1}^{m} \frac{D_0(i,j)F_{(\pi,D_0),t_k}(i,j)}{\pi b_{(\pi,D_0),t_k}}, & E_{(\pi,D_0),\mathcal{T}}[N_{in+1}] &= \sum_{k=1}^{m} \frac{t(i)f_{(\pi,D_0),t_k}(i)}{\pi b_{(\pi,D_0),t_k}}
\end{aligned}
$$
(6)

The equation describes the E-step of the EM algorithm. The following M-step computes new estimates for the parameters from the results of the E-step.

$$
\begin{aligned}
\hat{\pi}(i) &= \frac{E_{(\pi,D_0),\mathcal{T}}[B_i]}{m}, & \hat{D}_0(i,j) &= \frac{E_{(\pi,D_0),\mathcal{T}}[N_{ij}]}{E_{(\pi,D_0),\mathcal{T}}[Z_i]}, \\
\hat{t}(i) &= \frac{E_{(\pi,D_0),\mathcal{T}}[N_{in+1}]}{E_{(\pi,D_0),\mathcal{T}}[Z_i]}, & \hat{D}_0(i,i) &= -(\hat{t}(i) + \sum_{i \neq j}^{n} \hat{D}_0(i,j)).
\end{aligned}
$$
(7)

The iteration between (6) and (7) until the parameters are stable defines an EM algorithm for PHDs.

For MAPs the algorithm works similar but requires more effort since it is not sufficient to consider only the isolated values in a trace, instead the whole sequence has to be used in the E-step. Define first the following two vectors.

$$
\begin{aligned}
\boldsymbol{ff}^{(k)}_{(D_0,D_1)} &= \begin{cases} \pi & \text{if } k = 1 \\ \boldsymbol{ff}^{(k-1)}_{(D_0,D_1)} e^{D_0 t_{k-1}} D_1 & \text{if } 1 < k \le m \end{cases} \\
\boldsymbol{bb}^{(k)}_{(D_0,D_1)} &= \begin{cases} D_1 \mathbb{1} & \text{if } k = m \\ D_1 e^{D_0 t_{k+1}} \boldsymbol{bb}^{(k+1)}_{(D_0,D_1)} & \text{if } 1 \le k < m \end{cases}
\end{aligned}
$$
(8)

Vector $\boldsymbol{ff}^{(k)}$ is the forward vector describing the distribution immediately after the $(k-1)$th event in the trace and $\boldsymbol{bb}^{(k)}$ is the backward vector immediately after the events $m, \ldots, k+1$ occurred in backward direction. With these vectors the flow vectors and flow matrix for a single event can be defined.

$$
\boldsymbol{f}^{(k)}_{(D_0,D_1),t} = \boldsymbol{ff}^{(k)}_{(D_0,D_1)} e^{D_0 t}, \quad \boldsymbol{b}^{(k)}_{(D_0,D_1),t} = e^{D_0 t} \boldsymbol{bb}^{(k)}_{(D_0,D_1)}, \text{ and}
$$
$$
\boldsymbol{F}^{(k)}_{(D_0,D_1),t} = \int_0^t \left(\boldsymbol{f}^{(k)}_{(D_0,D_1),t-u} \right)^T \left(\boldsymbol{b}^{(k)}_{(D_0,D_1),u} \right)^T du.
$$
(9)

For the E-step of a MAP, the random variable M_{ij} is introduced that defines the number of times a transitions from state i to state j occurs that is accompanied by an event.

$$
\begin{aligned}
E_{(D_0,D_1),\mathcal{T}}[Z_i] &= \sum_{k=1}^{m} \frac{F^{(k)}_{(D_0,D_1),t_k}(i,i)}{\pi b^{(1)}_{(D_0,D_1),t_1}}, & E_{(D_0,D_1),\mathcal{T}}[N_{ij}] &= \sum_{k=1}^{m} \frac{D_0(i,j)F_{(D_0,D_1),t_k}(i,j)}{\pi b^{(1)}_{(D_0,D_1),t_1}}, \\
E_{(D_0,D_1),\mathcal{T}}[M_{ij}] &= \sum_{k=1}^{m-1} \frac{f^{(k)}_{(D_0,D_1),t_k}(i)D_1(i,j)b^{(k+1)}_{(D_0,D_1),t_{k+1}}}{\pi b^{(1)}_{(D_0,D_1),t_1}} &+ \frac{f^{(m)}_{(D_0,D_1),t_m}(i)D_1(i,j)\mathbb{1}}{\pi b^{(1)}_{(D_0,D_1),t_1}},
\end{aligned}
$$
(10)

Then the M-step is given by

$$\hat{D}_0(i,j) = \frac{E_{(D_0,D_1),\mathcal{T}}[N_{ij}]}{E_{(D_0,D_1),\mathcal{T}}[Z_i]} \text{ for } i \neq j, \ \hat{D}_1(i,j) = \frac{E_{(D_0,D_1),\mathcal{T}}[M_{ij}]}{E_{(D_0,D_1),\mathcal{T}}[Z_i]},$$

$$\hat{D}_0(i,i) = -\left(\sum_{j=1,i\neq j}^{n} \hat{D}_0(i,j) + \sum_{j=1}^{n} \hat{D}_1(i,j) \right). \tag{11}$$

Again the iteration of E-step (10) and M-step (11) defines the EM-algorithm.

3 An Expectation Maximization Algorithm Using Aggregated Traffic Traces

An EM algorithm using trace aggregation for a subclass of PHDs, namely Hyper-Erlang distributions, has been introduced in [26]. [26] proposes two different aggregation methods that will be summarized in the following section and extended to account for the additional requirements when fitting MAPs. Afterwards we will outline an EM algorithm with trace aggregation for general PHDs and MAPs.

3.1 Trace Aggregation

Let $\mathcal{T} = (t_1, t_2, \cdots, t_m)$ be a trace of e.g. inter-event times t_i. For trace aggregation the interval $[\min(\mathcal{T}), \max(\mathcal{T})]$ is divided into M subintervals $(\Delta_0, \Delta_1]$, $(\Delta_1, \Delta_2], \cdots, (\Delta_{M-1}, \Delta_M]$ with $0 \leq \Delta_0 < \min(\mathcal{T}) < \Delta_1 < \cdots < \Delta_{M-1} < \Delta_M = \max(\mathcal{T})$. [26] presented two aggregation methods that differ in the way how the interval boundaries Δ_i are chosen. In the uniform aggregation approach all intervals have the same width $\Delta = \Delta_i - \Delta_{i-1} = (\max(\mathcal{T}) - \Delta_0)/M$. Each interval i is then represented by a tuple $(\hat{t}_i, w_i)$, where $\hat{t}_i$ is the mean value of elements that fall within this interval and the weight w_i corresponds to the number of elements in the interval. More formally, let $J_i, i = 1, \cdots, M$ be sets of indices such that $j \in J_i$ if $t_j \in (\Delta_{i-1}, \Delta_i]$. Then, $w_i = |J_i|$ and $\hat{t}_i = \frac{1}{w_i} \sum_{j \in J_i} t_j$.

If the empirical distribution of the trace is heavy-tailed, uniform trace aggregation will produce a few intervals with lots of elements and many intervals with only few or even no elements. In these cases the logarithmic trace aggregation described in [26] provides better results. For logarithmic trace aggregation the intervals are chosen with equidistant width on a logarithmic scale, e.g. $(10^{-3}, 10^{-2}]$, $(10^{-2}, 10^{-1}]$, $(10^{-1}, 10^0]$, $(10^0, 10^1]$, $\cdots$. Let $s_{min} = \lfloor \log_{10} \min(\mathcal{T}) \rfloor$ and $s_{max} = \lceil \log_{10} \max(\mathcal{T}) \rceil$ be the smallest and largest logarithmic scale, respectively. Then, the trace is divided into the intervals $(10^s, 10^{s+1}]$, $s = s_{min}, \cdots, s_{max} - 1$, i.e. we have for the i-th interval $(\Delta_{i-1}, \Delta_i] = (10^{s_{min}+i-1}, 10^{s_{min}+i}]$. It is also possible to further divide the resulting intervals using uniform trace aggregation. Again, each interval i is then represented by a tuple $(\hat{t}_i, w_i)$. Intervals with $w_i = 0$ can be ignored for both aggregation types.

The aggregation approaches from [26] described above can be applied for PHD fitting but are not suitable for MAP fitting, because the order of the t_i and thereby the information about the correlation is lost. To save this information we introduce the vector $\mathcal{S} = (s_1, s_2, \cdots, s_m)$ with $s_j = i$ if $t_j \in (\Delta_{i-1}, \Delta_i)$, i.e. we store for each trace element the number of its interval. Thus, the aggregated trace $\mathcal{T}^*$ consists of M tuples $(\hat{t}_i, w_i)$ and the sequence $\mathcal{S}$.

3.2   EM Algorithms for PHD and MAP Fitting with Trace Aggregation

In the following we will modify the algorithms from Sect. 2 to allow for PHD and MAP fitting with aggregated traffic traces. We will first outline an algorithm for general PHDs which is a generalization of the approach from [26]. Afterwards the algorithm is extended to the case where MAPs are considered.

Assume that an aggregated traffic trace $\mathcal{T}^*$ is given by M tuples $(\hat{t}_i, w_i)$ and the sequence $\mathcal{S}$. For the description of the algorithm it does not matter how the intervals have been obtained, however, for the experimental results in the next section it is, of course, important which aggregation method has been used. For fitting the PHD we will only use $(\hat{t}_i, w_i)$, for fitting the MAP also $\mathcal{S}$ is required.

Fitting PHDs: The modifications on the EM algorithm for PHDs from Sect. 2 to allow for using aggregated traffic traces mostly affect the E-step of the algorithm.

In the original approach we have to compute the forward vector $\boldsymbol{f}_{(\pi,D_0),t}$, the backward vector $\boldsymbol{b}_{(\pi,D_0),t}$ and the flow matrix $\boldsymbol{F}_{(\pi,D_0),t}$ (cf. Eq. 3) for each trace element $t = t_1, t_2, \cdots, t_m$. Since these values are computed independent of each other, Eq. 3 can also be used for the aggregated trace, i.e. we compute $\boldsymbol{f}_{(\pi,D_0),t}$, $\boldsymbol{b}_{(\pi,D_0),t}$ and $\boldsymbol{F}_{(\pi,D_0),t}$ for each mean value of the intervals $t = \hat{t}_1, \hat{t}_2, \cdots, \hat{t}_M$. This leads to significant improvement of the runtime of the algorithm, because the time consuming computations of the matrix exponential and the integral in Eq. 3 have only to be done $M << m$ times.

In the E-step of the algorithm the weights w_i have to be considered, i.e. Eq. 6 becomes

$$
\begin{aligned}
E_{(\pi,D_0),\mathcal{T}^*}[B_i] &= \sum_{k=1}^{M} w_k \frac{\pi(i)\boldsymbol{f}_{(\pi,D_0),\hat{t}_k}(i)}{\pi\boldsymbol{b}_{(\pi,D_0),\hat{t}_k}} \\
E_{(\pi,D_0),\mathcal{T}^*}[Z_i] &= \sum_{k=1}^{M} w_k \frac{\boldsymbol{F}_{(\pi,D_0),\hat{t}_k}(i,i)}{\pi\boldsymbol{b}_{(\pi,D_0),\hat{t}_k}} \\
E_{(\pi,D_0),\mathcal{T}^*}[N_{ij}] &= \sum_{k=1}^{M} w_k \frac{D_0(i,j)\boldsymbol{F}_{(\pi,D_0),\hat{t}_k}(i,j)}{\pi\boldsymbol{b}_{(\pi,D_0),\hat{t}_k}} \\
E_{(\pi,D_0),\mathcal{T}^*}[N_{in+1}] &= \sum_{k=1}^{M} w_k \frac{t(i)\boldsymbol{f}_{(\pi,D_0),\hat{t}_k}(i)}{\pi\boldsymbol{b}_{(\pi,D_0),\hat{t}_k}}
\end{aligned}
\tag{12}
$$

The M-step needs not to be modified for fitting with an aggregated trace, i.e. Eq. 7 is used.

The steps for fitting PHDs with an EM algorithm and trace aggregation are summarized in Algorithm 1.

Algorithm 1. EM algorithm with trace aggregation for general PHDs

---

Input: Trace data $\mathcal{T} = t_1, \ldots, t_m$;
Output: PHD $(\boldsymbol{\pi}, \boldsymbol{D}_0)$;

1: Choose initial $(\boldsymbol{\pi}^{(0)}, \boldsymbol{D}_0^{(0)})$ and set $r = 0$;
2: Generate aggregated trace $\mathcal{T}^* = ((\hat{t}_1, w_1), (\hat{t}_2, w_2), \cdots (\hat{t}_M, w_M))$ from $\mathcal{T}$;
3: **repeat**
4:     Compute $\boldsymbol{f}_{(\boldsymbol{\pi}^{(r)}, \boldsymbol{D}_0^{(r)}), \hat{t}_i}$, $\boldsymbol{b}_{(\boldsymbol{\pi}^{(r)}, \boldsymbol{D}_0^{(r)}), \hat{t}_i}$ and $\boldsymbol{F}_{(\boldsymbol{\pi}^{(r)}, \boldsymbol{D}_0)^{(r)}, \hat{t}_i}$ for $i = 1, \cdots, M$ using Eq. 5;
5:     **E-step:** Compute the conditional expectations using Eq. 12;
6:     **M-step:** Compute $(\boldsymbol{\pi}^{(r+1)}, \boldsymbol{D}_0^{(r+1)})$ using Eq. 7;
7:     Set $r = r + 1$;
8: **until** $\|\boldsymbol{\pi}^{(r)} - \boldsymbol{\pi}^{(r-1)}\| + \|\boldsymbol{D}_0^{(r)} - \boldsymbol{D}_0^{(r-1)}\| < \epsilon$;
9: **return** $(\boldsymbol{\pi}^{(r)}, \boldsymbol{D}_0^{(r)})$;

Fitting MAPs: In the following we extend Algorithm 1 to allow for MAP fitting with aggregated traces. Considering trace aggregation for MAPs is more sophisticated than for PHDs, because the forward and backward vectors are not computed independently for each trace element any more (cf. Eq. 9), but contain the complete joint density from the first to the i-th trace element (for the forward vectors) or the complete joint density from the i-th to the last trace element (for the backward vectors). Moreover, these vectors are also needed for the computation of the flow matrix.

Note from Eq. 10, that for the estimation of the M_{ij} only the forward and backward vectors are needed. The flow matrix is needed for estimating Z_i and N_{ij}. However, these values can also be estimated using Eq. 12 reusing values from the EM fitting with aggregation for PHDs.

For the EM approach for MAPs with aggregated traffic traces we need additional matrices $M_{(\boldsymbol{\pi}, \boldsymbol{D}_0), t} = e^{\boldsymbol{D}_0 t}, t = \hat{t}_1, \cdots, \hat{t}_M$ which can be be computed using uniformization as follows.

$$\boldsymbol{V}^{(0)} = \boldsymbol{I}, \quad \boldsymbol{V}^{(k+1)} = \boldsymbol{V}^{(k)} \boldsymbol{P}_0, \quad \boldsymbol{M}_{(\boldsymbol{\pi}, \boldsymbol{D}_0), t} = \sum_{k=0}^{\infty} \beta(\alpha t, k) \boldsymbol{V}^{(k)}.$$

Then, we can define the forward and backward vectors for MAP fitting using the precomputed $\boldsymbol{M}_{(\boldsymbol{\pi}, \boldsymbol{D}_0), t}$ and the sequence $\mathcal{S} = (s_1, s_2, \cdots, s_m)$.

$$\tilde{\boldsymbol{ff}}_{(\boldsymbol{D}_0, \boldsymbol{D}_1)}^{(k)} = \begin{cases} \boldsymbol{\pi} & \text{if } k = 1 \\ \tilde{\boldsymbol{ff}}_{(\boldsymbol{D}_0, \boldsymbol{D}_1)}^{(k-1)} \boldsymbol{M}_{(\boldsymbol{\pi}, \boldsymbol{D}_0), \hat{t}_{s_{k-1}}} \boldsymbol{D}_1 & \text{if } 1 < k \le m \end{cases} \tag{13}$$

$$\tilde{\boldsymbol{f}}_{(\boldsymbol{D}_0, \boldsymbol{D}_1)}^{(k)} = \tilde{\boldsymbol{ff}}_{(\boldsymbol{D}_0, \boldsymbol{D}_1)}^{(k)} \boldsymbol{M}_{(\boldsymbol{\pi}, \boldsymbol{D}_0), \hat{t}_{s_k}}$$

$$\tilde{\boldsymbol{bb}}_{(\boldsymbol{D}_0, \boldsymbol{D}_1)}^{(k)} = \begin{cases} \boldsymbol{D}_1 \mathbb{1} & \text{if } k = m \\ \boldsymbol{D}_1 \boldsymbol{M}_{(\boldsymbol{\pi}, \boldsymbol{D}_0), \hat{t}_{s_{k+1}}} \tilde{\boldsymbol{bb}}_{(\boldsymbol{D}_0, \boldsymbol{D}_1)}^{(k+1)} & \text{if } 1 \le k < m \end{cases}$$

$$\tilde{\boldsymbol{b}}_{(\boldsymbol{D}_0, \boldsymbol{D}_1)}^{(k)} = \boldsymbol{M}_{(\boldsymbol{\pi}, \boldsymbol{D}_0), \hat{t}_{s_k}} \tilde{\boldsymbol{bb}}_{(\boldsymbol{D}_0, \boldsymbol{D}_1)}^{(k)}$$

Note, that the vectors are defined in a similar way as in Eqs. 8 and 9, but instead of computing the matrix exponential for the t_i we choose one of the precomputed

$M_{(\pi,D_0),t}$ according to s_i which indicates the interval (and thus the $\hat{t}_j$) that t_i falls in.

The E-step uses these precomputed vectors and matrices:

$$E_{(D_0,D_1),T^*}[Z_i] = \sum_{k=1}^{M} w_k \frac{F_{(\pi,D_0),\hat{t}_k}(i,i)}{\pi b_{(\pi,D_0),\hat{t}_k}} \tag{14}$$

$$E_{(D_0,D_1),T^*}[N_{ij}] = \sum_{k=1}^{M} w_k \frac{D_0(i,j)F_{(\pi,D_0),\hat{t}_k}(i,j)}{\pi b_{(\pi,D_0),\hat{t}_k}}$$

$$E_{(D_0,D_1),T^*}[M_{ij}] = \sum_{k=1}^{m-1} \frac{\tilde{f}^{(k)}_{(D_0,D_1)}(i)D_1(i,j)\tilde{b}^{(k+1)}_{(D_0,D_1)}(j)}{\pi \tilde{b}^{(1)}_{(D_0,D_1)}} + \frac{\tilde{f}^{(m)}_{(D_0,D_1)}(i)D_1(i,j)\mathbb{1}}{\pi \tilde{b}^{(1)}_{(D_0,D_1)}}$$

And finally, the M-step becomes

$$\hat{D}_0(i,j) = \frac{E_{(D_0,D_1),T^*}[N_{ij}]}{E_{(D_0,D_1),T^*}[Z_i]} \quad \text{for } i \neq j, \quad \hat{D}_1(i,j) = \frac{E_{(D_0,D_1),T^*}[M_{ij}]}{E_{(D_0,D_1),T^*}[Z_i]}$$

$$\hat{D}_0(i,i) = -\left(\sum_{j=1,i\neq j}^{n} \hat{D}_0(i,j) + \sum_{j=1}^{n} \hat{D}_1(i,j)\right) \tag{15}$$

Vector π is assumed to be the embedded stationary distribution after an event such that $\hat{\pi}$ is the solution of $\hat{\pi}\left(-\hat{D}_0\right)^{-1}\hat{D}_1 = \hat{\pi}$ subject to $\hat{\pi}\mathbb{1} = 1$.

Algorithm 2 summarizes our approach.

Algorithm 2. EM algorithm with trace aggregation for MAPs

Input: Trace data $T = t_1, \ldots, t_m$;
Output: MAP (D_0, D_1);
1: Choose initial $(D_0^{(0)}, D_1^{(0)})$ and set $r = 0$;
2: Generate aggregated trace $T^* = ((\hat{t}_1, w_1), (\hat{t}_2, w_2), \cdots (\hat{t}_M, w_M))$ and $S = (s_1, s_2, \cdots, s_m)$ from T;
3: repeat
4: Compute $f_{(\pi^{(r)},D_0^{(r)}),\hat{t}_i}$, $b_{(\pi^{(r)},D_0^{(r)}),\hat{t}_i}$, $F_{(\pi^{(r)},D_0)^{(r)},\hat{t}_i}$ and $M_{(\pi,D_0),\hat{t}_i}$ for $i = 1, \cdots, M$;
5: Compute $\tilde{f}^{(k)}_{(D_0,D_1)}$ and $\tilde{b}^{(k)}_{(D_0,D_1)}$ for $k = 1, \cdots, m$ according to Eq. 13;
6: **E-step:** Compute the conditional expectations using Eq. 14;
7: **M-step:** Compute $(D_0^{(r+1)}, D_1^{(r+1)})$ using Eq. 15;
8: Set $r = r + 1$;
9: until $\|D_0^{(r)} - D_0^{(r-1)}\| + \|D_1^{(r)} - D_1^{(r-1)}\| < \epsilon$;
10: return $(D_0^{(r)}, D_1^{(r)})$;

For the EM approach without trace aggregation the most time consuming part is the computation of the m forward vectors, the m backward vectors and the m flow matrices using e.g. randomization. For the approach with trace aggregation we have to compute M flow matrices with $M << m$ using randomization. Additionally, M matrix exponentials have to be computed and stored. Since $f_{(\pi,D_0),t} = \pi M_{(\pi,D_0),t}$ and $b_{(\pi,D_0),t} = M_{(\pi,D_0),t}t$ computation of those forward and backward vectors is cheap once $M_{(\pi,D_0),t}$ is known. The computation of $\tilde{f}^{(k)}_{(D_0,D_1)}$ and $\tilde{b}^{(k)}_{(D_0,D_1)}$ only consists of vector-matrix multiplications which is relatively cheap compared to the computation of the matrix exponential.

4 Experimental Results

For assessing the fitting quality of the presented EM algorithm we performed several experiments with synthetically generated traces and with traces from real systems. The synthetically generated traces have been created from a MAP and should be easier to fit than the real traces. However, the results provide hints on how many intervals are necessary for the algorithm to obtain good results.

For traces from computer and communication networks, [26] recommends using logarithmic trace aggregation, because with uniform trace aggregation few intervals contain the major part of the trace elements and many intervals contain only little or no trace elements. Consequently, we only present results using logarithmic trace aggregation. All experiments have been performed on a dual-core AMD Opteron Processor with 2.4 GHz and 16 GB RAM.

4.1 Synthetically Generated Traces

We generated 500.000 observations from the following MAP

$$D_0 = \begin{bmatrix} -1.733 & 0.064 & 0.923 \\ 0.159 & -2.289 & 0.040 \\ 2.015 & 0.101 & -2.344 \end{bmatrix}, \quad D_1 = \begin{bmatrix} 0.746 & 0.0 & 0.0 \\ 0.0 & 2.090 & 0.0 \\ 0.0 & 0.0 & 0.228 \end{bmatrix}$$

and fitted MAPs of order 3 using different numbers of intervals between 100 and 2000. Table 1 shows the log-likelihood values for the different interval numbers after 100 iterations of the EM algorithm. The results show that the best value was reached with 1000 intervals and cannot be further improved when increasing the number of intervals. For comparison, the original $MAP(3)$ has a log-likelihood value of -460207 for the trace. Using 1000 intervals our algorithm returned the following MAP

Table 1. Log-likelihood values for different interval numbers

Intervals	100	500	1000	2000
Log-likelihood	-460897	-460860	-460859	-460859

$$D_0 = \begin{bmatrix} -2.4646 & 0.222 & 0.051 \\ 0.449 & -1.4654 & 0.639 \\ 0.051 & 0.126 & -0.75706 \end{bmatrix}, \quad D_1 = \begin{bmatrix} 2.059 & 0.132 & 0.0006 \\ 0.145 & 0.222 & 0.0104 \\ 0.00006 & 0.004 & 0.576 \end{bmatrix}$$

Fig. 1 shows the log-likelihood values (left y-axis) and the total time consumption (right y-axis) after each of the 100 iterations. Note, that the log-likelihood values are the values for the original trace and not for the aggregated trace. As one can see, the largest improvement in the likelihood was obtained during the first 10 iterations. The time consumption is almost linear and overall

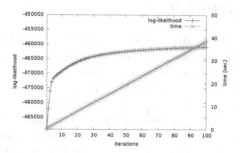

Fig. 1. Log-likelihood and time consumption for fitting a synthetically generated trace with a $MAP(3)$ and 1000 intervals

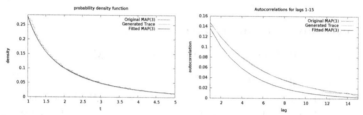

Fig. 2. Density and autocorrelations for the original MAP, the generated trace and the fitted MAP

the algorithm required about 40 seconds. Fig. 2 shows the probability density function and the lag-k autocorrelation coefficients for the original $MAP(3)$, the generated trace and the fitted MAP. As one can see, the density functions almost overlap completely, however, the fitted MAP slightly underestimated the autocorrelation.

4.2   Traces from a Real System

As real traces we used the two standard benchmark traces BC-pAug89 [18] and LBL-TCP-3 [27] from the Internet traffic archive (http://ita.ee.lbl.gov). The traces contain 1.000.000 and about 1.700.000 entries, respectively, and fitting them using an EM algorithm is very time consuming because of their size. We fitted MAPs of different order with a different number of intervals using our approach with trace aggregation. For comparison we also fitted MAPs using the EM algorithm from [4] that does not use trace aggregation and served as basis for our implementation. Fig. 3 shows the results for MAPs of order 5 fitted to the trace LBL-TCP-3. On the left y-axis the log-likelihood values are displayed, the right y-axis shows the total amount of time used for 50 iterations of the algorithms. The curves labeled with **agg** result from MAP EM fitting with trace aggregation using 1000 intervals, the curves labeled with **no agg** show the corresponding results from EM fitting without trace aggregation. As one can see, the log-likelihood values are almost identical for both algorithms, however,

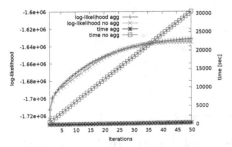

Fig. 3. Log-likelihood and time consumption for the trace LBL-TCP-3 and EM fitting with and without trace aggregation

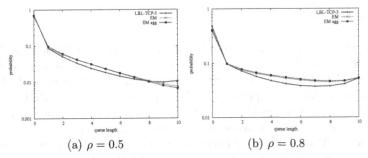

$$(a)\ \rho = 0.5 \qquad\qquad (b)\ \rho = 0.8$$

Fig. 4. Queueing Results for the trace LBL-TCP-3 and two fitted MAPs

without trace aggregation the algorithm needed over 8 hours and with trace aggregation the 50 iterations have been computed in less than 10 minutes.

To introduce another measure for comparing the fitting results aside from the likelihood we used the trace and the two fitted MAPs as arrival processes in a simple single-server queueing system with a capacity of 10 and exponentially distributed service times. Fig. 4 shows the queue length distribution from simulation runs with a utilization of $\rho = 0.5$ and $\rho = 0.8$. In both cases the two MAPs slightly overestimate the middle part of the queue length distribution resulting from the trace, but as expected from the almost identical likelihood values the two MAPs behave similar.

Fig. 5 shows the result for the trace BC-pAug89. Fig. 5(a) compares the time consumption and the log-likelihood when fitting MAPs of order 6 using an EM algorithm with and without trace aggregation, respectively, for the trace, which gives a similar picture as the results for the trace LBL-TCP-3. Fig. 5(b) contains the queueing results. Again both MAPs behave similarly.

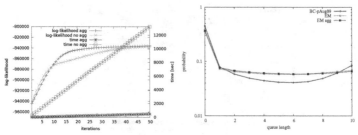

(a) Log-likelihood and time con- (b) Queueing results for $\rho = 0.8$
sumption

Fig. 5. Results for the trace BC-pAug89

5   Conclusions

The paper presents an EM algorithm for parameter fitting of *Phase Type Distri-butions* (PHDs) or *Markovian Arrival Processes* (MAPs). In contrast to known approaches, elements in the trace are first aggregated and then the EM algo-rithm is applied. A similar approach has been proposed before for PHDs but not for MAPs. Our experiments show that trace aggregation results in a dramatical improvement of the fitting times when the traces contain more than a few thou-sand elements. The value of the likelihood is not affected by trace aggregation which implies that the quality of the generated PHD or MAP is the same as if the process results from an EM algorithm applied to the original trace.

The approach can be extended by considering only specific matrix structures like acyclic matrices D_0 or use the EM algorithm for PHDs to determine the parameters of an acyclic distribution in canonical form as done in [24]. Further-more the approach can also be extended to fit the parameters of PHDs or MAPs according to grouped data as in [23,25].

References

1. Artalejo, J.R., Gomez-Corral, A., He, Q.M.: Markovian arrivals in stochastic mod-elling: a survey and some new results. Sort: Statistics and Operations Research Transactions 34(2), 101–156 (2010)
2. Asmussen, S., Nerman, O., Olsson, M.: Fitting phase-type distributions via the EM-algorithm. Scand. J. Stat. 23(4), 419–441 (1996)
3. Breuer, L.: An EM algorithm for batch Markovian arrival processes and its com-parison to a simpler estimation procedure. Annals OR 112(1-4), 123–138 (2002)
4. Buchholz, P.: An EM-algorithm for MAP fitting from real traffic data. In: Kemper, P., Sanders, W.H. (eds.) TOOLS 2003. LNCS, vol. 2794, pp. 218–236. Springer, Heidelberg (2003)
5. Buchholz, P., Felko, I., Kriege, J.: Input Modeling with Phase Type Distributions and Markov Models. Springer (to appear)
6. Buchholz, P., Kriege, J.: A heuristic approach for fitting MAPs to moments and joint moments. In: QEST, pp. 53–62 (2009)

7. Bux, W., Herzog, U.: The phase concept: approximation of measured data and performance analysis. In: Computer Performance, pp. 23–38 (1977)
8. Casale, G., Zhang, E.Z., Smirni, E.: KPC-toolbox: Simple yet effective trace fitting using Markovian arrival processes. In: QEST, pp. 83–92 (2008)
9. Feldmann, A., Whitt, W.: Fitting mixtures of exponentials to long-tail distributions to analyze network performance models. Performance Evaluation (1998)
10. Gerhardt, I., Nelson, B.L.: On capturing dependence in point processes: Matching moments and other techniques. Technical report, Northwestern Univ. (2009)
11. Heindl, A., Telek, M.: Output models of MAP/PH/1(/K) queues for an efficient network decomposition. Perform. Eval. 49(1/4), 321–339 (2002)
12. Horváth, A., Telek, M.: Matching more than three moments with acyclic phase type distributions. Stochastic Models 23, 167–194 (2007)
13. Horváth, G., Telek, M., Buchholz, P.: A MAP fitting approach with independent approximation of the inter-arrival time distribution and the lag-correlation. In: QEST, pp. 124–133. IEEE CS Press (2005)
14. Johnson, M.A., Taaffe, M.R.: Matching moments to phase distributions: Nonlinear programming approaches. Stochastic Models 2(6), 259–281 (1990)
15. El Abdouni Khayari, R., Sadre, R., Haverkort, B.: Fitting world-wide web request traces with the EM-algorithm. Performance Evaluation 52, 175–191 (2003)
16. Klemm, A., Lindemann, C., Lohmann, M.: Modeling IP traffic using the batch Markovian arrival process. Perform. Eval. 54(2), 149–173 (2003)
17. Kriege, J., Buchholz, P.: An Empirical Comparison of MAP Fitting Algorithms. In: Müller-Clostermann, B., Echtle, K., Rathgeb, E.P. (eds.) MMB & DFT 2010. LNCS, vol. 5987, pp. 259–273. Springer, Heidelberg (2010)
18. Leland, W.E., Taqqu, M.S., Willinger, W., Wilson, D.V.: On the self-similar nature of ethernet traffic (extended version). IEEE/ACM Trans. Netw. (1994)
19. McLachlan, G.J., Krishnan, T.: The EM Algorithm and Extensions. John Wiley and Sons (1997)
20. Neuts, M.F.: A versatile Markovian point process. Jour. of Appl. Probability (1979)
21. Neuts, M.F.: Matrix-geometric solutions in stochastic models. Johns Hopkins University Press (1981)
22. O'Cinneide, C.A.: Phase-type distributions: open problems and a few properties. Stochastic Models 15(4), 731–757 (1999)
23. Okamura, H., Dohi, T., Trivedi, K.S.: Markovian arrival process parameter estimation with group data. IEEE/ACM Trans. Netw. 17(4), 1326–1339 (2009)
24. Okamura, H., Dohi, T., Trivedi, K.S.: A refined EM algorithm for PH distributions. Perform. Eval. 68(10), 938–954 (2011)
25. Okamura, H., Dohi, T., Trivedi, K.S.: Improvement of expectation-maximization algorithm for phase-type distributions with grouped and truncated data. Applied Stochastic Models in Business and Industry 29(2), 141–156 (2012)
26. Panchenko, A., Thümmler, A.: Efficient phase-type fitting with aggregated traffic traces. Perform. Eval. 64(7-8), 629–645 (2007)
27. Paxson, V., Floyd, S.: Wide area traffic: the failure of Poisson modeling. IEEE/ACM Trans. Netw. 3(3), 226–244 (1995)
28. Stewart, W.J.: Introduction to the numerical solution of Markov chains. Princeton University Press (1994)
29. Thümmler, A., Buchholz, P., Telek, M.: A novel approach for phase-type fitting with the EM algorithm. IEEE Trans. Dep. Sec. Comput. 3(3), 245–258 (2006)

Modeling of Loss Processes Arising from Packet Flows at Bottleneck Links

Natalia M. Markovich[1,*] and Udo R. Krieger[2]

[1] Institute of Control Sciences
Russian Academy of Sciences
117997 Moscow, Russia
`markovic@ipu.rssi.ru`
[2] Faculty Information Systems and Applied Computer Science
Otto-Friedrich-University
D-96047 Bamberg, Germany
`udo.krieger@ieee.org`

Abstract. Packet video and voice are the dominant traffic sources in today's Internet. Numerous studies have dealt with the influence of packet loss on video and voice quality. We elaborate on the root causes of packet loss in the Internet and show by statistical methods how that affects the quality of transmitted real-time data. We evaluate the mean number of lost packets and the distribution of bit loss as quality indices of packet transmission at a bottleneck link with insufficient bandwidth. The latter information regarding the risk to lose packets for a known bandwidth of a bottleneck link can be transferred to customers.

Keywords: Packet traffic in Internet, geometric sums, cluster of exceedances, quantile, equivalent capacity, quality of transmission, bit loss.

1 Introduction

In this paper we consider a fundamental teletraffic issue arising from the transport of packet flows that are generated by real-time applications in high speed packet-switched networks. We study the packet loss process experienced by a flow at a single bottleneck link along its fixed route due to insufficient transport capacity and derive simple, measurable quality indices of this loss process. Our approach is based on the assumption that a bufferless queue models the link with regard to real-time flows in adequate manner and that the rate process induced by the flow is a sufficient description.

In this respect, our paper reflects an important application scenario in current multimedia Internet whose service pattern is dominated by the transport of live and on-demand video streaming. To investigate the quality-of-service (QoS) of the packet transport at the network layer and the quality-of-experience (QoE) of a video consumer, concise theoretical results on the impact of packet loss on the

* The first author was partly supported by the Russian Foundation for Basic Research, grant 13-08-00744 A.

K. Fischbach and U.R. Krieger (Eds.): MMB & DFT 2014, LNCS 8376, pp. 16–28, 2014.

QoS and QoE metrics are required (cf. [7]). The latter should provide a strong informativeness and allow an effective validation by measurement procedures. We try to fulfill both objectives by our statistically motivated teletraffic approach.

In this regard, this study extends our previous research efforts [14] - [16], where we have tried to understand the causes of packet loss during the transmission in Internet by purely statistical methods. It was found that the lack of an available (equivalent) transport capacity u at a bottleneck link constitutes one of the major causes. Considering the transmission of a packet flow generated by real-time applications along a series of routers, it is realistic to assume that the inter-arrival times $\{X_i\}_{i \geq 1}$ between consecutive packets are heavy-tail distributed with regularly varying tails (cf. [10], [11], [13]).

The rates of such a packet transmission process are usually approximated by ratios $R_i = Y_i / X_i$, where Y_i denotes the length of ith packet and X_i denotes the inter-arrival time between the ith and $(i+1)$th (or $(i-1)$th and ith) packet. Despite the fact that the related packet lengths $\{Y_i\}_{i \geq 1}$ are, by definition, light-tail distributed, these induced rates are distributed with a heavy tail inherited from $\{X_i\}_{i \geq 1}$. The heaviness of the tail and the dependence in the rate variables generate a cluster structure of the rate process. Clusters imply that conglomerates of observations of the underlying process $\{R_i\}_{i \geq 1}$ may exceed a sufficiently large bandwidth threshold u and cause a loss of packets since there is not sufficient transport capacity to handle these data on a considered link (see figure 1). This conclusion is derived from the assumption of a bufferless fluid model that describes the packet flow on the capacity-constrained bottleneck link which causes the loss. This assumption is rather strong, but it can be justified in the following way. In the fluid flow model each buffer would slightly increase the actual transport capacity along a path. However, these buffers in the routers are not unlimited and if the buffer of the bottleneck router is full, corresponding packets will be lost. To accommodate for this fact, one can simply model the available bandwidth by a slightly higher value than the actual link capacity of the router. Therefore, we use this well-known assumption on the bufferless fluid flow model throughout our paper. It is also used often in the domain of bandwidth estimation and the computation of an equivalent capacity assigned to a flow (cf. [6], [9], [20] among many others). Here, we will adopt the latter approach to define the transport capacity u of the bottleneck link from the perspective of a considered packet stream related to a real-time multimedia service (see also [6]).

As the loss of packets is arising in such clusters of packets, the sums of their packet lengths will generate a bit loss in the bufferless link model. Regarding more advanced packet-switched network protocols like live video streaming in peer-to-peer overlay networks, there may be other causes of packet loss. For instance, the departure of peers in a swarm or packets missing a playback deadline at the destination node during video transmission due to an insufficiently chosen playback delay can cause loss effects, too (cf. [3], [14]). Here, we shall focus solely on the packet loss due to a lack of transport capacity.

It is the objective of the present paper to attract appropriate statistical results on the loss process and to determine both the mean number of lost packets

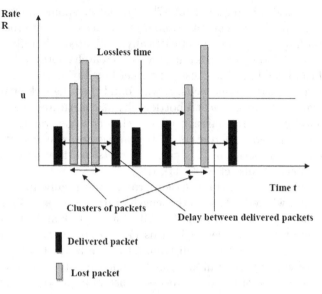

Fig. 1. Cluster structure of the loss process

in a cluster and the distribution of the bit loss for relatively large values of the capacity threshold u. Our approach is rather pragmatic in hope to adapt asymptotic statistical inferences to moderate size samples.

In [6] it was proposed to select the maximal sample rate $\max\{R_1, ..., R_n\}$ as value of the required bandwidth u that can be redundant. Moreover, due to the randomness of the sample such sample maxima can be considered as low or high quantile of the rate. Throughout the paper we select the $(1 - \rho)$th quantile x_ρ of R_i (i.e. $\mathbf{P}\{R_i > x_\rho\} = \rho$) as u and control the quality of the packet transport by ρ. However, the estimation of the quantile can become problematic if these packet rates $\{R_t\}_t$ are statistically dependent. This assumption is realistic due to a possible dependence of inter-arrival times between packets.

Regarding our analysis, we will rely on the fundamental statistical results about extreme values of a stationary stochastic processes like the rate process derived in [16]. In this paper it was proved that the distributions of cluster sizes and the inter-cluster sizes of exceedances (called lossless times) follow asymptotically a geometric law, irrespective of the marginal distribution of the rates, as the sample size $n \to \infty$ and when the threshold u is large. The inter-cluster size $T_1(u)$ means the number of non-exceedances between two consecutive clusters and the cluster size $T_2(u)$ implies the number of exceedances in the cluster, respectively, (see figure 1). Both random variables depend on u. More exactly, we determine the number of inter-arrival times between packets

$$T_1^*(u) = \min\{j > 1 : M_{1,j} \leq u, R_{j+1} > u | R_1 > u\}, \tag{1}$$

arising between clusters, and the number of inter-arrival times

$$T_2^*(u) = \min\{j > 1 : L_{1,j} > u, R_{j+1} \leq u | R_1 \leq u\}, \tag{2}$$

arising within a cluster. Here $M_{1,j} = \max\{R_2, .., R_j\}$, $M_{1,1} = -\infty$ and $L_{1,j} = \min\{R_2, ..., R_j\}$, $L_{1,1} = +\infty$. Note that

$$T_i(u) = T_i^*(u) - 1, \quad i \in \{1, 2\} \tag{3}$$

holds.

Hence, in our context of a bottleneck link the mean of $T_2(u)$ coincides with the mean number of lost packets. Moreover, the bit loss with regard to a given equivalent transport capacity u can be determined by

$$S_{T_2(u)} = \sum_{i=1}^{T_2(u)} Y_i. \tag{4}$$

As $T_2(u)$ follows asymptotically a geometric distribution, $S_{T_2(u)}$ can be called a geometric sum in asymptotic regime. Inferences regarding distributions of geometric sums (i.e., when the number of terms in the sum is geometrically distributed) are obtained in [2], [8], [17] among others. Our approach is different since $T_2(u)$ is geometrically distributed only asymptotically, i.e. for large sample sizes. The latter corresponds to large u in contrast to a small one considered in [2], [8]. Besides, $T_2(u)$ and Y_i may be mutually dependent. Their independence is necessarily assumed in [2], [8], [17].

Following [14] - [16] the quantile levels ρ and $q = 1 - \rho$ play the role of probabilities in the mentioned geometric distributions of $T_1(x_\rho)$ and $T_2(x_\rho)$, respectively, and ρ is included in further inferences regarding the distribution of the bit loss (cf. [16]).

The paper is organized as follows. In Section 2 we first propose new estimators of the quantile level $1 - \rho$, both for independent and dependent rates and give an algorithm for the latter case. In Section 3 the estimation of the mean number of lost packets and distribution of the bit loss are derived. Finally, some concluding remarks are presented in Section 4.

2   New Estimation of the Quantile Level of a Rate Process

We observe packets arriving to a destination node and the corresponding process $\{R_1, R_2, ..., R_n\}$ of packet rates. Let us assume that the process is strictly stationary with the marginal distribution function $F(x) = \mathbf{P}\{R_i \leq x\}, i \geq 1$. In the present context, we consider the approximate rates of packet transmissions that can be calculated as ratios $R_i = Y_i/X_i$ of the packet length Y_i to the corresponding inter-arrival time X_i. We denote the maximum of the process by $M_n = \max\{R_1, R_2, ..., R_n\}$.

We aim to find the value ρ, $\rho \in (0, 1)$, such that the quantile x_ρ of level $1 - \rho$ of the rate process $\{R_t\}$ is equal to a given threshold u, i.e. $u = x_\rho$ and $\mathbf{P}\{R_t \leq x_\rho\} = 1 - \rho$. We may think that u is the bottleneck bandwidth of a single link in a packet-switched network and that it is fixed for a short period of time. The value ρ will be used in Section 3 to evaluate control indices of the packet transmission, namely, the mean number of lost packets and the risk (or probability) to lose more than a fixed amount of bits.

As $F(x)$ is unknown and in case that the observations of the underlying rate process $\{R_t\}$ are independent, we can simply estimate it by the empirical distribution function $F_n(x) = 1/n \sum_{i=1}^{n} \mathbf{1}(x \geq R_i)$. Here $\mathbf{1}(A)$ denotes the indicator of the event A.

To find the required level ρ, we get

$$\rho = 1 - 1/n \sum_{i=1}^{n} \mathbf{1}(u \geq R_i). \tag{5}$$

The problem is that the observations $\{R_t\}$ are not necessarily independent in practice. In this case $F_n(x)$ may not be a uniformly consistent estimator of the distribution function $F(x)$.

Another problem may arise when $\{R_t\}$ are independent and heavy-tail distributed. To estimate high quantiles (i.e. close to 100%), one can use a parametric model of the tail function $\overline{F(x)} = \mathbf{P}\{R_1 > x\}$ that is usually taken as Pareto model $\mathbf{P}\{R_1 > x\} = l(x) \cdot x^{-\alpha}, x > 0$, where $l(x)$ is a slowly varying function at infinity, i.e. $\lim_{x \to \infty} l(tx)/l(x) = 1$ for all $t \geq 0$. (cf. [12, p. 4]). Then one can apply Weissman's quantile estimator (cf. Weissman [22], Markovich [12]). It means that

$$x_\rho^W = R_{(n-k)} \left((k+1)/(\rho(n+1)) \right)^{1/\widehat{\alpha}}$$

holds. Here $\widehat{\alpha}$ is an estimate of the tail index $\alpha > 0$ that determines the heaviness of the distribution tail and k is a number of the largest order statistics $R_{(1)} \leq R_{(2)} \cdots \leq R_{(n-k)} \leq \cdots \leq R_{(n)}$ used for the estimation. Then it is possible to find ρ assuming that $u = x_\rho$ (cf. [22], [12]).

In case that $\{R_t\}_{t=1,\ldots,n}$ are dependent and heavy-tail distributed, we can find the level of an extreme quantile, i.e., the quantile of the maxima M_n, which may be used as threshold u. The idea is to apply for this purpose the formula (5) using block-maxima data and further, to re-transform it to the level of a quantile of R_t (cf. [12]). Considering sufficiently large u, the exceedances of $\{R_t\}$ over u (i.e. rare extremal observations) are separated sufficiently far away from each other in time and, hence, are independent in some sense. Thus, one can use extreme quantiles as u.

Generally, one can approximate the distribution of the maxima by the expression

$$\mathbf{P}\{M_n \leq x_\rho\} \approx \mathbf{P}^{n\theta}\{R_1 \leq x_\rho\} = F^{n\theta}(x_\rho), \qquad n \in \mathbb{N}.$$

Here $\theta \in (0, 1]$ denotes the so called extremal index (see Robinson and Tawn [18]). In case that the observations of the process are independent, $\theta = 1$ holds. Hence, the value $n\theta$, which is less than n, indicates the number of stochastically "independent" observations within our sample $\{R_1, R_2, \ldots, R_n\}$.

Therefore, if we accept

$$F^{n\theta}(x_{\overline{\rho}}) = 1 - \overline{\rho}$$

and use $1 - \rho = (1 - \overline{\rho})^{1/(n\theta)}$, then we get the $(1 - \overline{\rho})$th quantile $x_{\overline{\rho}}$ of M_n. At the same time this is the $(1 - \rho)$th quantile of R_i.

To estimate θ for a given capacity threshold u, we may use the intervals estimator of Ferro and Segers [5]:

$$\bar{\theta}(u) = 2 \left(\sum_{i=1}^{N} (T_1^*(u))_i \right)^2 / (N \sum_{i=1}^{N} (T_1^*(u))_i^2). \tag{6}$$

Here $\{(T_1^*(u))_i, i = 1, ..., N\}$, is a sample of observations of the inter-cluster inter-arrival times $T_1^*(u)$ in (1). The number N of inter-cluster times is random and depends on the sample $\{R_1, R_2, ..., R_n\}$ and the threshold u. In contrast to other estimators (cf. [1]), this estimator has the advantage that it does not require a value of the block size as parameter.

In this context, it is usually recommended to select a proper value θ corresponding to a stability interval of the plot of $\bar{\theta}(u)$ against u (cf. [18]).

In the following algorithm we aim to find the level $(1 - \rho)$ of a quantile $x_{\bar{p}}$ of R_1 such that $x_{\bar{p}} \approx u$ holds, where $x_{\bar{p}}$ is the $(1 - \bar{p})$th quantile of M_n.

Estimation Algorithm of the Quantile Level ρ

We assume that the threshold u (i.e. the bottleneck bandwidth of a link) is known.

1. Regarding the process $\{R_i\}$, $i = \overline{1, n}$, divide the sample into blocks of equal size d and calculate the block maxima $M_1, ..., M_m$, $m = \lfloor n/d \rfloor$.[1]
2. Use $M_1, ..., M_m$ to find the level of the quantile $x_{\bar{p}}$ of maxima M_n, that is close to a given u, by rewriting formula (5):

$$\bar{p} = 1 - 1/m \sum_{i=1}^{m} \mathbf{1}(u \geq M_i).$$

3. For $u = x_{\bar{p}}$ count the inter-cluster times $\{(T_1^*(u))_i, i = 1, ..., N - 1\}$ by the observations $R_1, R_2, ..., R_n$ using (1).
4. Estimate the extremal index θ by formula (6).
5. Finally, calculate the quantile level of R_i by

$$\rho = 1 - (1 - \bar{p})^{1/(n\bar{\theta}(x_{\bar{p}}))}. \tag{7}$$

Remark 1. *The selection of d may be a challenge since it cannot be too large to avoid a small number of block maxima. One can take $d = \sqrt{n}$.*

3 Quality Control of Packet Transmission Processes at Bottleneck Links

A key issue in teletraffic engineering of high speed packet-switched networks is concerned with the control of the transmission processes by appropriate protocol

---

[1] $\lfloor A \rfloor$ denotes the integer part of A.

mechanisms. For this purpose adequate quality indices have to be defined and investigated. Regarding a flow of packets traversing a route from the source to the destination node, the number of packets and bits which are lost at a bottleneck link of finite bandwidth u, that is assigned to the flow on that route, constitute such performance measures. Dealing with real-time traffic we may model a router in front of this bottleneck link as bufferless queueing system with service rate u.

We shall use the value ρ obtained by (5) or (7) in Section 2, which is a novel estimate, to determine the mean number of lost packets and the probability of the bit loss arising from the rate exceedance of the considered level u. The latter indices reveal the quality of the packet transmission process along a path with this single bottleneck of bandwidth $u = x_\rho$.

Regarding the analysis of the loss process, we introduce the cluster size $T_2(u)$ of the exceedances arising from the rate process R_i of a packet flow beyond the capacity threshold u by (2) and (3). The latter determines the number of consecutive exceedances of this process $\{R_i = Y_i/X_i\}_i$ over the threshold u located between two consecutive non-exceedances (see figure 1). We also consider the sum of packet lengths over the cluster (4) assuming that all these packets in the clusters are lost at the bottleneck link if their corresponding rates $\{R_t\}$ exceed the channel capacity u (cf. [14], [15]). In this respect, $S_{T_2(u)}$ implies the bit loss in a cluster of exceedances as first quality index of the rate process defined by a flow. Then the expectation $\mathbf{E}T_2(u)$ denotes the mean number of lost packets per cluster as second quality index of a flow.

3.1 Estimation of the Mean Number of Lost Packets

It is derived by the results in [16] that under a specific mixing condition, similar to that in [5], the distribution of the discrete random variable $T_2(u)$ is asymptotically identical to a geometric distribution after an appropriate normalization. It depends on the extremal index θ of the rate process $\{R_i\}_i$, namely we get for $j \geq 2$

$$d_n P\{T_2(x_{\rho_n^*}) = j-1\} = d_n P\{T_2^*(x_{\rho_n^*}) = j\} \sim \chi_n (1-\chi_n)^{j-1}, \quad \text{as } n \to \infty, \quad (8)$$

where $d_n = \chi_n / \left(1 - (1-\chi_n)^{1/\theta}\right)$, $0 < \chi_n < 1$, and $q_n^\theta = \chi_n$ or $(1-q_n^*)^\theta = 1-\chi_n$ holds.[2] Here, ρ_n^* and q_n^* are related to ρ_n and q_n by following equations

$$q_n = 1 - \rho_n, \qquad q_n^* = 1 - \rho_n^*, \qquad \rho_n^* = (1 - q_n^\theta)^{1/\theta}.$$

Only high quantiles $x_{\rho_n^*}$ are appropriate as u in (8) such that $\rho_n^* \to 0$ holds as $n \to \infty$. In our terms, (8) follows for a bottleneck link with large bandwidth u.

Using (8), it holds for large n

$$\mathbf{E}T_2(x_{\rho_n^*}) \sim \frac{(1 - \rho_n^*) \cdot (\rho_n^*)^\theta}{\left(1 - (\rho_n^*)^\theta\right)^2}$$

---

[2] $f(x) \sim g(x)$ means that $f(x)/g(x) \to 1$ as $x \to a$, $x \in A$, where $f(x)$ and $g(x)$ are defined on some set A and a is a limit point of A.

and the following approximation of the mean cluster size, i.e., the mean number of lost packets in clusters,

$$\widehat{ET_2(x_\rho)} = C\frac{(1-\rho) \cdot \rho^{\overline{\theta}(x_\rho)}}{\left(1 - \rho^{\overline{\theta}(x_\rho)}\right)^2}$$

with a normalization constant $C > 0$ is obtained by methods from [16]. In the latter formula, the estimates (6) and (7) may be used instead of $\overline{\theta}(x_\rho)$ and ρ, respectively. Then the mean number of lost packets can be approximated by the geometric mean

$$\widehat{ET_2(x_\rho)} = C \, \rho/(1-\rho)$$

if $\theta = 1$ and ρ is close to zero which corresponds to independent single exceedances of R_t over a sufficiently large threshold $u = x_\rho$.

3.2   Estimation of the Bit-Loss Distribution

Apart of $\widehat{ET_2(x_\rho)}$, we propose in this paper to use quantiles x_η of the distribution of $S_{T_2(u)}$ as a quality characteristic of the packet transmission process at bottleneck links. Then the following probability

$$P\{S_{T_2(u)} > x_\eta\} = P\{\sum_{i=1}^{T_2(u)} Y_i > x_\eta\} = \eta$$

shows the risk to get a bit loss exceeding the critical value x_η with probability η for a given bottleneck bandwidth u.

It is our objective to find simple approximations of this probability. Evidently, we can assume that the packet lengths $\{Y_i\}_i$ are independent and identically light-tail distributed positive random variables with finite first and second moments, i.e., $EY_i = \alpha_1$ and $EY_i^2 = \alpha_2$ are positive constants. We again use the $(1 - \rho)$th quantile x_ρ of R_t as threshold u. In the following, we analyze four different cases in more detail.

Fixed Packet Lengths
First, we assume that all transported packets have the same packet length Y, e.g., the maximum size $Y = 1500$ bytes of IP packets in Ethernet, that defines a deterministic lengths distribution.

Then we get the simplest approximation

$$P\{S_{T_2(u)} > x_\eta\} = P\{T_2(u) > x_\eta/Y\}. \tag{9}$$

By (8) we then obtain for high quantiles $x_{\rho_n^*}$

$$P\{T_2(x_{\rho_n^*}) > x_\eta/Y\} = 1 - P\{T_2(x_{\rho_n^*}) \le x_\eta/Y\}$$
$$\le 1 - \sum_{j=1}^{\lfloor x_\eta/Y \rfloor} P\{T_2(x_{\rho_n^*}) = j\}$$

$$= 1 - (1/d_n) \sum_{j=1}^{\lfloor x_\eta/Y \rfloor} d_n \mathbf{P}\{T_2(x_{\rho_n^*}) = j\}$$

$$\sim 1 - (1/d_n) \sum_{j=1}^{\lfloor x_\eta/Y \rfloor} \chi_n (1 - \chi_n)^j$$

as $n \to \infty$. By (9) we get

$$\mathbf{P}\{S_{T_2(x_{\rho_n^*})} > x_\eta\} \sim 1 - (\chi_n/d_n)(1 - \chi_n) \sum_{j=0}^{\lfloor x_\eta/Y \rfloor - 1} (1 - \chi_n)^j$$

$$= 1 - \frac{1 - (1 - \chi_n)^{\lfloor x_\eta/Y \rfloor}}{d_n}(1 - \chi_n)$$

$$= 1 - \frac{q_n^*(1 - q_n^*)^\theta \left(1 - (1 - q_n^*)^{\theta \lfloor x_\eta/Y \rfloor}\right)}{1 - (1 - q_n^*)^\theta} \tag{10}$$

since $(1 - q_n^*)^\theta = 1 - \chi_n$ holds. Taking the last string of (10) equal to $0 \le \eta \le 1$, one can get the critical value x_η of the bit loss $S_{T_2(x_{\rho_n^*})}$ that can be exceeded with probability η for large n, i.e.,

$$\lfloor x_\eta/Y \rfloor = \ln A/(\theta \ln(1 - q_n^*)),$$

where $A = 1 - (1 - \eta)(1 - (1 - q_n^*)^\theta)/(q_n^*(1 - q_n^*)^\theta)$. As $\lfloor x \rfloor \le x$ holds for the integer part $\lfloor x \rfloor$ of any real number x, we get

$$x_\eta \ge Y \ln A/(\theta \ln(1 - q_n^*)).$$

When $\theta = 1$ holds, we obtain the simplest formula

$$x_\eta \ge Y \ln \eta/\ln(1 - q_n^*).$$

The case $\theta = 1$ may correspond only to a high quantile $x_{\rho_n^*}$ and a q_n^* which is close to 1.

Random Packet Length

Now we consider the second alternative that the packet lengths $\{Y_i\}_i$ are random. Then it is important to determine beforehand whether the cluster size $T_2(u)$ and the packet length Y_i are mutually independent or not. This dependence can be checked by methods described, for instance, in [4], [11], [21]. Besides, the approximation of $\mathbf{P}\{S_{T_2(x_\rho)} \ge x_\eta\}$ is different for small and large values of ρ which correspond to wide and narrow bottlenecks $u = x_\rho$, respectively. We shall consider the case that ρ is close to zero.

Mutually Dependent Packet Length and Cluster Size.

We first suppose that $T_2(u)$ and Y_i are mutually dependent. Regarding many applications of modern communication networks, this is a realistic assumption since $T_2(u)$

is determined by the rates R_t due to (2) and these rates may be dependent on the packet lengths and be independent of the inter-arrival times, like for Skype traffic (see, for instance, [4], [11], [13], [21]). Therefore, we get for $t \in [0,1]$

$$0 \leq P\{S_{T_2(x_{\rho_n^*})} > x_\eta\} \tag{11}$$
$$= P\{S_{T_2(x_{\rho_n^*})} > x_\eta, T_2(x_{\rho_n^*}) \leq \lfloor nt \rfloor\} + P\{S_{T_2(x_{\rho_n^*})} > x_\eta, T_2(x_{\rho_n^*}) > \lfloor nt \rfloor\}$$
$$\leq P\{S_{\lfloor nt \rfloor} > x_\eta\} + P\{T_2(x_{\rho_n^*}) > \lfloor nt \rfloor\}.$$

Taking into account the independence of $\{Y_1, ..., Y_n\}$ and assuming that $\alpha_2 > \alpha_1^2$, where $\mathbf{E}Y_i = \alpha_1$ and $\mathbf{E}Y_i^2 = \alpha_2$ hold, we estimate $P\{S_{\lfloor nt \rfloor} > x_\eta\}$ using exponential bounds (called the Bernstein inequalities) (see [19, Theorem 2.8][3]) as follows:

$$P\{S_{\lfloor nt \rfloor} > x_\eta\} \leq W(x_\eta) \tag{12}$$
$$= \begin{cases} \exp\left(-\dfrac{(x_\eta - \lfloor nt \rfloor \alpha_1)^2}{4\lfloor nt \rfloor(\alpha_2 - \alpha_1^2)}\right), & \alpha_1 \leq x_\eta/\lfloor nt \rfloor \leq \alpha_2 + \alpha_1 - \alpha_1^2; \\ \exp\left(-\dfrac{x_\eta - \lfloor nt \rfloor \alpha_1}{4}\right), & x_\eta/\lfloor nt \rfloor \geq \alpha_2 + \alpha_1 - \alpha_1^2. \end{cases}$$

Using the notation $(1 - q_n^*)^\theta = 1 - \chi_n$ and following [16], we obtain from (8)

$$P\{T_2(x_{\rho_n^*}) > \lfloor nt \rfloor\} = \sum_{j=\lfloor nt \rfloor+1}^{\infty} P\{T_2(x_{\rho_n^*}) = j\}$$

$$= \frac{1}{d_n} \sum_{j=\lfloor nt \rfloor+1}^{\infty} d_n P\{T_2(x_{\rho_n^*}) = j\}$$

$$\sim \frac{1}{d_n} \sum_{j=\lfloor nt \rfloor+1}^{\infty} \chi_n (1 - \chi_n)^j$$

$$= q_n^* (1 - q_n^*)^{\theta(\lfloor nt \rfloor+1)} / (1 - (1 - q_n^*)^\theta) = \varphi(q_n^*) \tag{13}$$

as $q_n^* \sim 1 - \tau/n$, $0 < \tau < \infty$ and $n \to \infty$. The condition $q_n^* \to 1$ corresponds to a large value u of the bottleneck bandwidth close to a 100% quantile of the rates $\{R_i\}_i$. The equivalence in (13) follows from the assumption $\sup_n \mathbf{E}(T_2^\varepsilon(x_{\rho_n})) < \infty$ for some $\varepsilon > 0$ in [16, Theorem 3].

Using (11)-(13), we obtain

$$P\{S_{T_2(x_{\rho_n^*})} > x_\eta\} \sim W(x_\eta) + \varphi(q_n^*)$$

as $n \to \infty$. Taking $W(x_\eta) + \varphi(q_n^*)$ equal to η, $0 \leq \eta \leq 1$, we can obtain x_η if $\eta > \varphi(q_n^*)$ is chosen.

---

[3] Theorem 2.8 states: Let $X_1, ..., X_n$ be iid and $S_n = \sum_{k=1}^n X_k$. Suppose that $\mathbf{E}X_k = 0$, $\sigma_k^2 = \mathbf{E}X_k^2 < \infty$, $k = 1, ..., n$, $B_n = \sum_{k=1}^n \sigma_k^2$ and that there exists a positive constant H such that $|\mathbf{E}X_k^m| \leq 1/2 m! \sigma_k^2 H^{m-2}$, $k = 1, ..., n$, for all integers $m \geq 2$. Then $\mathbf{P}\{S_n \geq x\} \leq e^{-x^2/(4B_n)}$ if $0 \leq x \leq B_n/H$, and $\mathbf{P}\{S_n \geq x\} \leq e^{-x/(4H)}$ if $x \geq B_n/H$ hold.

Regarding the simplest case when $\theta = 1$ holds, it follows that $\varphi(q_n^*) = (1 - q_n^*)^{\lfloor nt \rfloor + 1}$ holds. Hence, $\eta > (\rho_n^*)^{\lfloor nt \rfloor + 1}$ must be given. Denoting $\nu = \alpha_1^2 - \alpha_2 < 0$ and $\eta_0 = (\rho_n^*)^{\lfloor nt \rfloor + 1} + \exp(\lfloor nt \rfloor \nu/4)$, then we obtain from (12) that

$$
x_\eta = \begin{cases} \alpha_1 \lfloor nt \rfloor + 2\sqrt{\lfloor nt \rfloor \nu \ln(\eta - (\rho_n^*)^{\lfloor nt \rfloor + 1})}, & \eta \geq \eta_0; \\ \alpha_1 \lfloor nt \rfloor - 4\ln(\eta - (\rho_n^*)^{\lfloor nt \rfloor + 1}), & \eta \leq \eta_0 \end{cases}
$$

holds.

Mutually Independent Packet Length and Cluster Size. Let us assume now that $T_2(u)$ and Y_i are mutually independent. Despite the case is somewhat artificial, we have to consider it, too.[4] We also assume that a sufficiently large transport capacity u is available at the bottleneck link.

Due to (8) it follows for large n that

$$
\mathbf{P}\{S_{T_2(x_{\rho_n^*})} > x_\eta\} = \sum_{j=1}^{\infty} \mathbf{P}\{\sum_{i=1}^{j} Y_i > x_\eta\} \mathbf{P}\{T_2(x_{\rho_n^*}) = j\}
$$

$$
\leq \frac{1}{d_n} \sum_{j=1}^{\lfloor x_\eta/\alpha_1 \rfloor} d_n \mathbf{P}\{T_2(x_{\rho_n^*}) = j\} W_j(x_\eta) + \frac{1}{d_n} \sum_{j=\lfloor x_\eta/\alpha_1 \rfloor + 1}^{\infty} d_n \mathbf{P}\{T_2(x_{\rho_n^*}) = j\}
$$

$$
\sim \left(\chi_n \sum_{j=1}^{\lfloor x_\eta/\alpha_1 \rfloor} (1 - \chi_n)^j W_j(x_\eta) + \chi_n \sum_{j=\lfloor x_\eta/\alpha_1 \rfloor + 1}^{\infty} (1 - \chi_n)^j \right) / d_n
$$

$$
= \left(\chi_n \sum_{j=1}^{\lfloor x_\eta/\alpha_1 \rfloor} (1 - \chi_n)^j W_j(x_\eta) + (1 - \chi_n)^{\lfloor x_\eta/\alpha_1 \rfloor + 1} \right) / d_n
$$

$$
= q_n^* \sum_{j=1}^{\lfloor x_\eta/\alpha_1 \rfloor} (1 - q_n^*)^{\theta j} W_j(x_\eta) + \frac{q_n^*(1 - q_n^*)^{\theta(\lfloor x_\eta/\alpha_1 \rfloor + 1)}}{1 - (1 - q_n^*)^\theta} \tag{14}
$$

holds. Here we use the upper bound

$$
\mathbf{P}\{\sum_{i=1}^{j} Y_i > x_\eta\} \leq W_j(x_\eta) = \begin{cases} \exp\left(-\frac{x_\eta - j\alpha_1}{4}\right), & j \leq \lfloor x_\eta/(\alpha_1 - \nu) \rfloor, \\ \exp\left(-\frac{(x_\eta - j\alpha_1)^2}{4j(\alpha_2 - \alpha_1^2)}\right), & \lceil x_\eta/(\alpha_1 - \nu) \rceil \leq j \leq \lfloor x_\eta/\alpha_1 \rfloor \end{cases}
$$

with $-\nu = \alpha_2 - \alpha_1^2 > 0$. Taking the right hand side of (14) equal to η, a numerical inversion will yield a quantile estimate x_η.

In conclusion, we see that all four relevant cases yield simple formulae to approximate the quality indices of a packet flow which experiences a loss at a bottleneck link due to an insufficient transport capacity. Currently, a measurement campaign is prepared to validate the derived theoretical insights based on different voice and video streams traversing a bottleneck link with tunable bandwidth.

---

[4] The rate $R_i = Y_i/X_i = a$, where a is constant, provides an example when R_i and hence $T_2(u)$ do not depend on both Y_i and X_i. For any application the mutual dependence has to be checked.

4   Conclusions

In this paper we have considered a fundamental teletraffic issue arising from the control of packet transmission processes that are generated by real-time applications in high speed packet-switched networks. We have studied quality indices describing the loss process experienced by a packet flow at a single bottleneck link along a fixed route of the flow, where a given minimal transport capacity has been assigned to that flow at this specific link. Our approach is based on the assumption that a bufferless queue models the link with regard to real-time flows in adequate manner and that the induced rate process of the flow is a sufficient flow descriptor. We have defined the number of lost packets and the volume of lost bits as major quality indices that characterize the loss process of the considered flow at the bottleneck link.

We have realized that the loss process can be described by clusters of those packet rates exceeding the given bottleneck bandwidth of the capacity-constrained link. Extending fundamental results from statistical theory of extremes developed by our previous research [14] - [16], we were able to obtain the bit-loss distribution and its quantiles. The latter quantiles imply the critical levels of the bit loss for some given values of the bottleneck bandwidth and provide a simple tool for teletraffic engineering. Furthermore, we have obtained inferences for flow processes with both random and constant packet lengths of the underlying streams. Sufficiently high quantiles of the packet rates, which are close to 100%, are used to characterize the transport capacity of the bottleneck. If the packet rates are dependent random variables, the level of the latter quantile has been evaluated by means of quantiles of the block-maxima arising from the underlying rate process.

All these quantiles were obtained assuming that a bottleneck with a large transport capacity is available. Our proposed new statistical approach has the advantage that the latter equivalent capacity may be, in most cases, smaller than the sampled maximal rate proposed by the equivalent bandwidth concept of Guerin et al. [6]. Furthermore, the critical values of the bit loss can be derived from a simple real-time monitoring of flows. It can be used to inform the customers or their traffic sources about the probability to lose packets at a bottleneck link whose actual value of the transport capacity is only available for a short period.

In this way, new control protocols can be developed for adaptive flow control in teletraffic engineering and new engineering rules regarding the capacity assignment to real-time flows at critical links of high speed networks can be designed.

A validation of the proposed theoretical results based on measurements of the packet loss processes arising from the transport of multimedia packet flows along a single link with tunable bandwidth is the subject of our future research.

References

1. Beirlant, J., Goegebeur, Y., Teugels, J., Segers, J.: Statistics of Extremes: Theory and Applications. Wiley, Chichester (2004)
2. Bon, J.-L., Kalashnikov, V.: Some estimates of geometric sums. Statistics and Probability Letters 55, 89–97 (2001)

3. Dán, G., Fodor, V.: Delay asymptotics and scalability for peer-to-peer live streaming. IEEE Trans. Parallel Distrib. 20(10), 1499–1511 (2009)
4. D'Auria, B., Resnick, S.: Data network models of burstiness. Advances in Applied Probability 38, 373–404 (2006)
5. Ferro, C.A.T., Segers, J.: Inference for Clusters of Extreme Values. J. R. Statist. Soc. B 65, 545–556 (2003)
6. Guérin, R.A., Ahmadi, H., Naghshineh, M.: Equivalent Capacity and Its Application to Bandwidth Allocation in High-Speed Networks. IEEE Journal on Selected Areas in Communications 9(7), 968–981 (1991)
7. Hoßfeld, T., Schatz, R., Krieger, U.: QoE of YouTube Video Streaming for Current Internet Transport Protocols. In: Fischbach, K., Krieger, U.R. (eds.) MMB & DFT 2014. LNCS, vol. 8376, pp. 139–153. Springer, Heidelberg (2014)
8. Kalashnikov, V.: Geometric Sums: Bounds for Rare Events with Applications. Kluwer Academic Publishers, Dordrecht (1997)
9. Liu, F., Li, Z.: A Measurement and Modeling Study of P2P IPTV Applications. In: CIS 1, pp. 114–119. IEEE Computer Society (2008)
10. Markovich, N.M., Krieger, U.R.: Statistical Inspection and Analysis Techniques for Traffic Data Arising from the Internet. In: HETNETs 2004, Special Issue on "Convergent Multi-Service Networks and Next Generation Internet: Performance Modelling and Evaluation", pp. 72/1–72/9 (2006)
11. Markovich, N.M., Kilpi, J.: Bivariate statistical analysis of TCP-flow sizes and durations. Annals of Operations Research 170(1), 199–216 (2009)
12. Markovich, N.M.: Nonparametric Estimation of Univariate Heavy-Tailed Data. J. Wiley & Sons, Chichester (2007)
13. Markovich, N.M., Krieger, U.R.: Statistical Analysis and Modeling of Skype VoIP Flows. Computer Communications (COMCOM) 31(Suppl. 1), 11–21 (2010)
14. Markovich, N.M.: Quality Assessment of the Packet Transport of Peer-to-Peer Video Traffic in High-Speed Networks. Performance Evaluation 70, 28–44 (2013)
15. Markovich, N.M.: Analysis of Packet Transmission in Peer-to-Peer Overlay Networks. In: Preprints of the International IFAC Conference on Manufacturing Modelling, Management, and Control, MIM 2013, Saint-Petersburg, Russia, June 19-21, pp. 956–961 (2013)
16. Markovich, N.M.: Modeling Clusters of Extreme Values. Extremes (2013) (accepted), doi:10.1007/s10687-013-0176-3
17. Richards, A.: On upper bounds for the tail distribution of geometric sums of subexponential random variables. Queueing Systems 62, 229–242 (2009)
18. Robinson, M.E., Tawn, J.A.: Extremal analysis of processes sampled at different frequences. Journal of the Royal Statistical Society Series B 62(1), 117–135 (2000)
19. Petrov, V.V.: Limit Theorems of Probability Theory: Sequences of Independent Random Variables. Oxford University Press, New York (1995)
20. Qiu, D., Srikant, R.: Modeling and Performance Analysis of BitTorrent-Like Peer-to-Peer Systems. In: Proc. ACM SIGCOMM, pp. 367–377 (2004)
21. van de Meent, R., Mandjes, M.: Evaluation of 'user-oriented' and 'lack-box' traffic models for link provisioning. In: Proceedings of the 1st EuroNGI Conference on Next Generation Internet Networks Traffic Engineering, Rome, Italy. IEEE (2005)
22. Weissman, I.: Estimation of parameters and large quantiles based on the k largest observations. Journal of American Statistical Association 73, 812–815 (1978)

A Comparative Study of Traffic Properties for Web Pages Optimized for Mobile Hand-Held and Non-mobile Devices

Julius Flohr and Joachim Charzinski

Stuttgart Media University
University of Applied Sciences
Stuttgart, Germany
{jf053,charzinski}@hdm-stuttgart.de

Abstract. Even though the mobile Web is gaining more and more importance in the Web environment, relatively little is known about the traffic properties of Web pages optimized for mobile handheld devices (*MHDs*). This paper explores some characteristics of Web sites optimized for MHDs and compares them to their non-mobile counterparts. This is done using actively initiated measurements for which the homepages of the 500 most popular Web sites on the Internet have been contacted. The results show that most mobile versions of the pages are smaller than the non-mobile versions. The average mobile version of a homepage is about 30% smaller and similarly less complex as the non-mobile version.

1 Introduction

Mobile Web is on the rise. For 2013 the marketing analyst Gartner has identified the mobile device market as one of the largest trends in technology [15]. According to them, in 2013 the smartphone will overtake the PC as the most common web access device worldwide. While the exact crossover date is disputed, the general trend of smartphones and tablets being prefered for Web access is clear. This change in access technology has forced Web sites to adapt their pages to new input methods, screen sizes and resolutions. Even though web pages optimized for mobile access have been available for some time, relatively little is known which effect these adaptations have on the underlying network and how these pages optimized for mobile devices are different from their desktop counterparts. Both the browser identity string interpreted by the server and the possibly different behaviors of mobile and desktop browsers influence the difference in traffic characteristics between mobile and desktop browsing. Many studies of mobile network performance however still use the very simplistic and outdated Web traffic model from [12].

The work at hand gives an insight into this traffic aspect of the mobile Web. In order to make experiments reproducible, a predefined set of Web pages is used for actively initiated measurements similar to [4], but comparing the results obtained with a desktop client to those obtained with a mobile hand-held device

K. Fischbach and U.R. Krieger (Eds.): MMB & DFT 2014, LNCS 8376, pp. 29–42, 2014.
© Springer International Publishing Switzerland 2014

(MHD). The starting pages of the 500 most popular Internet services according to Alexa [13] are contacted and analyzed on a service level in order to provide 1:1 comparisons of the traffic caused by a mobile client and a desktop client, respectively, when visiting the same page. Even though this approach does not represent the usage behavior of any actual user group, it still helps to get an insight into the differences between web applications optimized for mobile and desktop browsers. The focus here is on the difference between desktop and mobile versions of the same Web pages and not on presenting a new representative traffic model.

The rest of this paper is organized as follows: Section 2 gives a short overview of related work. Section 3 explains in detail how the test environment has been setup, how the measurements have been analyzed and the methods for verification of the setup are described. The main results are presented in Section 4.

2   Related Work

As outlined in the previous section, MHDs nowadays play an important role in the landscape of modern web. While there has been a lot of research on the new challenges and possibilities of content adaptation and user interface design [1], relatively little is known about the traffic properties of real world Web pages and their composition in direct comparison to their non-mobile counterpart. One of the first publications in the mobile Web traffic field is by *Maier et al.* [10]. In early 2009 they analyzed anonymized packet level data of more than 20,000 residential DSL customers. For identification of packets belonging to a connection established by a MHD heuristics were used. They concluded that most of the mobile traffic is composed out of media content and mobile application downloads and that the majority of traffic is caused by Apple iOS devices. While this approach includes real-world traffic and app downloads, it has a bias towards the services used in a specific country by mobile devices connecting to the Internet via residential WLAN. The context of use will be different in other countries and when users are actually mobile. Apart from this, especially the mobile Web has changed in the past few years. In the same year *Falaki et al.* [5] published a paper for which they intercepted the mobile traffic of over 40 users on a device-level which allows a more detailed and fine grained traffic analysis. They found out that for the average user mobile traffic consisted of roughly 50 % browsing while each of email, maps and media contribute roughly 10 %. They further concluded that packet loss was the main factor which limited throughput on mobile devices.

The first paper presenting a comparative study of MHDs and non-mobile devices was by *Gember et al.* in 2011 [7]. They analyzed the traffic of two different campus wireless networks for three days and identified over 30.000 unique clients. They found that MHDs tend to have a low UDP usage and that their share of video traffic is greater than on non-MHDs but did not analyze traffic properties of Web pages in direct comparison.

3   Test Environment and Setup Verification

3.1   Test Environment and Setup

This section gives a detailed overview of the setup environment used to identify and eliminate systematic errors.

Data Generation and Collection. In order to gain a deeper understanding of the properties of services optimized for MHDs, a test setup has been chosen where measurements are initiated actively. As depicted in Figure 1, the setup

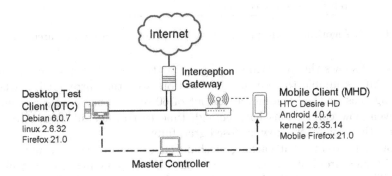

Fig. 1. Architectural Overview of Testing Environment

consists of four different entities: The Master Controller (MC), the Interception Gateway (IG), a Desktop Test Client (DTC) and a MHD. A "rooted" HTC Desire HD is used as MHD. The IG is a Linux VM responsible for recording and storing the traffic produced by the MHD and the DTC. For this task it has been configured to act as a router which connects the DTC and MHD to the Internet.

The MC is responsible for carrying out the whole experiment: It starts/stops the recording of traffic on the IG and triggers the request for a Web page on either MHD or DTC. Communication between MC and DTC/MHD is done via SSH and Android Debug Bridge[1], respectively. When recording the traffic of several different devices, it is necessary to differentiate between those. Doing so on IP level only would be possible but the IG stores the recorded traffic into one large binary file. For later analysis it is beneficial to be able to exactly match every packet not only to a device but also to which page request it belongs. These page requests almost always consist of several connections to multiple different hosts. Therefore, they are further on referred to as *Request Batches*. In order to be able to differentiate between Request Batches, the MC sends specially crafted UDP packets to the IG which are then written to binary recording. These packets contain information about the current device under test (DUT) and the requested home page.

---

[1] `https://developer.android.com/tools/help/adb.html`, accessed 07.17.2013.

---

tell IG to start recording
for *URL* in *URLList* **do**
   send UDP identifier "MHD", *URL*
   tell MHD to open *URL*
   wait for 60 seconds
   tell MHD to close browser window gracefully
   send UDP identifier "DTC" and *URL*
   tell DTC to open *URL*
   wait for 60 seconds
   tell DTC to close browser window gracefully
end for
tell IG to stop recording

Fig. 2. Algorithm Performed by Master Controller During Measurement

Figure 2 shows the algorithm performed by the MC during a measurement. As the MC is unable to receive a notification from the current DUT when a homepage has finished loading, a timeout of 60 seconds has been set to ensure that even slow connections have enough time to transfer all data. After this timeout, the browser window is closed gracefully.

In order to assure that caching mechanisms of the browsers do not interfer with the measurements, both browsers have been configured to start in safe mode. This means that the browser deletes all content from its internal caches as well as every cookie received during the session when it closes.

Data Analysis

Analysis of the data recorded is performed off-line: after the data have been recorded by the IG, the analysis is done with the help of several python scripts. First, one script iterates over every packet recorded and extracts relevant information for every request batch. This information is then stored in a SQLite database in order to decrease turn around times when performing actual statistical analysis. This is done by another python script.

First test measurements have revealed that current mobile operating systems and applications in general tend to contact the publisher on a frequent basis. E.g., the Android Operating System regularly sends TLS encrypted traffic to servers belonging to Google. In order to ensure that this communication is not interfering with the measurements, this communication has been identified and blacklisted for the analysis process. For the measurements performed during this research project, roughly 10 % of the traffic generated by the MHD was considered unwanted and was filtered out. There was no correlation between this background noise and the size of the requested page.

3.2   Selection of Web Browsers

Unfortunately, it is currently not possible to obtain reliable market share numbers for Web browsers on Android. Since Android 4.2 (Jelly Bean), Chrome has been the default browser[17]. Therefore, first tests were performed using this browser. However, it turned out that Chrome behaves even more unpredictably on the network interface than Firefox. This includes permanent sanity checks of DNS replies and reporting of network problems to Google. Therefore Firefox was selected as the browser for the measurements. By rooting the used MHD it was possible to use a version of tcpdump [16] which has been ported to the ARM microprocessor architecture [18] and thus to verify that Firefox and Chrome exhibit the same behavior on WLAN connections and wireless wide area network (*WWAN*) connections.

3.3   Setup Verification

In order to verify the test setup, an HTML test page was deployed on a server and requested several hundred times by both DUTs. After applying the whole tool chain on the recorded data, it was possible to validate the outcome with the known properties of the test page. It turned out that modern web browsers are using complicated heuristics [2] in order to maximize performance whilst minimizing data transfer volumes. This results in the Web browser not always fetching every HTML element on the page and therefore distorting the result. For Example, Firefox requests the favicon.ico, a small user-definable image for bookmarks [9], only on every second page visit.

In order to quantify the error introduced by this circumstance, the Mean Absolute Error (*MAE*) of the number of HTML elements retrieved (MAE_e) is calculated. The MAE is preferable over the mean square error in situations such as ours where data vary over multiple orders of magnitude [8].

$$MAE_e = \frac{1}{n} \sum_{i=1}^{n} |f_i - y_i| \tag{1}$$

where n is the sample size, f_i the measured value and y_i the real value. For the mobile Web browser, the calculated MAE_e is 0.011, for the desktop web browser it is 0.181. To verify that the error is independent of the number of page elements on a Website, the MAE_e has been calculated for different test pages with 1, 10 and 50 HTML elements. The resulting margin of error of the MAE_e was 0.002.

Since there is a tight dependency between the number of elements received from a server and bytes transferred, the MAE of the downstream volume, MAE_d, can easily be approximated by multiplying MAE_e with the mean size of the elements retrieved:

$$MAE_d = MAE_e (\frac{1}{n} \sum_{i=1}^{n} elementSize_i) \tag{2}$$

For the measurements performed during this experiment, this implies an error of 185kB for the DTC and 7kB for the MHD.

Table 1. Overview of key characteristics of collected data

	Pages visited	Unique hosts	No. of connections	Downstream Volume	No. of tracking pixels	No. of HTTP elements
MHD	500	4874	19378	342MB	689	21324
DTC	500	8362	28499	541MB	1953	42312
total	1000	11946	47877	883MB	2642	63636

Table 2. Per page characteristics

	Downstream Volume	HTML Elements Retrieved	Unique Host Contacts	Connect-ions	Web Bugs
MHD min	3KB	1	1	1	0
MHD max	29.5MB	497	65	371	25
MHD avg	684KB	44	10	38	1
DTC min	1KB	1	1	1	0
DTC max	65.8MB	475	118	382	69
DTC avg	1MB	83	17	57	4

4   Measurements and Main Results

For the actual experiment a list of the 500 most popular Web pages world wide [13] (retrieved May 24.2013) was used. Only these web pages have been opened. No other browsing was performed during the experiment. The usage behavior of this simulation does not represent an actual user group since it does not perform any interaction with the site at all. Still, it is able to give an insight to the properties of current state Web applications. Furthermore, this well-defined workload is a prerequisite for the direct comparison between desktop and mobile versions of the same page, and it allows detailed inspection of all packets without privacy issues. The measurements were performed on an ADSL2+ (Annex A) connection from German provider Alice with 16 Mbit/s downstream and 1024 kbit/s upstream. The whole measurement was performed three times and average values for each site visited were calculated in order to decrease the impact of stochastic errors. The measurements have been performed on June 07 2013 at 17:00, on June 12 2013 at 10:00 and on June 15 2013 at 23:00. An overview of the experiment characteristics is given in table 1.

In addition, table 2 gives a detailed overview of the minimum, maximum and average per page values of downstream volume, number of unique host contacts, number of connections and number of Web bugs when visiting the pages with the MHD and the DTC, respectively. For the DTC, six sites did not transfer any data. For the MHD, a total of 12 servers were not responding. Those pages have been excluded from the statistic.

4.1   Downstream Volumes

One of the most interesting metrics for describing a Web application is the amount of data transferred from the Web application to the client. For data collection, the lengths of all IP packets sent to the client were added, as long as the sender has not been blacklisted (cf. Section 3.1). Figure 3 depicts a comparative scatter plot where each point is defined by the amount of data sent to client when requesting the desktop and the MHD version of a web page. The plot indicates that a large amount of Web services deliver mobile versions which are smaller than their desktop counterpart. Most of the mobile versions are between one tenth and the same size as the traffic received by the desktop for the same URL. The empirical cumulative complementary distribution functions (ccdf) of MHD and DTC downstream volume per page are given in Figure 4. The distributions are similar in shape but over a wide range of sizes the mobile pages are around 1/3 of the size of the desktop pages.

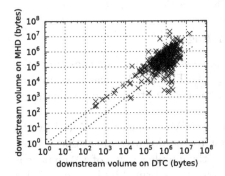

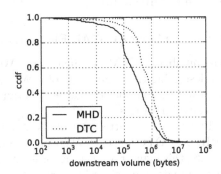

Fig. 3. Scatter plot of downstream volume received for every tested page. Helper lines are at $y = x$ and $y = x/10$.

Fig. 4. Cumulative Complementary Distribution Function (ccdf) of the number of bytes received per site request

However, Figure 3 also shows that a few sites deliver a MHD version of a page which is *larger* than its desktop counterpart. Analyzing the ccdf of the ratio of bytes received by the MHD versus the DTC for the same in Figure 5 reveals that nearly 20 % of the Web pages tested deliver more traffic to a mobile terminal than to a desktop computer. As Figure 3 shows, this happens mostly for pages of more than 100 kB. Most of the effect can be due to variations between subsequent retrievals of the same page (such as delivering different advertisements), but 5 % of the pages delivered more than 50 % more traffic to the MHD than to the DTC. This is often caused by an implementation error in a common Javascript video player: A lot of pages embed a Adobe Flash[2]-based video player on their desktop home page. Since most mobile hand-held devices don't support this technology, the mobile version of these pages often use a video player implemented in Javascript. However, there are some implementations of such players

---

[2] http://www.adobe.com/products/flash.html, accessed Dec. 20 2013.

which don't wait for user interaction but rather start downloading video files immediately after the homepage has been loaded.

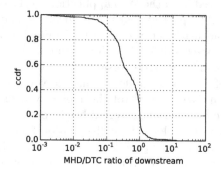

Fig. 5. Cumulative Complementary Distribution Function (ccdf) of the ratio of bytes received by MHD to bytes received by the desktop for the same page

4.2   Number of HTML Elements per Page

The number of HTML elements on a Web page is one of the key characteristics for describing the complexity of a Web page [3]. This number was measured by counting the number of packets containing an HTTP status code indicating a successful data transfer[3] [6].

Figure 6 is a scatter plot of the number of HTML elements retrieved by the MHD and DTC for each Web page. Similar to the downstream traffic volume results, this figure reveals that for most cases, the mobile version of a Web page is less complex than its desktop counterpart. This is confirmed by Figure 7, which shows the ccdf of the ratio of number of elements retrieved for each page.

As MHD displays are significantly smaller than desktop computer screens, it does not make sense to display the same number of images or the same size of videos on an MHD as on a desktop. The lower number of elements also is in line with the lower downstream volume of pages on the MHD that was already observed in Figure 5. Again, there are some (5 %) pages which delivered significantly (50 %) more elements to a mobile client than to the desktop.

4.3   Number of Connections and Unique Host Contacts

Another important metric for the complexity of a Web page is the number of connections opened and whether these connections are handled by one or multiple servers [3]. The number of connections was counted as the number of packets which had the TCP flags SYN and ACK set during data evaluation. This was combined with a list of IP addresses generated during a page request in order to decide whether the host had been contacted before. Figure 8 shows the number of connections, while Figure 9 depicts the number of unique hosts contacted for each page request.

---

[3] Status codes beginning with 2.

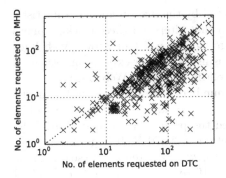

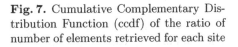

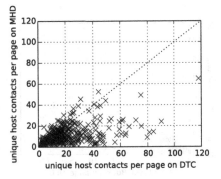

Fig. 6. Scatter plot of number of HTML elements received for every tested page. Helper line is at $y = x$.

Fig. 7. Cumulative Complementary Distribution Function (ccdf) of the ratio of number of elements retrieved for each site

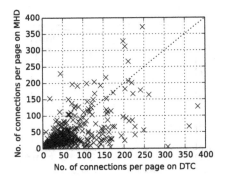

Fig. 8. Scatter plot of the number of connections established for every tested page. Helper line is at $y = x$.

Fig. 9. Scatter plot of the number of unique hosts contacted for every tested page. Helper line is at $y = x$.

Both metrics show that most mobile pages are less complex than their desktop counterpart versions, but there are also a few pages whose mobile versions are significantly more complex. Most of the points in both scatter plots correspond to the typical ratio of 3–4 connections per host (cf. Table 2), but especially in the upper part of Figure 8 it is visible that the extreme cases of more complex mobile pages caused the terminal to request many more elements from the servers but without increasing the number of servers correspondingly.

4.4   Web Bugs

Web Bugs are small, one pixel sized (often transparent) images which are not cachable. Advertising and user tracking code makes Web browsers request those images so that advertisers and trackers can profile users, e.g. to improve the match between advertisements and the current user's interests.

To identify Web Bugs in the data collected by the measurements, a heuristic was used: Ghostery [14] is a browser plugin that filters out these tracking pixels by matching every element of a Web page against a list of known Web bugs before actually requesting the element. This list of regular expressions was used to analyze the recorded traffic and thus identify all known Web Bugs.

Figure 10 displays a scatter plot of the number of Web Bugs identified in the mobile vs. desktop versions of each page. User tracking is also used on mobile Web pages, but not as excessively as when the pages were requested from the desktop computer, where some pages contained 20–70 Web bugs. Still, pages which are using tracking techniques on desktop web sites tend to do so on mobile pages as well but on a smaller scale. Figure 10 reveals that roughly 60 % of all tested web pages are tracking their users on the desktop version of their website while for the mobile version the number is around 50%. Note that the non-integer number of Web bugs comes from the fact that each page was loaded multiple times and in some cases the results varied slightly between the three replications.

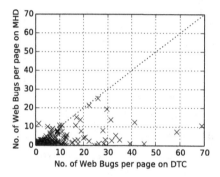

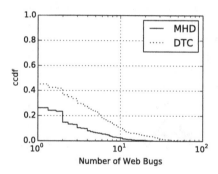

Fig. 10. Scatter plot of the number of detected Web Bugs for every tested page. Helper line is at $y = x$.

Fig. 11. Cumulative Complementary Distribution Function (ccdf) of the number of Web Bugs contained in tested Web pages

4.5 Usage of Content Delivery Networks

Content Delivery Networks are a technology for moving page content to a network of caching servers which are distributed around the world. This reduces the distance between the user and the server and therefore increases the usable data rate while latency is reduced and availability is increased [11]. To determine whether a Web page served data via a CDN, a heuristic was used: Before a client is able to establish a connection to a server on the Internet, the client first queries the Domain Name System (*DNS*) for the server's IP address using the Fully Qualified Domain Name (*FQDN*). From the DNS server's reply, the relation between FQDN and IP address is saved alongside with the downstream volume of every connection to the server's IP address. Further, the reverse DNS name of the IP address (lookup via in-addr.arpa) and the authoritative name

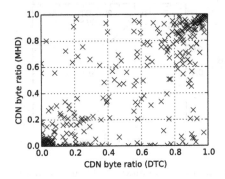

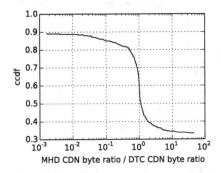

Fig. 12. Scatter plot of ratios (ratio of CDN traffic to all traffic) for MHD and DTC

Fig. 13. Cumulative Complementary Distribution Function (ccdf) of MHD CDN ratio to DTC CDN ratio

servers for the domain are retrieved. The information gathered from the DNS system is matched against a list of known CDN provider domains.

Figure 12 is a scatter plot of ratios (ratio of CDN traffic to all traffic) for the pages transferred to MHD and DTC. The plot shows that a large number of Web sites only delivers a small amount or nothing of its content via a Content Distribution Network whereas other pages rely heavily on CDNs. It is interesting to notice that the number of websites which use CDNs for their mobile version or for their desktop version is quite large. This is confirmed by Figure 13: 35 % of all Web sites tested delivered a significantly (factor 10) higher traffic share to mobiles than to desktops via CDNs (lower right end of the distribution in Figure 13). On the other hand, only 15 % of the sites delivered a significantly (factor 10) higher traffic share to desktops than to mobiles via CDNs (upper left end of the distribution in Figure 13).

4.6   Comparison to Past Results for Desktop

As the methodology used in the present paper is similar to [4], the present results can be compared to the results for a desktop with an empty cache ("S1") in [4] from Feb. 2009. Although this comparison does not cover the mobile client results and the list of top 500 sites has changed, it can give valuable insight on the recent long-term development of Web page size and complexity. This is a short summary of the main findings.

The **downstream volume** caused by the Web pages has increased by a factor of 2–4. In 2009, 70 % of the pages were larger than 300 kB, now 80 % are larger than 300kB. In 2009, 20 % of the pages were larger than 800 kB, now 20 % are larger than 2 MB. The average changed from 507 kB to 1 MB. The cumulative complementary distribution functions are depicted in Figure 14.

Page complexity in terms of the number of **elements** per page has increased slightly. The mean number of elements has increased from 64.7 to 83 per page, which is mainly an effect of the distribution head and tail, as shown in Figure 15.

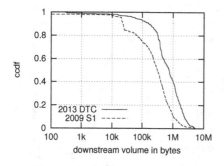

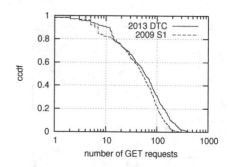

Fig. 14. Cumulative Complementary Distribution Function (ccdf) of downstream volume in current measurement (2013 DTC) and corresponding measurement from [4] (2009 S1)

Fig. 15. Cumulative Complementary Distribution Function (ccdf) of the number of GET requests per site in current measurement (2013 DTC) and corresponding measurement from [4] (2009 S1)

The share of pages with less than ten elements has dropped from 16 % in 2009 to 8 % in 2013 and the share of pages with more than 200 elements has increased from less than 2 % to 9 %.

Page complexity in terms of the number of **connections** and the number of unique **hosts** contacted has increased more significantly, as the distributions in Figures 16 and 17 indicate. Both measures have more than doubled in the past four years: The mean number of hosts contacted per page has increased from 7.6 to 17 and the average number of connections per page has risen from 25 to 57.

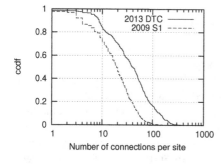

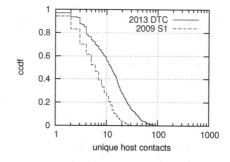

Fig. 16. Cumulative Complementary Distribution Function (ccdf) of the number of connections for each page in current measurement (2013 DTC) and corresponding measurement from [4] (2009 S1)

Fig. 17. Cumulative Complementary Distribution Function (ccdf) of the number of unique hosts contacted for each page in current measurement (2013 DTC) and corresponding measurement from [4] (2009 S1)

Note that these numbers do not only reflect traffic growth per page, as user preferences have also changed and the top 500 Web sites in 2013 are not the same as in 2009 – only 264 sites are part of both the 2009 and the 2013 top site lists. As this change of sites also reflects a change in user behavior, the above comparisons were performed on the full sets of 500 sites each.

5   Conclusion

Web pages look different on mobile clients than on desktops. This is due to servers delivering different or differently tailored content on the one hand and to mobile browsers behaving differently from desktop browsers on the other hand. In this paper, we assessed those differences with automated actively initiated measurements, requesting the same top 500 Web sites' landing pages on a desktop and on a mobile device. The measurements revealed that from most sites, mobile clients get significantly different content than desktops. In most cases (65 %), the mobile version is at least 10 % smaller than the desktop version, but in a few cases mobiles get much more traffic. The average mobile version is roughly 30 % smaller than the desktop version of the same page (684 kB vs. 1 MB).

A corresponding reduction of complexity is also observed with around 40 % fewer hosts contacted and connections required to load a mobile page compared to its desktop counterpart. If a site tracks user behavior on a desktop, it is likely to do so as well on a mobile, but with fewer tracking pixels ("Web Bugs") in total. Sites that do not use Web Bugs for desktops are also unlikely to use them with mobiles. However, they could still use other techniques for user tracking.

Overall, an increase of desktop traffic per page of a factor of 2–4 is observed compared to previous measurements from 2009. Page complexity has also increased since 2009, but only with a factor of around 2.

References

1. Anam, R., Ho, C.K., Lim, T.Y.: Web content adaptation for mobile devices: A greedy approach. International Journal of New Computer Architectures and their Applications (IJNCAA) 1(4), 1027–1042 (2011)
2. Babu, G.S., Srivatsa, S.: Design and implementation of web prefetching solution. International Journal of Engineering and Technology 2(1), 99–102 (2012)
3. Butkiewicz, M., Madhyastha, H.V., Sekar, V.: Understanding website complexity: measurements, metrics, and implications. In: Proceedings of the 2011 ACM SIGCOMM Conference on Internet Measurement, pp. 313–328. ACM (2011)
4. Charzinski, J.: Traffic Properties, Client Side Cachability and CDN Usage of Popular Web Sites. In: Müller-Clostermann, B., Echtle, K., Rathgeb, E.P. (eds.) MMB & DFT 2010. LNCS, vol. 5987, pp. 136–150. Springer, Heidelberg (2010)
5. Falaki, H., Lymberopoulos, D., Mahajan, R., Kandula, S., Estrin, D.: A first look at traffic on smartphones. In: Proceedings of the 10th Annual Conference on Internet Measurement, pp. 281–287. ACM (2010)

6. Fielding, R., Gettys, J., Mogul, J., Frystyk, H., Masinter, L., Leach, P., Berners-Lee, T.: Hypertext Transfer Protocol – HTTP/1.1. RFC 2616 (Draft Standard) (June 1999), http://www.ietf.org/rfc/rfc2616.txt, updated by RFCs 2817, 5785, 6266, 6585

7. Gember, A., Anand, A., Akella, A.: A comparative study of handheld and non-handheld traffic in campus Wi-Fi networks. In: Spring, N., Riley, G.F. (eds.) PAM 2011. LNCS, vol. 6579, pp. 173–183. Springer, Heidelberg (2011), http://dl.acm.org/citation.cfm?id=1987510.1987528

8. Hyndman, R.J., Koehler, A.B.: Another look at measures of forecast accuracy. International Journal of Forecasting 22(4), 679–688 (2006)

9. Jain, A.K.: User-definable images in bookmarks, US Patent App. 09/478,585 (January 6, 2000)

10. Maier, G., Schneider, F., Feldmann, A.: A first look at mobile hand-held device traffic. In: Krishnamurthy, A., Plattner, B. (eds.) PAM 2010. LNCS, vol. 6032, pp. 161–170. Springer, Heidelberg (2010), http://dl.acm.org/citation.cfm?id=1889324.1889341

11. Pallis, G., Vakali, A.: Insight and perspectives for content delivery networks. Communications of the ACM 49(1), 101–106 (2006)

12. 3GPP: TR 25.892, Feasibility Study for OFDM for UTRAN enhancement. 3GPP Technical Report (2004)

13. Alexa Internet Inc.: Top 1 million homepages, updated daily, http://s3.amazonaws.com/alexa-static/top-1m.csv.zip (accessed May 24, 2013)

14. Evidon, Inc.: Ghostery browser plugin, http://www.ghostery.com/ (accessed July 15, 2013)

15. Gartner, INC. Gartner identifies the top 10 strategic technology trends for 2013, http://www.gartner.com/newsroom/id/2209615 (accessed July 15, 2013)

16. tcpdump: http://www.tcpdump.org/ (accessed July 19, 2013)

17. ZDnet: http://www.zdnet.com/blog/networking/android-quietly-partners-up-with-chrome/2547 (accessed July 17, 2013)

18. Seal, D.: ARM architecture reference manual. Pearson Education (2000)

Construction Methods for MDD-Based State Space Representations of Unstructured Systems

Rüdiger Berndt, Peter Bazan, Kai-Steffen Hielscher, and Reinhard German

Friedrich-Alexander-Universität, Erlangen, Germany
ruediger.berndt@cs.fau.de
http://www7.cs.fau.de/~berndt

Abstract. Multi-valued Decision Diagrams (MDDs) are used in various fields of application. In performance evaluation, a compact representation of the state space of Markovian systems can often be achieved by using MDDs. It is well known that the size of the resulting MDD representation heavily depends on the variable ordering, i.e. the arrangement of the levels within the MDD. Markov models, derived from higher level descriptions of the system, often contain structural information. This information might give hints for an optimized variable ordering a priori, i.e. before the MDD is constructed. Whenever a model is described by constraints—considering the design space of a system, for example—there is a lack of such structural information. This is the reason why the MDD representation often consumes too much memory to be handled efficiently. In order to keep the memory consumption practicable, we have developed two optimization mechanisms. The presented examples demonstrate that efficient MDD representations of the feasible design space can be obtained, even for large unstructured systems.

Keywords: Unstructured systems, Design space, Multi-valued decision diagram, Variable ordering, Constraint computation sequence.

1 Introduction

Communication systems are often modeled with higher-level formalisms, including queuing networks [1], Stochastic Petri Nets (SPN) [1], stochastic process algebras [2, 3] or Unified Modeling Language (UML) models [4]. However, the state space representations derived from higher-level models might still be too large to be stored explicitly. This problem can be addressed by using efficient storage structures such as decision diagrams. In general, Binary Decision Diagrams (BDDs) encode binary functions [5], whereas Multi-valued Decision Diagrams (MDDs) encode multi-valued functions [6]. Both structures are suited to represent the state space of a model.

Tools providing efficient symbolic state space generation algorithms are, among others, the probabilistic symbolic model checker PRISM [7], the qualitative and quantitative analyzer of Generalized Stochastic Petri Nets (GSPNs) MAR-CIE [8], or the stochastic model checking analyzer for reliability and timing SMART [9].

K. Fischbach and U.R. Krieger (Eds.): MMB & DFT 2014, LNCS 8376, pp. 43–56, 2014.
© Springer International Publishing Switzerland 2014

To reduce the memory consumption of decision diagrams, static variable orderings make use of the model's structure to find a good ordering a priori. Dynamic variable ordering modifies the arrangement of the decision diagram's levels after the construction. In order to keep the size of the decision diagram small, dynamic ordering can also be applied during the construction is in progress.

In this article we introduce two new optimization techniques for the construction of MDD-based state space representations considering large unstructured systems. The first one, *Mass-Spring-Relaxation* (MSR), has been designed to determine good static variable orderings. The performance of the second technique, *BestFit*, is superior to the one of the *SortLevel* method, which has been introduced in [22]. In general, both methods are applied during the construction of the MDD and determine a constraint computation sequence to keep the size of intermediate MDDs small. The applicability of the new methods is demonstrated by successfully constructing the feasible design space of six real-world automotive configuration problems. Among others, these MDD representations can later be used to verify consistency rules as stated in [23].

This article is organized as follows: in section 2 we give an overview of related work. Section 3 introduces the formal model for the description of unstructured systems and the new construction methods. In section 4 the toolchain is explained, first. Afterwards, an example of a structured and an unstructured system are discussed. Section 5 concludes our work.

2   Related Work

In [10], an overview of AND/OR Multi-valued Decision Diagrams (AOMDDs) as a compiled data structure for constraint networks is given. Decision diagrams and the problem of determining optimal variable orderings are covered in many scientific articles. Finding an optimal ordering for binary or multi-valued decision diagrams is known to be NP-complete [11].

A survey of static variable ordering methods, i.e. heuristics to establish an adequate variable arrangement prior to the actual state space construction, is presented in [12]. The tool MARCIE, for example, provides built-in computation of static variable orderings, and the tool SMART implements static variable ordering methods presented in [13].

Dynamic variable ordering is achieved by swapping two adjacent levels in a decision diagram. Algorithms restricting successive swaps to a window of a maximal and a minimal level are presented in [14] and [15]. By performing all variable permutations within this window only, a local optimization is achieved. This window is then moved over the whole decision diagram's range of levels. The sifting algorithm [16] widens the window without increasing the computational effort because only one variable is moved up or down, respectively.

Beside these two basic methods, many other algorithms have been proposed. Freely distributed software packages which provide variable ordering algorithms are given, for example, by the Colorado University Decision Diagram Package (CUDD) [17] and JINC [18].

Hadzic et. al. [19] provide a method to solve the problem of interactive configuration. The authors describe a two-phase approach in order to avoid time-consuming search effort in the configuration process. The offline phase yields a pre-compiled binary decision diagram representing the space of solutions—i.e. valid configurations. In the following, this structure is the basis for the online phase where the actual configuration is performed. Doing so allows to move the computational effort to the offline phase.

3   Construction Methods

This chapter presents two new methods which are used for the construction of unstructured systems' feasible design spaces; it is organized as follows. Firstly, a formal model for the description of unstructured systems will be introduced in section 3.1. Based on that, in section 3.2, the new *MSR* algorithm is developed. This method computes appropriate static variable orderings for unstructured systems. Finally, the last section introduces a new method to optimize the constraint computation sequence.

3.1   Design Space, Constraints, and Feasible Design Space

This section introduces the formal model for the description of unstructured systems. The finite, non-empty set of distinct symbols $A := \{a_1, \ldots, a_n\}$ is denoted as the set of *attributes*. The partition $V := \{V_1, \ldots, V_m\}$ of A is referred to as the set of *variables*. For a given A and V, the set

$$W := V_1 \times \cdots \times V_m \tag{1}$$

can be derived. This set will henceforth be denoted as the *design space*.

In order to express that certain combinations of attributes, and thus elements within the design space, are infeasible, *constraints* are introduced in the following way. A *constraint* is an m-tuple $c := (P_1, \ldots, P_m)$, $P_i \subseteq V_i$, which induces the set:

$$W(c) := P_1 \times \cdots \times P_m \tag{2}$$

Therefore, each constraint imposes a relation among a subset of variables $\hat{V} \subseteq V$. This set is referred to as the constraint's scope:

$$s(c) := \{V_i | V_i \neq P_i, 1 \leq i \leq m\} \tag{3}$$

Let the set of constraints be denoted as $R := \{c_1, \ldots, c_k\}$. Hence, for a given A, V, and R, the *feasible design space* can be derived as follows:

$$\overline{W}(R) := W \setminus \bigcup_{1 \leq i \leq k} W(c_i) \tag{4}$$

Fig. 1 illustrates an example of the formal model. Here, the design space W, the constraint c_1, and the feasible design space $\overline{W}(R) = W \setminus W(c_1)$ are

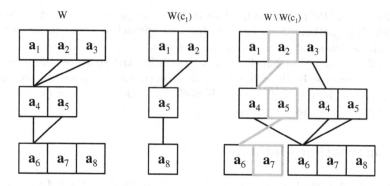

Fig. 1. Design space W, a constraint c_1, and the feasible design space $\overline{W}(R)$

represented by an MDD. The different levels of the MDDs correspond to the variables $V_i \in V$. Each path, starting from the top to the bottom node, yields one element of W, $W(c_1)$, and $W \setminus W(c_1)$, respectively. The gray lines of $W \setminus W(c_1)$ represent the element $(a2, a5, a7)$.

Given A, V, and R, no structural information on the system is available, and the sole knowledge on relations among variables is within the scopes of constraints. This information is the basis for the *Mass-Spring-Relaxation* method (MSR) to obtain static variable orderings.

3.2   Mass-Spring-Relaxation

The *MSR* method is inspired by algorithms known, among others, from the field of Sensor And Actor Networks (SANETs)—considering, for example, fault tolerant and robust localization [20]. It is based upon the idea of connecting mass points with linear-elastic springs. Hence, according to *Hooke's law*, each mass point m_i is affected by the force

$$F_i := \sum_j F_{i,j} = \sum_j d(m_i, m_j) \cdot K_{i,j} \tag{5}$$

The terms $F_{i,j}$ denote the forces between all mass points m_j being connected to m_i via springs. The term $d(m_i, m_j)$, furthermore, depicts the distance between the two mass points m_i and m_j. The scalar constant $K_{i,j}$ represents the spring constant for the spring connecting m_i and m_j. Regarding SANET applications, mass-spring-relaxation algorithms aim on finding positions for the mass points such that the sum of the corresponding forces is minimized. In the following, this idea is applied to unstructured systems to identify adequate static variable orderings.

First, for each pair of variables V_i, V_j, with $(i \neq j)$, a spring and the according spring constant $K_{i,j}$ are derived from the set of constraints R as follows:

$$K_{i,j} := n(i, j) + |V_i| + |V_j| = K_{j,i}, \quad \text{where} \tag{6}$$

$$n(i, j) := |\{c \in R | V_i, V_j \in s(c)\}| \tag{7}$$

In order to determine a distance between variables, all $V_i \in V$ are mapped to positions X_i in the interval $[0,1] \in \mathbb{R}$. For each variable $V_i \in V$ a force F_i can be calculated by the following term:

$$F_i := \sum_j F_{i,j} = \sum_j (X_j - X_i) \cdot K_{i,j} \tag{8}$$

Given the vector $\mathbf{F}$ of the forces, the vector $\mathbf{X}$ of the positions, and the matrix $\mathbf{K}$ of the spring constants, the whole system can be written as a system of linear equations:

$$\mathbf{K} \cdot \mathbf{X} = \mathbf{F} \tag{9}$$

Now, one variable V_{i_0} is selected and mapped to the position 0, and another variable V_{i_1} is selected and mapped to the position 1. The positions X_{i_0} and X_{i_1} are treated as constants, whereas the positions of the remaining variables $V_j \in V$ are regarded as unknowns.

According to the application within the SANET domain, the sum of forces affecting each variable $V_i \in V$ is to be minimized. In our case, all F_i with $i \neq i_0, i_1$ are set to zero. With these additional conditions, now the linear equation system (9) can be solved. For a resulting $\mathbf{X}$, the following weighting function, which takes into account that $|F_{i,j}| = |F_{j,i}|$, is defined:

$$w(\mathbf{X}) := \sum_{i<j} |F_{i,j}| \tag{10}$$

The linear equation system (9) is solved for each combination of variables $V_{i_0}, V_{i_1} \in V$. From the set of the resulting $\frac{m \cdot (m-1)}{2}$ solutions, we choose a solution $\mathbf{X}_{min}$ given that $w(\mathbf{X}_{min})$ is a minimum. For $\mathbf{X}_{min}$ a variable ordering is obtained by transferring the natural ordering ($\leq$) of the positions in $\mathbb{R}$ to the set of variables V.

The complexity of the algorithm is given by $\mathcal{O}(m^5)$: number of combinations $\mathcal{O}(m^2)$, Gaussian elimination of an $m \times m$ matrix: $\mathcal{O}(m^3)$. However, the run time can be reduced by exploiting the sparseness of the matrix.

3.3   Best-Fit

According to (4), the feasible design space is obtained by subtracting the union of all constraints from the set W. The toolchain implements this operation by successively subtracting constraints from the MDD. This sequence is referred to as *constraint computation sequence*, and does not only determine the dynamics of memory consumption during dynamic variable ordering, but also affects the process of constructing the MDD after having identified a good variable ordering. For large unstructured systems and an arbitrary computation sequence, it is not always possible to construct the MDD representation because intermediate MDD representations might exceed the memory limitations. Therefore we introduce the new method *BestFit* to keep the size of intermediate MDDs small.

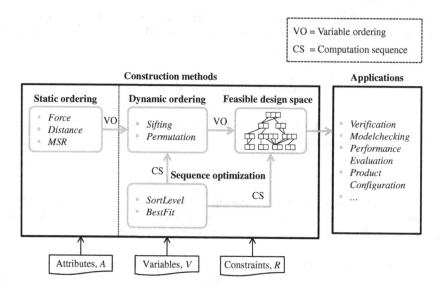

Fig. 2. Toolchain for the construction methods

During the construction of $\overline{W}(R)$ the best fitting constraints are subtracted first. Let an intermediate $\overline{W}(R_i)$ with $R_i \subset R$ be given. Now, each $c \in R \setminus R_i$ is subtracted from $\overline{W}(R_i)$. The best fitting constraint c is the one with the *least memory consumption* regarding the MDD representation of $\overline{W}(R_i) \setminus W(c)$. Accordingly, a flatter growth of memory consumption is obtained, but computational costs increase. Therefore, by taking only a limited number $R_j \subset R \setminus R_i$ of constraints into account, the computational costs can be reduced again.

The efficiency of the method can be further improved in the following way: in each step t, the set R_{j_t} is constructed such that all $|R_{j_{t-1}}|/2$ best fitting constraints of the preceding step $t - 1$ become elements of the new R_{j_t}. The enhanced computation sequence—obtained during MDD construction—can be memorized and applied whenever the MDD has to be constructed again. This results in a significant speed up.

4   Application

This chapter demonstrates the capability of the new construction methods. In Section 4.1, we first describe the toolchain for the construction of the MDD-based design space representations of unstructured systems described by constraints. The subsequent section introduces our first example, a component-based Generalized Stochastic Petri Net (GSPN). By exploiting information on the model's structure, a good static variable ordering is obtained. Still, the memory consumption of the MDD representation can be further reduced by applying dynamic variable ordering.

Table 1. Memory consumption (in [MB]) of four different variable orderings regarding the Petri net example's state space

Dynamic variable ordering	Variable orderings			
	Model structure	Random		
	A	B	C	D
No	2.1	144	142	137
Sifting	0.53	0.54	0.57	0.59

Table 2. Dimensions and results of the automotive configuration problems

Problem	Cardinality			Performance	
	Attributes	Variables	Constraints	Size [MB]	Time [Sec.]
P1	989	168	2487	41	14
P2	1001	176	3040	25	9
P3	943	174	4679	2	13
P4	1240	181	4413	48	47
P5	1116	160	3844	120	188
P6	781	157	2161	1	6

The second example introduces six configuration problems of the automotive application domain (section 4.3). These problems do not contain structural information. We demonstrate that the application of the *MSR* method yields good a priori variable orderings. Combining the initial *MSR* ordering along with the application of dynamic variable ordering and the *BestFit* computation sequence yields MDD representations with least memory consumption.

4.1   Toolchain

The toolchain (see Fig. 2) is written in C++ and consists of two stages: the first stage deals with finding an appropriate static variable ordering. For this purpose the following approaches were implemented: *Force* [21], *Distance*, and the new *MSR* method. The *MSR* approach has been specifically designed with regard to unstructured systems and, in our examples, yields the best a priori variable ordering.

During the second stage the MDD representation of the feasible design space is computed. For the application of dynamic variable ordering, the methods *Permutation* [15] and *Sifting* [16] are available. The specification of a window size allows to control the computational cost of each algorithm. Dynamic variable ordering is combined with one of the two built-in sequence optimization methods, *BestFit* and *SortLevel*.

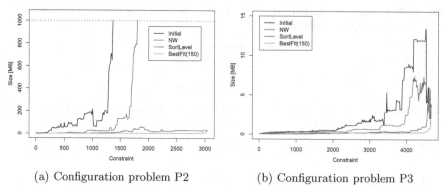

(a) Configuration problem P2   (b) Configuration problem P3

Fig. 3. Dynamics of memory consumption with regard to four different computation sequences

4.2   Structured State Space Example

Structural information is useful for the construction of the MDD-based state space representation and can often be derived from high level descriptions of the model. If the information is used to determine a static variable ordering, it is assumed that the size of the MDD representation can be kept small. This is demonstrated with the help of a component-based GSPN example as illustrated in Fig. 4:

Seven clients can send messages to seven servers via *Channel Send*. *Client 1* sends messages to *Server 1*, *Client 2* to *Server 2*, and so forth. Each message has a type t to indicate the communicating pair of client and server. The servers reply to the corresponding clients via *Channel Receive*. The capacity of all places within this GSPN is one. Accordingly, a transition is disabled if at least one outgoing arc is connected to a place containing a token. The initial tokens of the channels are of the type $t = 0$ and the initial tokens of client *Client x* and *Server x* are of type $t = x$. Therefore the token types are from the range 0 to 7. Tokens of each type might follow the arcs which are not marked.

Whenever an arc, connecting a place with a transition, is marked with a token type t, only tokens of type t will enable this transition. In the case that an arc from a transition to a place is marked with t, a token of type t is moved to the place after the transition has fired. This GSPN is confusion free due to its structure, the place capacities, and the given token types. Therefore the underlying Continuous Time Markov Chain (CTMC) can be constructed without problems.

However, for our example only the reachable state space was computed in advance and stored to be reused, because the goal was to investigate the effect of different variable orderings. The reachable state space of this example contains 1.1 million states. For this example no static ordering algorithm like MSR is used. The initial variable ordering is derived from the structure of the model instead. This ordering yields an MDD which consumes 2.1 MB. When applying dynamic variable ordering—Sifting—the memory consumption can be reduced

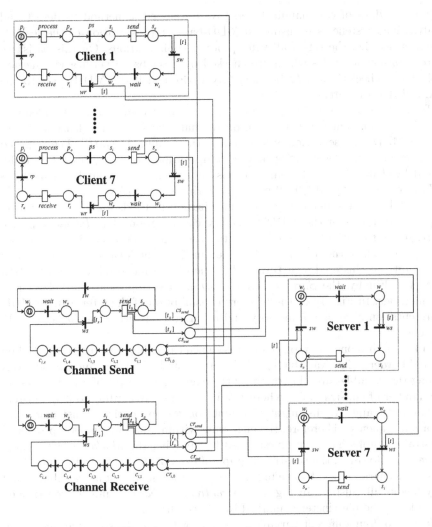

Fig. 4. GSPN with seven server and seven client components

to 0.53 MB (variable ordering A in Table 1). Considering random static variable orderings (B, C, and D in Table 1), the corresponding dynamically optimized MDDs require similar amounts of memory; even though the initial memory consumptions vary from 137MB to 144MB. In contrast to that, the MDD using variable ordering A initially consumes 2.1 MB, only. Thus, variable orderings derived from the model structure can significantly reduce the initial size. Still, using dynamic optimization, the memory consumption can be further decreased.

4.3 Unstructured Design Space Example

Highly customizable products and mass customization—as increasing trends of the last years—are mainly responsible for an immense growth of complexity within the data of car manufacturers. We developed a method to detect and analyze inconsistencies by using an MDD-based representation of the feasible design space, i.e. the set of all valid product configurations. On this basis, we stated consistency rules which are checked by a set-based verification method [23]. These checks can only be efficiently performed if the MDD fits into the RAM of the computer.

Table 2 depicts the dimensions of six real-world configuration problems of a major car manufacturer. In addition to that, the size of the feasible design space's MDD representation is provided in the column *Size[MB]*. The required computation time—using an optimized computation sequence (*BestFit*)— is depicted by *Time [Sec.]*. All computations have been carried out by using a 2.8 GHz Intel Core 2 Quad Q9550 processor with 8 GB of RAM.

Fig. 3 depicts the behavior of the optimization methods for the computation sequence in terms of the MDD's memory consumption. The *Initial* sequence corresponds to the sequence of the data base. The *NW* curve is obtained by the application of the algorithm described in [24]. The idea of this approach is to exploit the clustered structure within the constraint graph of configuration problems. Finally, the *SortLevel* and *BestFit* curve represent the behavior of our methods. In Fig. 3 (a), the memory consumption of the intermediate MDD representation exceeds the memory limitation of 1 GB using the *Initial* or *NW* sequence.

In Fig. 5, the constraint graph of P1 is shown (including an extract, marked by the red border). Each variable $V_i \in V$ is represented by a node, and the relations among the variables are illustrated by the edges. The weight of an edge depicts the number of constraints c_k where $\{V_i, V_j\} \in s(c_k)$. According to [24], clusters within constraint graphs might give hints on an appropriate constraint computation sequence. Therefore, the clustering within our configuration problems' constraint graphs has been investigated by applying the *Markov Cluster Algorithm* [25]. However, the constraint graph of each of the configuration problems P1 - P6 is characterized by one big cluster—containing almost all variables—and only few small clusters. In Fig. 5, the *central variable* (i.e. mostly constrained variable) of the big cluster is marked by a green frame.

In Fig. 6, four different variable orderings of P1 are shown. Each line represents a variable $V_i \in V$. The length of a variable's line depicts the number of constraints c_j where $V_i \in s(c_j)$. The arrangement of the lines, starting from the top to the bottom, corresponds to the arrangement of the MDD's levels. Fig 6 (a), (b) and (c) represent the static variable orderings obtained from the algorithms of the toolchain. The variable ordering of Fig. 6 (d) is established due to dynamic variable ordering (Sifting, window size 5), starting with the *MSR* ordering. Considering all configuration problems, the *MSR* algorithm yields the best a priori orderings insofar as time-consuming dynamic ordering (cf. window size) can be avoided and, in addition to that, the corresponding dynamically obtained variable ordering requires the least memory consumption (cf. Table 2, *Size[MB]*) compared to the other static approaches.

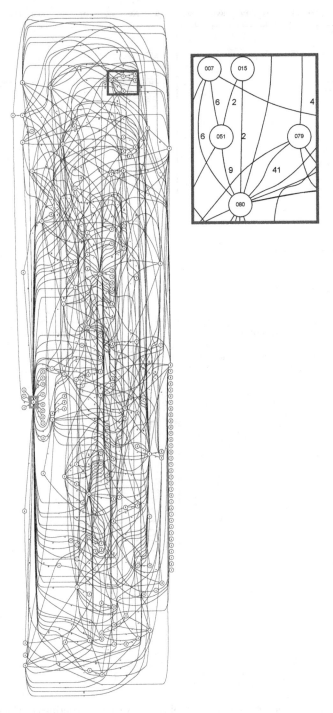

Fig. 5. An unstructured system's constraint graph (configuration problem, P1)

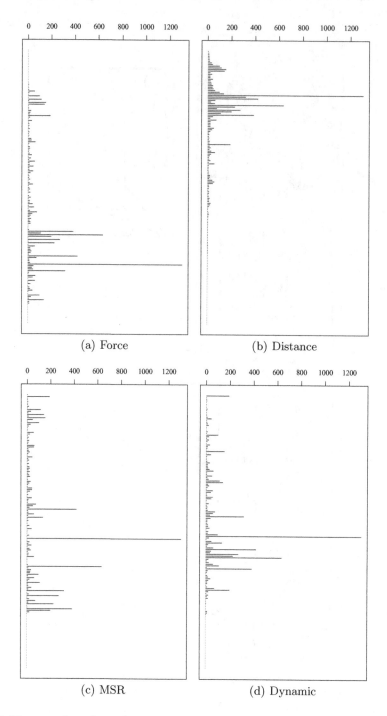

(a) Force

(b) Distance

(c) MSR

(d) Dynamic

Fig. 6. Three static and one dynamically obtained variable orderings of the configuration problem P1

5   Conclusion

In this article we have presented two new methods for the construction of MDD-based state space representations of large unstructured systems and compared them with algorithms from literature. For the automotive configuration problems, the first method, *MSR*, yields the best static variable orderings. This approach exploits information on the relations among variables which are induced by the set of constraints.

The second method, *BestFit*, is applied in combination with dynamic variable ordering and determines a constraint computation sequence. This sequence yields a flatter growth of the MDD's memory consumption compared with the sequences of the other applied algorithms. We also presented our toolchain which realizes the described methods. The applicability of the two new methods has been demonstrated by computing the MDD-based feasible design space of six large real-world configuration problems of the automotive domain. Considering all implemented algorithms, the feasible design space of the automotive configuration problems could only be successfully constructed by the application of our methods (*MSR*, *BestFit*, and *SortLevel*).

It is important to realize that the variable orderings and the computation sequences can be memorized by the toolchain and used again to efficiently reconstruct the MDD representations without applying time-consuming dynamic variable ordering and sequence optimization. This is necessary, among others, when the set of constraints is changed.

References

1. Bolch, G., Greiner, S., de Meer, H., Trivedi, K.S.: Queueing Networks and Markov Chains, 2nd edn. John Wiley and Sons, New York (2006)
2. Hillston, J., Ribaudo, M.: Stochastic process algebras: a new approach to performance modeling. In: Modeling and Simulation of Advanced Computer Systems, pp. 235–256, Gordon Breach (1998)
3. Hermanns, H., Herzog, U., Katoen, J.-P.: Process algebra for performance evaluation. Theoretical Computer Science 274(12), 43–87 (2002)
4. Trowitzsch, J., Jerzynek, D., Zimmermann, A.: A toolkit for performability evaluation based on stochastic UML state machines. In: VALUETOOLS 2007, p. 30 (2007)
5. Bryant, R.E.: Graph-based algorithms for Boolean function manipulation. IEEE Transactions on Computers C-35 (8), 677–691 (1986)
6. Kam, T., Villa, T., Brayton, R.K., Sangiovanni-Vincentelli, A.: Multivalued decision diagrams: theory and applications. Multiple-Valued Logic 4(1-2), 9–62 (1998)
7. Kwiatkowska, M., Norman, G., Parker, D.: PRISM 4.0: Verification of Probabilistic Real-Time Systems. In: Gopalakrishnan, G., Qadeer, S. (eds.) CAV 2011. LNCS, vol. 6806, pp. 585–591. Springer, Heidelberg (2011)
8. Heiner, M., Rohr, C., Schwarick, M.: MARCIE – Model Checking and Reachability Analysis Done Efficiently. In: Colom, J.-M., Desel, J. (eds.) PETRI NETS 2013. LNCS, vol. 7927, pp. 389–399. Springer, Heidelberg (2013)
9. Ciardo, G., Jones III, R.L., Miner, A.S., Siminiceanu, R.: Logic and stochastic modeling with SMART. Perform. Eval (PE) 63(6), 578–608 (2006)

10. Mateescu, R., Marinescu, R., Dechter, R.: AND/OR Multi-valued Decision Diagrams for Constraint Optimization. In: Bessière, C. (ed.) CP 2007. LNCS, vol. 4741, pp. 498–513. Springer, Heidelberg (2007)
11. Bollig, B., Wegener, I.: Improving the Variable Ordering of OBDDs Is NP-Complete. IEEE Transactions on Computers 45(9) (1996)
12. Rice, M., Kulhari, S.: A Survey of Static Variable Ordering Heuristics for Efficient BDD/MDD Construction, Technical Report, UC Riverside (2008)
13. Siminiceanu, R.I., Ciardo, G.: New Metrics for Static Variable Ordering in Decision Diagrams. In: Hermanns, H., Palsberg, J. (eds.) TACAS 2006. LNCS, vol. 3920, pp. 90–104. Springer, Heidelberg (2006)
14. Fujita, M., Matsunaga, Y., Kakuda, T.: On variable ordering of binary decision diagrams for the application of multi-level logic synthesis. In: Proceedings of the Conference on European Design Automation (EURO-DAC 1991), pp. 50–54. IEEE Computer Society Press, Los Alamitos (1991)
15. Ishiura, N., Sawada, H., Yajima, S.: Minimazation of Binary Decision Diagrams Based on Exchanges of Variables. In: ICCAD 1991, pp. 472–475 (1991)
16. Rudell, R.: Dynamic variable ordering for ordered binary decision diagrams. In: ICCAD 1993, pp. 42–47 (1993)
17. Somenzi, F.: CUDD: Colorado University Decision Diagram Package, Release 2.4.2. User's Manual and Programmer's Manual (February 2009)
18. Ossowski, J., Baier, C.: A uniform framework for weighted decision diagrams and its implementation. STTT 10(5), 425–441 (2008)
19. Hadzic, T., Subbarayan, S., Jensen, R.M., Andersen, H.R., Moller, J., Hulgaard, H.: Fast Backtrack-free Product Configuration using a Precompiled Solution Space Representation. In: PETO Conference, DTU-TRYK, pp. 131–138 (2004)
20. Eckert, J., Villanueva, F., German, R., Dressler, F.: Distributed Mass-Spring-Relaxation for Anchor-Free Self-Localization in Sensor and Actor Networks. In: Proceedings of 20th International Conference on Computer Communications and Networks (ICCCN), pp. 1–8 (2011)
21. Aloul, A.F., Markov, L.I., Sakallah, A.K.: FORCE: A Fast and Easy-to-Implement Variable-Ordering Heuristic. In: Great Lakes Symposium on VLSI (GLSVLSI), Washington, D.C., pp. 116–119 (2003)
22. Berndt, R., Bazan, P., Hielscher, K.-S.: MDD-based Verification of Car Manufacturing Data. In: 3rd International Conference on Computational Intelligence, Modelling and Simulation (CIMSiM), pp. 187–193 (2011)
23. Berndt, R., Bazan, P., Hielscher, K.-S., German, R., Lukasiewycz, M.: Multi-valued Decision Diagrams for the Verification of Consistency in Automotive Product Data. In: Proceedings of the 12th International Conference on Quality Software (QSIC), pp. 189–192 (2012)
24. Narodytska, N., Walsh, T.: Constraint and variable ordering heuristics for compiling configuration problems. In: Proceedings of the 20th International Joint Conference on Artificial Intelligence, pp. 149–154 (2007)
25. van Dongen, S.: A cluster algorithm for graphs, Technical Report INS-R0010, National Research Institute for Mathematics and Computer Science in the Netherlands, Amsterdam (May 2000)

Performance Analysis of Computing Servers — A Case Study Exploiting a New GSPN Semantics

Joost-Pieter Katoen[1], Thomas Noll[1], Thomas Santen[2],
Dirk Seifert[2], and Hao Wu[1,*]

[1] Software Modeling and Verification Group
RWTH Aachen University, Germany
{katoen,noll,hao.wu}@cs.rwth-aachen.de
[2] Advanced Technology Labs (ATL) Europe
Microsoft Research, Aachen, Germany
{thomas.santen,dirk.seifert}@microsoft.com

Abstract. Generalised Stochastic Petri Nets (GSPNs) are a widely used modeling formalism in the field of performance and dependability analysis. Their semantics and analysis is restricted to "well-defined", i.e., confusion-free, nets. Recently, a new GSPN semantics has been defined that covers confused nets and for confusion-free nets is equivalent to the existing GSPN semantics. The key is the usage of a non-deterministic extension of CTMCs. A simple GSPN semantics results, but the question remains what kind of quantitative properties can be obtained from such expressive models. To that end, this paper studies several performance aspects of a GSPN that models a server system providing computing services so as to host the applications of diverse customers ("infrastructure as a service"). Employing this model with different parameter settings, we perform various analyses using the MaMa tool chain that supports the new GSPN semantics. We analyse the sensitivity of the GSPN model w.r.t. its major parameters –processing failure and machine suspension probabilities– by exploiting the native support of non-determinism. The case study shows that a wide range of performance metrics can still be obtained using the new semantics, albeit at the price of requiring more resources (in particular, computation time).

Keywords: Computing Services, Model-Based Analysis, Generalized Stochastic Petri Nets, Markov Automata.

1   Introduction

Goal of the paper. The goal of this paper is to introduce an industrial case study that demonstrates the application of a newly developed semantics [1,2] of Generalised Stochastic Petri Nets (GSPN). This semantics covers basically every GSPN, in particular those which exhibit non-determinism that, e.g., is due to the presence of confusion. This paper presents a simple, abstract GSPN model of a

* Supported by ATL, the RWTH Aachen University Seed Fund, and the EU FP7 SENSATION project.

K. Fischbach and U.R. Krieger (Eds.): MMB & DFT 2014, LNCS 8376, pp. 57–72, 2014.

computing service, and analyses its performance properties from both a customer and a provider point of view. We do so by exploiting the MaMa tool chain [3] which supports the new GSPN semantics and relies on various algorithms from Markov decision theory.

Computing services. The growing cost of installing and managing computer systems leads to outsourcing of computing services to providers. We use the term computing services to refer to any kind of server system providing computing resources such as physical or virtual machines in order to host the applications of diverse customers. Examples of such systems are hosting centers that provide out-sourced computing capabilities to customers. If these resources are accessible via Internet, one speaks about cloud computing. In particular, the most basic form of cloud service, the so-called infrastructure-as-a-service model, conforms to this setting, providing physical or virtual machines to the customer. Here, the cloud OS can support large numbers of machines and has the ability to scale services up and down according to customers' varying requirements. Quality of service and cost efficiency are important factors from both the customer's and the provider's perspective.

Focus of this study. This paper investigates non-functional properties of a simple computing service. We are in particular interested in the performance under several users' requirements. Questions of interest are, e.g., how to scale the server system, i.e., how many machines are needed to achieve a certain service level? When can certain bottleneck situations such as long waiting times occur? An important focus is on the sensitivity of these performance aspects when varying the two main system parameters – the rate of processing failures and the rate of putting machines into suspended mode. Apart from these performance issues, we are also interested in power consumption by computing services.

Approach. The computing server is succinctly modelled as a GSPN [4]. Machines can be either operational ("ready") or stand-by ("suspended"), and randomly switch between these modes. Job loads are generated by a Poisson process, and job processing may randomly fail. It is a closed model, i.e., jobs that have been processed return to a pool from which new job requests can be generated. Two user profiles are considered: scientific computing tasks with high computational demands and small (or large) client populations, and web service tasks with low computational demands and large client populations. The GSPN is analysed using the recently developed MaMa tool chain[1]. Put in a nutshell, the GSPN is mapped onto a Markov automaton (MA; [5]), an extension of a continuous-time Markov chain with non-determinism, and analysed using several new algorithms [3]. The capability to deal with non-determinism allows for analysing non well-defined GSPNs; in fact, the new GSPN-semantics is (weak) bisimulation equivalent to the classical GSPN semantics [1]. We exploit non-determinism for analysing the sensitivity of various performance metrics w.r.t. variations of the main system parameters. The response-time distribution in steady state is obtained by a combination of the PASTA theorem and the tagged token technique.

---

[1] Publicly available at: http://wwwhome.cs.utwente.nl/~timmer/mama/.

Main results and findings. GSPNs turn out to be a convenient modelling formalism in our setting; the resulting model is succinct and easily extendible. Our analysis gives useful insight into the initial number of ready machines so as to keep the time until jobs cannot directly be processed below a certain threshold, and to keep the long-run average number of queued jobs at a minimum. This is valuable information to adequately dimension the computing server. The response-time distribution shows that being in equilibrium, the system can guarantee a reasonably low response time in the majority of cases when job requests are organised in a FIFO queue. Taking a random service policy however gives rise to a substantial increase in response time. The sensitivity analyses reveal that the failure rate has not a significant impact on the expected time until no ready machine is available but has a large influence on reaching 50% and 90% job queue capacity.

Main contributions. To summarize, our main scientific contributions are:
1. a simple GSPN model for computing servers in which machines can be operational ("ready") or stand-by ("suspended"), and job processing may randomly fail;
2. an extensive set of evaluation results focusing on expected durations until given system occupancies, long-run objectives, response-time distribution and energy consumption;
3. a sensitivity analysis of the two major model parameters –processing failures and machine down rates– by exploiting non-determinism;
4. a first industrial case study using the recent GSPN-to-Markov automata semantics [1] and accompanying analysis algorithms [3].

Organization of this paper. Sect. 2 briefly introduces GSPNs, their mapping onto MA, and the analysis algorithms. Sect. 3 presents the GSPN model of the computing server. Sect. 4 is the main section of the paper and presents our evaluation results. Sect. 5 discusses related work, and Sect. 6 concludes.

2   Modeling Formalism: GSPNs

The scenario. In this paper we analyse an exemplary service offering computing resources. We explore two scenarios: first, an application that is supposed to process a number of jobs as they occur, for example, in scientific calculations for weather forecasts, or biometric and medical simulations. Typically, such jobs are long running and processing is requested with a proportionally low frequency. Often they are executed in batches. The second scenario reflects a web service. Here jobs are running much shorter but they occur at a considerably higher frequency. In both scenarios we analyse the influence of various parameters on the overall performance of the service. For example, an insufficient number of available machines impacts the response time of the service, as jobs have to be queued until they can be processed. If new instances are requested, the time to start these instances delays their availability. Furthermore, instances can be detracted from the user due to application failures or for maintenance reasons. On the other hand, an over-dimensioned number of available (and mostly idling) machines unnecessarily increases the costs to run the service as well as the energy consumption of the data center. In the following we introduce our formal model that enables such analyses.

GSPNs. Generalised Stochastic Petri Nets (GSPNs) [4] are a modelling formalism for concurrent systems involving randomly timed behaviour. GSPNs inherit from Petri nets the underlying bipartite graph structure, partitioned into *places* and *transitions* and extend this by distinguishing between *timed* and *immediate* transitions. The latter can fire instantaneously and in zero time upon activation. The firing time of a timed transition is governed by a rate which uniquely defines a negative exponential distribution. A special form of timed transitions is of type *n-Server*, meaning that the given rate is multiplied by the number of predecessor tokens to yield the actual transition rate. Timed transitions are depicted as non-solid bars labelled by "n-Server", if applicable, while immediate transitions are depicted as solid bars. An example of a GSPN is shown in Fig. 2.

GSPN semantics. The semantics of a GSPN may conceptually be considered as consisting of two stages [4]. The first (abstract) stage describes when and which transitions may fire, and with what likelihood. This basically conforms to playing the token game of a net. The second stage defines the underlying stochastic process –typically a continuous-time Markov chain (CTMC)– which represents the intended stochastic behaviour captured in the first stage. This CTMC is obtained by amalgamating sequences of immediate firings. Performance analysis of the GSPN then amounts to analysing the transient or steady-state behaviour of its underlying CTMC. This trajectory works fine for well-defined GSPNs, i.e., nets that are confusion-free. Recently, a new GSPN semantics has been proposed [1] that covers all definable GSPNs, in particular nets that contain confusion. The semantics is defined in terms of Markov automata (MA), which are basically transition systems in which transitions are either labelled with the action τ (representing the firing of an immediate transition), or with the rate of an exponential distribution. The target of an action transition is a discrete probability distribution over the states while for a rate-labelled transition it is simply a state. For confusion-free GSPNs, this semantics is (weakly) bisimilar to the two-phase GSPN semantics. States in MA correspond to markings of the net. It falls outside the scope of this paper to give a full-fledged treatment of this semantics; we rather present a simple example, see Fig. 1. The example net is confused, as transitions t_1 and t_2 are not in conflict, but firing transition t_1 leads to a conflict between t_2 and t_3, which does not occur if t_2 fires before t_1. Transitions t_2 and t_3 are weighted so that in a marking $\{p_2, p_3\}$ in which both transitions are enabled, t_2 fires with probability $\frac{w_2}{w_2+w_3}$ and t_3 with its complement probability. Fig. 1 depicts the MA semantics of this net. Here, states correspond to sets of net places that contain a token. In the initial state, there is a non-deterministic choice between the transitions t_1 and t_2. In this paper, we

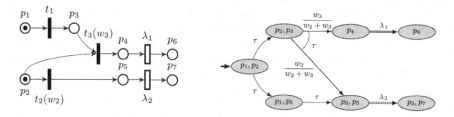

Fig. 1. A simple confused GSPN (left) and its MA semantics (right)

will exploit non-determinism for analysing the sensitivity of various performance metrics w.r.t. some rates in the net. The MAMA tool chain [3] realizes the new semantics via a translation to process algebra. This tool is used in our analysis of the computing server.

Performance metrics. We consider three basic measures on (possibly confused) GSPNs. *Long-run* average measures are the pendant to steady-state probabilities in CTMCs. Given a state m in an MA, i.e., a marking in the net, and a set T of target states, this measure is the minimal (or maximal) fraction of time spent in some state in T in the long run, when starting in m. In absence of non-determinism, the minimal and maximal long-run average coincide. The computation of long-run averages on MA can be reduced to a combination of several standard algorithms on Markov decision processes (MDPs); for details we refer to [3]. The (minimal or maximal) *expected time* of reaching a set T of target states from a given state m can be obtained by a reduction to a stochastic shortest-path problem. Such problems can efficiently be solved by linear programming. The third measure is determining *timed reachability probabilities*. They are the pendant to transient probabilities in CTMCs. Given a set T of target states, a given state m and a deadline d, the central question here is to determine the minimal (or maximal) probability of reaching some state in T within time d when starting in m. Such problems are a bit more involved and can be tackled using discretisation techniques. Further details are outside the scope of this paper and are provided in [3].

3   A GSPN Model of the Computing Server

Figure 2 shows our GSPN model of a computing server. The places, transitions, and parameters have the following interpretation:

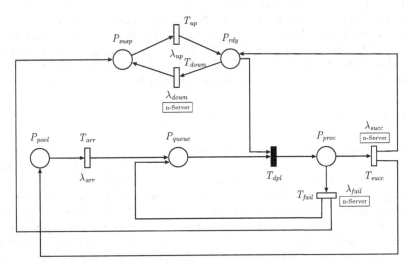

Fig. 2. GSPN model of computing server

P_{pool} represents the pool of job requests. After successful processing, they re-enter this place.

P_{queue} models the waiting queue of the system. Job requests enter this place via T_{arr} with rate λ_{arr}, and re-enter the queue if their processing fails.

T_{dpl} immediately deploys a waiting request on a (ready) machine if available.

P_{proc} represents the actively executing requests. From here, the jobs are either returned via T_{succ} to P_{pool} (with rate λ_{succ}) after successful completion, or the machine fails (or is preempted by the provider). In the former case, $1/\lambda_{succ}$ gives the expected execution time. In the latter case, $1/\lambda_{fail}$ is the mean time between failures, and requests are enqueued again via T_{fail}.

P_{rdy}/P_{susp} divide the available machines into two categories. The first ("ready") can directly process service requests, while the second ("suspended") first need to be set up to become ready. Two associated transitions, T_{up} and T_{down} with respective rates λ_{up} and λ_{down}, represent the corresponding startup and shutdown operations that are taken when additional machines are required or when they are idle, respectively. In particular, λ_{up} models the booting time of a machine by an exponential distribution. Initially we assume that all machines in the server are ready. Note that T_{dpl} requires P_{rdy} to be non-empty in order to process requests, and that a machine re-enters P_{rdy} after successful processing of a request. If processing is aborted via T_{fail}, the machine becomes suspended as it has to be restarted (in case of failure) or reallocated (in case of preemption).

Note that transitions T_{succ}, T_{fail} and T_{down} are marked as "n-Server" to reflect the fact that the respective rates refer to single requests and machines. Since we assume the failed machines can only be rebooted one by one, T_{up} is not marked as "n-Server". Moreover, the computing server with different types of services and machines can be easily modeled from the "simple" one by using *colored* GSPN or assigning immediate transitions with weights (when the probabilistic distribution of such types of services (machines) is known), and these extended semantics can again be translated into MA semantics without extra effort.

This GSPN is specified using the Petri Net Markup Language (PNML), which is a standardized XML-based interchange format for Petri nets [6]. Many tools can be used to generate Petri Nets in PNML notation, such as the Platform-Independent Petri Net Editor (PIPE). Using the MaMa tool chain, the GSPN is automatically mapped onto a Markov automaton for further analysis.

4   Quantitative Evaluation of the GSPN Model

This section presents the results of evaluating our GSPN model. They are obtained by using the recently developed MaMa tool chain that supports the mapping of GSPNs onto Markov automata and their quantitative assessment. We first present some statistics about the underlying state space size, detailing the user profiles –scientific computing tasks and web service tasks– that are used, and the set of properties considered. Due to space limitations, we focus on presenting the main outcomes. Sect. 4.2 presents the results for expected-time and long-run metrics for scientific computing and web-service tasks. These figures give insight into the quantitative behaviour of the computing system, and provide useful information concerning dimensioning the system in terms of the (initial) number of ready machines. Sect. 4.3 investigates the sensitivity of our evaluation results on varying the parameters λ_{fail} and λ_{down}. Sect. 4.4 considers the long-run energy consumption, whereas Sect. 4.5 focuses on the response-time distribution of user requests. The latter results are of interest to both service providers and users. All experiments are obtained on a AMD 48-core CPU @ 2.2 GHz, 192 GB RAM and Linux kernel 2.6.32.

4.1   Experimental Setup

State space. The state space of the GSPN model is determined by two parameters: the size of the client population and the initial number of ready machines. They are respectively represented by $\mathcal{I}(P_{pool})$ and $\mathcal{I}(P_{rdy})$ where $\mathcal{I}(P)$ denotes the initial number of tokens in place P. The state space sizes are summarized in Table 1 where the last column indicates the state space generation time (in seconds).

User profiles. We consider two application scenarios: scientific computing and web-services. In the scientific computing setting, tasks arrive at a relatively low rate and have a substantial processing time (usually ranging from minutes to hours). Web-service tasks such as bing search queries arrive much more frequently and have a short processing time, typically in the range of seconds.

Table 1. GSPN state space statistics

$\mathcal{I}(P_{rdy})$	$\mathcal{I}(P_{pool})$	# states	# trans.	time
100	100	20,201	55,250	23s
100	500	100,601	255,650	79s
100	1000	201,101	506,150	153s
100	2000	402,101	1,007,150	314s
100	2500	502,601	1,257,650	387s
200	1000	401,201	1,021,300	321s
250	1000	501,251	1,282,625	394s

Table 2. Parameter settings for the application scenarios

Our parameters settings are listed in Table 2, where the time unit is one minute. Scientific computing tasks

	λ_{arr}	λ_{succ}	λ_{fail}	λ_{up}	λ_{down}
Scientific computing	1.667	0.1	0.00208	0.05	0.005
Web service	180	20	0.006	0.05	0.005

arrive at a rate of 100 requests per hour ($\lambda_{arr} = 1.667$), and require a processing time of 10 min ($\lambda_{succ} = 0.1$), failures occur once per eight hours, booting a machine requires 20 min, and a ready machine suspends once every 200 min (please bear in mind that transition T_{down} is of type n-Server). Three web service requests are issued per second, and each requires an average execution time of three seconds. The scientific computing case is considered for a small client population, i.e., $\mathcal{I}(P_{pool}) = 100$, and a large one, i.e., $\mathcal{I}(P_{pool}) = 500$. The web service setting is of interest only for a large client population.

Properties. For each scenario, we consider the following six properties:

p1. The expected time until P_{queue} exceeds 90% of its capacity
p2. The expected time until P_{queue} exceeds 50% of its capacity
p3. The expected time[2] until no ready machine is available for requests in P_{queue}
p4. The average long-run occupancy of P_{queue}
p5. The average long-run occupancy of P_{proc}

---

[2] In some dedicated cases, we also study the probability until this phenomenon happens within a given deadline. This *timed reachability* property is however more complex to evaluate.

The verification times are listed in Table 3. It clearly shows that expected-time properties are simpler to analyse than long-run properties.

This is due to the fact that the former involve a single LP problem to be solved, whereas the latter require a (non-trivial) graph decomposition as well as solving of several LP problems.

Table 3. Property evaluation times per scenario

	p1	p2	p3	p4	p5
s_{small}	12m2s	5m52s	1m13s	18h44m	6h30m
s_{large}	6h6m	1h54m	10m13s	495h28m	109h16m
w_{large}	5h6m	1h39m	9m52s	402h38m	50h35m

Moreover, evaluating **p4** requires $\mathcal{I}(P_{pool}) \cdot \mathcal{I}(P_{rdy})$ iterations when using value iteration, whereas the other long-run properties require $\mathcal{I}(P_{rdy})$ iterations. This explains the difference in runtimes between the long-run properties. We stress that these runtimes should not be compared to evaluating similar properties on CTMCs; as MA include non-determinism, the algorithms are intrinsically more complex and have a higher time complexity.

4.2   Expected-Time and Long-Run Properties

Expected-time properties. First consider the properties **p1** and **p2**, i.e., the expected time until P_{queue} reaches 90% and 50% of its capacity, respectively. For a small population, the capacity of P_{queue}, denoted C_{queue}, equals $\mathcal{I}(P_{pool}) = 100$. Analysing these properties boils down to computing the expected time from the initial marking to the set of markings satisfying $\mathcal{M}(P_{queue})/C_{queue} \geq p\%$ where $\mathcal{M}(P)$ refers to the current marking of place P. The evaluation results are shown in Fig. 3 (left) for $p = 90\%$ and Fig. 3 (right) for $p = 50\%$, where the number of initial ready machines (x-axis) is varying. They suggest that about 25 initial ready machines is a rather good choice.

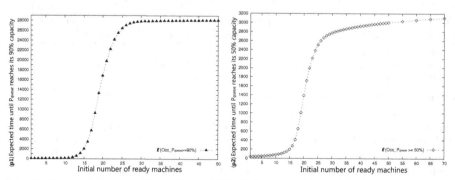

Fig. 3. Expected time until exceeding 90% (left) and 50% (right) of client queue capacity for scenario s_{small}

Property **p3** refers to the expected time until there is no more ready machine available for waiting requests in P_{queue}. We check this by determining the expected time from the initial marking to the set of markings where $\mathcal{M}(P_{queue}) > 0$ and $\mathcal{M}(P_{rdy}) = 0$. The results are plotted in Fig. 4 (left). To get more insight into the likelihood of encountering this situation, we also evaluate the probability to reach this state within a given time frame d. As the computation of

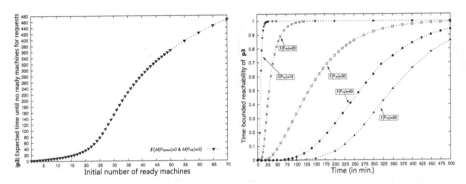

Fig. 4. Expected-time and timed reachability probabilities until client requests wait

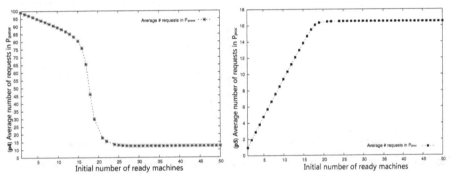

Fig. 5. Long-run average number of tasks in P_{queue} (left) and P_{proc} (right) for s_{small}

these probabilities is very time-consuming, we let the initial number of ready machines vary from 10 to 50. The results for varying d (along the x-axis, in minutes) and different values of $\mathcal{I}(P_{rdy})$ are plotted in Fig. 4 (right). Clearly, the timed reachability probabilities rapidly approach one for a relatively small number of machines (e.g., 10 or 20), but this effect substantially diminishes on increasing this number. The evaluation times for obtaining the latter results ranges from around 28 s for 10 machines up to nearly 60 h for 50 machines where we have set an accuracy of 10^{-1}.

Long-run properties. For a set T of target states, let $\mathcal{L}(T)$ denote the long-run average fraction of time of residing in T. The set of target states where exactly $i \in \mathbb{N}$ tokens are in place P is denoted as $T_i(P) = \{\mathcal{M} \mid \mathcal{M}(P) = i\}$. The long-run average number of tokens in place P, denoted $\mathcal{L}(\# P)$, in our GSPN model is then given by $\mathcal{L}(\# P) = \sum_{i \in \mathbb{N}} \mathcal{L}(T_i(P)) \cdot i$. The average number of waiting (in P_{queue}) and processing tasks (in P_{proc}) are shown in Fig. 5 (left) and Fig. 5 (right), respectively. Our results indicate that an equilibrium is reached for about 25 initial ready machines. To show the impact of the size of the client population, we check both properties for $\mathcal{I}(P_{rdy}) = 500$, see Fig. 6. The results indicate an (expected) increase of waiting requests in P_{queue}, whereas the average number of processing requests is only negligibly affected.

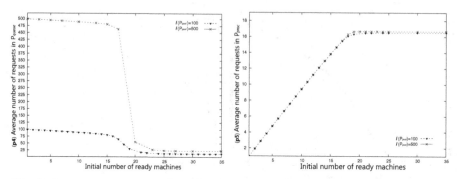

Fig. 6. Long-run average number of tasks in P_{queue} (left) and P_{proc} (right) for $\mathbf{s}_{large}$

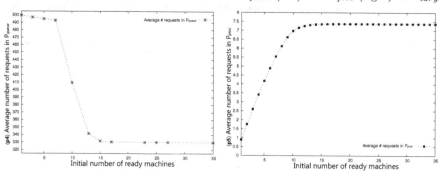

Fig. 7. Long-run average number of tasks in P_{queue} (left) and P_{proc} (right) for $\mathbf{w}_{large}$

Web-service tasks. We evaluated all properties also for the web-service setting. In contrast to the scientific computing case, jobs have a short processing time but arrive at a substantially higher rate (cf. the parameter settings in Table 2). Due to space reasons, we only present the results of the long-run properties **p4** and **p5** (see Fig. 7). Whereas for the scientific computing application scenario, a stable situation is reached for about 25 ready machines, this is now the case for 15 machines. In that case, the average number of concurrently processing tasks in the server will be around 7.5, and there are about 330 tasks on average waiting in the queue.

4.3 Sensitivity Analysis

In order to a get a better insight into the influence of two important modelling parameters –the failure rate λ_{fail} of job processing and the rate λ_{down} of ready machines becoming suspended– we carry out a sensitivity analysis by exploiting the native support of non-determinism in our setting. (Note that such an analysis is not possible using the classical GSPN semantics for "deterministic" nets.)

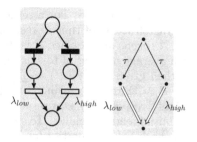

Fig. 8. Non-determinism in GSPN and MA

This is done as follows. We first only vary λ_{fail}. In the underlying MA, this is accomplished by adding two internal (immediate) transitions which are directly followed by two timed transitions with rates λ_{low} and λ_{high}, respectively (see Fig. 8). The benefit of this approach is that when analysing our properties, we obtain *bounds*. For instance, for the expected-time properties, we would obtain minimal and maximal expected-time values. This means in particular, that for any failure rate between λ_{low} and λ_{high}, the expected time lies between the obtained bounds. The analysis algorithms in the MAMA tool chain obtain these bounds from the adapted GSPN (and thus MA) by running a single algorithm. We first vary the failure rate λ_{fail} from 0.00208 ($\approx$ 480 min) to 0.00312 ($\approx$ 320 min) and 0.00416 ($\approx$ 240 min) respectively, then reduce the failure rate λ_{fail} to 0.00156 ($\approx$ 640 min) and 0.00104 ($\approx$ 960 min) respectively. The obtained results for the expected-time properties are shown in Fig. 9 and 10.

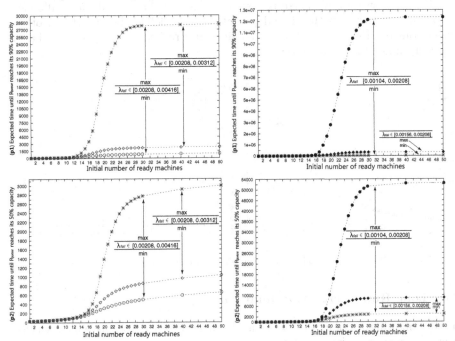

Fig. 9. Evaluation results for properties **p1** and **p2** by varying λ_{fail}

From these results, we make three observations. First, we consider the number of clients for which the lower and upper expected times start to become distinct. On increasing λ_{fail}, i.e., with shorter average failure intervals, the minimal and maximal expected times start to differ for $\mathcal{I}(P_{pool}) = 14$, 15 and 22 in **p1**, **p2**, and **p3**, respectively. On decreasing λ_{fail}, i.e. with longer average failure intervals, these points shift to 17, 18, and 24, respectively. Secondly, we observe (e.g., from both the right curves) a significant impact on the difference between minimal and maximal expected times when increasing the minimal failure rate. Reducing $\lambda_{fail} = 0.00208$ to just one half (0.00104) results in an increase of about 400 times of the expected time (after reaching an equilibrium), whereas a reduction to 0.00156 (= three quarters) results in just an increase by a factor of 11 (cf. Fig. 9 (top right)). This is because transition T_{fail} (with rate λ_{fail}) has a two-fold effect on the number of tasks in P_{queue} in our GSPN model. First, T_{fail} has a more direct effect on tasks in P_{queue} than T_{succ} (λ_{succ}). If a task is successfully processed, it arrives in P_{pool} and waits for turning to be a new request. Here, T_{arr} is not an n-Server type time transition. However, if the processing of a task has failed, it will directly arrive in P_{queue} (and thus increases the number of waiting tasks). Second, T_{fail} also affects the availability of ready machines in P_{rdy}. If the task is successfully finished, the ready machine goes back to P_{rdy} and does not need to re-initialize. But if it has failed, the machine serving the task needs to be restarted. Note that the startup of a suspended machine (transition T_{up}) is not a n-Server typed transition. As a result, these twofold effects will cause a superposed influence on the growth of the number of tasks in P_{queue} and hence have a strong impact on the expected-time property. The third observation we make is that λ_{fail} does not have significant influence on **p3** in comparison with **p1** and **p2** (cf. Fig. 10 (left)). The results of other evaluations (cf. Fig. 10 (right)) also confirm that rather than λ_{fail}, λ_{down} has a stronger impact on property **p3**.

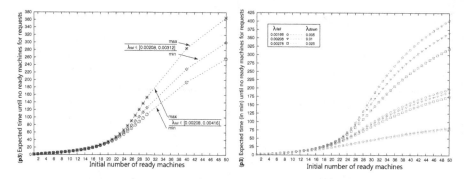

Fig. 10. Checking **p3** by varying λ_{fail}

4.4 Long-Run Energy Consumption

In the following section, we are going to answer two questions which service providers may especially be interested in: what is the operating cost and the quality of service of their computing server? To answer these questions, we try to estimate the long-run energy consumption of the server and the response-time distribution of requests as respective metrics for these two parameters.

We assume that active machines (i.e., those in P_{proc}) have a power consumption of 40 W [7], ready machines (P_{rdy}) have a power consumption of 20 W (50% of the active value), and suspended machines (P_{susp}) have a power consumption of 8 W (20% of active). Furthermore, if we initialize m ready machines in P_{rdy}, in the long run these will be distributed to three possible places P_{susp}, P_{rdy} and P_{proc}. In other words, at any moment the overall number of machines in these three places will be m. Thus we can compute the power consumption of the server in the long run based on the steady-state probabilities. After we have determined the average number of machines in these places in the long run, which can be analogously derived as **p4**, the overall power consumption in the long run is computed as

$$P = 40 \ W \cdot \mathcal{L}(\#P_{susp}) + 20 \ W \cdot \mathcal{L}(\#P_{rdy}) + 8 \ W \cdot \mathcal{L}(\#P_{proc}).$$

The results are shown in Fig. 11 (left) for failure rate $\lambda_{fail} = 0.00208$. We observe that λ_{down} and $\mathcal{I}(P_{rdy})$ do not significantly influence the average number of active machines in P_{proc} in the long run; they are always around 16 (cf. Fig. 5 (right)). Although the more ready machines we initialize in P_{rdy} (i.e. $\mathcal{I}(P_{rdy})$), the more redundant machines will be in P_{rdy} and P_{susp}. Their distribution is controlled by λ_{down}. If there are few redundant machines, e.g., $\mathcal{I}(P_{rdy}) = 20$ (i.e., only about 4 machines left for λ_{down} to distribute these to P_{rdy} and P_{susp}), then the energy consumption only varies in a small range. In contrast, if $\mathcal{I}(P_{rdy}) = 40$, we notice that when λ_{down} is 0.0025, about 23.10 machines are suspended, 0.65 are ready, and 16.25 are active on average, whereas when λ_{down} is 0.001, about 9.61 machines are suspended, 13.73 are idle, and 16.66 are active on average. This wide range distribution of suspended and ready machines caused by λ_{down} yields a drastic increase of energy consumption as shown in Fig. 11 when $\mathcal{I}(P_{rdy})$ is large. On the one hand, keeping a certain number of ready machines in P_{rdy} guarantees a better response time of requests, on the other hand, too many redundant ready machines lead to a higher energy consumption.

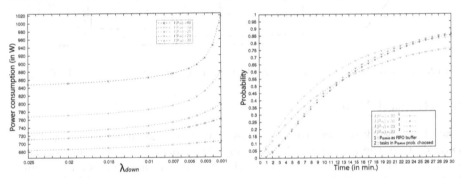

Fig. 11. Power consumption and response-time distribution of computing server

4.5   Response-Time Distribution in Steady State

Now we compute the response-time distribution in steady state approximately [3]based on a combination of the PASTA theorem [8] and tagged-token techniques [9] for GSPNs. From the former we know that an arrival of a Poisson process sees the system as if it was arriving at a random instance of time (i.e. the system in steady state). Since the steady-state probabilities of the computing server can easily be computed from the resulting MA by using the MAMA tool, the response-time distribution in steady state can be computed by tagging a customer's job and following the tagged request until it has been successfully processed in the server which is in steady state. The right side of Fig. 12 illustrates the tagged task (represented by $*$ at P_{queue}) in the computing server (with

---

[3] Since our model is closed.

$\lambda_{fail} = 0.00208$, $\lambda_{down} = 0.001$, $\mathcal{I}(P_{rdy}) = 30$) which is just in a steady state with probability 0.00192925986. The number attached to each place represents the current number of tokens in that place. By adding a boolean variable to each place P_{queue}, P_{proc} and P_{pool} indicating the position of the tagged request, the response-time distribution is then obtained via a time-bounded reachability computation using the MaMa tool. Note that adding a tagged token increases the state space. The left side of Fig. 12 shows the advantage of using probabilistic transitions in MAs during our computation. They are used for setting up the initial probabilistic distribution for different steady states of the server. After these steps, we can again generate the MA and compute the response-time distribution, all with the MaMa tool. The result is shown in Fig. 11 on the right.

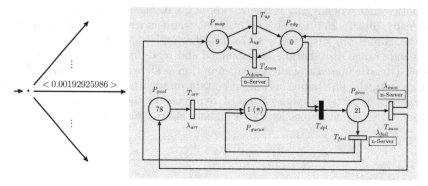

Fig. 12. Computing server in steady state with tagged token (∗) placed in P_{queue}

5   Related Work

The closest work on performance evaluation that is similar to our work was carried out in the field of cloud computing. Appropriate stochastic models have recently been proposed in [10,11,12,7]. [10] describes a prototype tool for translating expressions of probabilistic resource usage patterns into Markov decision processes with rewards. This allows to check costing and usage queries expressed by reward-augmented probabilistic temporal logic (PCTL). [13] models cloud computing systems with migration by CTMCs using PRISM, verifying some quantitative properties such as the time-bounded probability of migration operation in the cloud computing system. [12] introduces a stochastic reward net model for the IaaS cloud, based on which resiliency metrics are computed by changing the job arrival rate and the number of available PMs. [11,7] models a cloud computing server as different kinds of scalable interacting stochastic (sub)models. In [11], interaction happens when results from sub-models are used as input for other sub-models. In the end, two quality-of-service metrics, the effective job rejection probability and the effective mean response delay, are obtained. [7] represents the IaaS cloud with tiered service offerings by three pools for hot, warm and cold virtual machines, which have different response time and power consumption characteristics, respectively. These pools are represented by interacting stochastic sub-models (basically CTMCs), from which the power consumption and performance metrics are computed.

Another strand of research is based on queueing theory. [14,15,16] analytically evaluates the performance of cloud computing services. [14] proposes an approximation method to compute the probability and cumulative distribution of the response time by applying the inverse Laplace-Stieltjes transformation (LTS) on the LTS of total response time obtained analytically. [15] models the cloud computing server by a M/G/m/m+r queueing system. Here, quantitative properties such as the distributions of the number of tasks and of waiting and response times etc., are analytically computed. Besides cloud computing, [9] presents a general distributed computing technique for response-time analysis with GSPN models based on Laplace transformation and its inversion [17,18].

6   Concluding Remarks

This paper has presented a simple GSPN for computing servers in which virtual machines can be stand-by or operational, and the processing of requests may randomly fail. Our analysis has focused on both long-run and expected-time properties that give insight into the number of required virtual machines so as to yield a given service level (i.e., low response time, and low probability of lack of processing power). A sensitivity analysis by exploiting non-determinism in the GSPN model shows the influence of the failure probability. Finally, long run energy consumption was analysed. The exploited analysis algorithms are based on analysing Markov automata, and are more intricate –hence more time-consuming– than those for classical (confusion-free) GSPN which are based on CTMCs. Although our original net does not exhibit confusion, the one used for the sensitivity analysis does. Future work will focus on improving the performance of the analysis algorithms.

References

1. Eisentraut, C., Hermanns, H., Katoen, J.-P., Zhang, L.: A semantics for every GSPN. In: Colom, J.-M., Desel, J. (eds.) PETRI NETS 2013. LNCS, vol. 7927, pp. 90–109. Springer, Heidelberg (2013)
2. Katoen, J.P.: GSPNs revisited: Simple semantics and new analysis algorithms. In: Application of Concurrency to System Design (ACSD), pp. 6–11. IEEE (2012)
3. Guck, D., Hatefi, H., Hermanns, H., Katoen, J.-P., Timmer, M.: Modelling, reduction and analysis of Markov automata. In: Joshi, K., Siegle, M., Stoelinga, M., D'Argenio, P.R. (eds.) QEST 2013. LNCS, vol. 8054, pp. 55–71. Springer, Heidelberg (2013)
4. Ajmone Marsan, M., Balbo, G., Conte, G., Donatelli, S., Franceschinis, G.: Modelling with Generalized Stochastic Petri Nets. John Wiley & Sons (1995)
5. Eisentraut, C., Hermanns, H., Zhang, L.: On probabilistic automata in continuous time. In: LICS, pp. 342–351. IEEE Computer Society (2010)
6. Billington, J., Christensen, S., van Hee, K.M., Kindler, E., Kummer, O., Petrucci, L., Post, R., Stehno, C., Weber, M.: The Petri Net Markup Language: Concepts, technology, and tools. In: van der Aalst, W.M.P., Best, E. (eds.) ICATPN 2003. LNCS, vol. 2679, pp. 483–505. Springer, Heidelberg (2003)

7. Ghosh, R., Naik, V.K., Trivedi, K.S.: Power-performance trade-offs in Iaas cloud: A scalable analytic approach. In: Dependable Systems and Networks Workshops, pp. 152–157 (2011)
8. Wolff, R.W.: Poisson arrivals see time averages. Operations Research 30, 223–231 (1982)
9. Dingle, N.J., Knottenbelt, W.J.: Automated customer-centric performance analysis of Generalised Stochastic Petri Nets using tagged tokens. In: PASM 2008. ENTCS, vol. 232, pp. 75–88 (2009)
10. Johnson, K., Reed, S., Calinescu, R.: Specification and quantitative analysis of probabilistic cloud deployment patterns. In: Eder, K., Lourenço, J., Shehory, O. (eds.) HVC 2011. LNCS, vol. 7261, pp. 145–159. Springer, Heidelberg (2012)
11. Ghosh, R., Trivedi, K.S., Naik, V.K., Kim, D.S.: End-to-end performability analysis for Infrastructure-as-a-Service cloud: An interacting stochastic models approach. In: IEEE Pacific Rim International Symposium on Dependable Computing (PRDC), pp. 125–132. IEEE CS (2010)
12. Ghosh, R., Longo, F., Naik, V.K., Trivedi, K.S.: Quantifying resiliency of Iaas cloud. In: IEEE Symposium on Reliable Distributed Systems (SRDS), pp. 343–347. IEEE (2010)
13. Kikuchi, S., Matsumoto, Y.: Performance modeling of concurrent live migration operations in cloud computing systems using PRISM probabilistic model checker. In: IEEE Int. Conf. on Cloud Computing (IEEE CLOUD), pp. 49–56. IEEE (2011)
14. Xiong, K., Perros, H.G.: Service performance and analysis in cloud computing. In: IEEE Congress on Services, Part I (SERVICES I), pp. 693–700. IEEE Computer Society (2009)
15. Khazaei, H., Misic, J.V., Misic, V.B.: Performance analysis of cloud computing centers using M/G/m/m+r queuing systems. IEEE Trans. Parallel Distrib. Syst. 23, 936–943 (2012)
16. Yang, B., Tan, F., Dai, Y.S., Guo, S.: Performance evaluation of cloud service considering fault recovery. In: Jaatun, M.G., Zhao, G., Rong, C. (eds.) Cloud Computing. LNCS, vol. 5931, pp. 571–576. Springer, Heidelberg (2009)
17. Abate, J., Whitt, W.: The Fourier-series method for inverting transforms of probability distributions. Queueing Syst. 10, 5–87 (1992)
18. Harrison, P.G., Knottenbelt, W.J.: Passage time distributions in large Markov chains. In: Int. Conf. on Measurements and Modeling of Computer Systems (SIGMETRICS), pp. 77–85. ACM (2002)

Modeling and Performance Analysis of a Node in Fault Tolerant Wireless Sensor Networks

Ruslan Krenzler and Hans Daduna

University of Hamburg, Department of Mathematics
Center of Mathematical Statistics and Stochastic Processes
{daduna,ruslan.krenzler}@math.uni-hamburg.de

Abstract. We develop a separable model for a referenced node in a fault tolerant (disruption tolerant) wireless sensor network, which encompasses the message queue of the node and an inner and an outer environment for describing details of the transmission protocols. We prove that the system has steady state of product form for the queue and its environment. We discuss several modifications and the relation of our approach to that in previous papers in the literature.

Keywords: Wireless sensor nodes, fault tolerant networks, separability, environment, closed form steady state, interacting processes.

1 Introduction

Modeling fault tolerant (disruption tolerant) wireless sensor networks (DSN) is a challenging task due to the specific constraints imposed on the network structure and the principles the nodes have to follow to maintain connectedness of the network. The complexity of the models increases furthermore if the nodes are mobile and if energy efficiency is required. A typical way to resolve the latter problem is to reduce energy consumption by laying a node in sleep status whenever this is possible. In sleep status all activities of the node are either completely or almost completely interrupted. Clearly, this will have implications for availability of connections in the network.

In active mode the node undertakes several activities: Gathering data and putting the resulting data packets into its queue, receiving packets from other nodes which are placed in its queue (and relaying these packets when they arrive at the head of the node's queue), and processing the packets in the queue. Mobility requires routing decisions and routing evaluation which is connected with localization procedures.

Analytical performance analysis of DSN found in the literature usually follows a two-step procedure. (1) Investigate a single ("referenced") node, and (2) combine by some approximation procedure the interacting nodes to a separable network, for a review see [16]. More detailed study of a specific node model is [9], other typical examples for the two-step procedure are [10], [18].

Our study is in part motivated by research in [17]. The protocol for the pervasive information gathering and processing described there (for more details

K. Fischbach and U.R. Krieger (Eds.): MMB & DFT 2014, LNCS 8376, pp. 73–87, 2014.
© Springer International Publishing Switzerland 2014

on this protocol see [17]) consists basically on two "key components", (i) for data transmission, governed by "nodal delivery probabilities", and (ii) for queue management, governed by "message fault tolerances". Both of these components are complex and their interaction is a challenging problem for any modeling procedure.

[17] proceed as follows: In a first part "an overview of the dynamic delay/fault-tolerant mobile sensor network data delivery scheme" is provided with detailed recipes for the update procedure of the "nodal delivery probability" and the "message fault tolerance". In a second part complexity even of the single node's model is drastically reduced by not including the dynamics of these characteristics into the detailed analytical model. The authors argue: "While it is desirable to accurately analyze the data delivery scheme . . . , this is not practical given its complexity in data transmission and queue management [17][p. 3290]. Consequently, for characterizing the behavior of a sensor node, (i) they fix for the node the nodal delivery probability as a constant depending mainly on the number of other nodes in its one-hop neighborhood, and (ii) the message fault tolerances are set to constant = 1, which means that no copy of a sent out message is kept by the sending node.

The aim of our presentation is to show that at least modeling of a single node and its **bidirectional interaction with the network**, can be done much more detailed than described in the cited literature, while still upcoming with closed formulas for the steady state behavior and important structural theorems for the interaction between node and the network in equilibrium. An main observation will be that it is possible to reduce the complexity of the interacting processes in a similar way by **separability of the steady state** as complexity is reduced in the celebrated Jackson and Gordon-Newell networks.

Our result will not rely on a specific version of a DSN setting, and we will explain how to adapt our procedure with the selected model from [17] to other settings. We believe that the principles of our modeling procedure are rather generally to apply. Our procedure is:

Starting from the detailed description of a dynamic disruption/fault-tolerant mobile sensor node's data delivery scheme in [17], we develop an analytical model of a single node, the "referenced node" (RN) in the spirit of [17], [10], and [18], and others. The key component of our sensor node model is a queueing system of M/M/1-type for the message queue management. Development of this queue is influenced by other processes which represent the specific features of the DSN. These processes will be considered as an environment for the queue with a **vice-versa** interaction.

We point out that we will make modeling simplifications as well, especially we will focus on the first key component, the data transmission, and will only include marginal parts of the queue management. To reduce technical effort we will discretize all state spaces. This simplification can be removed leading to Markov processes with general state spaces.

Related Work: There are two main approaches for analytical modeling of DSN. The first is by direct construction of Markov processes and numerically solving the balance equation to obtain performance metrics from this. Typical examples are [2] and [3]. Jiang and Walrand studied the closely related CSMA protocol for the IEEE 802.11 Wireless Networks, and found explicit expressions for the stationary distribution of the network, see [5] and the references there. A single node and its environment is described in [9], exploiting matrix-geometrical methods.

The second approach is by utilizing stochastic network models with product form steady state. From this it is easy to obtain performance metrics. One often pays with oversimplification. But experience with the OR models for classical computer and communications systems is, that many systems are robust against deviations from, e.g., assumptions on service distributions. Using product form models usually one usually proceeds in the two-step construction, described above. For an idealized sensor network with sleep and active periods of the nodes Liu and Tong Lee [10] applied this procedure. Mehmet Ali and Gu [11] used a generalized Jackson network with unreliable nodes to model a DSN. From the product form steady state in [14] the authors derive relevant performance metrics. Wu, Wang, Dang, and Lin [17] used a classical Jackson network to model "delay/fault-tolerant mobile sensor networks". A detailed analysis of a DSN with the aid of queueing network models is performed by Qiu, Feng, Xia, Wu, and Zhou [12]. The networks are not of product form but similar to Mehmet Ali and Gu [11] it is assumed that separability can be applied.

Our research in this paper is part of an ongoing project which focusses on investigations of queueing networks in a random environment. The aim is to find structures which show the asymptotic properties of separable networks (a) for the internal structure of Jackson-type or BCMP networks, and (b) for the interaction of the service network with the environment. Predecessors of our present work are e.g., [13] (environment determines the availability of unreliable network nodes), [15] (environment consists of an attached inventory, where stockout lets the service process break down until replenishment arrives). A survey on related queueing-inventory systems is [8]. Recent results on single nodes are in [6], [7], with more relevant references.

The paper is structured as follows. In Section 2 we describe in detail the features of transmission and queue management protocols which we will incorporate into our model. Section 3 contains the main result on separability of the queue-environment interaction. In Section 4 we present details which can be further incorporated into the model, as well as possibilities to reduce complexity for easier computations. Some examples are presented in detail.

2 Model Description

We consider a single mobile sensor node in a DSN (disruption tolerant wireless sensor network). Due to mobility and changing external conditions, this "referenced node" (RN) observes a varying environment with which the RN strongly interacts The functioning of the RN is governed by the following principles which select the relevant features and incorporate several interacting processes.

- Length of the packet queue of the RN ($\in \mathbb{N}_0$),
- number of active nodes in the one-hop neighborhood (the "outer environment") and the nodal delivery status of these neighbors,
- nodal delivery status of the RN (part of the "inner or local environment"),
- modus of the RN (active $= 1$, sleep $= 0$) (part of the "inner environment").

It follows that the referenced node RN can communicate with other nodes if and only if RN is **active** $(= 1)$ **and** the number of active nodes in the outer environment is > 0 (for short we say, the outer environment then is **on** (> 0)).

When RN is active $(= 1)$ and outer environment on (> 0), the stream of packets arriving at the packet queue of RN is the superposition of data gathering and receiving packets from other nodes. Following [17][p. 3291] we assume that the superposition process is a Poisson-λ process, and processing a packet in the queue needs an exponential-μ distributed time. The inter arrival times and service times are an independent set of variables.

Whenever RN is in sleep mode or the outer environment is off, all sensing, relaying, and sending activities of RN are frozen. This assumption is posed for simplicity, and is different from e.g. [10], who allow during this periods data gathering by the node, but is in line with e.g. [18].

Whenever RN is ready to send, it sends a packet to a one-hop neighbor. The routing decision is made on the basis of the nodal delivery status of the neighbors. The packet is send to the neighbor node with maximal nodal delivery value, say ζ, if there are ties these are broken by a pure random decision (with equal probability).

The nodal delivery values are on a scale $D := \{1, 2, \ldots, d\}$ with $d < \infty$ the highest value. Whenever RN has send a packet to a node with delivery value ζ, it updates its own delivery value ξ as follows

$$\xi \to \begin{cases} \xi + 1, \text{ if } \xi < \zeta; \\ \xi - 1, \text{ if } \xi > \zeta; \\ \xi, \quad \text{ if } \xi = \zeta. \end{cases} \tag{1}$$

Moreover, RN maintains a timer to adjust its nodal delivery value [17][p. 3288]: Whenever there has been no transmission within a time interval $\bar{\Delta}$, a timeout occurs and the delivery value ξ is updated (because RN could not transmit data during an interval $\bar{\Delta}$) as follows

$$\xi \to \begin{cases} \xi - 1, \text{ if } \xi > 1; \\ \xi, \quad \text{ if } \xi = 1. \end{cases} \tag{2}$$

The length of the interval $\bar{\Delta}$ is Erlang-distributed with phase parameter δ and $T \geq 1$ phases (approximating a deterministic timer [17]). Whenever a transmission of RN occurs, the running timer is interrupted and immediately restarted. The phases are counted in decreasing order $T, T - 1, \ldots, 1$. When the timer expires (the last phase, counted $= 1$, ends), it is reset to its maximal value T. The successive sampled timer intervals are independent and independent of the other activities.

Remark: In [17][p. 3288] the nodal delivery values are probabilities, i.e., on scale $[0, 1]$, our rescaling is only for technical simplifications.

Message fault tolerances for the packets are introduced to estimate the importance of a stored (replication of a) message. Replications of some sent packets are stored for another transmission sometime later on. Whenever a copy of the sent message is stored at the end of the local queue, its message fault tolerance value is increased depending on the delivery values of the receiver. This will make the DSN less vulnerable against packet losses and will on the other hand not flood the network with too much messy packets.

Handling "message fault tolerance" is suppressed in the analytical single node model in [17]. We incorporate a simplified scheme in our model by the

Assumption on Generating Redundancy: Whenever RN has send a packet, it will store that packet with probability $f > 0$ at the end of its local queue. The storage decision is independent of the past. We assume in our first approach that $f = 0$ holds (as in [17]), $f > 0$ will be dealt with in Section 4.

Definition 1. *The "outer environment process" describes the development of N nodes, which constitute the one-hop neighborhood of RN, and is assumed to be an irreducible homogeneous Markov process*

$$O = (O(t) : t \geq 0), \qquad \text{with state space} \quad E_o := (\{0\} \cup D)^N \,,$$

where 0 in coordinate number k stands for "the k-th node is not available for RN", while $\eta_k > 0$ in coordinate k stands for "the k-th node is available for RN and has a nodal delivery value $\eta_k \in D$".

The generator of O is denoted by $Q_o = (q_o(y, y') : y, y' \in E_o)$ and the unique steady state distribution of O is denoted by $\theta_o = (\theta_o(y) : y \in E_o)$.

We abbreviate for $\eta = (\eta_1, \dots, \eta_N) \in E_o$: $g(\eta) := \max\{\eta_1, \dots, \eta_N\}$, and shall say that the outer environment is "quiet" if $g = 0$ holds.

RN can communicate with other nodes iff RN is active $= 1$ **and** $g \neq 0$ holds.

Example 2. *Several properties and components of the following environment process are taken from the model in [17]. (1) Reduction to a fixed cell where all other sensors are accessible, i.e., the one-hop neighborhood with N nodes is sufficient. (2) Independence of sensor nodes in the cell, which leads to (3) below and to the processes describing the behavior of the neighbors of RN are independent Markov processes with state space $\{0, 1, 2, \dots, d\}$. (3) Retrials are independent with identical success probability which is expressed in (3).*

In the model [17][Section 3] is not incorporated that as long as a node, say node j, is active its nodal delivery value evolves as a random walk on D as indicated by (1) and (2) which are taken from [17][Section 2.A.(1)]. For simplicity, we assume that this random walk is Markov for its own, with upward jump rate $w_j^+(\eta_j)$ for node j in state $\eta_j < d$, and downward jump rate $w_j^-(\eta_j)$ in state $\eta_j > 1$. Its steady state is with normalization G_j

$$p_j(\eta_j) = G_j^{-1} \prod_{k=2}^{\eta_j} \frac{w_j^+(k-1)}{w_j^-(k)}, \quad \eta_j = 1, \dots, d \,.$$

With the help of these steady state probabilities and constant rates $a_j, b_j > 0$ we incorporate additionally the active/sleep behavior (see Definition 4 below) of the nodes in the neighborhood into the positive local transition rates for node j as

$$q_{oj}(0, \eta_j) = b_j \cdot p_j(\eta_j), \quad \text{and} \quad q_{oj}(\eta_j, 0) = a_j, \quad \eta_j = 1, \dots, d.$$

The positive transition rates of O are for $j = 1, \dots, N$, and $\eta_j \in \{1, \dots, d\}$

$$q_o((\eta_1, \dots, \eta_{j-1}, 0, \eta_{j+1}, \dots, \eta_N); (\eta_1, \dots, \eta_{j-1}, \eta_j, \eta_{j+1}, \dots, \eta_N)) = b_j \cdot p_j(\eta_j),$$
$$\text{and } q_o((\eta_1, \dots, \eta_{j-1}, \eta_j, \eta_{j+1}, \dots, \eta_N); (\eta_1, \dots, \eta_{j-1}, 0, \eta_{j+1}, \dots, \eta_N)) = a_j. \quad (3)$$

The environment process O is ergodic with steady state probabilities

$$\theta_o(\eta_1, \dots, \eta_N) = \prod_{j=1}^{N} \left(\frac{a_j}{a_j + b_j} \right)^{1_{(\eta_j = 0)}} \left(\frac{b_j}{a_j + b_j} \cdot p_j(\eta_j) \right)^{1_{(\eta_j \neq 0)}}, (\eta_1, \dots, \eta_N) \in E_o.$$

The outer environment is quiet with probability $\theta_o(0, \dots, 0) = \prod_{j=1}^{N}(a_j/(a_j + b_j))$, and for $k = 1, \dots, d$ the probability that $\{g \geq k\}$ holds is

$$1 - \prod_{j=1}^{N} \left(\frac{a_j}{a_j + b_j} + \frac{b_j}{a_j + b_j} \sum_{\eta_j = 1}^{k-1} p_j(\eta_j) \right). \quad (4)$$

Definition 3. *The inner (local) environment of RN is a stochastic process, which is not Markov for its own*

$$I = (I(t) : t \geq 0), \quad \text{with state space} \quad E_i := \Delta \times D,$$

where $(t, \xi) \in \Delta \times D$ indicates that the timer is in phase t and the nodal delivery status of RN is ξ. Recall: 1 stands for lowest, d for highest delivery value, $\Delta := \{1, \dots, T\}$ are the possible residual exponential-δ phases of the running timer.

Definition 4. *Active and sleep phases of RN are governed by an alternating renewal process*

$$A = (A(t) : t \geq 0), \quad \text{with state space} \quad E_a := \{0, 1\},$$

where 1 stands for "active" and 0 stands for "sleep". The dwell time in the active status is exponential-α, whereas in sleep status exponential-β. The unique steady state distribution of A is $\theta_a = (\theta_a(0), \theta_a(1)) = (\beta/(\alpha + \beta), \alpha/(\alpha + \beta))$.
During RN's sleep times all its activities are frozen: Sending, receiving, timer.

Definition 5. *The queue length process of RN is a process, which is not Markov for its own*

$$X = (X(t) : t \geq 0), \quad \text{with state space} \quad \mathbb{N}_0,$$

where $X(t)$ counts the number of packets stored in RN, either under transmission (in service) or waiting. Whenever RN is sleeping or the outer environment is *quiet, there is no service possible, the packet on the service place is stored there, and no new arrival is admitted until RN becomes active again* **and** *there are active nodes in the outer environment.*

Note, that whenever RN is in active mode, its timer is running, irrespective of the status of the outer environment O.

Assumption 6. *We make the following natural assumption: The processes O and A are independent and independent of the set of inter arrival and service times, and of the timer intervals.*

Note, that independence of A and O from the timer is for free if the timer is deterministic. A direct consequence of the definitions and Assumption 6 is

Proposition 7. *With $Y := (A, I, O)$ the process $Z := (X, Y) = (X, A, I, O)$ is a homogeneous Markov process, which is irreducible on state space*

$$E := \mathbb{N}_0 \times E_a \times E_i \times E_o = \mathbb{N}_0 \times \{0,1\} \times \Delta \times D \times (\{0\} \cup D)^N .$$

We denote the generator of Z by $Q = (q(z, z') : z, z' \in E)$, and, when it exists, the (then uniquely defined) steady state distribution of Z, by $\pi = (\pi(z) : z \in E)$.

In general the queue length process X and its environment Y are strongly dependent. In one direction, the environment can shut down the service and arrival process, while in the other direction transmission of a message changes the nodal delivery value and resets the timer. We emphasize that in the first case the environment changes and the queue length stays at its present value, while in the second case the queue length **and** the environment jump concurrently. This property is discussed in Remark 2 below in comparison with the literature.

3   Steady State Behavior

We assume in the following that the node and its environment can stabilize in the long run, i.e., the joint process $Z = (X, Y)$ is ergodic, which implies that a steady state of Z exist. Recall from p. 76: When RN is able to communicate, the arrival rate is λ, the service rate is μ.

Proposition 8. *Z is ergodic on E iff $\lambda < \mu$. Then its unique stationary distribution π fulfills for all $(n, a, t, \xi, \eta) \in \mathbb{N}_0 \times \{0,1\} \times \Delta \times D \times (\{0\} \cup D)^N$*

$$\pi(n, a, t, \xi, \eta) = \left(1 - \frac{\lambda}{\mu}\right) \left(\frac{\lambda}{\mu}\right)^n \cdot \theta(a, t, \xi, \eta) , \tag{5}$$

where θ is a (unique) probability distribution on $\{0,1\} \times \Delta \times D \times (\{0\} \cup D)^N$.

Proof. In the balance equations for Z we abbreviate $-q_o(\eta, \eta) =: q_o(\eta), \eta \in E_o$, and when no restriction is posed, a variable runs through all admissible values. Recall $g(\eta) := \max(\eta_1, \ldots, \eta_N)$.

For $g(\eta) \neq 0, t < T, a = 1 : \pi(n, 1, t, \xi, \eta)[\lambda + \mu 1_{(n>0)} + \alpha + \delta + q_o(\eta)]$

$= \pi(n - 1, 1, t, \xi, \eta)\lambda 1_{(n>0)} + \pi(n, 0, t, \xi, \eta)\beta + \pi(n, 1, t + 1, \xi, \eta)\delta$

$+ \sum_{\gamma \in E_o - \{\eta\}} \pi(n, 1, t, \xi, \gamma)q_o(\gamma, \eta)$

For $g(\eta) \neq 0, a = 1 : \pi(n, 1, T, \xi, \eta)[\lambda + \mu 1_{(n>0)} + \alpha + \delta + q_o(\eta)]$ $\qquad(6)$

$= \pi(n - 1, 1, T, \xi, \eta)\lambda 1_{(n>0)} + \pi(n, 0, T, \xi, \eta)\beta + \sum_{\gamma \in E_o - \{\eta\}} \pi(n, 1, T, \xi, \gamma)q_o(\gamma, \eta)$

$+ \pi(n, 1, 1, \xi, \eta)\delta 1_{(\xi=1)} + \pi(n, 1, 1, \xi + 1, \eta)\delta 1_{(\xi<d)} + \sum_{s=1}^{T} \pi(n + 1, 1, s, \xi, \eta)\mu 1_{(\xi=g(\eta))}$

$+ \sum_{s=1}^{T} \pi(n + 1, 1, s, \xi - 1, \eta)\mu 1_{(0<\xi-1<g(\eta))} + \sum_{s=1}^{T} \pi(n + 1, 1, s, \xi + 1, \eta)\mu 1_{(d \geq \xi+1>g(\eta)>0)}$

For η with $g(\eta) = 0, t < T, a = 1 : \pi(n, 1, t, \xi, \eta)[\alpha + \delta + q_o(\eta)]$

$= \pi(n, 0, t, \xi, \eta)\beta + \pi(n, 1, t + 1, \xi, \eta)\delta + \sum_{\gamma \in E_o - \{\eta\}} \pi(n, 1, t, \xi, \gamma)q_o(\gamma, \eta)$

For η with $g(\eta) = 0, a = 1 : \pi(n, 1, T, \xi, \eta)[\alpha + \delta + q_o(\eta)] = \pi(n, 0, T, \xi, \eta)\beta$

$+ \sum_{\gamma \in E_o - \{\eta\}} \pi(n, 1, T, \xi, \gamma)q_o(\gamma, \eta) + \pi(n, 1, 1, \xi, \eta)\delta 1_{(\xi=1)} + \pi(n, 1, 1, \xi + 1, \eta)\delta 1_{(\xi<d)}$

For $a = 0 : \quad \pi(n, 0, t, \xi, \eta)[\beta + q_o(\eta)] = \pi(n, 1, t, \xi, \eta)\alpha + \sum_{\gamma \in E_o - \{\eta\}} \pi(n, 0, t, \xi, \gamma)q_o(\gamma, \eta)$

Inserting $\pi(n, a, t, \xi, \eta) = \left(1 - \frac{\lambda}{\mu}\right)\left(\frac{\lambda}{\mu}\right)^n \cdot \theta(a, t, \xi, \eta)$ into these equations reveals that the queue length terms $\left(1 - \frac{\lambda}{\mu}\right)\left(\frac{\lambda}{\mu}\right)^n$ cancel completely, which yields the following set of reduced equations.

For $g(\eta) \neq 0, t < T$, and $a = 1 : \theta(1, t, \xi, \eta)[\lambda + \alpha + \delta + q_o(\eta)] = \theta(0, t, \xi, \eta)\beta$

$+ \theta(1, t + 1, \xi, \eta)\delta + \sum_{\gamma \in E_o - \{\eta\}} \theta(1, t, \xi, \gamma)q_o(\gamma, \eta)$

For $g(\eta) \neq 0, a = 1 : \theta(1, T, \xi, \eta)[\lambda + \alpha + \delta + q_o(\eta)] = \theta(0, T, \xi, \eta)\beta$

$+ \sum_{\gamma \in E_o - \{\eta\}} \theta(1, T, \xi, \gamma)q_o(\gamma, \eta) + \theta(1, 1, \xi, \eta)\delta 1_{(\xi=1)} + \theta(1, 1, \xi + 1, \eta)\delta 1_{(\xi<d)}$

$+ \sum_{s=1}^{T} \theta(1, s, \xi, \eta)\lambda 1_{(\xi=g(\eta))} + \sum_{s=1}^{T} \theta(1, s, \xi - 1, \eta)\lambda 1_{(0<\xi-1<g(\eta))}$

$+ \sum_{s=1}^{T} \theta(1, s, \xi + 1, \eta)\lambda 1_{(d \geq \xi+1>g(\eta)>0)}$

For η with $g(\eta) = 0, t < T, a = 1 : \theta(1, t, \xi, \eta)[\alpha + \delta + q_o(\eta)]$

$= \theta(0, t, \xi, \eta)\beta + \theta(1, t + 1, \xi, \eta)\delta + \sum_{\gamma \in e_o - \{\eta\}} \theta(1, t, \xi, \gamma)q_o(\gamma, \eta)$

For η with $g(\eta) = 0, a = 1 : \theta(1, T, \xi, \eta)[\alpha + \delta + q_o(\eta)] = \theta(0, T, \xi, \eta)\beta$

$$+ \sum_{\gamma \in E_o - \{\eta\}} \theta(1, T, \xi, \gamma) q_o(\gamma, \eta) + \theta(1, 1, \xi, \eta) \delta 1_{(\xi=1)} + \theta(1, 1, \xi+1, \eta) \delta 1_{(\xi<d)}$$

For $a = 0$: $\quad \theta(0, t, \xi, \eta)[\beta + q_o(\eta)] = \theta(1, t, \xi, \eta)\alpha + \sum_{\gamma \in E_o - \{\eta\}} \theta(0, t, \xi, \gamma) q_o(\gamma, \eta)$

With elementary, but tedious computations it can be shown that this is a "generator equation", i.e., there exists some continuous time Markov process on the finite state space $K := \{0, 1\} \times \Delta \times D \times (\{0\} \cup D)^N$ with generator matrix $Q_{red} = (q_{red}(y, y') : y, y' \in K$ such that the reduced system of equations is $\theta \cdot Q_{red} = 0$. The main effort is to show that the row sums of Q_{red} are zero.

This generator equation has a unique probability solution because K is finite and Q_{red} is irreducible.

The result of Proposition 8 is surprising. Obviously, the queueing process X which is the central unit of the message handling and transmission management system and the environment process Y strongly interact. Nevertheless, in steady state and in the long run the joint steady state distribution for a fixed time instant is the independent coupling of the respective marginal steady state distributions. This resembles the independence of the marginal queue lengths in a stationary Jackson network [4]. The new feature here is that X and Y are processes of very different structure, while in Jackson's theorem the queue lengths are processes of similar nature.

Similarly, as it is well known in the case of Jackson networks, our result does not say that X and Y are independent processes. There are correlations over time in $(Z(s), Z(t))$ for $0 \le s < t$ and for different time instants there are correlations between $X(s)$ and $Y(t)$. The investigation of this correlation structure is part of our ongoing research.

Another remarkable property of the system following from Proposition 8 is an invariance property: Whenever for a pair λ, μ with $\lambda < \mu$ we have computed the marginal environment steady state θ, this is the θ as function of λ (not of μ!) for all other pairs with $\lambda < \mu$. This is of interest in cases of a complicated environment, where $\theta \cdot Q_{red} = 0$ may be not easy to obtain.

Remark 1. From the very definition of the active-sleep process A and the outer environment process O and Assumption 6 it follows that the marginal distribution of A is θ_a given in Definition 4 and the marginal distribution of O is θ_o indicated in Definition 1.

The solution θ of $\theta \cdot Q_{red} = 0$, found in the proof of Proposition 8 in general does not factorize further. But even if we cannot factorize θ further it is helpful by reducing an infinite linear system of equations to a finite system.

Remark 2. Boucherie [1] considered vector processes of independent coordinates, where restriction on the transitions are imposed as follows: A coordinate process, say S_j, by entering a specified subset A_j of its state space, where he competes with a second process, say S_k for resources (which can be used by only one process at a time) shut down S_k completely, as long as it stays in A_j. This is similar to our "vector process". The difference is: In [1] it is assumed that only one coordinate of the vector process can change at time, and the starting point are independent Markov processes. Neither property is required here: Not all processes used for the construction are independent, and there occur simultaneous jumps of the queue and the environment, as can be seen in (6).

4   Extensions and Refinements

Modeling the Outer Environment
The Markov process O to describe the development of the outer environment is constructed in Definition 1 in the spirit of the neighborhood construction of [17]. Note, that there dynamics of the nodal delivery values are substituted by a fixed value. Into our process O we have incorporated dynamics of nodal delivery values without much effort, still obtaining explicit expressions.

Our modeling procedure offers to incorporate much more versatile dynamical schemes. This can be seen from the proof of Proposition 8: It is not necessary that the set $\{g = 0\} \subset E_o$ is single valued. There may be more states of the outer environment which do not allow RN to communicate with its neighbors for different reasons.

On the other side this flexibility offers model reductions. Starting from a complex environment space E'_o with rates $q'_o(k, \ell)$ and some "decision function" (other than the simple maximum) $g' : U' \to \{0, 1, \ldots, d\}$ we can reduce complexity via $U'' := g(U') := \{0, 1, \ldots, d\}$ and assume that the functional process $g(O)$ is Markovian itself. Reasonable (approximate) transition rates then are

$$q''_o(k, \ell) := S(k, \ell)^{-1} \sum_{\eta \in U, g'(\eta)=k} \sum_{\varsigma \in U, g'(\varsigma)=\ell} q'_o(\eta, \varsigma),$$

where $S(k, \ell) = \sum_{\eta \in U', g'(\eta)=k} \sum_{\varsigma \in U', g'(\varsigma)=\ell} 1_{(q'_o(\eta,\varsigma)>0)}$ is the number of positive transitions from $\{g' = k\}$ to $\{g' = \ell\}$.

More reduction is obtained if we distinguish in the status of the outer environment only states 0 (= no active neighbor = quiet outer environment) and 1 (= at least one active neighbor).

In any case: The proof of Proposition 8 applies without changes.

Example 9. *Consider the outer environment E_o from Definition 1. Then $g(E_o) = \{0, 1, \ldots, d\}$ and from (4) the probability of $\{g = 0\}$ is $p(0) = \prod_{j=1}^N (a_j/(a_j + b_j))$, while the maximal nodal delivery value in the neighborhood is $k \geq 1$ (i.e., $\{g = k\}$) with probability $p(k) :=$*

$$\prod_{j=1}^N \left(\frac{a_j}{a_j + b_j} + \frac{b_j}{a_j + b_j} \sum_{\eta_j=1}^k p_j(\eta_j) \right) - \prod_{j=1}^N \left(\frac{a_j}{a_j + b_j} + \frac{b_j}{a_j + b_j} \sum_{\eta_j=1}^{k-1} p_j(\eta_j) \right).$$

A kernel to generate dynamics for this equilibrium is with positive transition rates

$$q(i, i+1) = \ell(i), \quad i = 0, 1, \ldots, d-1, \quad \text{and} \quad q(i, i-1) = m(i), \quad i = 1, \ldots, d,$$

with $\ell(i) = 1/p(i)$ for $i = 0, 1, \ldots, d-1$ and $m(i) = 1/p(i)$ for $i = 1, \ldots, d$. This yields a reversible dynamics with the required target distribution.

Example 10. *Consider the outer environment E_o from Definition 1 with $D :=$ $\{1\}$, i.e., we distinguish only whether the N nodes of RN's one-hop neighborhood are available or not. Then $E_o = \{(0,1)\}^N$ and the positive transition rates for O are, for $j = 1, \ldots, N$, and $\eta_j = 1$*

$$q_o((\eta_1, \ldots, \eta_{j-1}, 0, \eta_{j+1}, \ldots, \eta_N); (\eta_1, \ldots, \eta_{j-1}, \eta_j, \eta_{j+1}, \ldots, \eta_N)) = b_j, \quad and$$
$$q_o((\eta_1, \ldots, \eta_{j-1}, \eta_j, \eta_{j+1}, \ldots, \eta_N); (\eta_1, \ldots, \eta_{j-1}, 0, \eta_{j+1}, \ldots, \eta_N)) = a_j.$$

The environment process O is ergodic and the steady state probabilities are

$$\theta_o(\eta_1, \ldots, \eta_N) = \prod_{j=1}^{N} \left(\frac{a_j}{a_j + b_j}\right)^{1_{(\eta_j=0)}} \left(\frac{b_j}{a_j + b_j}\right)^{1_{(\eta_j=1)}}, \quad \forall (\eta_1, \ldots, \eta_N) \in E_o.$$

The outer environment is quiet with probability $\theta_o(0, \ldots, 0) = \prod_{j=1}^{N}(a_j/(a_j + b_j))$.

Modeling Fault Tolerance

The introduction of fault tolerance values for any message and its updating in course of transmitting a message and possibly restoring it in the message queue of RN tries to support the resilience of the network without flooding it with messages. Modeling this in a detailed way would need to introduce for the messages different types which change over time and, if we follow the details of the protocol in [17], type-dependent priorities and reordering of the packets according to the fault tolerance values. As the authors in that paper noticed, such scheme probably can not be modeled analytically in full detail. So message replication is skipped in their model.

A simple way to incorporate the effect of increasing queue lengths by a randomized message replication is to estimate an overall replication probability $f \in [0, 1]$ for sent messages and consider the message queue as a feedback queue: If a message is served, it is fed back with feedback probability $f > 0$ to the tail of the queue. We immediately obtain the

Corollary 11. *Let the message queue be a feedback queue with feedback probability $f > 0$. Z is ergodic on E iff $\lambda < \mu(1-f)$. Then its unique stationary distribution π_f fulfills for all $(n, a, t, \xi, \eta) \in \mathbb{N}_0 \times \{0, 1\} \times \Delta \times D \times (\{0\} \cup D)^N$*

$$\pi_f(n, a, t, \xi, \eta) = \left(1 - \frac{\lambda}{\mu(1-f)}\right)\left(\frac{\lambda}{\mu(1-f)}\right)^n \cdot \theta(a, t, \xi, \eta),$$

with θ the distribution on $\{0, 1\} \times \Delta \times D \times (\{0\} \cup D)^N$ from Proposition 8.

The result says that with replication probability f the load of the referenced node is the same as without replication but with a prolongation of the transmission time according to service rate $\mu(1-f)$.

Although with the corollary we are in a position to adapt the load of the message queue better to the situation with message replication we have to pay for this with a slight drawback, which may be not obvious. The protocol in [17] declares that the nodal delivery value is updated every time a message is sent out. In the model described in Corollary 11 updating is formally done only when a message is sent out and no feedback occurs.

Without going into the details we mention only that we can remedy this drawback by introducing an additional update process which updates RN's nodal delivery value according to the scheme (1) at time points generated by a Poisson-μf process when RN is active.

Intensity of the Arrival Process

In [17], [10], [18]), the arrivals at the message queue of RN are assumed to be generated by two independent Poisson processes. A Poisson-r process generates the data for RN, while a Poisson-ℓ process is generated by the nodes in the neighborhood of RN. The intensity of the Poisson-ℓ process is determined by the states of the outer environment. ℓ is typically computed as a gross value on the basis of the environments steady state. An example is given in [17][p. 3291]. In a similar way we can, starting from the information decoded in the distribution θ from Proposition 8, estimate the overall arrival rate ℓ at RN from the outside. We then set $\lambda := r + \ell$.

Reducing the Dimension of the Environment Process

The reduction of complexity described above leave the dimension of the state space of Z invariant while diminishing the sizes of components. Further reduction can be obtained by incorporating the effects of the outer environment into the transition regime of the inner environment and by canceling thereafter the component process O. The resulting process $Z := (X, Y) = (X, A, I)$ will be a homogeneous irreducible strong Markov process on $E := \mathbb{N}_0 \times E_a \times E_i = \mathbb{N}_0 \times \{0, 1\} \times \Delta \times D$. The development of the nodal delivery status of RN is governed by the timer $\bar{\Delta}$ as before via (2) and by the rule that whenever RN has send a packet, it updates its delivery value ξ as follows

$$
\xi \to \begin{cases} \xi + 1, \text{ with probability } r^+(\xi) & \text{if } \xi < d; \\ \xi - 1, \text{ with probability } r^-(\xi) & \text{if } \xi > 1; \\ \xi, \quad \text{ with probability } 1 - r^+(\xi)1_{(\xi<d)} - r^-(\xi)1_{(\xi>1)} & \text{if } 1 \le \xi \le d. \end{cases}
$$

As in Proposition 8 then follows for the system with no replication of sent messages ($f = 0$) the first part of the next statement, while the second part is again surprising.

Corollary 12. *Z is ergodic on the reduced state space $E = \mathbb{N}_0 \times E_a \times E_i = \mathbb{N}_0 \times \{0, 1\} \times \Delta \times D$ iff $\lambda < \mu$. Then its unique stationary distribution π fulfills*

$$
\pi(n, a, t, \xi) = \left(1 - \frac{\lambda}{\mu}\right)\left(\frac{\lambda}{\mu}\right)^n \cdot \theta(a, t, \xi), \quad \forall(n, a, t, \xi) \in \mathbb{N}_0 \times \{0, 1\} \times \Delta \times D,
$$

where θ is a uniquely defined probability distribution on $\{0, 1\} \times \Delta \times D$.

Moreover, θ factorizes completely for $(a, t, \xi) \in \{0, 1\} \times \Delta \times D$ according to

$$
\theta(a, t, \xi) = \left(\frac{\beta}{\alpha + \beta}\right)^a \cdot \left(\frac{\alpha}{\alpha + \beta}\right)^{1-a} \cdot \left(\frac{\delta}{\lambda + \delta}\right)^{T-t} K_{\Delta}^{-1} \cdot \psi(\xi). \tag{7}
$$

Here $K_\Delta = \frac{\delta}{\lambda}\left(\frac{\lambda+\delta}{\delta} - \left(\frac{\delta}{\lambda+\delta}\right)^{T-1}\right)$ is the normalization for the timer distribution, and ψ is a probability on D, the marginal nodal delivery value distribution.

Proof. Whenever there is no restriction for a variable indicated, it runs through all admissible values. The steady state equations for Z are then

For $t < T$, $a = 1$: $\pi(n, 1, t, \xi)[\lambda + \mu 1_{(n>0)} + \alpha + \delta]$
$= \pi(n-1, 1, t, \xi)\lambda 1_{(n>0)} + \pi(n, 0, t, \xi)\beta + \pi(n, 1, t+1, \xi)\delta$

For $a = 1$: $\pi(n, 1, T, \xi)[\lambda + \mu 1_{(n>0)} + \alpha + \delta] = \pi(n-1, 1, T, \xi)\lambda 1_{(n>0)}$

$+ \pi(n, 1, 1, \xi)\delta 1_{(\xi=1)} + \sum_{s=1}^{T} \pi(n+1, 1, s, \xi-1)\mu r^+(\xi-1)1_{(\xi>1)}$

$+ \pi(n, 1, 1, \xi+1)\delta 1_{(\xi<d)} + \sum_{s=1}^{T} \pi(n+1, 1, s, \xi+1)\mu r^-(\xi+1)1_{(\xi<d)}$

$+ \pi(n, 0, T, \xi)\beta + \sum_{s=1}^{T} \pi(n+1, 1, s, \xi)\mu[1 - r^+(\xi)1_{(\xi<d)} - r^-(\xi)1_{(\xi>1)}]$

For $a = 0$: $\pi(n, 0, t, \xi)\beta = \pi(n, 1, t, \xi)\alpha$

Inserting $\pi(n, a, t, \xi) = \left(1 - \frac{\lambda}{\mu}\right)\left(\frac{\lambda}{\mu}\right)^n \cdot \left(\frac{\beta}{\alpha+\beta}\right)^a \cdot \left(\frac{\alpha}{\alpha+\beta}\right)^{1-a} \cdot \phi(t, \xi)$, where ϕ is a function of (t, ξ) only, into these equations reveals that the terms $\left(1 - \frac{\lambda}{\mu}\right)\left(\frac{\lambda}{\mu}\right)^n \cdot \left(\frac{\beta}{\alpha+\beta}\right)^a \cdot \left(\frac{\alpha}{\alpha+\beta}\right)^{1-a}$ cancel completely, yielding a set of reduced equations:

For $t < T$: $\phi(t, \xi)[\lambda + \delta] = \phi(t+1, \xi)\delta$
$\phi(T, \xi)[\lambda + \delta]$

$= \phi(1, \xi)\delta 1_{(\xi=1)} + \sum_{s=1}^{T} \phi(s, \xi-1)\lambda r^+(\xi-1)1_{(\xi>1)} + \phi(1, \xi+1)\delta 1_{(\xi<d)}$

$+ \sum_{s=1}^{T} \phi(s, \xi+1)\lambda r^-(\xi+1)1_{(\xi<d)} + \sum_{s=1}^{T} \phi(s, \xi)\lambda[1 - r^+(\xi)1_{(\xi<d)} - r^-(\xi)1_{(\xi>1)}]$

For $t = 1, \ldots, T$, the first equation yields $\phi(t, \xi) = \phi(T, \xi)(\delta/(\lambda+\delta))^{T-t}$, and we set $\phi(t, \xi) = \left(\frac{\delta}{\lambda+\delta}\right)^{T-t} K_\Delta^{-1} \cdot \psi(\xi)$ for some function $\psi(\xi)$. The first equation is solved obviously by this expression, and the second turns into $\psi(\xi)[\lambda + \delta] =$

$\psi(\xi)\left(\frac{\delta}{\lambda+\delta}\right)^{T-1}\delta 1_{(\xi=1)} + \sum_{s=1}^{T}\psi(\xi-1)\left(\frac{\delta}{\lambda+\delta}\right)^{T-s}\lambda r^+(\xi-1)1_{(\xi>1)}$

$+ \psi(\xi+1)\left(\frac{\delta}{\lambda+\delta}\right)^{T-1}\delta 1_{(\xi<d)} + \sum_{s=1}^{T}\psi(\xi+1)\left(\frac{\delta}{\lambda+\delta}\right)^{T-s}\lambda r^-(\xi+1)1_{(\xi<d)}$

$$+ \sum_{s=1}^{T} \psi(\xi) \left(\frac{\delta}{\lambda + \delta} \right)^{T-s} \lambda[1 - r^+(\xi)1_{(\xi<d)} - r^-(\xi)1_{(\xi>1)}]$$

Recall that $\sum_{s=1}^{T} \left(\frac{\delta}{\lambda+\delta} \right)^{T-s} = K_\Delta$ and $\frac{1}{\lambda+\delta} K_\Delta \lambda = \delta \left[\frac{\lambda+\delta}{\delta} - \left(\frac{\delta}{\lambda+\delta} \right)^{T-1} \right]$. Dividing by $\lambda + \delta$ and utilizing this property yields $\psi(\xi) =$

$$\psi(\xi) \left(\frac{\delta}{\lambda+\delta} \right)^T 1_{(\xi=1)} + \psi(\xi-1)(1 - \left(\frac{\delta}{\lambda+\delta} \right)^T) r^+(\xi-1)1_{(\xi>1)}$$

$$+\psi(\xi+1) \left(\frac{\delta}{\lambda+\delta} \right)^T 1_{(\xi<d)} + \psi(\xi+1)(1 - \left(\frac{\delta}{\lambda+\delta} \right)^T) r^-(\xi+1)1_{(\xi<d)}$$

$$+\psi(\xi)(1 - \left(\frac{\delta}{\lambda+\delta} \right)^T)[1 - r^+(\xi)1_{(\xi<d)} - r^-(\xi)1_{(\xi>1)}]$$

Taking $\psi(1)$ as unknown, this is a two-term recursion for the $\psi(\xi)$, which are uniquely determined up to the factor $\psi(1)$, which is determined from $\psi(1)+\ldots+\psi(d) = 1$. This must hold, because the proposed product form for θ, respectively π, is by ergodicity of Z a probability.

Comments: The marginal timer distribution reveals that the most probable timer value is T. The geometrical decay of the residual timer state probabilities is faster when the arrival intensity increases. This reflects the timer policy: The timer is reset to T whenever a message is sent out.

It is not intuitive that (i) the timer distribution is independent of α and β, because the timer is interrupted whenever RN is in sleep mode, and (ii) the timer and the active-sleep processes are at fixed times independent.

Corollary 13. *In the setting of Corollary 12 in steady state the throughput of RN is*

$$TH(RN) = \lambda \left(1 - \frac{\beta}{\alpha+\beta} - \psi(0)\frac{\alpha}{\alpha+\beta} \right).$$

Acknowledgement. We thank three referees for their constructive suggestions which enhanced the presentation of our paper.

References

1. Boucherie, R.J.: A characterization of independence for competing Markov chains with applications to stochastic Petri nets. IEEE Transactions of Software Engineering 20(7), 536–544 (1994)
2. Chiasserini, C.-F., Garetto, M.: An analytical model for wireless sensor networks with sleeping nodes. IEEE Transactions on Mobile Computing 5(12), 1706–1718 (2006)
3. Chen, Z., Lin, C., Wen, H., Yin, H.: An analytical model for evaluating IEEE 802.15.4 CSMA/CA protocol in low-rate wireless application. In: Advanced Information Networking and Applications Workshops, AINAW 2007, vol. 2, pp. 899–904 (2007)

4. Jackson, J.R.: Networks of waiting lines. Operations Research 5, 518–521 (1957)
5. Jiang, L., Walrand, J.: A distributed CSMA algorithm for throughput and utility maximization in wireless networks. IEEE/ACM Transactions on Networking 18(3), 960–972 (2010)
6. Krenzler, R., Daduna, H.: Loss systems in a random environment - steady state analysis. Preprint, Center of Mathematical Statistics und Stochastic Processes, University of Hamburg, No. 2012-04 (2012)
7. Krenzler, R., Daduna, H.: Loss systems in a random environment - embedded Markov chain analysis. Preprint, Center of Mathematical Statistics und Stochastic Processes, University of Hamburg, No. 2013-02 (2013)
8. Krishnamoorthy, A., Lakshmy, B., Manikandan, R.: A survey on inventory models with positive service time. OPSEARCH 48, 153–169 (2011)
9. Li, W.W.: Several characteristics of active/sleep model in wireless sensor networks. In: New Technologies, Mobility and Security (NTMS), pp. 1–5 (2011)
10. Liu, J., Tong Lee, T.: A framework for performance modeling of wireless sensor networks. In: 2005 IEEE International Conference on Communications, ICC 2005, vol. 2, pp. 1075–1081 (2005)
11. Mehmet Ali, M.K., Gu, H.: Performance analysis of a wireless sensor network. In: IEEE Wireless Communications and Networking Conference, vol. 2, pp. 1166–1171 (2006)
12. Qiu, T., Feng, L., Xia, F., Wu, G., Zhou, Y.: A packet buffer evaluation method exploiting queueing theory for wireless sensor networks. Computer Science and Information Systems 8(4), 1027–1049 (2011)
13. Sauer, C., Daduna, H.: Availability formulas and performance measures for separable degradable networks. Economic Quality Control 18, 165–194 (2003)
14. Sauer, C., Daduna, H.: Separable networks with unreliable servers. In: Charzinski, J., Lehnert, R., Tran-Gia, P. (eds.) Providing QoS in Heterogeneous Environments. Teletraffic Science and Engineering, vol. 5b, pp. 821–830. Elsevier Science, Amsterdam (2003)
15. Schwarz, M., Sauer, C., Daduna, H., Kulik, R., Szekli, R.: M/M/1 queueing systems with inventory. Queueing Systems and Their Applications 54, 55–78 (2006)
16. Wang, Y., Dang, H., Wu, H.H.: A survey on analytic studies of Delay-Tolerant Mobile Sensor Networks. Wireless Communications and Mobile Computing 7, 1197–1208 (2007)
17. Wu, H., Wang, Y., Dang, H., Lin, F.: Analytic, Simulation, and Empirical Evaluation of Delay/Fault-Tolerant Mobile Sensor Networks. IEEE Transactions on Wireless Communications 6(9), 3287–3296 (2007)
18. Zhang, Y., Li, W.: An energy-based stochastic model for wireless sensor networks. Wireless Sensor Networks 3(9), 322–328 (2011)

Modeling Responsiveness of Decentralized Service Discovery in Wireless Mesh Networks

Andreas Dittrich[1], Björn Lichtblau[2], Rafael Rezende[1], and Miroslaw Malek[1]

[1] Advanced Learning and Research Institute (ALaRI)
Università della Svizzera italiana, Lugano, Switzerland
{andreas.dittrich,ribeiror,malekm}@usi.ch
[2] Humboldt-Universität zu Berlin, Berlin, Germany
lichtbla@informatik.hu-berlin.de

Abstract. In service networks, discovery plays a crucial role as a layer where providers can be published and enumerated. This work focuses on the responsiveness of the discovery layer, the probability to operate successfully within a deadline, even in the presence of faults. It proposes a hierarchy of stochastic models for decentralized discovery and uses it to describe the discovery of a single service using three popular protocols. A methodology to use the model hierarchy in wireless mesh networks is introduced. Given a pair requester and provider, a discovery protocol and a deadline, it generates specific model instances and calculates responsiveness. Furthermore, this paper introduces a new metric, the expected responsiveness distance d_{er}, to estimate the maximum distance from a provider where requesters can still discover it with a required responsiveness. Using monitoring data from the DES testbed at Freie Universität Berlin, it is shown how responsiveness and d_{er} of the protocols change depending on the position of nodes and the link qualities in the network.

Keywords: Real-time systems, Responsiveness, Service discovery, Wireless mesh networks, Markov Models, Probabilistic Breadth-First Search.

1 Introduction

Service-oriented architecture (SOA) describes a paradigm where services are the building blocks of system design. SOA introduces several principles to support its paradigm. Among them is discoverability, which means that structured data is added to services to be effectively published, discovered and interpreted. Communication of this data is done by *service discovery* (SD). Using SD, service instances can be enumerated and sorted according to functional and non-functional requirements, facilitating autonomous mechanisms like optimization of service compositions or fall-back to correctly operating instances in case of failure.

If discovery fails, a service cannot be available. Comprehensive service dependability evaluation thus needs to consider the discovery process. This is traditionally neglected, however. Since SD is a time-critical operation, one key dependability property is *responsiveness* – the probability to perform some action on time even

K. Fischbach and U.R. Krieger (Eds.): MMB & DFT 2014, LNCS 8376, pp. 88–102, 2014.

in the presence of faults [14]. For SD, responsiveness quantifies the probability that a required ratio of present service instances is found within a deadline. Due to the diversity of usage scenarios and the dynamics of modern networks, it is not trivial to predict. This problem is exemplified in unreliable networks with more complex fault behavior, such as self-organized *wireless mesh networks* (WMNs), where the quality of links is constantly changing and heavily affected by external interference, fading effects and multi-path propagation.

This work provides a hierarchy of stochastic models to evaluate responsiveness of decentralized SD in unreliable networks. It provides a methodology to apply these models to WMNs. Because of a high variability of link quality in such networks, the responsiveness is expected to change significantly with the positions of requester and provider. The methodology thus considers the *user-perceived* responsiveness of given communication partners. It estimates packet loss probabilities and transmission time distributions for each link on the communication paths between the partners and generates specific model instances to assess SD responsiveness. This facilitates the evaluation of responsiveness in common SD scenarios, to provide hints on the suitability of current protocols and detect their shortcomings in WMNs. The provided solution is expected to spur future research on service dependability which includes the discovery layer.

The remainder of this paper is structured as follows. After brief background information and related work in Sections 2 and 3, the problem is described in Section 4. A hierarchy of stochastic models to evaluate SD responsiveness is introduced in Section 5, followed by a methodology that uses these models in Section 6. The case study in Section 7 shows the responsiveness of SD in different scenarios. Results are explained and interpreted. Section 8 concludes the work.

2 Service Discovery

SD is realized with three different architectures. In two-party or decentralized architecture, service clients and providing instances communicate directly with each other. In three-party or centralized architecture, this communication is handled by a registry. Hybrid architectures can switch between these two on demand. SD describes service instances with a unique identifier, optionally a service type and other structured information relevant to a service user. Syntax and semantics of this information are known to discovery clients.

Discoverability requires the ability to both publish a service instance and to discover it. All discovery protocols supply these two basic types of operation. A providing service instance can publish its presence either directly to the network via multi- or broadcast or to a registry, also known as registration. Clients use discovery to enumerate providing instances passively, by listening to *publish* messages or actively, through discovery requests with subsequent responses, if providers are available. Responses are either sent directly from providers or from the registry, via uni- or multicast. The use of multicast generally causes higher load on the network than unicast. However, it may suppress requests from other clients by responding proactively and greatly simplifies distributed cache maintenance. In WMNs, efficient flooding poses a great challenge so using multicast should be considered carefully.

In *Internet Protocol* (IP) networks, three different discovery protocols are prevalent: *Service Location Protocol* (SLP), *Simple Service Discovery Protocol* (SSDP) and *Domain Name System based Service Discovery* (DNS-SD). DNS-SD as part of the Zeroconf protocol family is referred to by that name throughout this paper. Especially, SSDP and Zeroconf can be found in a plethora of embedded devices, such as printers, network-attached storage or cameras. The protocols transmit messages using the lightweight *user datagram protocol* (UDP). UDP is an unreliable transport so recovery operations are done by the SD protocols themselves. Fail-stop faults may be classified as regular exhibition of network dynamics and are recovered by goodbye messages. Crash, omission and timing faults are recovered by request retries and timeouts. The number of retries and the time between them vary among the protocols. Zeroconf and SLP specify an initial retry timeout and then double it every period. In SSDP, the requester may choose a timeout in a specified interval for every period. Values for the individual intervals are shown in Table 1. Quantitative analysis of specific properties to justify these strategies, responsiveness in particular, is practically non existent.

Table 1. Service discovery retry intervals for the studied protocols

	$t_{retry}(1)$	$t_{retry}(2)$	$t_{retry}(3)$	$t_{retry}(4)$	$t_{retry}(5)$
Zeroconf	$1s$	$2s$	$4s$	$8s$	$16s$
SLP	$2s$	$4s$	$8s$	$16s$	$32s$
SSDP (min/max)	$1s/5s$	$1s/5s$	$1s/5s$	$1s/5s$	$1s/5s$

Most widely used for IP networking in WMNs is *Optimized Link State Routing* (OLSR). OLSR nodes proactively search for routes and cooperatively create a spanning tree that covers the whole topology. A number of different metropolitan networks, such as in Athens, Berlin and Leipzig successfully employ OLSR.

3   Related Work

An overview of decentralized discovery protocols can be found in [22] and [11]. Dabrowski et al. did an experiment-based analysis of various dependability properties in existing discovery protocols [6,7,8]. Among them, related to responsiveness is *update effectiveness*, the probability to restore a consistent state after failure. They did not consider active SD responsiveness during regular operation. Furthermore, the widespread Zeroconf protocol is not considered, the responsiveness of which has been evaluated in experiments in [10]. The paper at hand aims to provide analytical methods to reproduce the results in [10].

The automatic generation of steady-state service availability models from service descriptions and infrastructure information is presented in [15]. A related approach with state-of-the-art tool support can be found in [9], which has been extended to support instantaneous availability evaluation in [19]. However, none can be easily adapted for responsiveness evaluation and their complexity is prohibitive in highly connected WMNs. A work inspirational to this paper describes dependability analysis using directed acyclic graphs [20]. The paper at hand combines a network topology and a discovery operation in a Markov model that reflects such a graph. A related model has been used for a cost-estimation of automatic network address assignment in Zeroconf [4].

General problems and challenges in WMNs are presented in [1]. There are several approaches to model packet transmission delays at the 802.11 MAC level, e.g. [17,18], which will not be considered due to their complexity. Bianchi [2] developed a Markov model to compute the 802.11 *Distributed Coordination Function* (DCF) saturation throughput. It assumes a known finite number of terminals, ideal channel conditions and all nodes in one collision domain. These assumptions do not hold for the WMNs targeted in this work. Instead of a detailed modeling of low-level MAC operations, we favor an approach that encompasses application layer protocols. Our delay estimation is based on the *expected transmission count* (ETX) metric [5] used by OLSR with packet transmission delays as defined in the 802.11 standard [12], related to, but more efficient than [16].

4 Problem Statement

A methodology is needed to quantify *user-perceived* responsiveness of decentralized SD in WMNs. The user-perceived scope is defined by the position of requester and provider and the time of discovery. The methodology needs to use a stochastic model to evaluate responsiveness and an automated procedure that covers the following steps: (1) Define SD scenario that contains requester and provider, protocol and deadline for the SD operation. (2) Gather monitoring data from the network and prepare that data as input parameters of the model. (3) Instantiate specific models using these parameters and the scenario definition. (4) Evaluate user-perceived responsiveness by solving these model instances.

The methodology should support evaluation of three different variants of SD responsiveness. First, the responsiveness for different requester-provider pairs, second, the average responsiveness of a specific provider for all requesters in the network. Third, a novel metric, the *expected responsiveness distance* should be investigated, to estimate the maximum distance from a provider where requesters are expected to discover it with a required responsiveness (see Definition 1). This work focuses on IP networks and their most common discovery protocols: Zeroconf, SSDP and SLP. Routing is done by the prevalent OLSR protocol.

Definition 1. *Given a service discovery deadline t_D with a required responsiveness $R_{req}(t_D)$, a set of service providers S and sets of clients $C_d, d \in \mathbb{N}^+$ with d denoting the minimum hop distance of each client in C_d from all providers in S. Let $R_{avg,d}(t_D)$ be the average responsiveness when discovering S from C_d. The expected responsiveness distance d_{er} is the maximum d where $R_{avg,d}(t_D) \geq R_{req}(t_D)$ and $\forall d' \in \mathbb{N}^+, d' < d : R_{avg,d'}(t_D) \geq R_{req}(t_D)$.*

5   Modeling Service Discovery

When doing SD, the number of requesters and providers may vary. For instance, multiple clients might request a single service. One client could discover all existing providers in the network to choose one meeting best its requirements. We will now focus on decentralized SD by a single client. Any such SD operation can be described with a generic family of Markov models, which includes three types of states: (1) A single state named req_0 defines the beginning of an SD operation, when the initial request has been sent. (2) Two absorbing states ok and $error$ define the successful or unsuccessful end of an SD operation. (3) A set containing every state between the first two types where not all required responses have been received and the final deadline has not been reached.

The Markov model family is parametric in two parameters: number of retries and required coverage. The maximum number of retries n describes the first dimension of the model family. Beginning from req_0, it defines a chain of retry states req_i, $i = 1...n$, that stand for "retry i has been sent". From every retry state the model can transition into ok in case a sufficient number of responses was gathered. If not it will transition to the next retry state and eventually from req_n to $error$. The parameter required coverage describes how many responses need to be received before an SD operation is called successful and is the second dimension of the model family. The retry states req_i, $i = 1...n$ become a set of states that relate to the success ratio when doing retry i. The size of this set can be arbitrary but for example, if three services need to be found for successful operation, there could be three states req_{ij}, $j = 0, 1, 2$ for every retry i that stand for "retry i has been sent and j responses have been received so far".

Estimating the transition probabilities within this Markov model family is not trivial. In the following, we propose a hierarchy of stochastic models where the probabilities of these high level discovery models are calculated by low level models based on link quality data measured in the network.

5.1   Service Discovery Model

To demonstrate the model hierarchy, we will now instantiate a specific model for discovery of a single service within a deadline $t_D = 5s$ using the Zeroconf protocol. The number of retries n can be derived by examining the retry strategy of the discovery protocol under analysis (see Table 1). Given the times in seconds $t_{retry}(i), i \in \mathbb{N}^+$ between retries $i - 1$ and i with $t_{retry}(0) = 0$. The total time $t_{total}(r)$ after the beginning of a discovery operation when sending retry r is calculated according to Equation 1.

$$t_{total}(0) = 0, \quad t_{total}(r) = \sum_{i=1}^{r} t_{retry}(i) \quad , r \in \mathbb{N}^+ \tag{1}$$

For Zeroconf, $t_{total}(2) < t_D < t_{total}(3)$. So, $n = 2$ retries will be sent. The resulting regular Markov model instance is depicted in Figure 1: In short, retries continue to be sent until a response is received, triggering a transition to the *ok* state. If no response is received after retry n has been sent and before t_D, the operation is considered failed by transitioning to state *error*. So, the discovery operation is successful as soon as the first response packet arrives at the requester. Transitions between the retry states will only happen if no response has been received until the specific retry timeout.

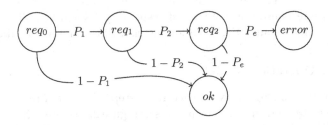

Fig. 1. Markov chain for single service discovery

There are two related probabilities in Figure 1: $P_r, 1 \leq r < n$ is the probability that no discovery response was received between $t_{total}(r) - t_{retry}(r)$ and $t_{total}(r)$. P_e is the probability that no response was received between $t_{total}(n)$ and t_D. Arrival times of responses to a specific request r can be considered as a random variable X_r. Equation 2 describes the cumulative distribution of this variable, the probability that a response to request r has arrived by time t or, the *responsiveness* $R_r(t)$ of a single request-response operation for request r.

$$F_{X_r}(t) = P\{X_r \leq t\} = R_r(t) \tag{2}$$

Knowing this, Equation 3 calculates the probability that a response to request r arrives in a specific time interval.

$$P\{t_x \leq X_r \leq t_y\} = R_r(t_y) - R_r(t_x) \tag{3}$$

Functions $Pr : \mathbb{N}^+ \to [0,1]$ and $Pe : \mathbb{N}^+ \to [0,1]$, as defined in Equations 4 and 5, can now calculate P_r and P_e such that $Pr(r) = P_r$ and $Pe(n) = P_e$.

$$Pr(r) = \prod_{i=1}^{r} \left(1 - \frac{R_i(t_{total}(r)) - R_i(t_{total}(r-1))}{1 - R_i(t_{total}(r-1))} \right) \tag{4}$$

$$Pe(n) = \prod_{i=1}^{n} \left(1 - \frac{R_i(t_D) - R_i(t_{total}(n))}{1 - R_i(t_{total}(n))} \right) \tag{5}$$

Since Equation 5 is a special case of Equation 4, only Equation 4 is explained in detail. A retry is forced when no response packet arrived until the retry timeout, so the product multiplies the individual probabilities for non-arrival of responses to each request that has been sent so far. The probability for the response to request i to arrive *within the specific interval* is described by the quotient. The numerator describes the unconditional probability for a response to arrive within the specified interval. But, deducting from the structure of the Markov model, it cannot have arrived before. That condition is given in the denominator. The quotient, thus, gives the probability that a response to request i is received in the specified time interval, provided it has not arrived before. It is then subtracted from 1 to get the probability of non-arrival.

Missing is a specification to calculate the functions $R_r(t)$. One way would be to measure response times of request-response pairs and fit a distribution to them. We provide an analytical solution instead, using a retry operation model.

5.2   Retry Operation Model

When discovering a single service, each retry step relates to a request-response pair, described by the semi-Markov process in Figure 2. In state Rq, a request has been sent. When it arrives at the destination, the provider will send a response, triggering a transition to state Rp. As soon as this response arrives back at the requester, the model enters state ok. If one of the messages gets lost, it will transition to state $error$.

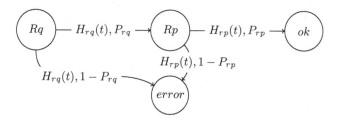

Fig. 2. Semi-Markov chain for a single request-response pair

In case messages arrive (with a probability of P_x), they have a certain distribution of arrival times. This is described by $H_x(t)$, the sojourn time distribution for state x. The cumulative distribution function of time to absorption in state ok now calculates $R_r(t)$. Since t is relative to the beginning of the SD operation, $R_r(t)$ is in fact parametrized by the location $t_{total}(r)$, the time at which retry r is being initiated. The retry operation model is independent of a concrete network infrastructure. It has no knowledge of how to calculate the probabilities and transition time distributions. Providing concrete values of P_x and $H_x(t)$ for specific SD pairs on demand is the purpose of the network mapping model.

5.3   Network Mapping Model

Mapping requests and responses to the network under analysis means providing models that calculate P_x and $H_x(t)$ in the retry operation model (see Figure 2) by taking into account the details of the used communication mechanism, unicast or multicast. This mapping is dependent on the concrete network infrastructure. In this case, we provide models for a WMN running OLSR. Different networks could need diverse models, but, provided they estimate P_x and $H_x(t)$, these could be used in the proposed model hierarchy as well.

Unicast Model. A unicast message follows the shortest path according to the routing metric. In OLSR, every node periodically calculates that shortest path and saves the next hop for every destination. A unicast message is sent to the next hop node which then decides to forward according to its own next hop information for the destination. We use an algorithm that calculates the unicast path hop by hop based on the next hop information on each node. If no such global information is available, using the shortest path known to the first node remains a viable, albeit less accurate solution.

Since there is only one path with n nodes and $m = n - 1$ links, this can be modeled as a simple semi-Markov chain of n states. Each state $k_i, i = 1...n - 1$ stands for "message forwarded by node i", state k_n means "message arrived at node n". The links between nodes i and $i + 1$ become transitions $k_i \rightarrow k_{i+1}$. Further, there is a transition from $k_i, i = 1...n - 1$ to *error* to account for packet loss. State transition probabilities $P_{k_i,k_{i+1}}$ are calculated from the currently monitored packet transmission probabilities of the link between nodes i and $i+1$ (see Section 6), taking into account that unicasts will be retransmitted up to seven times if not acknowledged by the receiving node. The estimation of sojourn time distributions $H_{k_i,k_{i+1}}(t)$ is described in Section 5.4. The resulting unicast chain is then integrated into the retry operation model in Figure 2 – for a unicast response, for example, by merging states k_i and Rp, k_n and ok as well as the two error states. The rest of the chain replaces transition $Rp \rightarrow ok$.

Multicast Model. In theory, modeling the traversal of a multicast discovery packet should consider all possible paths between source and destination. This redundancy has been taken into account in [9] but finding all paths between two nodes is NP-complete, a prohibitive complexity especially in networks with high connectivity, such as WMNs. Since the vast majority of those paths has a very low probability of traversal and their impact on the responsiveness of the multicast communication would be minor, this work instead uses *probabilistic breadth-first search* (PBFS) [13] to derive an estimation of the multicast path length. In PBFS, node neighbors are only considered if the edge between a node and its neighbor succeeds a random roll against its transmission probability, as monitored by the routing layer (see Section 6). This way, each run of PBFS realistically simulates how a multicast packet would traverse the WMN. PBFS is sampled a sufficient number of times to approximate with which probability the destination node could be reached. This reflects P_x in the retry operation model, for example, P_{rq} for a multicast request. We additionally store the probability for each path length in case of arrival to later estimate the distribution of sojourn time $H_x(t)$ in Section 5.4.

5.4   Transmission Time Distributions

Estimations for sojourn time distributions in the network mapping models are based on the (re-)transmission and potential back-off periods defined in the 802.11 standard [12]. For transmission times over links, we assume the lowest data rate, which is correct for multicasts. Unicasts, however, will transmit at higher data rates if possible, reducing the time for individual retry transmissions. The estimation thus presents an upper bound for the transmission time as dependent on the data rate. The estimation also ignores additional contention due to internal traffic or external interference, which affects the upper limit of transmission times. To account for this, a certain percentage of packets is assumed to arrive *after* the estimated maximum transmission time for both uni- and multicasts. The bounds calculated from these assumptions are fitted to an exponential distribution for the transmission time. For the unicast model, this is done for each transition $k_i \rightarrow k_{i+1}, i = 1...n - 1$ and provides $H_{k_i,k_{i+1}}(t)$. In the multicast model, one distribution function is generated for each possible path length given by PBFS. The distributions are then weighted with the corresponding probability for their length and combined in a single function $H_x(t)$.

6   Methodology

To calculate the SD responsiveness for given pairs of requester and provider in a network, the model layers described in Section 5 need to be generated bottom-up using the following steps:

1. Define a scenario which consists of (1) the SD communication partners requester and provider, (2) the discovery protocol and (3) a deadline for the SD operation.
2. Generate low level network mapping models for individual requests and responses between the SD pair requester and provider based on the communication mechanisms of the protocol, uni- or multicast (see Sections 5.3, 5.4).
3. Integrate the network mapping models from Step 2 in the semi-Markov chain for the retry model (see Section 5.2). This chain calculates the responsiveness of an individual retry over time.
4. Calculate the number of retries n based on the defined protocol and deadline. This defines the structure of the high level discovery model (see Section 5.1).
5. Estimate the state transitions probabilities in the discovery model, using Equations 4 and 5. In these equations, $R_n(t)$ is the cumulative probability for absorption at time t in state ok in the retry model from Step 3.

The discovery model can then be solved. The steady-state probability of arrival in state ok in this model is the probability that an SD operation as specified in the scenario is successful, given the current monitored state of the network. The methodology has been implemented in a Python framework that carries out all necessary steps. More complex stochastic analysis is performed using the SHARPE tool [21].

All monitoring data is gathered on demand from the routing layer. This approach is least invasive and can be used in every network where the routing layer provides the needed data. OLSR nodes use probe messages to measure link qualities for every neighbor. Given the forward delivery ratio d_f and reverse delivery ratio d_r, ETX is defined as the reciprocal of $(d_f \cdot d_r)$. This information allows to construct a complete network graph with edges weighted by their ETX value. In the graph, nodes are annotated with meta information from their local OLSR routing table that includes the next hop for every other reachable node in the network.

7   Case Study

To demonstrate how the proposed methodology can be used to estimate the responsiveness in common use cases of SD, the three protocols explained in Section 2 are now evaluated in three different scenarios using measured data from a real-life WMN, the *distributed embedded systems* (DES) testbed at *Freie Universität Berlin* (FUB). This testbed consists of around 130 wireless nodes that are spread over multiple campus buildings of FUB. Due to space limitations, we refer to a complete description of the testbed in [3]. For the sake of traceability, node identifiers in this text reflect the actual hostnames in the testbed.

In this case study, OLSR was used in version 0.6.5.2. It provides a valid reference for the real world application of the methodology. All monitoring was done by OLSR. Topology data was gathered with OLSR's JSON plug-in and then integrated into the network model using the Python framework. The testbed was configured and data gathered with different transmission power levels to obtain different topologies. Retry intervals of the discovery protocols are set according to the standards as described in Section 2. Since SSDP does not have fixed intervals, it is assessed in two different configurations reflecting the minimum and maximum interval as defined in the standard.

7.1   Scenario 1 – Single Pair Responsiveness

First, the responsiveness of a single pair requester and provider is evaluated over time. In order to investigate also how the responsiveness changes with the distance between nodes, two different pairs were chosen. One pair *(t9-105, t9-154)* is within the main cloud *t9*, a dense and well-connected part of the WMN consisting of 56 nodes (see Figure 3a). The other pair *(t9-105, a3-119)* covers almost the maximum distance in the network (see Figure 3b). In both cases, node *t9-105* is the requester. The results clearly show that as the distance between requester and provider increases, overall responsiveness decreases.

The difference in responsiveness among the protocols is apparent. With increasing deadlines the responsiveness of the Zeroconf protocol is consistently lower compared to the other protocols. This is because Zeroconf uses multicast for both requests and responses. Multicast packets will not be resent seven times before considered lost, so the danger of packet loss is much higher. The positive

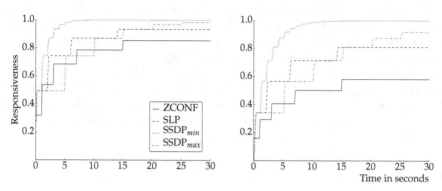

(a) Within same cloud, provider *t9-154*   (b) Maximum distance, provider *a3-119*

Fig. 3. Discovery responsiveness over time for different providers requested from *t9-105*

effects of multicast responses for multiple communication pairs, as pointed out in Section 2, cannot be considered in this analysis. Also not included are the effects of additional load on the network caused by discovery. Since retries are considered independent events, lower retry intervals will lead to a higher responsiveness. While this assumption can be justified for retry intervals in the order of seconds – discovery packets are only a few bytes in size – it cannot hold for ever-lower intervals. So, although SSDP with a minimum interval ranks consistently best, the increased load might not be in the best interest of the service network as a whole. More in-depth research is needed on that matter. However, it can be deducted that with low deadlines, the chosen retry interval is more relevant for responsiveness than the communication mechanism (i.e., unicast vs. multicast). In general, current SD protocols struggle to achieve a high responsiveness in WMNs, even over short distances.

7.2   Scenario 2 – Average Provider Responsiveness

The second scenario covers the average responsiveness of a single provider over time when requested from an arbitrary client in the network. To demonstrate how the models capture topology changes, this scenario uses data measured in two different topologies that were generated with different radio power settings. The focus lies on provider *t9-154* from Section 7.1, which is well centered within the network so it provides a good reference to see the effects of overall link quality on responsiveness. Figure 4 shows the results.

The main observation is that the average responsiveness when discovering node *t9-154* is quite high due to its prominent, almost optimal position in the network. With high quality radio links, depicted in Figure 4a, all protocols quickly reach a responsiveness of over 90%. Responsiveness is considerably decreased for lower quality wireless connections (see Figure 4b). With deadlines above 15 seconds, there is a consistent ranking of the discovery protocols, with

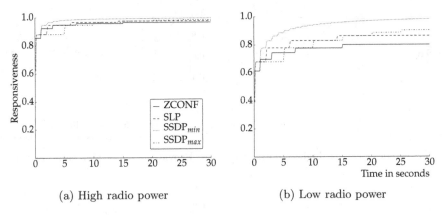

(a) High radio power   (b) Low radio power

Fig. 4. Average responsiveness over time for provider *t9-154* in different topologies

Zeroconf again having the lowest responsiveness. The ranking is identical for different link qualities, only the overall values are different. Due to different retry strategies of the protocols, however, this behavior is not consistent for lower deadlines. This underlines the findings from the Scenario 1: With deadlines close to the individual retry intervals, the chosen interval is more relevant for responsiveness than the communication mechanism. In summary, it can be said that purely multicast based SD as in Zeroconf is justified when positive effects for multiple communication partners are expected. For single discovery operations among few partners, responding via unicast like in SSDP and SLP provides higher responsiveness because of its more reliable communication mechanism. Among SSDP and SLP, the specific retry strategy until the deadline is the main factor impacting responsiveness.

7.3   Scenario 3 – Expected Responsiveness Distance

The last scenario covers the *expected responsiveness distance* d_{er} from Definition 1. The responsiveness of two different providers, *t9-154* and *a3-119*, is calculated when requested from every client in the network. Then, the responsiveness is averaged for requesters at the same distance of these providers. Again, the used data was measured in two different topologies that were generated with different radio power settings. The discovery deadline is set to five seconds. Results are illustrated in Figure 5.

The ranking among the protocols is not the same as in the previous scenarios. This is due to the chosen, realistically short deadline of five seconds. The retry strategy until this deadline has an important impact and the maximum retry timeout for SSDP simply did not force enough retries to account for lost messages. It can also be recognized in Figure 5d, that badly placed providers risk a very low d_{er} with decreasing link quality. The d_{er} for the different protocols with a required responsiveness $R_{req} = 0.8$ is summarized in Table 2. It should

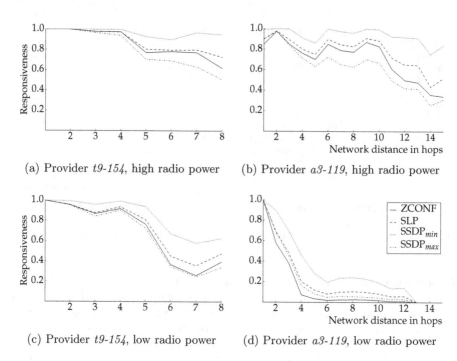

(a) Provider *t9-154*, high radio power

(b) Provider *a3-119*, high radio power

(c) Provider *t9-154*, low radio power

(d) Provider *a3-119*, low radio power

Fig. 5. Average responsiveness over number of hops for providers *t9-154* and *a3-119* in two different topologies

be noted that the maximum d_{er} depends on the eccentricity ϵ of the provider node, the greatest distance from any other node.

As can be seen in Figure 5, the average responsiveness is not always decreasing over distance. This happens because hop count as the chosen distance metric does not necessarily reflect the quality of a path. In fact, longer paths might be of higher quality. The hop distance is, however, an intuitive metric that in this case presents the lower bound for d_{er}. If needed, a more realistic, quality-based distance metric should be used to increase accuracy.

Table 2. Expected responsiveness distance d_{er} of the studied protocols with a deadline of five seconds (ϵ = provider eccentricity, R_{req} = required responsiveness, RPS = radio power setting). A higher d_{er} is generally desired.

Provider	ϵ	R_{req}	*RPS*	Zeroconf	SLP	SSDP (min)	SSDP (max)
t9-154	8	0.8	high	4	5	8	4
			low	4	5	5	4
a3-119	15	0.8	high	3	4	13	3
			low	1	1	2	1

8   Conclusion

Dependability evaluation of *service discovery* (SD) in dynamic and decentralized networks remains challenging. This work proposes a stochastic model family to evaluate the user-perceived responsiveness of SD, the probability to find providers within a deadline, even in the presence of faults. The family consists of a hierarchy of Markov and semi-Markov processes that are parametrized to allow instantiation for diverse SD scenarios and use current network monitoring data as input. To put the models into use, a methodology has been introduced that works specifically in wireless mesh networks with proactive routing. Upon request, it generates and solves model instances for specific SD scenarios.

Using data from the DES testbed at Freie Universität Berlin, responsiveness was evaluated for the three most prevalent SD protocols in IP networks. First, the responsiveness for different pairs of requester and provider has been compared. Second, the average responsiveness of a single provider, depending on the topology, has been analyzed. Results demonstrate that responsiveness varies dramatically depending on the position of nodes in the network and the overall link quality. The results further indicate that, with short deadlines close to the individual retry intervals, the right retry timing strategy is more important than the communication mechanism. With longer deadlines, using the more reliable unicast instead of multicast consistently improves responsiveness. In either case, the fixed strategies of current SD protocols struggle to achieve a high responsiveness in these dynamic and inherently unreliable networks. Finally, a new metric *expected responsiveness distance* d_{er} has been introduced, estimating the maximum hop distance from a provider at which nodes can discover it with a required responsiveness. To deploy a responsive service with a minimum number of nodes, every requester in the network should be within the d_{er} of at least one provider. The d_{er} of two different providers has been evaluated and the results underline the importance of position when placing service instances.

Future work will include a comprehensive experimental validation of the model, also in centralized and hybrid SD architectures. The model could then be used to develop novel discovery protocols that, for example, support variable retry intervals depending on the state of the network. Finally, the model facilitates comprehensive service availability evaluation that includes also the discovery layer.

References

1. Akyildiz, I.F., Wang, X.: A survey on wireless mesh networks. IEEE Communications Magazine 43(9), S23–S30 (2005)
2. Bianchi, G.: Performance analysis of the IEEE 802.11 distributed coordination function. IEEE Journal on Selected Areas in Communications 18(3), 535–547 (2000)
3. Blywis, B., Günes, M., Juraschek, F., Hahm, O.: Properties and topology of the DES-testbed. Tech. Rep. TR-B-11-02, FU Berlin, Germany (March 2011)
4. Bohnenkamp, H., van der Stok, P., Hermanns, H., Vaandrager, F.: Cost-optimization of the IPv4 zeroconf protocol. In: International Conference on Dependable Systems and Networks, pp. 531–540. IEEE (June 2003)

5. Couto, D.S.J.D., Aguayo, D., Bicket, J., Morris, R.: A high-throughput path metric for multi-hop wireless routing. In: 9th Annual International Conference on Mobile Computing and Networking, pp. 134–146. ACM (2003)

6. Dabrowski, C.E., Mills, K.L.: Understanding self-healing in service-discovery systems. In: Workshop on Self-healing Systems (WOSS), pp. 15–20. ACM (2002)

7. Dabrowski, C.E., Mills, K.L., Elder, J.: Understanding consistency maintenance in service discovery architectures during communication failure. In: 3rd International Workshop on Software and Performance (WOSP), pp. 168–178. ACM (2002)

8. Dabrowski, C.E., Mills, K.L., Elder, J.: Understanding consistency maintenance in service discovery architectures in response to message loss. In: 4th Annual International Workshop on Active Middleware Services, pp. 51–60 (2002)

9. Dittrich, A., Kaitovic, I., Murillo, C., Rezende, R.: A model for evaluation of user-perceived service properties. In: International Symposium on Parallel Distributed Processing, Workshops and Phd Forum (IPDPSW), pp. 1508–1517. IEEE (May 2013)

10. Dittrich, A., Salfner, F.: Experimental responsiveness evaluation of decentralized service discovery. In: International Symposium on Parallel Distributed Processing, Workshops and Phd Forum (IPDPSW), pp. 1–7. IEEE (April 2010)

11. Edwards, W.K.: Discovery systems in ubiquitous computing. IEEE Pervasive Computing 5(2), 70–77 (2006)

12. IEEE standard for information technology – telecommunications and information exchange between systems – [. . .]. IEEE Std 802.11-2012. IEEE Standards Association, pp. 1–2793 (2012)

13. Lichtblau, B., Dittrich, A.: Probabilistic breadth-first search – a method for evaluation of network-wide broadcast protocols. In: International Conference on New Technologies, Mobility and Security (NTMS). IEEE (to appear, April 2014)

14. Malek, M.: Responsive systems: A marriage between real time and fault tolerance. In: Cin, M.D., Hohl, W. (eds.) Fault-Tolerant Computing Systems, Informatik-Fachberichte, vol. 283, pp. 1–17. Springer (1991)

15. Milanovic, N., Milic, B.: Automatic generation of service availability models. IEEE Trans. on Services Computing 4(1), 56–69 (2011)

16. Naimi, A.M., Jacquet, P.: One-hop delay estimation in 802.11 ad hoc networks using the OLSR protocol. Tech. Rep. RR-5327, INRIA, Le Chesnay, France (2004)

17. Oliveira, R., Bernardo, L., Pinto, P.: Modelling delay on IEEE 802.11 MAC protocol for unicast and broadcast nonsaturated traffic. In: Wireless Communications and Networking Conference (WCNC), pp. 463–467. IEEE (March 2007)

18. Raptis, P., Vitsas, V., Paparrizos, K.: Packet delay metrics for IEEE 802.11 distributed coordination function. Mobile Networks and Applications 14(6), 772–781 (2009)

19. Rezende, R., Dittrich, A., Malek, M.: User-perceived instantaneous service availability evaluation. In: Pacific Rim International Symposium on Dependable Computing (PRDC), pp. 273–282. IEEE (December 2013)

20. Sahner, R.A., Trivedi, K.S.: Performance and reliability analysis using directed acyclic graphs. IEEE Trans. on Software Engineering SE-13 (10), 1105–1114 (1987)

21. Trivedi, K.S.: SHARPE (symbolic hierarchical automated reliability and performance evaluator). Software (February 2010), http://sharpe.pratt.duke.edu

22. Zhu, F., W. Mutka, M., M. Ni, L.: Service discovery in pervasive computing environments. IEEE Pervasive Computing 4, 81–90 (2005)

Performance Evaluation of Forward Error Correction Mechanisms for Android Devices Based on Raptor Codes

Philipp M. Eittenberger and Udo R. Krieger

Faculty of Information Systems and Applied Computer Science
Otto-Friedrich-University
D-96047 Bamberg, Germany
udo.krieger@ieee.org

Abstract. We present a performance analysis concerning the application of Raptor codes as forward error correction mechanism at the application layer of Android devices. At first, a short overview on practical aspects of the implementation of Raptor coding is given. Subsequently, methods to increase the coding performance on ARM processors are presented and their impact is evaluated by representative experiments on different mobile devices. Finally, we assess the performance of our enhanced Raptor code implementation. Compared to a baseline Java implementation it achieves performance gains of up to 1200 %.

Keywords: Performance measurements, forward error correction, Raptor codes, Android device.

1 Introduction

Considering wireless broadcast or multicast services, Raptor codes have emerged as a dominant forward error correction mechanism at the application layer by multiple standard specifications. They are an ideal supplement to increase the dissemination performance of point-to-multipoint and multipoint-to-multipoint communication in wireless and cellular networks. Due to the growing number of mobile devices, in particular Android phones and tablets, their implementation on these devices and an analysis of the computational complexity of Raptor codes as error-correction mechanism is an important, but to a large extent not yet answered question.

Forward error correction (FEC) at the application layer is mainly necessary when the error correction at the physical layer is not able to provide error-free data transfer due to poor conditions of a communication channel. It is often encountered in wireless and cellular networks and has many possible reasons such as shadowing, fading, interference etc., which may lead to severe packet loss. However, using application-layer forward error correction (AL-FEC), such as Raptor codes, lost packets can be reconstructed to perform a reliable content delivery.

K. Fischbach and U.R. Krieger (Eds.): MMB & DFT 2014, LNCS 8376, pp. 103–119, 2014.

In the last years, several standards have incorporated Raptor codes in their specifications for content delivery. For instance, the 3rd Generation Partnership Project (3GPP) uses the standardized Raptor code version 10 ($R10$) in its specification for Multimedia Broadcast/Multicast Services (MBMS) [2]. The Digital Video Broadcasting project (DVB) uses the same Raptor code in the specification for handheld devices (DVB-H) [1] and for IPTV [3], and there is another IPTV related specification by ITU [4]. Recently, 3GPP adopted the MBMS standard for UMTS/LTE [5], which uses R10 as AL-FEC as well. The large spread of Raptor codes in standards and specifications is mainly due to their capacity achieving performance, i.e., they achieve nearly the ideal code performance under any loss condition on the channel. However, in particular for Point-to-Multipoint (P2MP) communication, such as MBMS, (cf. [14], [6], [15]) and Multipoint-to-Multipoint (MP2MP) communication, like Peer-to-Peer (P2P) systems (cf. [8]), Raptor codes can provide even more benefits. Let us consider a broadcast delivery system, where a server transmits video content over a broadcast network, e.g., over an LTE network. Due to the heterogeneous system and channel conditions, the forward error correction schemes at the physical layer are not able to provide sufficient reliability. Moreover, in the case of packet loss, the nature of P2MP transmission would require a large negotiation overhead between the sender and the receivers. The application of an automatic repeat request (ARQ) retransmission scheme would immensely increase the size of the feedback channel. Given AL-FEC, a feedback channel is neither desirable nor necessary at all in this case. Due to these reasons, the practical elimination of the feedback channel and the decoding of Raptor codes in linear time, the latter have emerged as a dominant AL-FEC mechanism for wireless broadcast or multicast services.

Raptor codes, as representative of the class of fountain codes, have the desirable property of *ratelessness*; i.e., they have theoretically the ability to generate an unlimited amount of uniquely encoded data on-the-fly. This property completely eliminates the need for any fine grained content reconciliation in MP2MP communication. If we take as an example P2P live streaming as proposed by Wu and Li [20], fine grained chunk scheduling would not be necessary any more since a receiving peer could restore the original data. A slightly larger amount of encoded data from any set of encoders, i.e. peers, is simply needed. As every received uniquely encoded symbol of a data chunk is useful for the decoding of the original data, Raptor codes could reduce the chunk scheduling problem to a bandwidth allocation problem.

We see that Raptor codes constitute an ideal supplement for unreliable, but lightweight transport protocols in order to increase the dissemination performance of P2MP and MP2MP communication in wireless and cellular networks. This creates a strong motivation for our work to investigate the performance of the Raptor code version 10 on Android devices. With regard to mobile devices, it is vital to perform the Raptor coding as power efficient as possible in order to ensure a maximum battery lifetime. To the best of our knowledge, and despite the growing number of smartphones, especially Android phones and tablets, the implementation and computational complexity evaluation of Raptor codes on these devices have not been investigated yet.

The paper is organized as follows. First, a short overview on practical aspects of the implementation of Raptor coding is given. Then methods to increase the coding performance on ARM processors are presented and their impact is evaluated on different mobile devices. Thereafter, we assess the performance of our enhanced Raptor code implementation and show that it achieves performance gains of up to 1200 % compared to a baseline Java implementation. Finally, a conclusion is given in Section 5.

2   Raptor Codes as Forward Error Correction Mechanism

Fountain codes have the ability to generate potentially unlimited, uniquely encoded data on-the-fly. **Rap**id **Tor**nado codes belong to the class of fountain codes. They have been developed by Amin Shokrollahi [18] as an advancement of Tornado codes [12]. Raptor codes represent an improvement over Luby transform codes (LT codes) [10] and the first practical class of a fountain code with nearly optimal error-correction functionality. Here we provide a brief description of Raptor coding operations. Regarding their theoretical properties, we refer to [18] and [11].

We assume that a data file is divided into n data blocks, each consisting of a set of K *input symbols* $t = (x_1, ..., x_K)$ with a symbol size of T bytes. In this context the term "symbol" represents a data unit. A fountain code can theoretically provide an unlimited supply of uniquely encoded *output symbols* $z = (z_1, ..., z_n)$. This desirable property is called *ratelessness*. The decoder can recover the source symbols from any set of $\Theta = K(1+\varepsilon), \varepsilon > 0$, encoded symbols, where Θ is slightly larger than K. The surplus of symbols $\varepsilon \times K$ is called the overhead of the code. These additional symbols are also called *repair symbols*.

Fountain codes do not guarantee the successful decoding by K symbols. The probability of a decoding failure, however, decreases with each additional symbol. The possibility that each receiver is able to decode the encoded symbols generated by different rateless code encoders if both use the same rateless code and the same parameter setting (symbol size, block size) is another desirable aspect. Due to this property content reconciliation can be avoided. There is, for instance, no need for any fine grained chunk scheduling in P2P networks (cf. [7]).

2.1   Application-Layer FEC Using Raptor Codes

To enable the data dissemination using Raptor codes, the encoded symbol(s) must be packetized and annotated with information needed for the decoding process. At first, the source data is segmented into n blocks. The size K of each block in terms of symbols and the size of each symbol T can be dynamically adjusted due to the rateless property of Raptor Codes [11]. Every block is marked with a unique identifier (BlockID). Then the Raptor code is applied independently on each block.

Every block consists of K source symbols of T bytes. If the last symbol of a block is smaller, it is padded by zeros up to size T. All symbols of one block get consecutive identifiers (SymbolID), which indicate the seed values of a random number generator. The header of each encoded symbol includes the BlockID, the SymbolID and the symbol size T. This information is necessary to ensure that the receiver can match the symbol to the correct block and is able to decode the data successfully. When the receiver reaches a threshold of Θ encoded symbols, it starts to decode the particular block. If the decoding was not successful, the receiver waits for additional symbols and is able to proceed incrementally with the decoding.

Before the encoding and transmission of one block can start, the participants must agree upon the block and symbol sizes. Therefore, a special message containing the block header information must be exchanged. As long as the symbol size T is comparatively bigger than the header, the additional information of the exchanged message introduces only a small overhead.

2.2   Raptor Encoding

A Raptor code can be regarded as a regular linear block code. Thus, it is suitable to present its operations by generator matrices without an exposition of its theoretical details. Our implementation of Raptor coding closely follows the specification of an *R10* code first given in [2] and after that in many others standards (cf. [3], [5], [13]). The specification in [2] uses a combination of a low density parity check (LDPC) precode with an LT code. The rateless property of the Raptor code is a result of the LT code, while the increased performance is due to the LDPC code [18]. By design the R10 is able to support up to 8,192 source symbols and 65,536 encoded symbols.

The Raptor encoding consists of two phases. In the *pre-code phase* a generator matrix $\boldsymbol{A}$ is used to compute *intermediate symbols* $\boldsymbol{c} = (c_1, \ldots, c_L)$ using the K source symbols $(L > K)$ (see figure 1).

First Encoding Phase: The Code Constraint Processor. In the first step of the pre-coding phase a column vector $\boldsymbol{D}$ is constructed consisting of $Z = S + H$ zero symbols followed by K source symbols,

$$\boldsymbol{D}_{[0:L-1]} = [\boldsymbol{Z}^T \boldsymbol{t}^T]^T$$

with $L = S + H + K$. The size of S is chosen such that it is the smallest prime integer that satisfies $S \geq \lceil (0.01 \times K) \rceil + X$ with $X(X - 1) \geq 2K$. The parameter H is the smallest integer that satisfies

$$\binom{H}{\lceil H/2 \rceil} \geq K + S.$$

To produce the intermediate symbols, $\boldsymbol{D}$ is multiplied by the inverse of the pre-code generator matrix $\boldsymbol{A}$,

$$\boldsymbol{c}_{[0:L-1]} = \boldsymbol{A}_{L \times L}^{-1} \cdot \boldsymbol{D}_{[0:L-1]}.$$

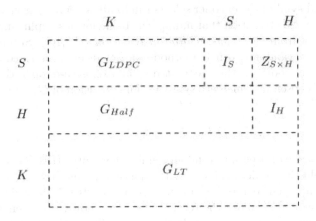

Fig. 1. Block diagram of the pre-code generator matrix $\boldsymbol{A}$

The matrix $\boldsymbol{A}$ consists of several sub-matrices (as depicted in Figure 1): $\boldsymbol{G}_{LDPC}$ is the $S \times K$ generator matrix of the LDPC symbols defined by

$$\boldsymbol{G}_{LDPC} \cdot [c[0], ..., c[K-1]]^T = [c[K], ..., c[K+S-1]]^T.$$

$\boldsymbol{G}_{Half}$ defined by

$$\boldsymbol{G}_{Half} \cdot [c[0], ..., c[L-1]]^T = [x[0], ..., x[K-1]]^T.$$

is a $H \times (K+S)$ higher density check matrix of so called *half symbols* (due to the fact that the columns of this submatrix have a relative weight of approximately $1/2$), which are produced by the usage of a binary reflected Gray code[1]. $\boldsymbol{G}_{LT}$ is the $K \times L$ generator matrix of a LT code included in $\boldsymbol{A}$ to make the overall Raptor code systematic. It is defined as

$$\boldsymbol{G}_{LT} \cdot [c[0], ..., c[L-1]]^T = [x[0], ..., x[K-1]]^T.$$

$\boldsymbol{I}_X$ represents a $X \times X$ identity matrix and $\boldsymbol{Z}_{S \times H}$ denotes a $S \times H$ zero matrix.

Second Encoding Phase: LT Encoding. In the second phase the LT encoder semi-randomly selects sets of intermediate symbols $\boldsymbol{c}$ and generates the output symbols $\boldsymbol{z} = (z_1, ..., z_\Theta)$ such that

$$\boldsymbol{G}_{LT} \cdot \boldsymbol{c} = \boldsymbol{z}_{[0:\Theta-1]}$$

with $\Theta \geq K$ holds. One must ensure that $\boldsymbol{A}$ is invertible at the receiver. Thus, Θ is chosen to be greater than K to compensate for the possible loss of symbols during a transmission and to ensure the successful decoding at the receiver. For

---

[1] In a Gray sequence two successive values differ only in a single bit position.

each encoded symbol the encoder selects randomly a degree d from a specifically designed degree distribution that mimics the behavior of sampling uniformly and independently from the *robust soliton distribution* (cf. [10]). Subsequently, the encoder selects randomly a neighborhood of d connected intermediate symbols. Each output symbol z_x is then generated by an exclusive-or operation (XORing) of the set of chosen intermediate symbols. The inclusion of G_{LT} in A makes the Raptor Code systematic such that (cf. [18], [11])

$$z[i] = D[H + S + i] \text{ for } 0 \le i \le K - 1$$

holds. The usage of a pseudo random number generator (PRNG) has been proposed to yield the random values. By relying on a pseudo-random process, some initial value has to be determined as the seed of the PRNG. Regarding the decoding of the encoded symbols, the receiver needs to know the chosen degree d and the set of chosen intermediate symbols. One possibility to inform the decoder is given by the transmission of the initial value used as a seed of the PRNG.

Regarding the application of Raptor codes in MP2MP communication, the very important condition that each encoder uses a unique seed value for its PRNG must be met. Otherwise, encoders with the same seed value would produce the same output symbols and such redundantly encoded symbols would increase the overhead rate.

2.3   Raptor Decoding

The receiver starts the decoding process upon reception of a given number of encoded symbols larger than the threshold Θ. The latter is the minimum amount of symbols that makes the pre-code matrix A invertible and thereby, the decoding successful (as subsequently described). As Raptor encoding and decoding are in principle symmetric operations, the decoder starts with the application of the pre-code on the set of received symbols and afterwards it applies the LT code.

As A is a bit matrix that satisfies $A \times c = D$, the decoding is equivalent to decode c from known A and D. Hence, it can only be successful if A has full rank over GF(2). To avoid the computationally expensive matrix multiplication, the decoding is combined with the inversion of A such that all operations on A are also performed on the corresponding symbols of the received symbols' vector. The intermediate symbols c are obtained by

$$c_{[0:L-1]} = [Z^T z'^T]^T \cdot A_{M \times L}^{-1}.$$

The input vector z' containing the received N', $K \le N' \le N$, encoded symbols is padded with $S + H$ zeros, such that it has the size $M = N + S + H$. Using row XORing and row and column exchange operations and after discarding $M - L$ rows, the matrix $A_{M \times L}^{-1}$ is converted into the identity matrix $I_{L \times L}$. Upon successful decoding of c, the missing source symbols can be restored by applying G_{LT} on c according to

$$t_{[0:K-1]} = G_{LT} \cdot c_{[0:L-1]}.$$

2.4   Representation of the Pre-code Matrix A

Raptor codes are the ideal candidate of an FEC mechanism applied at the application layer (AL-FEC) of P2MP and MP2MP communication due to their excellent performance, the minimal overhead, approaching very closely an ideal fountain code, and their ability to efficiently support dynamically adjusted block sizes. RFC 5053 [13] states that their speed of decoding relies heavily upon "... maintaining a sparse representation of A [...], although this is not described here". We have considered two approaches regarding the internal matrix representation. In the *WORD* scheme a matrix entry occupies the word length of the CPU, which is typically 32 bits. It is contrary to the *PACKED WORD* approach, where 32 matrix entries are stored in one word and each entry is accessed by bit shifts. In the later performance evaluation we have used the *PACKED WORD* pattern due to its significantly reduced memory footprint. However, if matrix entries are accessed often, the bit shifting operations of the *PACKED WORD* matrix representation have a negative effect on the coding performance. Due to the sparseness of the matrix A, more sophisticated representations are desirable, but were not investigated in this study (see [17] for further information).

2.5   Decoding the Pre-code Matrix A

Two main approaches can be distinguished to decode the pre-code matrix A. *Message passing* (MP) algorithms have low complexity, but not optimal error-correction performance. Belief propagation (BP) proposed in [18] is one instance of such an algorithm. *Maximum Likelihood* (ML) methods have a nearly optimal error-correction capacity at the expense of higher computational complexity. ML decoding over a *binary erasure channel* reduces to the solution of a system of linear equations. Therefore, the most prominent representative of this approach is Gaussian elimination (GE). The main operations of GE over GF(2) are given by the exchange and the XORing of rows, which is potentially costly. To combine the optimality of ML methods with the efficiency of the BP approach, Shokrollahi [18] developed *inactivation decoding*. It uses in the first phase BP and in the second phase GE to solve the remaining system. However, the inversion of the reduced submatrix is still the main performance bottleneck. In general, the matrix inversion is the most expensive computational operation, accounting for up to 92 % of the computing time (see [17]; therein an implementation by an embedded system platform based on the NIOS II soft-core processor is used, which is running on an Altera Stratix III FPGA).

In our R10 implementation, we have used the enhanced, incremental version of the Inactivation Decoding Gaussian Elimination matrix inversion algorithm proposed by Mladenov et al. [16]. Profiling subsequent encoding and decoding operations of the C implementation of the R10 code, we found that around 60 % of the CPU time is spent for XORing rows. To increase the performance of the coding process, we therefore focus in this study on the acceleration of this part.

Table 1. Device Specification

Device Name	CPU Name	CPU Freq. (GHz)	Cores	Instr. Set	RAM	Level 1 Cache	Level 2 Cache
Samsung Galaxy Tab GT-P1000	Samsung Exynos 3110	1.0	1	ARMv7	512 MB	32KiB	512 KiB
Huawei S7-301u MediaPad	Qualcomm Snapdragon MSM8260	1.2	2	ARMv7	512 MB	32KiB per core	512 KiB per core
Google Nexus 7	Nvidia Tegra 3 T30L	1.3	4+1	ARMv7	1024 MB	32KiB per core	1024 KiB per core

3   Raptor Coding on Android Devices

It is a goal of our study to find those parameters that maximize the encoding and decoding speed and yield an excellent transmission performance. As we are particularly interested in the performance that can be achieved in practice on Android devices, we will investigate in the following experiments the best trade-off between performance and computational complexity regarding an implementation of Raptor code version 10 (R10). In comparison to Apple products the hardware base of Android certified devices is much more heterogeneous. Thus, there is a high diversity of mobile CPUs from many different vendors, making investigations and performance evaluations much more manifold.

In our performance experiments we have used three different off-the-shelf Android tablet PCs. They incorporate three different mobile CPUs. Samsung's Galaxy Tab GT-P1000 uses the in-house developed Exynos 3110 chip (known as "Hummingbird") running at 1.0 GHz. MediaPad by Huawei applies Qualcomm's Snapdragon S3 dual core running at 1.2 GHz. The third test device is given by Google's Nexus 7, which uses NVIDIA's Tegra 3 CPU. The latter is a quad core with a 5th battery-saver core that handles low-power tasks. In Nexus 7 it operates at 1.3 GHz. All three devices have a level 1 cache of 32 KiB per core. Details about the particular hardware specification are provided in Table 1. The choice of these devices was mainly motivated by their CPUs since they represent the leading manufacturers of mobile ARM processors.

We have applied a *single threaded* implementation of Raptor codes. Thus, we did not take advantage of the multi-core architecture of these devices. A multi-threaded performance evaluation could also be misleading since the Galaxy Tab has only a single core. We note, however, that there are opportunities for future performance optimizations by parallel execution of Raptor coding.

3.1   Implementation of R10 by Java and C with ARM NEON Support

Given the heterogeneous hardware base, Java always is the first choice of every Android app since it enables portability and ensures code reuse. Using the fastest parameter combinations for encoding and decoding, first performance measurements of a Java based version of R10 code were conducted on the Galaxy Tab and yielded average encoding and decoding throughputs of approximately 700 Kbit/s and 800 Kbit/s, respectively (cf. [7]). Profiling the application we found that the performance suffers mainly by a slow implementation of some functions of the standard Java library in Android. The re-implementation of these critical methods improved the performance by a factor of up to 10.

In a next step a C version of R10 was connected via the *Java Native Interface* (JNI) to the Android app. In addition, as of ARM architecture ARMv7, the instruction set has been enriched by an advanced single instruction, multiple data (SIMD) extension. It is a 64/128 bit hybrid SIMD data processing architecture called *NEON* providing hardware support to handle parallel data sets. NEON instructions operate on 32 registers, which are 64 bits wide, and in dual mode on 16 registers, which are 128 bit wide. They perform the same operation on multiple data points simultaneously. Thus, NEON is truly beneficial for audio and video coding operations. But the performance of simple tasks like XORing plain data arrays may be accelerated by parallelization, too. To investigate the possible performance gain of NEON regarding XOR operations, we have incorporated additional NEON support into the C version of our R10 implementation.

3.2   XOR Performance on ARM CPUs

Regarding the R10 code more than 60 % of the processing time is spent in XORing symbols during subsequent encoding and decoding operations. To improve the performance of this atomic operation of standardized Raptor codes, it is essential to increase this XOR performance. Therefore, we have conducted a performance evaluation of possible improvements presented in this section. As a reference, we performed XOR throughput measurements in C.

NEON intrinsics provide an intermediate step of SIMD code generation between code vectorization and writing assembler code. They offer similar functionality to inline assembly, masking, however, the low-level behavior in a high-level language. We have used this possibility to parallelize the XOR operations loading four integers simultaneously at a 128 bit wide register level. Due to space limitations, we will not discuss the details here.

In a third approach the same functionality is implemented in inline assembly exploiting the full potential of the NEON instructions. Here, all 16 32-bit registers are loaded in parallel, subsequently XORed and stored.

Figures 2 and 3 show the resulting performance of these three approaches on the Galaxy Tab and Nexus 7, respectively, for different data array sizes ranging from 2^2 to 2^{17} bits. The arrays have been filled with randomly generated data and XORed 10,000 times for each array size after a warm-up phase, whose results were discarded. The figures display the average XOR throughput with confidence intervals at a confidence level of 99 %. Under the condition that the random variables are independent and identically distributed, the Glivenko-Cantelli theorem states that the empirical distribution function converges with probability 1 to the true CDF with a growing number of observations.

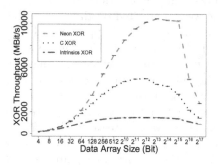

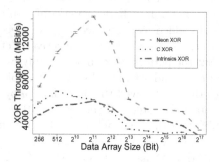

Fig. 2. XOR Performance on Exynos 3110 (Samsung Galaxy Tab)

Fig. 3. XOR Performance on Tegra 3 T30L (Google Nexus 7)

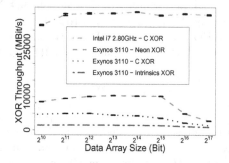

Fig. 4. XOR Performance Comparison: i7 2.8 GHz vs. Exynos 3110

The performance acceleration by NEON instructions can be clearly seen, at best more than doubling the speed compared to plain C code. The Galaxy Tab achieves a maximal average throughput of more than 10 Gbit/s for an array size of 8192 bits. Nexus 7 achieves a maximal average throughput of more than 14 Gbit/s with an array size of 2048 bits. After reaching the maximum, the performance is steeply decreasing due to the effects of cache misses. Interestingly, NEON intrinsics fail badly for such a simple task like XORing data. Only on Nexus 7 the intrinsic XOR surpasses the performance of the C XOR w.r.t. data array sizes greater than 2048 bits. Therefore, Neon intrinsics were not considered in the following experiments. However, despite that NEON is mainly aimed to parallelize more complex operations, we found that even for such simple tasks like XORing data arrays, the NEON instruction set already yields a tremendous performance boost. To compare the achieved performance, Figure 4 shows the results of the Galaxy Tab operating at 1 GHz and those arising from the same task on an Intel i7 CPU with 2.8 GHz while XORing data on one CPU core. The single core of i7 achieves average speeds of more than 30 Gbit/s using the simple C code. Due to the much larger level 1 cache of the i7, the performance degradation by cache misses happens comparatively later, i.e., for much larger data array sizes. However, in relation to the CPU frequency and the power consumption of both CPUs, the performance of the ARM processors is remarkable.

4   Performance Evaluation of Raptor Coding

To exploit the full potential of Raptor codes as FEC mechanism at the application layer of Android devices, the following important questions have to be answered: What are the adequate symbol and block sizes? How do these parameter settings influence the performance of the coding processes? The reason is that, in comparison to CPUs of desktops, CPUs in mobile devices have different cache sizes. Therefore, different symbol sizes and block sizes may result in different encoding and decoding throughput. These items matter since we are operating on handheld devices that rely primarily on a battery, and higher performance simply may result in less battery consumption.

Thus, we have performed an extensive measurement campaign to provide answers to these questions. Thereby, we can investigate the foundations for a future application of Raptor codes in the domain of mobile, wireless computing. Due to page restrictions, it is not possible to present all gathered results. Here, we discuss only those cases that are the most representative ones regarding a particular device. We are mainly interested in the basic parameter settings and the corresponding achievable decoding performance on a device under test. Considering scenarios of the mentioned standards, e.g., MBMS or DVB-H, data encoding is not performed on handheld devices, but it is restricted to a dedicated infrastructure. Therefore, we will omit the encoding results, but we found that the achievable encoding performance is similar to that of decoding.

4.1   Selection of Symbol and Block Size

At first, the influence of the symbol size T on the decoding time is investigated. Theoretically, Raptor codes have a linear decoding time $O(K\ log(1/\varepsilon))$. Thus, by choosing the symbol size and block size as large as possible, the total amount of time could be decreased. However, as the R10 relies heavily on the matrix inversion algorithm, which accounts for up to 92 % of the computing time [17], this theoretical optimum cannot be reached by this approach for large block sizes. In this context, we also have to determine an optimal block size K. This is necessary to achieve a good trade-off between the overhead of repair symbols combined with their required decoding time and the delay that the receiver encounters while it waits to reach the decoding threshold Θ. Our investigation seeks to minimize the start up delay and the amount of time needed for the encoding and decoding processes. A too large block size will cause an excessive start up delay of the receiver, whereas a smaller block size at the beginning of the transmission could decrease it. The main issue concerns the efficiency in terms of decoding speed and the resulting overhead rate.

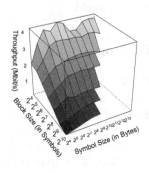

Fig. 5. Decoding Throughput - Java - Galaxy Tab

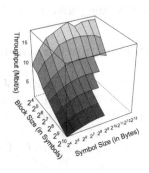

Fig. 6. Decoding Throughput - C - Galaxy Tab

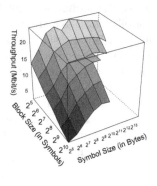

Fig. 7. Decoding Throughput - NEON - Galaxy Tab

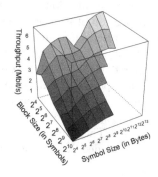

Fig. 8. Decoding Throughput - Java - Nexus 7

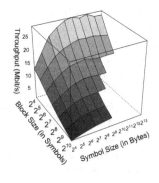

Fig. 9. Decoding Throughput - C - Nexus 7

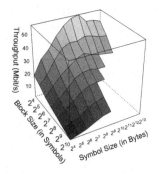

Fig. 10. Decoding Throughput - NEON - Nexus 7

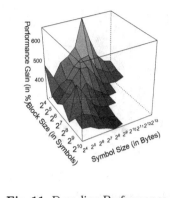

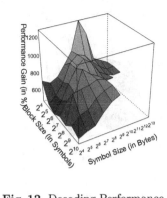

Fig. 11. Decoding Performance Gain in % - C vs. Java - Nexus 7

Fig. 12. Decoding Performance Gain in % - NEON vs. Java - Nexus7

By our experiments we have investigated a range of block sizes with $K \in \{32, 64, 128, 256, 512, 1024, 2048, 4096\}$ symbols and symbols with a size of $T \in \{16, 32, 64, 128, 256, 512, 1024, 2048\}$ bytes.

After a warm-up phase, randomly generated data were encoded and decoded a 100 times on the particular test devices for every combination of the block and symbol size. The resulting average throughput of the decoding process on the Galaxy Tab is depicted in figures 5, 6 and 7. The effect of the higher complexity of the matrix inversion with increasing block sizes is clearly visible in all three settings. Furthermore, it can be seen that small block sizes are beneficial in terms of encoding speed. The influence of the symbol size on the performance is also visible. Larger symbols increase the performance up to a maximum at a symbol size of 512 bytes on the Galaxy Tab. Symbol sizes greater than 512 bytes have an adverse effect as the performance slowly decreases due to cache misses. Regarding encoding and decoding speed the same experiment was performed on MediaPad and Nexus 7. The achieved mean decoding performance on Nexus 7 for all three XORing methods are depicted in figures 8 to 10. Using the NEON instruction set, it is possible to achieve average encoding and decoding throughputs of more than 35 and 50 Mbit/s, respectively, for a given symbol size of 1024 bytes and a block size of 16 symbols. Figure 14 shows the measured average decoding throughput on MediaPad. By the NEON enhanced version, a maximal speed of 40 Mbit/s was achieved for a symbol size of 512 bytes and a block size of 16 symbols.

The relative performance gain of the C implementation compared to the Java version on Nexus 7 is shown in figure 11. C code achieves an up to 600 % higher decoding performance for small block sizes. The comparison between the NEON extended version and the plain Java code is illustrated in figure 12. The NEON version provides a performance acceleration of more than 1200 %. Interestingly, in both comparisons spikes of relative performance gains have been measured for a symbol size of 512 bytes, which does not induce the achievable maximal throughput on Nexus 7. The spikes occur in both cases due to an anomalous

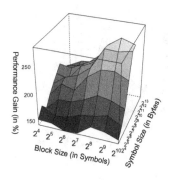
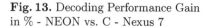

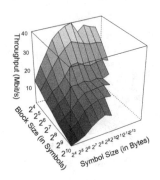

Fig. 13. Decoding Performance Gain in % - NEON vs. C - Nexus 7

Fig. 14. Decoding Throughput - NEON - MediaPad

drop in performance of the Java code for symbol sizes from 64 to 2048 bytes (compare with figure 8).

The achieved relative performance improvement by the NEON enhanced version compared to the C implementation is depicted in figure 13. Larger symbol and block sizes tend to increase the relative performance gains (up to 250 %) of the NEON version.

4.2   The Number of Required Repair Symbols

The next issue concerns the number of repair symbols that are needed for a successful decoding of each block. As each additional repair symbol increases the overhead, i.e. the threshold Θ that ensures a successful decoding with high probability, an adequate number has to be chosen. However, even if the decoding should fail, a retry with a slightly higher number Θ will yield a success with very high probability.

For all combinations of the block and symbol sizes we have performed the presented encoding and decoding experiments with 9 repair symbols. We use very conservative confidence intervals based on Wilson's score interval [19] with a confidence level of 95 %. Gasiba et al. [9] report that on average $K+2$ symbols are sufficient to recover from transmission errors. They have investigated source block sizes of $K \in \{100, 1000\}$ with $T = 512$ bytes. As the symbol size T has no influence on the decoding probability, the results of our experiments do not confirm their value Θ. We used 10 extra repair symbols in all experiments, which ensures a decoding success with a probability of more than 99.9 % in most of the settings. Regarding larger block sizes the obtained overhead rate is still very close to that of an ideal fountain code. From the perspective of a required small overhead rate, large block sizes are necessary. However, if it is chosen too large, the receiver will have to wait for the reception of the Θ symbols, leading to longer decoding delays. Both cases always demand a compromise between coding speed and overhead.

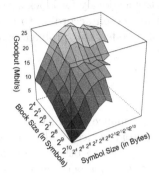

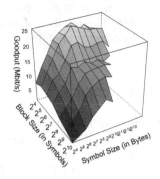

Fig. 15. Decoding Goodput (Measured in C) - NEON - MediaPad

Fig. 16. Decoding Goodput (Measured in Java) - NEON - MediaPad

4.3 Overhead Rate of Repair Symbols and Resulting Goodput

It remains to determine the influence of the overhead rate of those required repair symbols ensuring the successful decoding on the achievable goodput. The latter is simply defined as the size of the input data divided by the time needed for encoding/decoding without taking into account the amount of necessary repair symbols. Thus, block sizes chosen too small have an adverse effect on the overall performance as they induce a comparably higher number of necessary repair symbols to ensure the successful decoding. For small block sizes, e.g., with $K = 10$ symbols, ε can be as high as 110 %, whereas ε drops to less than 1 % for block sizes greater than 1600 symbols. The following figures illustrate the influence of the block size respectively the overhead rate on the achievable goodput. Figure 14 shows the achieved decoding throughput on MediaPad for the NEON extended R10 implementation. Figure 15 displays the actual goodput of this experiment (the measurements have been conducted in the native C code). Due to the comparatively higher number of repair symbols for very small block sizes, the best trade-off between coding speed and overhead is achieved for 32 symbols, despite the fact that the throughput for 16 symbols is superior in all experiments. Figure 16 displays the same goodput measurement after the data conversion from C code through JNI to the Java Android app. This means that the timings of these measurements have been conducted in the Java space. One can hardly observe any differences in both plots, which implies that data conversion from C to Java is not a performance bottleneck.

In conclusion, the results of the parameter evaluation w.r.t. R10 show that as long as the level 1 cache of a mobile CPU has a size of 32 KiB, symbol sizes between 512 and 1024 bytes achieve the best coding throughput. The block size in terms of used symbols has to be determined in relation to the specific requirements if plain goodput performance of the Raptor coding is needed. A block size of 32 symbols works best. If coding performance is not important, but the overhead rate, then large block sizes should be chosen. However, one has to be aware that the coding performance decreases tremendously for block sizes beyond 1024. The number of repair symbols must be chosen according to the required decoding probability. Using an incremental decoder, this problem can be mitigated.

5 Conclusion

In this paper we have investigated the achievable performance of a FEC mechanism that is applied at the application layer of Android devices and derived from an efficiently implemented Raptor coding. Compared to other fountain codes, like Online or LT codes, Raptor codes have a superior performance in terms of coding speed and overhead rate. Considering the application of Raptor codes in the domain of AL-FEC on mobile devices, our first insights derived from several realized experiments are promising.

We have used a performance evaluation of the Raptor decoding process, supported by efficient implementations on different devices, to determine a suitable parametrization of the proposed procedure. Furthermore, we have proposed a simple approach to increase the coding performance by using the NEON instruction set on ARMv7 CPUs. These results can be employed for a successful future deployment of Raptor codes. Given large block sizes only a small overhead rate is required and the necessary transmission rates can be supported easily. The next generation of mobile CPUs will enable an even higher degree of parallelization, e.g., Tegra 4 offers CUDA support, and Exynos 5 supports OpenCL. Thus, more opportunities for future performance optimizations are provided. A more sophisticated, compressed representation of the pre-code matrix A may provide another viable option to increase the coding speed.

In conclusion, our performance results have proved that an efficient R10 implementation of Raptor codes can achieve the coding speed, that is required for an AL-FEC scheme on Android devices to enable a significant acceleration of the data dissemination in P2MP and MP2MP communication.

Acknowledgments. The authors express their sincere appreciation to Todor Mladenov for his guidance regarding Raptor coding. Furthermore, they would like to thank Marcel Großmann for his assistance regarding the Android measurements.

References

1. ETSI TS 102 034 V 1.3.1: Digital Video Broadcasting (DVB); IP datacast over DVB-H: Content Delivery Protocols (CDP) (2005)
2. 3GPP TS 26.346: Technical Specification Group Services and System Aspects; Multimedia Broadcast/Multicast Services (MBMS); Protocols and Codecs (2007)
3. ETSI TS 102 034 V1.4.1: Digital Video Broadcasting (DVB); Transport of MPEG-2 TS based DVB services over IP based networks (2009)
4. ITU-T H.701, Series H: Audiovisual and multimedia systems IPTV multimedia services and applications for IPTV - General aspects content delivery error recovery for IPTV services (2009)

5. ETSI TS 126 346 V10.3.0: Universal Mobile Telecommunications System (UMTS); LTE; Multimedia Broadcast/Multicast Service (MBMS); Protocols and Codecs (2012)
6. Cataldi, P., Grangetto, M., Tillo, T., Magli, E., Olmo, G.: Sliding-window Raptor codes for efficient scalable wireless video broadcasting with unequal loss protection. IEEE Transactions on Image Processing 19(6), 1491–1503 (2010)
7. Eittenberger, P.M.: Raptorstream: Boosting mobile peer-to-peer streaming with Raptor codes. In: Proceedings of the ACM SIGCOMM 2012, Helsinki, pp. 291–292 (2012)
8. Eittenberger, P.M., Mladenov, T., Krieger, U.R.: Raptor Codes for P2P Streaming. In: Proceedings 20th Euromicro, Garching (2012)
9. Gasiba, T., Stockhammer, T., Xu, W.: Reliable and efficient download delivery with Raptor codes. In: 6th International ITG-Conference on Source and Channel Coding (TURBOCODING), Munich, pp. 1–6 (2006)
10. Luby, M.: LT codes. In: 43rd Annual IEEE Symposium on Foundations of Computer Science, FOCS 2002, Vancouver, pp. 271–280 (2002)
11. Luby, M., Gasiba, T., Stockhammer, T., Watson, M.: Reliable multimedia download delivery in cellular broadcast networks. IEEE Transactions on Broadcasting 53(1), 235–246 (2007)
12. Luby, M., Mitzenmacher, M., Shokrollahi, A., Spielman, D., Stemann, V.: Practical loss-resilient codes. In: Proceedings of the Twenty-ninth Annual ACM Symposium on Theory of Computing, STOC 1997, El Paso, TX, pp. 150–159 (1997)
13. Luby, M., Shokrollahi, A., Watson, M., Stockhammer, T.: RFC 5053 (2007)
14. McAuley, A.J.: Reliable broadband communication using a burst erasure correcting code. In: Proceedings of ACM SIGCOMM 1990, Philadelphia, PA, pp. 297–306 (1990)
15. Mladenov, T., Nooshabadi, S., Kim, K.: MBMS Raptor codes design trade-offs for IPTV. IEEE Transactions on Consumer Electronics 56, 1264–1269 (2010)
16. Mladenov, T., Nooshabadi, S., Kim, K.: Efficient incremental Raptor decoding over BEC for 3GPP MBMS and DVB IP-datacast services. IEEE Transactions on Broadcasting 57(2), 313–318 (2011)
17. Mladenov, T., Nooshabadi, S., Montiel-Nelson, J.A., Kim, K.: Decoding of Raptor codes on embedded systems. Microprocessors and Microsystems - Embedded Hardware Design 36, 375–382 (2012)
18. Shokrollahi, A.: Raptor codes. IEEE Transactions on Information Theory 52, 2551–2567 (2006)
19. Wilson, E.B.: Probable Inference, the Law of Succession, and Statistical Inference. Journal of the American Statistical Association 22(158), 209–212 (1927)
20. Wu, C., Li, B.: rStream: Resilient peer-to-peer streaming with rateless codes. In: Proceedings of the 13th ACM MULTIMEDIA 2005, Singapore, pp. 307–310 (2005)

Evaluation of Caching Strategies
Based on Access Statistics of Past Requests

Gerhard Hasslinger and Konstantinos Ntougias

Deutsche Telekom Technik, Fixed Mobile Engineering, Darmstadt, Germany
gerhard.hasslinger@telekom.de, kostas_ntougias@yahoo.gr

Abstract. Delivery of popular content on the Internet usually does not rely on a single server but is supported by content delivery networks (CDNs) that reactively store requested content in distributed cache servers. CDNs strengthen the availability and downloading throughput. Moreover, they shorten transport paths when caches in the proximity of requesting users are preferred.

We study how the cache hit rate as the main efficiency criterion of web caches depends on the request statistics and the caching strategy that selects which content should be placed in or evicted from a cache. Although the least recently used (LRU) strategy seems to be widely deployed in web caches, our comparison in simulations and analytic case studies reveals essentially higher hit rates for alternatives based on the complete request statistics in the past under the realistic assumption of Zipf distributed user requests.

Keywords: Web caching, replacement strategies, least recently used (LRU), least frequently used (LFU), sliding window, geometric fading, cache hit rate analysis and simulation, Zipf distributed requests.

1   Introduction

Traditionally, there are two main application areas for caching [2][26]:

- Caching in computing systems to accelerate data access with the help of fast storage media and
- web caching in order to shorten transport paths and delays for data on the Internet.

We focus on web caching being applied in different variants including content delivery networks (CDNs) e.g. for Google YouTube or Akamai [1] based on distributed server and storage systems on network nodes as well as on user devices. The latter case of client side caching can completely avoid data transport but has a limited although still considerable traffic saving potential due to repeated requests of a user or a small user group to the same content [10]. Network caches can only partially shorten the transport path but mutual sharing of content among a larger user population strengthens their efficiency. Then requests for content are governed by Zipf's law, also known as 80:20 or 90:10 rule, such that most of the requests (80-90%) are addressing a small subset (10-20%) of popular objects, e.g. HTML pages, images, videos etc. Zipf's law has been confirmed to provide a valid approximation for request pattern to web content in many measurement studies [5][8][15][17][19][28][32].

K. Fischbach and U.R. Krieger (Eds.): MMB & DFT 2014, LNCS 8376, pp. 120–135, 2014.
© Springer International Publishing Switzerland 2014

Zipf distributed requests make small caches already quite efficient. Based on the independent reference model (IRM) assuming a stream of independent and identically distributed (i.i.d.) requests to a set of N objects [2][14][22], the optimum hit rate in a cache for M ($M \leq N$) objects is obtained by holding the most popular objects in the cache. Then the hit rate equals the sum of the top M access probabilities. In fact, web caches for a large user population have to deal with slowly varying distributions of object popularity where new objects are raising and others are falling in the popularity ranking [11][33]. Therefore the cache replacement policy has to be flexible for updating the cache content over time in order to achieve an optimum hit rate.

The main focus of our work is on the efficiency of cache replacement strategies, which rank the objects by assigning a score value based on a metric that evaluates user behavior from the access log of past requests. Several classes of replacement policies are studied in literature [26]. Recency-based replacement policies exploit the temporal locality of the request stream on a short time scale. The least recently used (LRU) principle is a simple to implement and often applied scheme [12][25][27][31], which puts the most recently requested object in the highest rank and evicts an object from a cache of size M, as soon as M other objects have been addressed more recently.

Frequency-based replacement policies count the number of requests per object providing more information about the past than LRU. The least frequently used (LFU) strategy keeps objects with highest request count in the cache which is optimal for a static independent request model, but does not react to changing popularity of object.

Many variations of caching strategies have been proposed and evaluated which combine LRU and LFU [23] or include other utility functions e.g., size, detailed cost saving criteria, validity deadline for objects etc. [4][7][18][21][22][25][26][27]. The HTTPbis working group at the Internet Engineering Task Force is currently specifying the data exchange between content sources and web caches with regard to various preconditions for caching in order to avoid outdated or invalid content and to enforce recommendations and policies of content providers [13].

Within this framework we assume that the considered objects are all cacheable and we study two variants of frequency-/recency-based caching strategies:

- Sliding window (W-LFU) [22], which restricts the LFU principle to request counts within a window of the K most recent requests and

- Geometric fading [23], which weights former requests by a decreasing factor ρ^k for the kth recent request and ranks the objects according to the sum of weights.

Both considered caching strategies, sliding window and geometric fading, are approaching the LFU strategy as one extreme case for $K \to \infty$ and $\rho \to 1$ as well as the LRU strategy on the other extreme for $K \leq M$ with LRU tie breaking and for $\rho < 0.5$.

A comparative study of sliding window and pure, "perfect" LFU [22] for unlimited window size K determines the effect of the window size on the hit rate for i.i.d. requests and for a special Zipf-like distribution as given in equation (1) with $\beta = 1$. In this case, an analytical bound is obtained for the degradation of the hit rate below the optimum value for unlimited LFU. The study [22] also evaluates sliding window (W-LFU) for a trace which shows partly increasing hit rate also for small window size because of changing popularity of objects in longer history during the trace.

Geometric fading has been evaluated in comparison to its extreme cases LRU and LFU as the main focus of [23] based on several traces of access pattern for database systems. However, for the same comparison we observe completely different results in Section 5 considering Zipf distributed user requests in web applications.

Although LRU still seems to be the most widely used replacement policy among web caching solutions [25][31], our simulation results show essential deficits of the achievable LRU hit rate compared to statistics based strategies. Similar experience seems to be reported in only few studies in literature. An extended LRU caching variant [24] is found to outperform LRU hit rates by 5-20% for workloads from buffer and disk storage scenarios. With regard to web caching, a study [30] reports 10-15% hit rate deficit of LRU compared to a history LRU variant regarding up to 6 past requests and evaluation examples in [15] indicate inefficiencies of LRU for Zipf distributed random requests.

We proceed in Section 2 with a closer look on Zipf's law and its effect on caching. Section 3 defines and characterizes main properties of the proposed cache replacement strategies, sliding window LFU and geometric fading. In Section 4, the deficits in the LRU hit rate are studied for the static independent request model by constructing and analyzing the supposed worst case. The performance of the statistics based strategies is evaluated in Section 5 against LRU in simulations for Zipf distributed request patterns, including a comparison of approximations of the LRU hit rate. Section 6 is briefly discussing more general caching criteria and the final Section 7 presents our conclusions and open issues for further study.

2   Request Patterns for Content on the Internet: The Relevance of Zipf Laws with Slowly Varying or Static Popularity

Measurements of request patterns for content on the Internet usually reveal Zipf distributions to provide a useful approximation of the popularity. As a main property of Zipf's law, a considerable portion of the requests refer to a small set of top ranked objects. In particular, a Zipf distribution $A(R)$ on a finite set of N objects

$$A(R) = \alpha R^{-\beta} \quad \text{where} \quad \beta > 0; \; \sum_{R=1}^{N} A(R) = 1 \; \Rightarrow \; \alpha = A(1) = 1/\sum_{R=1}^{N} A(R) \qquad (1)$$

attributes decreasing request probabilities $A(R)$ to the objects such that $R = 1, ..., N$ marks their popularity rank. The exponent β determines the decay in request frequencies or probabilities. The skewness of the distribution is increasing with β.

The relevance of the Zipf's law in access statistics on the Internet has been confirmed in many case studies, e.g. for page requests on popular web sites by Breslau et al. [5], for video platforms like YouTube [8], for Amazon book selling ranks or P2P networks [3][33]. The frequency of words in a long text, the size of organizations or the number of links to web sites are other examples exhibiting Zipf law distributions which seem to be fundamental for natural growth processes and relationships among a large set of objects <en.wikipedia.org/wiki/Zipf's_law>. In more detail, the Zipf distribution form is often limited to a subset of most popular objects whereas a long tail of low popularity objects usually does not follow the simple form (1) with a single parameter [15][17][28] but requires extensions for improved fitting.

The parameter β of Zipf approximations to request patterns in web applications is usually in the range $0.5 < \beta < 1$. Breslau et al. [5] recommend $0.64 < \beta < 0.85$ for fitting of a number of web request traces while other studies obtain β close to 1. Then the probability to address the set of the top 1% of objects is in the range of 10% - 40% [18]. A concentration on a small set of objects leads to high cache hit rates when the most popular objects can be kept in the cache.

If the request probability of cacheable objects is constant over time such that requests from a large user population can be assumed to be independent and identically distributed then the caching strategy for maximum hit rate would be to keep the most popular objects constantly in the cache. However, the popularity of web objects is changing over time. Investigations are observing dynamics in popularity on the time scale of days, weeks, or months [3][8][32][33]. In [3][11] the typical request profile of popular objects in P2P networks is characterized by a fast growth towards maximum popularity followed by a long slowly decreasing phase. The measurement study [33] shows only 1-3% of change in the top 100, top 1 000, and top 10 000 Gnutella network files within a daily drift. On the other hand, web caches with a large user popularity are often processing thousands of requests per hour.

The conclusions of slowly varying popularity for web caching strategies are twofold: An efficient web cache has to react on changing request preferences by including new objects when they are becoming popular. Nevertheless, when the dynamics is low and replacements are necessary only in the order of thousand or more requests then the cache content and the hit rate can be kept close to the static popularity case by keeping popular objects in the cache over long time periods.

In the sequel, we investigate different caching strategies which react to dynamic changes in request pattern over time but we consider the independent reference model with static popularity and i.i.d. requests as the most relevant criterion providing an upper bound on the hit rate. In Section 6 an overview on references to an extended set of caching criteria is given with regard to costs and benefits of delivering an object from the cache [2][7], whereas we focus on the hit rate as the main performance gain.

3   LRU and Statistics Based Cache Replacement Strategies

3.1   Least Recently Used (LRU)

LRU is a simple replacement policy with classical applications in computing and database systems and also widely used for web caching. LRU is easy to implement as a double chained list of M objects for fixed cache size M with insertion of recently requested object from the top and eviction of objects at the bottom. The Squid web proxy solution uses LRU as stated in the guide [31] "*LRU is the default policy, not only for Squid, but for most other caching products as well.*". The Dropbox content delivery service also applies LRU in client caches. A recent Dropbox TechBlog [25] is discussing LRU performance tradeoffs with reference to problems shown in [24] but finally concludes "*Overall, the caching algorithm you want to use is usually LRU, since it is theoretically very good and in practice both simple and efficient.*"

However, the reasoning leading to this conclusion mainly considers deterministic and periodic request sequences as worst case scenarios of LRU and alternatives. Those cases may be relevant in computing systems performing accesses in program loops, whereas random and Zipf distributed requests are observed in measurement and trace studies for web caching with different effect. In accordance with results for other proposed strategies in [24][30], our theoretical as well as simulative performance evaluation in Sections 4 and 5 confirm severe deficits of LRU hit rates for web caching, making it worthwhile to consider more elaborate strategies involving request statistics from the past.

3.2   Replacement Methods Based on Request Statistics

We study two basic alternatives of cache replacement strategies with a limited memory of the past:

- Sliding Window: The cache holds those objects which have the highest request frequency over a sliding window of the last K requests.

- Geometric Fading: The cache holds those objects that have the highest sum of weights for past requests, where the kth request in the past is assigned a geometrically decreasing weight ρ^k ($0 < \rho < 1$).

The policies compute a score or weight function for the frequencies of past requests to an object in order to estimate the request probabilities, which are unknown a priori. Fig. 1 illustrates the ranking of objects for caching with the considered strategies for an example sequence of requests. Both statistics-based strategies provide a single parameter, i.e. the size K of the sliding window and the fading factor ρ, which determines the backlog of the memory into the past. In this way they employ an aging mechanism to avoid cache pollution with objects that decrease in popularity over time.

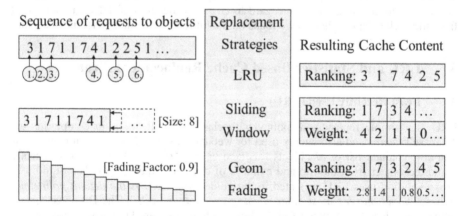

Fig. 1. Comparison of LRU, sliding window and geometric fading strategies

Geometric fading is equivalent to LRU for $\rho \leq \frac{1}{2}$, since then the weight of the last request exceeds the sum of all previous scores. The same holds for the sliding window mechanism for $K \leq M$ when we implement it with LRU as a tie breaker for deciding on the eviction if several objects have the same request frequency count. For $K \to \infty$

and $\rho \to 1$, both methods approach an infinite count statistics over the past corresponding to least frequently used (LFU). When the cache is filled at the start without much backlog information being available, the short-term statistics corresponding to small K may largely deviate from the long-term steady state behaviour.

In practice, the popularity of objects in the web is observed to be slowly changing [3][8][33]. As a consequence, pure LFU with an unlimited count statistics is expected to degrade in the long-term behavior since it would keep outdated formerly popular objects in the cache without sufficient response to dynamic popularity.

A window of size K stands for a fixed backlog whereas geometric fading introduces a slowly decreasing influence over time. Both strategies can establish a comparable backlog when $\rho = K/(K+1) \Leftrightarrow \Sigma_{j \geq 1}\, \rho^j = \rho/(1-\rho) = K$. It is mandatory to adapt the aging parameters K and ρ to the rate of change in the objects' popularity. This can be done again based on statistics of the user request behavior or by evaluation and tuning for optimum cache performance as illustrated in Section 5, Fig. 4. The minimum score of objects in the cache indicates how many requests to a new object have to be encountered until it will enter the cache.

3.3   Implementation Effort of Replacement Methods

Least Recently Used

A main advantage for the widely applied LRU strategy is the simple and efficient implementation as a double chained stack of M objects. An update per request is done at constant effort for putting the requested object on top of the LRU stack.

Sliding Window

The sliding window statistics requires some more updating effort. The count of the requested object is incremented and the count of another object is decremented, corresponding to the oldest request being dropped from the sliding window. Cached objects are sorted due to their score. For updating an object with in- or decremented count an extended double chained list is sufficient with constant updating effort per request similar to [29], despite of more complex LFU implementation proposals [23]. Moreover, the sliding window has to be stored as a cyclic list of size K, in order to determine the oldest request in the sliding window and to overwrite it by the recent request. Nonetheless, the entire processing effort per request can be kept constant.

Geometric Fading

On first glance, an update per request for geometric fading has to increment the weight of the new requested object and to multiply the aging factor ρ to the weights of all objects, which would mean an enormous $O(N)$ effort. But instead of decreasing the weight of all objects by a factor ρ, we can equivalently increase the weight only for the new requested object by a reciprocal factor $1/\rho$ each time, i.e. the weight to be added for a new request is initiated with 1 and then is growing to $(1/\rho)^k$ after k requests. This procedure has the same aging effect due to an inflation of weights for new requests. The only problem is that the weight will approach the maximum number in floating-point representation over time. Therefore the weights of cached objects have to be readjusted by dividing them by $(1/\rho)^k$ when a threshold is reached.

In this way, the updating effort for geometric fading is reduced to the order $O(\log(M))$ for reinserting the requested object at an upward position in the cache.

The survey [26] refers to a similar ρ-aging method, where the scores of all objects are reduced by a factor ρ not for each request but in longer time intervals, e.g. once an hour, thus essentially reducing the effort per request.

4   Deficits of LRU Hit Rates for Random i.i.d. Requests

We start the evaluation of the LRU caching performance by looking for worst case examples of the achievable LRU hit rate for the independent reference model (IRM [2][22]). In this way, we would like to check whether it is usual or extreme to outperform the LRU hit rate by up to 20% as shown in examples in [24][30]. In particular, we introduce the following preconditions and notations:

- A set of N objects $O = (o_1, o_2, ..., o_N)$ includes all cacheable data that is requested over a considered time period by the user population.

- The cache has a fixed size for storing $M \ll N$ objects, since in practice the cache size is very small compared with the size of all objects available for web caching.

- We assume that requests address the objects according to a random, independent and identically distributed (i.i.d.) sequence, such that a request refers to an object o_k with probability p_k, where the objects are assumed to be ordered according to their popularity $p_1 \geq p_2 \geq ... \geq p_N$.

Under these assumptions, the optimum replacement policy keeps the M most popular objects in the cache, since then the hit rate reaches its maximum value $h_{OPT} = \Sigma_{k=1}^{M} p_k$.

This can be achieved with LFU policy in the long term steady state case $h_{OPT} = h_{LFU}$.

Considering small cache size ($M = 1$)

Deficits of LRU are inevitable without full awareness of the objects' popularity and can be illustrated starting from the smallest cache size $M = 1$. Then the worst case for LRU is encountered when the top object is much more popular than the others, i.e. when $p_1 \gg \varepsilon \geq p_2 \geq p_3 \geq ... \geq p_N$. Then under the LRU policy, o_1 is found in the cache with probability p_1 whereas one of the other objects has been addressed most recently with probability $1 - p_1$. As the LRU hit rate we obtain

$$h_{LRU} \leq p_1 \cdot p_1 + (1 - p_1) \cdot \varepsilon \approx p_1^2. \tag{2}$$

We conclude that the absolute difference between $h_{OPT} = p_1$ and $h_{LRU} \approx p_1^2$ can be as large as $h_{OPT} - h_{LRU} \approx 25\%$ for $p_1 = 0.5$ and the relative difference $h_{LRU} / h_{OPT} \approx p_1$ can be arbitrary large for small p_1, e.g., 1% LRU versus 10% optimum hit rate for $p = 0.1$.

Analysis for arbitrary cache size M

For larger caches, the degradation of LRU hit rates can even exceed 25%, when we follow the considered case for arbitrary size M with access probabilities

$$p_1 = p_2 = ... = p_M = p \gg \varepsilon = p_{M+1} = p_{M+2} = ... = p_N \tag{3}$$

where again the top M objects are much more popular than the others and the optimum hit rate is given by $h_{OPT} = \Sigma_{k=1}^{M} p_k = Mp$.

For the independent request model, an analytical formula for the LRU hit rate is known, see e.g. equation (6) in [18], but requires exponential computation effort in M and hence can be evaluated only for small caches. For realistic cache size, approximations have been proposed by [9][12][14][15][18], as compared in Table 1 of Section 5.

However, under the assumptions of equation (3) the iterative approximation according to [18] still allows for an exact analysis, because only two classes of objects need to be distinguished: The set of M popular objects $O_{POP} = \{o_1, o_2, ..., o_M\}$, each of which has request probability p, and the remaining $N - M$ objects, each of which has negligible request probability $\varepsilon << p$. Let $p_{LRU}(j, k)$ denote the probability that j popular objects from the set O_{POP} are found in an LRU cache of size k. Then the LRU hit rate h_{LRU} for a cache of size M can be expressed as

$$h_{LRU} = \Sigma_j \, p_{LRU}(j, M)[\, j \cdot p + (M - j) \cdot \varepsilon\,] \approx \Sigma_j \, j \cdot p \cdot p_{LRU}(j, M). \tag{4}$$

We can set up an iterative computation scheme for the probabilities $p_{LRU}(j, k)$ for increasing cache size $k = 1, 2, ..., M$. Initially we obtain

$$p_{LRU}(0, 1) = 1 - M \cdot p \quad \text{and} \quad p_{LRU}(1, 1) = M \cdot p \tag{5}$$

for $k = 1$ according to the probability that the last request referred to an object outside or inside O_{Pop}. In general, the probability $p_{LRU}(j, k)$ can be determined from a combination of cases with j or $j - 1$ objects in a cache of size $k - 1$ when we consider the situation after a new object has been put on top of the cache. Then the former top k object is evicted from the cache, whereas the former top $1, ... , (k - 1)$ objects in the cache and the new object are building a cache of size k.

$$p_{LRU}(j,k) = p(j,k-1)\frac{1-Mp-(k-1-j)\varepsilon}{1-jp-(k-1-j)\varepsilon} + p(j-1,k-1)\frac{(M-j+1)p}{1-(j-1)p-(k-j)\varepsilon}. \tag{6}$$

Both ratios in equation (6) express conditional probabilities that the new object is outside or inside the set O_{POP} provided that j popular objects (or $j - 1$, respectively) are excluded, since they are already in the cache of size $k - 1$. A corresponding number of non-popular elements is also excluded. Equation (6) holds for $0 < j < k$. If we presume $p_{LRU}(k, k-1) = p_{LRU}(-1, k-1) = 0$ then (6) is valid for $j = 0, k$ as well.

Evaluation of the equations (4)-(6) reveals that LRU hit rates are more than 25% below the optimum in a wide range of $0.38 \leq M \cdot p \leq 0.78$ with a maximum of 28.9% for $M \cdot p \approx 0.58$, provided that ε is small, i.e. $\varepsilon < 0.01p$ and for $M \geq 5$. Moreover, for small caches, LRU shows substantial relative degradation e.g. down from 20% to 4% and then seems inappropriate. We suppose that the considered case (3) is the worst case scenario for LRU hit rate degradation for independent references, although we lack a formal proof. Therefore it would be sufficient to show that the LRU hit rate is always decreasing when the probabilities p_j, p_k of two objects o_j, o_k are smoothed, i.e. are both changed to $(p_j + p_k)/2$.

As compared to the performance evaluation based on realistic web cache traces with Zipf distributed requests in [18][24][30], the 5%-20% differences in the hit rate between LRU and proposed alternative strategies are about half as large as the previously derived case. Statistics based strategies are still experienced to exploit most of the optimum hit rate as confirmed in the following simulation studies.

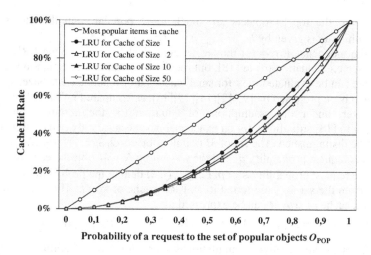

Fig. 2. Analysis of severe deficits of LRU cache hit rates

5   Evaluation of Replacement Methods by Simulation

We use simulations in order to investigate the performance of caching strategies under Zipf distributed user requests. We compare LRU with sliding window and geometric fading for independent Zipf distributed requests. We include $N = 1\,000$ objects, whereas the cache size M and the parameter β of the Zipf distribution are varying. The hit rate is evaluated as the main performance criterion. Simulation results are obtained from a series of 10-20 independent simulation runs, each of which includes at least 4 000 i.i.d. Zipf distributed requests. In this way, we have a preliminary check of the variability of the obtained hit rates and we were able to tune the length of simulation runs in order to keep the estimated standard deviation in the series of simulation runs for each result below 1%. First we study the long-term behavior and therefore the hit rate evaluation excludes a sufficiently long starting phase. Later on, a closer look on the transient behavior shows that the strategies involving request statistics can have a long starting phase before the behavior stabilizes towards steady state behavior, whereas LRU can be assumed in steady state as soon as the cache is completely filled.

Fig. 3 presents the simulation results of the replacement strategies for different cache sizes ($M = 5$, 10, 20, 50 and 100), Zipf distribution exponents ($\beta = 0.6$, 0.8 and 0.99), and for a maximum window size $K = 4\,000$ and a fading factor $\rho = 0.99999$. Then the sliding window as well as the geometric fading strategy come close to pure LFU since the request count statistics is large enough to provide a good sample for representing the Zipf request distribution.

The obtained results reflect the expected behavior: The curves of statistics-based strategies almost achieve the optimum hit rate $h_{\mathrm{OPT}} = \Sigma_{k=1}^{M} p_k$ whereas LRU stays 5 - 18% below. The deviation of the statistics based strategies is negligible for small cache size but is increasing up to 3% for $M = 100$. In general, the figures confirm the efficiency of web caching for Zipf distributed requests already when the cache size covers only 1‰ - 1% of the relevant objects and especially when the parameter β is close to 1 corresponding to a strong concentration of requests on popular objects.

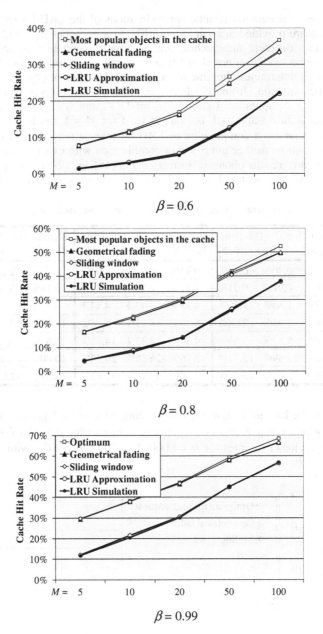

Fig. 3. Hit rates of the caching strategies for Zipf distributed requests $A(R) = \alpha R^{-\beta}$

In addition to simulation results, approximations of the LRU hit rate for independent requests are provided in a curve according to approaches in [9][12][14][15][18]. There are two different approaches: An iterative computation of the hit rate for increasing cache size is proposed in [9] and slightly improved in [18]. The approach in [12][14][15] determines the time for requests to M different objects as the root of a characteristic equation, from which the hit rate of the objects is obtained. This approach has a computational complexity of O(N) and is asymptotically exact for large M. The iterative approach is exact at least for $M = 1$ and has a complexity of O(MN). Since an exact computation of LRU hit rates is feasible up to $M \approx 10$ [18], the approach can be further improved in combination with exact results for small M. Table 1 compares results obtained from eq. (1) in [15], eq. (7-8) in [18], and eq. (1-2) in [9], which coincide with only minor deviations over the complete range.

Table 1. Comparison of LRU cache hit rate approximations for Zipf distributions

M	Results for $\beta = 0.6$ from			Results for $\beta = 0.8$ from			Results for $\beta = 0.95$ from		
	[9][14]	[18]	[12]	[9][14]	[18]	[12]	[9][14]	[18]	[12]
1	0,30%	0,30%	0,30%	0,93%	0,94%	0,94%	2,18%	2,24%	2,24%
3	0,91%	0,91%	0,91%	2,71%	2,74%	2,75%	6,18%	6,30%	6,34%
5	1,50%	1,50%	1,50%	4,38%	4,43%	4,44%	9,72%	9,86%	9,96%
10	2,93%	2,94%	2,94%	8,16%	8,21%	8,26%	16,94%	17,01%	17,25%
20	5,64%	5,65%	5,66%	14,30%	14,32%	14,42%	26,53%	26,52%	26,79%
50	12,68%	12,69%	12,71%	26,16%	26,16%	26,24%	40,80%	40,80%	40,90%
100	22,03%	22,03%	22,05%	37,78%	37,78%	37,82%	52,61%	52,62%	52,66%

In Fig. 4, the hit rate is evaluated for sliding window and geometric fading with increasing window size K and corresponding fading factor $\rho = K/(K+1)$. We pick one of the previous examples for $N = 1\,000$, $M = 100$ and $\beta = 0.8$ with $h_{LRU} \approx 37.8\%$ and $h_{LFU} \approx 52.8\%$.

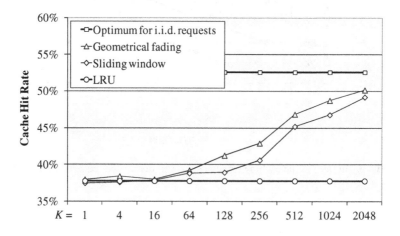

Fig. 4. Sliding window and geom. fading: Hit rate for varying K, ρ ($\rho = K/(K+1)$)

The curves for geometric fading and sliding window start at the LRU hit rate without much improvement for $K \leq 2^6$. In the range $K = 2^6, ..., K = 2^{11}$ the hit rate is improving by several percent with each doubling step towards the optimum hit rate level. Geometric fading starts to improve about one step earlier because memory of previous requests is present in the object's score over longer time even for small fading factors, whereas sliding window strictly deletes any memory beyond the window size K. The evaluation of the impact of the window size on the hit rate is useful in order to determine an appropriate choice of the parameters K and ρ for both statistics based methods.

Finally, we demonstrate the transient behavior for the same example with $N = 1000$, $M = 100$ and $\beta = 0.8$ with regard to several characteristics of the cache, in particular

- the mean popularity rank of the objects in the cache,
- the number of top 100 objects stored in the cache of size $M = 100$ and
- the hit rate.

A window size $K = 4000$ and a corresponding fading factor ρ is assumed in order to observe a long term behavior close to the unlimited LFU caching strategy. The evaluation shows one figure per interval of 100 requests, i.e. a 40% hit rate in the 3rd interval corresponds to 40 hits occurring among the requests no. 201 - 300. Fig. 5 shows that the mean object rank in the cache starts in the range of 250 - 300 out of 1000 objects and then is fast decreasing towards the expected long term value of 50.5 when the cache tends to collect the top 100 objects.

Accordingly, the number of top 100 objects found in the cache starts around 30 and is increasing to about 80. In examples for $M \leq 10$ the cache content often consists of all top M objects already after 1000 requests. Fig. 6 shows the corresponding curves of the hit rate starting from a low level due to limited statistics being available and converging to the LRU hit rate in the course of the simulation run. In all cases a similar behavior of the sliding window and geometric fading strategy is apparent in the curves of Fig. 5 - Fig. 6.

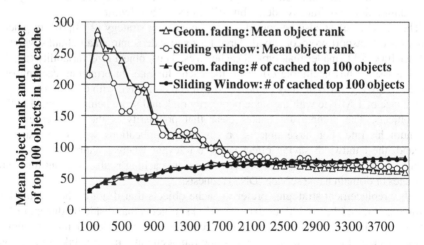

Fig. 5. Transient behavior: Mean rank and number of top 100 objects in the cache

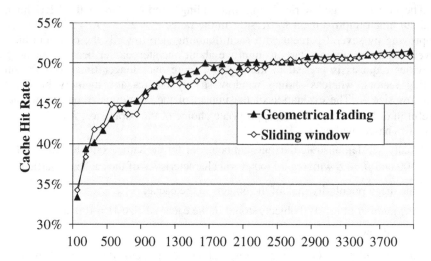

Fig. 6. Increasing hit rate for transient behavior over intervals of 100 requests

6   Generalized Caching Criteria

In general, there are many more aspects to be considered in the decision for caching requested objects beyond statistics on past requests for achieving the optimum hit rate. A current IETF standardization draft document [13] on HTTP caching refers to a list of preconditions for cacheability based on information to be exchanged between the origin server and the cache, such as expiration date, cache directives ("no-store", only for "private" i.e. client side caches etc.) and cache control extensions. Depending on the status with regard to those criteria, an object may be delivered from the cache with or without revalidation from the origin server, where cache delivery with revalidation does not improve delay but still can save bandwidth.

The object size can also be considered in the caching strategy [2][8][26]. In practice, codecs and transport protocols divide large files and videos into small chunks which are at least 1000-fold smaller than typical cache sizes. Thus, object size variability (e.g. bin-packing issues) has negligible effect on the cache hit rate. In principle, caching of an object of size e.g. j MByte may be broken down and compared with caching of j objects of unit size of 1 MByte with the same popularity rank and score being attributed to those unit objects. The comparison makes clear that popularity is the main criterion for optimum hit rate. For large objects or streaming applications with high bandwidth demand, the bandwidth saving effect is more relevant whereas shorter delays are the main caching advantage for small objects. Therefore caching is also relevant for control messages or domain name service (DNS) requests.

Other replacement strategies prefer to cache objects that if not cached would have to traverse limited-bandwidth or expensive links, objects that reside on distant or busy servers, or objects with stringent quality requirements in order to further improve performance and reduce costs. Finally, some replacement strategies take into account the "freshness" [13] of the objects in order to avoid consistency misses and thus improve the hit rate. Several function-based replacement policies can be found in the literature [7][26] that use cost functions which exploit such information (e.g. link bandwidth, server load, object age etc.) in order to estimate cost savings for objects indicating the benefits related with their caching.

7   Conclusions and Outlook

Requests for popular content on the Internet are prevalently served by overlay caching systems in content delivery networks. The efficiency of web caching is promoted by Zipf distributed user requests and a growing portion of traffic via the HTTP protocol.

However, our evaluation of cache replacement strategies in comparison of the most commonly used LRU policy with two strategies based on statistics of past requests reveals deficits of the LRU cache hit rate of up to 28.9% in a worst case analysis and still 10-20% in simulations of realistic web caching environments. Similar experience seems to be present in literature only in a few studies of the performance of alternative strategies based on traces for requests to content on the Internet. Especially the hit rate potential of small caches is scarcely used by LRU.

The considered caching strategies are adaptable to changing popularity of objects, but we assume the optimum caching efficiency to closely approach the static case of independent and identically Zipf distributed requests. The modeling and analysis of changing popularity of objects and proposals for improved strategies are for further study, e.g. with prediction of increasing and decreasing phases in the popularity profile of objects.

Acknowledgements. We would like to thank an anonymous reviewer for extending our awareness of related work. This work has been performed partially in the framework of the European EU ICT STREP SmartenIT (FP7-ICT-2011-317846) as well as the MEVICO project founded by the German Federal Ministry of Education and Research (BMBF).

References

[1] Akamai, State of the Internet, Quarterly Report Series (2013),
      http://www.akamai.com
[2] Bahat, O., Makowski, M.: Optimal replacement policies for non-uniform cache objects with optional eviction. In: Proc. IEEE Infocom Conference, San Francisco, CA, USA (2003)
[3] Bolla, R., et al.: Modeling file popularity in peer-to-peer file sharing systems. In: Proc. 14th ASMTA Conf., Prague, Czech Republic, pp. 149–155 (2007)
[4] Braun, L., et al.: Analyzing caching benefits for YouTube traffic in edge networks: A measurement-based evaluation. In: IEEE Network Operations & Management Symposium, Maui, Hawaii, USA (2012)
[5] Breslau, L., et al.: Web caching and Zipf-like distributions: Evidence and implications. In: Proc. IEEE Infocom (1999)
[6] Buyya, R., Pathan, M., Vakali, A. (eds.): Content delivery networks. LNEE, vol. 9. Springer, Heidelberg (2008)

[7] Cao, P., Irani, S.: Cost aware WWW caching algorithms. In: Proc. USENIX Symposium, Monterey, CA, USA (1997)

[8] Cha, M., et al.: I tube, you tube, everybody tubes: Analyzing the world's largest user generated content video system. In: Internet Measurement Conference, IMC 2007, San Diego, USA (2007)

[9] Che, H., Tung, Y., Wang, Z.: Hierarchical web caching systems: modeling, design and experimental results. IEEE JSAC 20(7), 1305–1314 (2002)

[10] Charzinski, J.: Traffic properties, client side cachability and CDN usage of popular web sites. In: Müller-Clostermann, B., Echtle, K., Rathgeb, E.P. (eds.) MMB & DFT 2010. LNCS, vol. 5987, pp. 136–150. Springer, Heidelberg (2010)

[11] Cohen, B.: Incentives build robustness in BitTorrent (2003), http://bitconjurer.org/BitTorrent/bittorrentecon.pdf

[12] Dan, A., Towsely, D.: An approximate analysis of the LRU and FIFO buffer replacement schemes. SIGMETRICS Perform. Eval. Rev. 18, 143–152 (1990)

[13] Fielding, R., et al.: Hypertext transfer protocol HTTP/1.1: Caching, Internet-Draft, work in progr. (2013), http://tools.ietf.org/html/draft-ietf-httpbis-p6-cache-22

[14] Fricker, C., Robert, P., Roberts, J.: A versatile and accurate approximation for LRU cache performance. In: Proc. 24th International Teletraffic Congress, Kraków, Poland (2012)

[15] Fricker, C., et al.: Impact of traffic mix on caching performance in a content-centric network. In: IEEE INFOCOM 2012 Workshops, pp. 310–315 (2012)

[16] Gill, P., et al.: YouTube traffic characterization: A view from the edge. In: Internet Measurement Conference, IMC 2007, San Diego, USA (2007)

[17] Guo, L., et al.: Does Internet media traffic really follow Zipf-like distributions? In: ACM SIGMETRICS (2007)

[18] Hasslinger, G., Hohlfeld, O.: Efficiency of caches for content distribution on the Internet. In: Proc. 22nd International Teletraffic Congress, Amsterdam, The Netherlands (2010)

[19] Hasslinger, G., Hartleb, F., Beckhaus, T.: User access to popular data on the internet and approaches for IP traffic flow optimization. In: Al-Begain, K., Fiems, D., Horváth, G. (eds.) ASMTA 2009. LNCS, vol. 5513, pp. 42–55. Springer, Heidelberg (2009)

[20] Hasslinger, G., Hartleb, F.: Content delivery and caching from a network provider's perspective. Special Issue on Internet based Content Delivery, Computer Networks 55, 3991–4006 (2011)

[21] Kandavanam, G., Botvich, D., Balasubranmaniam, S.: PaCRA: A path-aware content replication approach to support QoS guaranteed video on demand service in metropolitan IPTV networks. In: IEEE/IFIP Network Operations & Mgnt. Symp. NOMS, pp. 591–598 (2010)

[22] Karakostas, G., Serpanos, D.N.: Exploitation of different types of localities for web caching. In: Proc. 7th IEEE Symposium on Computers and Communications (ISCC), pp. 207–212 (2002)

[23] Lee, D., et al.: LRFU: A spectrum of policies that subsumes the least recently used and least frequently used policies. IEEE Transactions on Computers 50(12), 1352–1361 (2001)

[24] Megiddo, N., Modha, S.: Outperforming LRU with an adaptive replacement cache algorithm. IEEE Computer 37(4), 4–11 (2004)

[25] Panchekha, P.: Caching in theory and practice, Dropbox TechBlog (2012), https://tech.dropbox.com/2012/10/caching-in-theory-and-practice

[26] Podlipnik, S., Böszörmenyi, L.: A survey of web cache replacement strategies. ACM Computer Surveys, 374–398 (2003)

[27] Rabinovich, M., Spatscheck, O.: Web caching and replication. Addison-Wesley, Boston (2002)

[28] Reed, W.J.: The Pareto, Zipf and other power laws. Economics Letters 74(1), 15–19 (2001)

[29] Shah, K., Mitra, A., Matani, D.: An O(1) algorithm for implementing the LFU cache eviction scheme accessible from, `http://dhruvbird.com/lfu.pdf` or `http://en.wikipedia.org/wiki/Least_frequently_used` (2010)

[30] Vakali, A.I.: LRU-based algorithms for web cache replacement. In: Bauknecht, K., Madria, S.K., Pernul, G. (eds.) EC-Web 2000. LNCS, vol. 1875, pp. 409–418. Springer, Heidelberg (2000)

[31] Wessels, D.: Squid: The definitive guide. O'Reilly (2004)

[32] Williams, A., et al.: Web workload characterization: Ten years later. In: Tang, X., et al. (eds.) Web Content Delivery, pp. 3–21. Springer (2005)

[33] Zhao, S., Stutzbach, D., Rejaie, R.: Characterizing files in the modern Gnutella network: A measurement study. SPIE/ACM Proc. Multimedia Computing and Networking (2006)

QoE of YouTube Video Streaming
for Current Internet Transport Protocols

Tobias Hoßfeld[1], Raimund Schatz[2], and Udo R. Krieger[3]

[1] University of Würzburg, Institute of Computer Science, Würzburg, Germany
`hossfeld@informatik.uni-wuerzburg.de`
[2] Telecommunications Research Center Vienna - FTW, Vienna, Austria
`schatz@ftw.at`
[3] Otto-Friedrich University Bamberg, Bamberg, Germany
`udo.krieger@uni-bamberg.de`

Abstract. Video streaming currently dominates global Internet traffic and will be of even increasing importance in the future. In this paper we assess the impact of the underlying transport protocol on the user perceived quality for video streaming using YouTube as example. In particular, we investigate whether UDP or TCP fits better for Video-on-Demand delivery from the end user's perspective, when the video is transmitted over a bottleneck link. For UDP based streaming, the bottleneck link results in spatial and temporal video artifacts, decreasing the video quality. In contrast, in the case of TCP based streaming, the displayed content itself is not disturbed but playback suffers from stalling due to rebuffering. The results of subjective user studies for both scenarios are analyzed in order to assess the transport protocol influences on Quality of Experience of YouTube. To this end, application-level measurements are conducted for YouTube streaming over a network bottleneck in order to develop models for realistic stalling patterns. Furthermore, mapping functions are derived that accurately describe the relationship between network-level impairments and QoE for both protocols.

Keywords: YouTube, Quality of Experience, Stalling, TCP, Loss, UDP.

1 Introduction

Video streaming dominates global Internet traffic and is expected to account for 57 % of all consumer Internet traffic in 2014 generating over 23 exabytes per month [1]. It can be distinguished between delivery of live video streaming with on-the-fly encoding, like IPTV or Facetime, and delivery of pre-encoded video, so called Video-on-Demand (VoD). The most prominent VoD portal is YouTube which accounts for more than two billion video streams daily [2].

The transport of video streams in the Internet is currently realized either with TCP or UDP. However, due to the diverse features of these protocols their application has a huge impact on the streaming behavior. The usage of TCP guarantees the delivery of undisturbed video content since the protocol itself cares for the retransmissions of corrupted or lost packets. Further, it adapts the

K. Fischbach and U.R. Krieger (Eds.): MMB & DFT 2014, LNCS 8376, pp. 136–150, 2014.

transport rate to network congestion, thus minimizing packet loss. If the available bandwidth is lower than the required video bit rate the video transmission lasts longer than the video playback. Thus, the playback is interrupted which is referred to as *stalling*. Hence, in case of TCP the video playback rather than the video itself is disturbed. In contrast, UDP does not perform bandwidth adaptation or guarantee packet delivery, but it transmits the data with the same bit rate as forwarded by the application. Thus, network congestion leads to lost packets which occur as artifacts or jumps in the stream. Hence, the user experiences a *degraded video quality* in terms of visual impairments.

The question arises which transport protocol is more appropriate from the end user's point of view, i.e. the Quality of Experience (QoE). To answer this question we consider a bottleneck scenario in which network capacity is limited. Thus, the available network bandwidth may be lower than the required video bit rate and the user may suffer from stalling and quality degradation for TCP and UDP, respectively. In order to compare the impact of the transport protocols on the QoE, two subjective user studies are presented. In previous work [3], we quantified the impact of stalling on QoE, while [4] executed user surveys to evaluate QoE of video streaming with lost packets.

The contribution of this paper is twofold. First, an intensive YouTube measurement study is conducted in order to quantify the relevant application-level QoS parameters for YouTube over a bottleneck. In particular, the observed stalling patterns are modeled in terms of stalling frequency and stalling length. Second, YouTube video streaming via TCP and via UDP is compared from the end-user perspective by means of subjective user studies [3,4]. The comparison is realized by transforming the results of the subjective tests to the common denominator in the considered scenario, that is the network bandwidth limitation due to the bottleneck. Since [3] provides first a YouTube QoE model for given stalling pattern, the work presented here is the first comparing QoE – and in particular YouTube QoE – for different transport protocols.

The reminder of this paper is structured as follows. Section 2 shows the application-level measurements for YouTube over a bottleneck. This includes the video characteristics in terms of duration and video bit rate as well as the observed stalling patterns which is required to later map the bottleneck bandwidth to QoE. The subjective user study on QoE for YouTube video streaming in the presence of stalling, which means via TCP, is reviewed in Section 3. The QoE model for UDP based transmission of YouTube videos is presented in Section 4. The results of the subjective tests are compared and discussed in Section 5. Finally, Section 6 concludes this work and discusses further research issues.

2   Measurement of YouTube Application-Level QoS

In the considered bottleneck scenario for TCP, the available network bandwidth B is limited. When downloading a video which is encoded at a video bit rate $V > B$, stalling may occur. The number N of stallings during the video playout as well as the length L of a single stalling event will both affect the QoE. However, the stalling pattern even in the bottleneck scenario with constant network capacity may be quite complex, since several factors interact and influence the stalling pattern, (a) YouTube's implementation of flow control on application layer [5], (b) TCP's flow control on transport layer, (c) variabe bit rate due to the used video encoding, (d) implementation of the video player and its video buffer.

Therefore, we derive in the following a simple model for the observed stalling patterns based on an application-level measurement study. In Section 2.1, the measurement setup is explained. The observed stalling patterns over the dedicated bottleneck are analyzed in Section 2.2. The notation and variables frequently used throughout this paper are summarized in Table 1.

2.1   Setup of Application-Level Measurements

Our YouTube TCP measurement campaign took place from July to August, 2011 during which more than 37,000 YouTube videos were requested, about 35 GByte of data traffic was captured, and more than 1,000 videos were analyzed frame by frame in detail. In addition, 266,245 video descriptions were downloaded from YouTube containing the duration of the videos.

For measuring YouTube video streaming over a bottleneck, the measurement setup included three different components. (1) *Bandwidth shaper.* A network emulation software was used to limit the upload and download bandwidth. In our experiments, the "NetLimiter" bandwidth shaper was applied. (2) *YouTube user simulation.* This component simulated a user watching YouTube videos in his browser. Therefore, a local Apache web server was configured and web pages were dynamically generated, which call the YouTube API for embedding and playing the YouTube video. The embedding of the YouTube videos in an own web page is necessary for monitoring the appliction-level QoS. In order to obtain a random snapshot on YouTube, we randomly searched for videos via the YouTube API and used a public dictionary of english words as keyword for the YouTube search request. (3) *QoS monitor.* The video player status ("playing", "buffering", "ended") and the used buffer size (in terms of number of bytes loaded for the current video) were monitored within the generated web page using Javascript. At the end of the simulation (i.e. when the simulated user completely watched the video, after a certain timeout, or in case of any player errors), the stalling monitoring information and the buffer status were written to a logfile. Further, the network packet traces were captured using wireshark and tshark. As a result, both network-level QoS parameters (from the packet traces) and application-level QoS parameters (the stalling patterns) were captured.

The QoS monitor component provided the data for analyzing the stalling pattern on application level. The YouTube API specifies an event called "onStateChange" which is fired whenever the state of the player changes. For each event, e.g. when the video player switches between buffering of data and playing the video, the current timestamp, the number of bytes loaded, as well as an identifier for the event itself are recorded by the QoS monitor. However, it has to be noted that the timer resolution depends on the actual JavaScript implementation within the browser used. In our experiments, we used the Internet explorer within Windows 7 which shows a timer resolution of about 16 ms.

Table 1. Notation and variables frequently used

Variables	
V	total bit rate of video in (kbps)
D	duration of video in (s)
B	bandwidth limitation in (kbps)
N	number of stalling events
L	duration of a single stalling event
F	stalling frequency $F = N/D$ in (1/s)
R	packet loss ratio
ρ	throughput normalized by video bitrate, i.e. $\rho = B/V$
Functions	
$f_L(N)$	mapping function between number N of stalling events and MOS values for stalling events of length L via TCP
$g_v(R)$	mapping function between packet loss ratio R and MOS values for videos with resolution v (CIF, 4CIF) via UDP
$\Upsilon_L(\rho)$	mapping function between normalized throughput ρ and MOS values for stalling events of length L via TCP
$\Upsilon_v(\rho)$	mapping function between normalized throughput ρ and MOS values for videos with resolution v (CIF, 4CIF) via UDP

For analyzing the video files, the video contents were extracted from the packet traces. The YouTube API specifies a set of calls for requesting videos via HTTP. Via pattern matching, these HTTP requests and corresponding HTTP objects were identified. YouTube uses DNS translation and URL redirection, as the actual video contents are located on various caching servers, see [6,7,8]. The video contents were then reassembled from the corresponding TCP stream.

The video file itself was parsed by implementing a perl module which analyzed the video frames and extracted meta-information from the video file. As a result, video information like video bit rate, video resolution, used audio and video codecs, or video size and duration were extracted. Furthermore, for each video frame in the video stream, information about the video playback times of frames, the size of the video frames, as well as the type of frames (key frame or interframe) were extracted.

2.2 Observed Stalling Patterns over Bottleneck

The aim of this section is to model the observed stalling patterns when the YouTube video is streamed over a bottleneck. The subjective user studies [3] summarized in Section 3 quantify QoE depending on the number N of stalling events and the length L of a single stalling event. A mapping function $f_L(N)$ between the stalling parameters as application-level QoS and the QoE in terms of mean opinion score (MOS) values is provided. Now, we derive the influence of the bottleneck capacity B on the observed stalling pattern in the following. In particular, we depict two exemplary bandwidth limitations, that are $B = 384$ kbps as typical bandwidth of UMTS cell phones and $B = 450$ kbps which is roughly the median of the video bit rate V as observed in our measurement campaign, see the technical report [9] for more details.

Stalling Frequency. The stalling frequency F is defined as the ratio of the number of stalling events and the duration D of the video, i.e. $F = N/D$. First, the correlation of F with several influence factors was investigated in terms of Pearson's linear correlation coefficient given in brackets: 1. frame rate (-0.03), 2. video duration (-0.35), 3. median of stalling length (0.37), 4. number of stallings (0.47), 5. mean stalling length (-0.58), 6. video bit rate (0.87). Thus, there is no significant correlation between stalling frequency and frame rate, number and length of stalling, or the video duration. The stalling frequency is strongly correlated only with the video bit rate.

Figure 1 depicts the stalling frequency depending on the normalized video demand x for two different bandwidth limitations. The normalized video demand is defined as the ratio of the video bit rate V and the bottleneck capacity B, i.e. $x = V/B$. The measurement results for each video clip are plotted with "$\diamond$" marker and "$+$" marker for $B = 384$ kbps and $B = 450$ kbps, respectively. As a result, we see that the measurement results – for both bottleneck capacities – lie in the same area. In particular, the measured frequencies with the corresponding measured video demands can be well fitted by an exponential function which we found by minimizing the least square errors,

$$F(x) = -1.09e^{-1.18x} + 0.36 \, . \tag{1}$$

The resulting coefficient of determination of the fitting function F and the measurement data is $D = 0.943$. However, there are several outliers which lie above the dashed line in Figure 1. About $15.22\,\%$ of the video clips are assumed to be outliers. We found no statistical correlation between these values of F and any other variables. An in-depth analysis of the packet traces as well as of the video contents did not reveal a clear reason for this. However, we assume that these outliers are caused by the implementation of the video player itself. Considering the correlation coefficients of F and the video bitrate V without the outliers leads to 0.955 and 0.958 for $B = 384$ kbps and $B = 450$ kbps, respectively.

Thus, when the bottleneck capacity is equal to the video bit rate, i.e. $x = 1$, the stalling frequency is $F(1) = 0.021$. In that case, a one minute video clip will already stall once due to the variable video bit rate. According to the curve fitting function, the stalling frequency will converge and it is $\lim_{x \to \infty} F(x) = 0.357$. Hence, a one minute clip will stall at most 21 times. However, from QoS perspective, this is not relevant, such high video demands may cause the player to crash anyway. From QoE perspective this is either not relevant, since the user is already annoyed when a few stalling events happen (see Section 3).

Stalling Length. Next, we take a closer look at the length L of single stalling events. For each video clip, we measured the durations of each stalling event. Then, we computed several statistical measures per video clip, including mean and median of the stalling length over the stalling events of an individual clip. However, we found no correlation between the statistical measures of the stalling time and any other variable, i.e. video frame rate, stalling frequency, video bit rate, video duration, number of stallings.

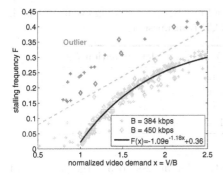 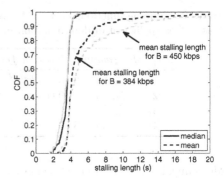

Fig. 1. Measured and fitted stalling frequency F depending on the normalized video demand x as ratio of video bit rate V and bottleneck capacity B

Fig. 2. Median and mean of the stalling length for two different bottleneck capacities of $B = 384$ kbps and $B = 450$ kbps, respectively

Figure 2 shows the CDF of the median and the mean stalling length for the two different network capacities B. It can be seen that the curves for the mean stalling length differ with B. Nevertheless, the minimum of the average stalling length is about 2 s and for most videos the mean stalling length is below 6 s. However, there are several videos which show an even larger mean stalling length. A closer look at the individual application level stalling traces revealed that this large average stalling length was mostly caused by one large single stalling event during the playout of the individual video clip. These video clips correspond to the outliers as identified for the stalling frequency in Figure 1.

We therefore take a closer look at the median of the stalling length to attenuate the impact of large single stalling events. In that case, the CDFs of the median of the stalling length for the two different network capacities are very close together and no impact of the bottleneck capacity on the median can be observed. In particular, the observed stalling lengths are mainly between 2 s and 5 s. Because of this observation and no correlations with other variables, we conclude that the implementation of the video playout buffer determines mainly the stalling length.

Summarizing this section, the stalling pattern of a video can be described by stalling frequency F and stalling length L. The stalling frequency is determined by the ratio of video bit rate and bottleneck capacity. The length of a single stalling event is in the order of a few seconds and lies between 2 s and 6 s mainly.

3   Subjective Study on YouTube Video Delivery via TCP

For linking the stalling patterns for YouTube video streaming via TCP to the user perceived quality, we briefly summarize our former subjective user study [3,10] conducted by means of crowdsourcing. Crowdsourcing means to outsource a task (like video quality testing) to a large, anonymous crowd of users in the form of an open call. Crowdsourcing platforms in the Internet, like Amazon

Table 2. Mapping functions between MOS and number N of stalling events of length L as well as coefficient of determination for TCP transmission

length L	mapping function $f_L(N)$	coef. of determination R_L^2
1 s	$f_1(N) = 3.26 \cdot e^{-0.37 \cdot N} + 1.65$	0.941
2 s	$f_2(N) = 2.99 \cdot e^{-0.69 \cdot N} + 1.95$	0.923
3 s	$f_3(N) = 2.99 \cdot e^{-0.96 \cdot N} + 2.01$	0.997
4 s	$f_4(N) = 3.35 \cdot e^{-0.89 \cdot N} + 1.62$	0.978

Mechanical Turk or Microworkers.com [11], offer access to a large number of internationally widespread users in the Internet and distribute the work submitted by an employer among the users. The work is typically organized at a finer granularity and large jobs (like a QoE test campaign) are split into cheap (micro-)tasks that can be rapidly performed by the crowd.

With crowdsourcing, subjective user studies can be efficiently conducted at low costs with adequate user numbers for obtaining statistically significant QoE scores [12]. However, reliability of results cannot be trusted because of the anonymity and remoteness of participants (cf. [13] and references therein): some subjects may submit incorrect results in order to maximize their income by completing as many tasks as possible; others just may not work correctly due to lack of supervision. In [3,14], we showed that results quality are an inherent problem of crowdsourcing, but can be dramatically improved by filtering based on additional test design measures, e.g. by including consistency and content questions, as well as application usage monitoring.

In several crowdsourcing campaigns, we focused on quantifying the impact of stalling on YouTube QoE and varied (1) the number of stalling events from $N = 0$ to $N = 6$ as well as (2) the length of a single stalling event from $L = 1$ s to $L = 4$ s. The stalling events were periodically simulated, i.e. every D/N seconds a single stalling event of constant duration L occured. The duration of all test videos was 30 s. We also considered the influence of (3) the different crowdsourcing campaigns, (4) the test video id in order to take into account the type of video as well as the resolution, used codec settings, etc. Further, we asked the users to additionally rate (5) whether they liked the content.

As an outcome of this subjective study, we found that the stalling parameters N and L clearly dominate the user ratings and are the key influence factors. Surprisingly, the user ratings are statistically independent from the video parameters (like resolution of the YouTube videos, video motion, type of content like news or music clip, etc.) or whether the users liked the content or not.

For quantifying the impact of stalling on QoE, the subjective user ratings for a particular stalling pattern are averaged resulting into a so-called mean opinion score (MOS) according to ITU-T Recommendation ITU-T P.800.1 [15]. MOS takes on the values 1 = bad, 2 = poor, 3 = fair, 4 = good, and 5 = excellent. Figure 3 depicts the MOS values for one and three seconds stalling length for varying number of stalling events. In addition, the MOS values are fitted according the IQX hypothesis as discussed in [16]. The IQX hypothesis formulates a

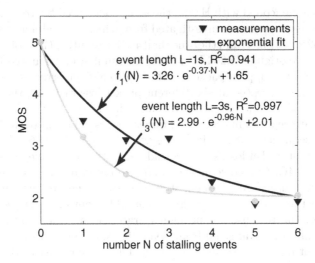

Fig. 3. MOS values for one and three seconds stalling length in case of TCP based video streaming

fundamentail relationship between QoE and an impairment factor corresponding to the QoS. According to the IQX hypothesis, the change of QoE depends on the current level of QoE – the expectation level– given the same amount of change of the QoS value. Mathematically, this relationship can be expressed by a differential equation

$$\frac{\partial QoE}{\partial QoS} = -\beta(QoE - \gamma) \tag{2}$$

which can be easily solved as an exponential functional relationship between QoE and QoS.

In the context of YouTube QoE for TCP based video streaming, the number of stallings is considered as impairment. Hence, QoE in terms of MOS is described by an exponential function. The mapping functions between the number N of stalling events of length L are given in Table 2 which also shows the coefficients of determination R_L^2 for the different fitting functions being close to perfect match, i.e. $R_L^2 = 1$.

The results in Figure 3 show that users tend to be highly dissatisfied with two ore more stalling events per clip. However, for the case of a stalling length of 1 s, the user ratings are substantially better for same number of stallings. Nonetheless, users are likely to be dissatisfied in case of four or more stalling events, independent of the stalling duration.

4   Quality Assessment of UDP-Based Video Transmission

For assessing the user perceived quality of YouTube video streaming using the UDP transport protocol, we rely on a publicly available database, that is the "EPFL-PoliMI video quality assessment database" at http://vqa.como.polimi.it/. Its video streams are encoded with H.264, the same codec used by YouTube. Twelve different video sequences were investigated from which one half has a spatial CIF resolution (352×240 pixel) and the other half 4CIF resolution (704×480 pixel). For each of the twelve original H.264 bit-streams, a number of corrupted bit-streams were generated, by dropping packets according to a given error pattern. The error patterns were generated at six different packet loss ratios R, that are 0.1 %, 0.4 %, 1 %, 3 %, 5 %, 10 %. Furthermore, two different types of error patterns are considered, that are random errors and bursty errors. Thus, in total, 72 CIF and 72 4CIF video sequences with packet losses as well as the original 6 CIF and 6 4CIF sequences without packet losses were considered in the subjective tests.

The CIF and 4CIF video sequences were presented in two separate test sessions to the test users. At the end of each video sequence, the subjects were asked to rate the quality using a five-point ITU continuous adjectival scale. Using a slider, the test users continuously rate the instantaneously perceived quality using an adjectival scale from "bad" to "excellent", which corresponds to an equivalent numerical scale from 0 to 5. Thus, in contrast to the subjective user study in the previous section 3, "bad" quality rating y is any continuous value between 0 and 1, i.e. $0 \leq y \leq 1$, while "excellent" quality rating means $4 < y \leq 5$. In total, fourty naive subjects took part in the subjective tests. More details on the subjective test can be found in [17,4].

Figure 4 shows the MOS depending on the simulated packet loss ratio R for the two different resolutions CIF and 4CIF. For each packet loss ratio R and each video resolution, the subjective ratings from all test users (across the different video contents and the type of error pattern) were averaged to obtain the corresponding MOS value. It can be seen that the MOS strongly decays with increasing network impairment in terms of packet loss.

To this end, we consider the packet loss ratio as impairment factor on the QoE. Hence, we can apply again the IQX hypothesis in order to derive a mapping function between the QoS impairment, i.e. the packet loss ratio, and the QoE in terms of MOS. As a result, we obtain an exponential mapping function between QoE and QoS which is depicted as solid line in Figure 4. Furthermore, the mapping function itself is shown in the plot. Again, we see a very good match of the mapping function and the measured MOS values which is quantified by the coefficient of determination being close to a perfect match.

As a result, we see that in the case of UDP-based video streaming, packet loss is a key influence factor on QoE. In contrast, the resolution of the video contents (CIF vs. 4CIF) has only a minor impact on the MOS.

5   Comparison of Youtube QoE for TCP and UDP

For quantifying the influence of the transport protocol on the QoE, we consider now the bottleneck scenario with a given bottleneck capacity B. In case of TCP based video streaming, the bottleneck may lead to stalling as QoE impairment. According to our findings in Section 2 a given bottleneck link capacity results in a certain stalling pattern, i.e. a certain stalling frequency F and a certain stalling

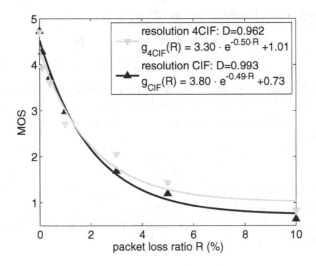

Fig. 4. MOS values and mapping function between packet loss ratio R for UDP based streaming

length L. With the YouTube QoE model in Section 3, the stalling pattern can then be mapped to a MOS. In case of UDP based video streaming, the bottleneck link capacity may lead to packet loss as QoE impairment. Then, the QoE model from Section 4 can be applied to quantify the QoE in terms of MOS for a given packet loss ratio R. Hence, in both cases, TCP or UDP based video streaming, the bottleneck link capacity is mapped to MOS. In the following, we show how this mapping is applied in case of TCP (Section 5.1) and UDP (Section 5.2). In order to have a fair comparison between UDP and TCP based transmission of video contents, we neglect any initial delays. Finally, Section 5.3 compares both protocols from the end user perspective, when the video stream is delivered over a bottleneck.

5.1 TCP Based Video Streaming with Stalling

The download time T_d of a video of duration D which is encoded with average video bitrate V depends on the capacity B of the bottleneck,

$$T_d = \frac{V \cdot D}{B} .$$

(3)

Thus, the total stalling time T_s follows as difference $T_d - D$ between the download time and the video duration,

$$T_s = \left(\frac{V}{B} - 1 \right) D .$$

(4)

Then, the number N of stalling events of length L is

$$N = \left(\frac{V}{B} - 1\right) \frac{D}{L} = \left(\frac{1}{\rho} - 1\right) \frac{D}{L}. \tag{5}$$

Together with the normalized throughput ρ which is defined as the ratio between the bandwidth limitation B and the video bitrate V, i.e. $\rho = \frac{B}{V}$, we arrive at the following mapping function Υ_L between the normalized throughput and the MOS value,

$$\Upsilon_L(\rho) = f_L\left(\left(\frac{1}{\rho} - 1\right)\frac{D}{L}\right), \tag{6}$$

where $f_L(N)$ is defined as in Section 3 in Figure 3 or Table 2.

In addition to this simple model for obtaining the stalling pattern to a given bottleneck capacity B, we can use the fitting function in Eq.(1) which returns the stalling frequency $F = N/D$ for given $V/B = 1/\rho$.

5.2   UDP Based Streaming with Packet Loss

During the video of length D, about $\frac{D \cdot B}{S}$ packets of size S are downloaded with a download bandwidth B. Since the video (encoded with bitrate V) consists of $\frac{D \cdot V}{S}$ packets, the packet loss ratio follows as

$$R = 1 - \frac{B}{V}. \tag{7}$$

Accordingly, the mapping Υ_v between the normalized throughput $\rho = \frac{B}{V}$ and the MOS value is derived as

$$\Upsilon_v(\rho) = f_v(1 - \rho) \tag{8}$$

using the mapping function $f_v(R)$ between the packet loss ratio R and the MOS value as defined in Section 4 for a given video resolution v.

5.3   Comparison of QoE for TCP and UDP Based Delivery of YouTube Videos

In this section, we combine the results from the previous subsections in order to compare the QoE for YouTube video streaming over a bottleneck with capacity B. For TCP based transmission, this results in stalling which degrades the QoE; for UDP based transmission, the bottleneck results into packet loss and corresponding visual impairments of the video.

Thus, for the current two Internet protocols, TCP and UDP, the same QoS impairment in terms of the bottleneck bandwidth will lead to completely different QoE impairments. Thus, it is possible to evaluate which kind of stalling pattern (in terms of number of stallings and length of a single stalling event) corresponds to which packet loss ratio, such that the user experiences the same

QoE. Figure 5a shows the number N of stallings on the x-axis and the corresponding packet loss ratio R on the y-axis which result in the same MOS value, which is indicated by the color of the point. Two different curves are depicted according to a stalling length of $L = 1\,\text{s}$ and $L = 4\,\text{s}$. For the mapping between packet loss and MOS we used the CIF resolution. For example, $N = 2$ stallings of length $L = 4\,\text{s}$ correspond to a packet loss ratio $R = 2\,\%$ and lead to a MOS value about 2, i.e. bad quality. It can be seen, that the transformation between both impairment factors is quite complex and non-linear.

Finally, we compare both protocols, TCP and UDP, for a given bottleneck bandwidth B in terms of MOS. In particular, we use the normalized throughput ρ as ratio of the bottleneck bandwidth B and the video bitrate V. Then, we can directly use the mapping functions in Eq.(6) and in Eq.(8) based on the subjective user studies presented in Section 3 and in Section 4 for TCP and UDP, respectively.

Figure 5b shows the numerical results depending on the normalized throughput ρ. In case of TCP, we use the mapping functions based on the four different stalling length from $L = 1\,\text{s}$ to $L = 4\,\text{s}$. In addition, the measurement results from Section 2.2 are used. For the different videos streamed over a bottleneck, we measured the video bitrate, the duration of the video, the observed number of stallings, and the median of the stalling length. These values are used as input in Eq.(6) to obtain a MOS value. The first observation is that the measured stalling values mapped to MOS are in the range of the curves $\Upsilon_L(\rho)$.

In case of UDP, the MOS values are plotted for the CIF and the 4CIF resolution with respect to ρ in Figure 5b. The second observation is that UDP always performs worse than TCP from the end user perspective. Hence, for the same bottleneck capacity, the end user will likely more tolerate the resulting stalling in case of TCP than the resulting video quality degradation in case of UDP.

The results indicate that TCP based video streaming actually used by YouTube outperforms UDP based video streaming in terms of user perceived quality for network bottleneck scenarios. However, it has to be noted that also techniques for

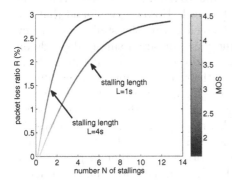

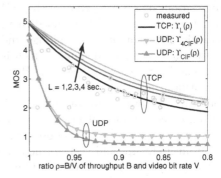

(a) MOS color plot wrt. stalling frequency (TCP) and packet loss ratio (UDP).

(b) Investigation of different bottleneck capacities with videos in CIF resolution.

Fig. 5. Comparison of UDP and TCP streaming in terms of Mean Opinion Scores

overcoming the video quality degradation due to packet losses in case of UDP do exist. By allowing buffering as well as additional retransmission mechanisms on the application layer, UDP based streaming approach might be enhanced significantly and even keep up with TCP. Furthermore, we have restricted the results of this paper to the bottleneck scenario. Therefore, it would be interesting to investigate if the results can be transfered to lossy links scenarios or if UDP might be the appropriate choice for such scenarios, as the TCP throughput is approximately proportional to $1/\sqrt{R}$, cf. [18]. In addition, an investigation of other transport protocols like DCCP and SCTP would reveal their ability for video streaming and identify the optimal transport protocol for a YouTube like streaming service.

6   Conclusions and Future Work

Quality of Experience as a subjective measure of the end-customer's quality perception has become a key concept for analyzing Internet applications like YouTube video streaming from the end user's perspective. Therefore, in this article we have taken a closer look at the impact of the current Internet transport protocols on QoE for YouTube video streaming. In particular, we have investigated the quality degradations which occur in case of network bandwidth bottlenecks in case of TCP and UDP based video streaming.

For UDP based video streaming, a network bottleneck may result into packet loss and therefore visual impairments of the video contents. In contrast, TCP based video streaming, as currently implemented by YouTube, will not suffer from video quality degradation, i.e. the video content itself is not disturbed, however the bottleneck may lead to stalling of the video stream. The question arises which of both protocols is more appropriate in case of a bottleneck from the end user's perspective.

Therefore, we conducted a large-scale measurement study of YouTube video streaming over a bottleneck, in order to derive and model the resulting stalling pattern. This stalling pattern is non-trivial, due to a number of interactions and correlations on several layers of the ISO/OSI stack. However, we found that the stalling patterns can be modeled in the following way: the stalling frequency as ratio of the number of stallings and the video duration simply depends on the normalized video demand, which is the ratio of the video bit rate and the bottleneck link capacity (see 1). However, their relation follows a non-linear exponential function. The median of the length of a single stalling event was found to be between two seconds and four seconds. With these two parameters, the observed stalling pattern can be modeled for a given bottleneck bandwidth.

As second contribution, we presented the results of two subjective user studies from literature and transformed them accordingly in order to predict user perceived quality for a given bottleneck bandwidth. The first subjective measurement campaign considers QoE when stalling occurs in case of TCP video streaming. The second subjective measurement study allows to quantify QoE when packets get lost in case of UDP video streaming. Finally, this allows to compare the influence of UDP and TCP in the bottleneck scenario. Our results show that TCP outperforms UDP for any given bottleneck bandwidth. Furthermore, we have seen that some basic considerations regarding the observed stalling pattern also enable accurate results in terms of predicted QoE.

This work represents an important first step towards the appropriate selection of network protocols and functionality according to the demands and properties of Internet services based on the strict integration of the actual end user's perspective. This QoE optimized selection may be realized by means of functional composition, network virtualization or other frameworks such as the Framework for Internet Innovation [19]. Future work has to deal with application-network interaction in general. For example adaptive streaming [20] may overcome limitations in the network by reducing the application requirements, but adequate QoE models taking into account video quality adaptation have to be derived.

Acknowledgments. This work was partly funded by Deutsche Forschungsgemeinschaft (DFG) under grants HO 4770/1-1 and TR257/31-1, in the framework of the EU ICT Project SmartenIt (FP7-2012-ICT-317846), the project U-0 funded by the Austrian competence center program COMET, and the COST QUALINET Action IC1003. The authors alone are responsible for the content.

References

1. Cisco Systems Inc.: Cisco Visual Networking Index: Forecast and Methodology, 2009-2014 (June 2010)
2. Shiels, M.: YouTube at five- 2 bn views a day (2011)
3. Hoßfeld, T., Schatz, R., Seufert, M., Hirth, M., Zinner, T., Tran-Gia, P.: Quantification of YouTube QoE via Crowdsourcing. In: IEEE International Workshop on Multimedia Quality of Experience - Modeling, Evaluation, and Directions (MQoE 2011), Dana Point, CA, USA (December 2011)
4. De Simone, F., Tagliasacchi, M., Naccari, M., Tubaro, S., Ebrahimi, T.: H.264/AVC video database for the evaluation of quality metrics. In: Proceedings of the 35th International Conference on Acoustics, Speech, and Signal Processing, ICASSP 2010 (2010)
5. Alcock, S., Nelson, R.: Application flow control in youtube video streams. SIGCOMM Comput. Commun. Rev. 41 (April 2011)
6. Nygren, E., Sitaraman, R.K., Sun, J.: The akamai network: a platform for high-performance internet applications. SIGOPS Oper. Syst. Rev. 44 (August 2010)
7. Mori, T., Kawahara, R., Hasegawa, H., Shimogawa, S.: Characterizing traffic flows originating from large-scale video sharing services. In: Ricciato, F., Mellia, M., Biersack, E. (eds.) TMA 2010. LNCS, vol. 6003, pp. 17–31. Springer, Heidelberg (2010)
8. Adhikari, V., Jain, S., Zhang, Z.: Where do you tube? uncovering youtube server selection strategy. In: IEEE ICCCN 2011 (July 2011)
9. Hoßfeld, T., Zinner, T., Schatz, R., Seufert, M., Tran-Gia, P.: Transport Protocol Influences on YouTube QoE. Technical Report 482, Uni. Würzburg (July 2011)

10. Hoßfeld, T., Schatz, R., Biersack, E., Plissonneau, L.: Internet Video Delivery in YouTube: From Traffic Measurements to Quality of Experience. In: Biersack, E., Callegari, C., Matijasevic, M. (eds.) Data Traffic Monitoring and Analysis: From Measurement, Classification and Anomaly Detection to Quality of Experience. Springer's Computer Communications and Networks series (2013)
11. Hirth, M., Hoßfeld, T., Tran-Gia, P.: Anatomy of a Crowdsourcing Platform - Using the Example of Microworkers.com. In: Workshop on Future Internet and Next Generation Networks (FINGNet), Seoul, Korea (June 2011)
12. Chen, K., Chang, C., Wu, C., Chang, Y., Lei, C., Sinica, C.: Quadrant of Euphoria: A Crowdsourcing Platform for QoE Assessment. IEEE Network 24(2) (March 2010)
13. Hirth, M., Hoßfeld, T., Tran-Gia, P.: Cost-Optimal Validation Mechanisms and Cheat-Detection for Crowdsourcing Platforms. In: Workshop on Future Internet and Next Generation Networks, Seoul, Korea (June 2011)
14. Hoßfeld, T., Keimel, C., Hirth, M., Gardlo, B., Habigt, J., Diepold, K., Tran-Gia, P.: CrowdTesting: A Novel Methodology for Subjective User Studies and QoE Evaluation. Technical Report 486, University of Würzburg (February 2013)
15. ITU-T Rec. P.800.1: Mean opinion score (mos) terminology (February 2003)
16. Fiedler, M., Hoßfeld, T., Tran-Gia, P.: A Generic Quantitative Relationship between Quality of Experience and Quality of Service. IEEE Network Special Issue on Improving QoE for Network Services (June 2010)
17. De Simone, F., Naccari, M., Tagliasacchi, M., Dufaux, F., Tubaro, S., Ebrahimi, T.: Subjective assessment of H.264/AVC video sequences transmitted over a noisy channel. In: Proceedings of the First International Workshop on Quality of Multimedia Experience, QoMEX 2009 (2009)
18. Padhye, J., Firoiu, V., Towsley, D., Kurose, J.: Modeling tcp throughput: a simple model and its empirical validation. SIGCOMM Comput. Commun. Rev. 28 (October 1998)
19. Koponen, T., et al.: Architecting for innovation. SIGCOMM Comput. Commun. Rev. 41 (2011)
20. Sieber, C., Hoßfeld, T., Zinner, T., Tran-Gia, P., Timmerer, C.: Implementation and User-centric Comparison of a Novel Adaptation Logic for DASH with SVC. In: IFIP/IEEE International Workshop on Quality of Experience Centric Management (QCMan), Ghent, Belgium (May 2013)

Increasing the Coverage of Vantage Points in Distributed Active Network Measurements by Crowdsourcing

Valentin Burger, Matthias Hirth, Christian Schwartz,
Tobias Hoßfeld, and Phuoc Tran-Gia

University of Würzburg, Germany
Chair of Communication Networks

Abstract. Internet video constitutes more than half of all consumer traffic. Most of the video traffic is delivered by content delivery networks (CDNs). The huge amount of traffic from video CDNs poses problems to access providers. To understand and monitor the impact of video traffic on access networks and the topology of CDNs, distributed active measurements are needed. Recently used measurement platforms are mainly hosted in National Research and Education Networks (NRENs). However, the view of these platforms on the CDN is very limited, since the coverage of NRENs is low in developing countries. Furthermore, campus networks do not reflect the characteristics of end user access networks. We propose to use crowdsourcing to increase the coverage of vantage points in distributed active network measurements. In this study, we compare measurements of a global CDN conducted in PlanetLab with measurements assigned to workers of a crowdsourcing platform. Thus, the coverage of vantage points and the sampled part of the global video CDN are analyzed. Our results show that the capability of PlanetLab to measure global CDNs is rather low, since the vast majority of requests is directed to the US. By using a crowdsourcing platform we obtain a diverse set of vantage points that reveals more than twice as many autonomous systems deploying video servers.

1 Introduction

Internet video constitutes more than half of all consumer Internet traffic globally, and its percentage will further increase [4]. Most of the video traffic is delivered by content delivery networks (CDNs). Today the world's largest video CDN is YouTube. Since Google took over YouTube in 2006 the infrastructure of the video delivery platform has grown to be a global content delivery network. The global expansion of the CDN was also necessary to cope with growing demand of user demands and the high expectations on the video playback. Therefore, content delivery networks try to bring content geographically close to users. However, the traffic from content delivery networks is highly asymmetric and produces a large amount of costly inter-domain traffic [11]. Especially Internet Service Providers (ISPs) providing access to many end users have problems to

K. Fischbach and U.R. Krieger (Eds.): MMB & DFT 2014, LNCS 8376, pp. 151–161, 2014.

deal with the huge amount of traffic originating from YouTube. Furthermore, the Google CDN is constantly growing and changing, which makes it difficult for access providers to adapt their infrastructure accordingly.

To understand and monitor the impact of YouTube traffic on ISPs and the topology of CDNs appropriate measurements are aquired. Due to YouTube's load-balancing and caching mechanisms the YouTube video server selection is highly dependent on the location of the measurement points. Hence, we need a globally distributed measurement platform to perform active measurements to uncover the location of YouTube servers. Recent work [1,2] has performed such measurements in PlanetLab [13], a global test bed that provides measurement nodes at universities and research institutes. The problem is that probes disseminated from PlanetLab nodes origin solely from National Research and Education Networks (NRENs). This may not reflect the perspective of access ISPs which have a different connection to the YouTube CDN with different peering or transit agreements.

To achieve a better view on the YouTube CDN from the perspective of end users in access networks we use a commercial crowdsourcing platform to recruit regular Internet users as measurement probes. Thus, we increase the coverage of vantage points for the distributed measurement of the YouTube CDN. To evaluate the impact of the measurement platform and the coverage of their vantage point, we perform the same measurements using PlanetLab nodes and crowdsourcing users and compare the obtained results.

Our measurements show that distributed measurements in PlanetLab are not capable to capture a globally distributed network, since the PlanetLab nodes are located in NRENs where the view on the Internet is limited. We demonstrate that recruiting users via crowdsourcing platforms as measurement probes can offer a complementary view on the Internet, since they provide access to real end users devices located out side of these dedicated research networks. This complementary view can help to gain a better understanding of the characteristics of Video CDNs. Concepts like ALTO or economic traffic management (ETM) [7] need a global view of the CDN structure to optimize traffic beyond the borders of ISPs. Finally, models for simulation and performance evaluation of mechanisms incorporating CDNs need to apply the characteristics identified by crowd sourced network measurements.

This paper is structured as follows: Section 2 explains the basic structure and functionality of the YouTube CDN, give as short overview of the concept of crowdsourcing, and the reviews work related. The measurements conducted in the PlanetLab and via crowdsourcing are described in Section 3. In Section 4 we details on the measurement results and their importance for the design of distributed network measurements. We conclude this work in Section 5.

2   Background and Related Work

In this section, we briefly describe the structure of the YouTube video CDN and give a short introduction in the principles of crowdsourcing. Further, we summarize related work in the field of distributed active measurements of CDNs as well as work related to crowdsourcing aided network measurements.

2.1 Evolution and Structure of Content Delivery Networks

Since the launch of the YouTube service content delivery has drastically changed. The number of users watching videos on demand has massively increased and the bandwidth to access videos is much higher. Furthermore, the increased bandwidth enables web services to be interactive by using dynamic server- or client-side scripts. The appearance of dynamic services and the increasing quality of multimedia content raised user expectations and the demand on the servers. To bring content in high quality to end-users with low latency and to deal with increasing demand, content providers have to replicate and distribute the content to get it close to end-users. Thus, content delivery networks such as the Google CDN evolved.

The global expansion of the CDNs also changes the structure of the Internet. Google has set up a global backbone which interconnects Google's data centers to important edge points of presence. Since these points of presence are distributed across the globe, Google can offer direct peering links to access networks with many end users. Such, access network providers save transit costs, while Google is able to offer services with low latency. To bring content even closer to users ISPs can deploy Google servers inside their own network to serve popular content, including YouTube videos [5].

To select the closest server for a content request and to implement load balancing CDNs use the Domain Name System (DNS). Typically a user watches a YouTube video by visiting a YouTube video URL with a web browser. The browser then contacts the local DNS server to resolve the hostname. Thereafter, the HTTP request is directed to a front end web server that returns an HTML page including URLs for default and fallback video servers. These URLs are again resolved by DNS servers to physical video servers, which stream the content. The last DNS resolution can happen repeatedly until a server with enough capacity is found to serve the request. Thus, load balancing between the servers is achieved [1].

2.2 Crowdsourcing

Crowdsourcing is an emerging service in the Internet that enables outsourcing jobs to a large, anonymous crowd of users [16]. So called *Crowdsourcing platforms* acts as mediator between the users submitting the tasks, the *employers*, and the users willing to complete these tasks, the *workers*. All interactions between workers and employers are usually managed through these platforms and no direct communication exits, resulting in a very loose worker-employer relationship. The complexity of Crowdsourcing tasks varies between simple transcriptions of single words [17] and even research and development tasks [10]. Usually, the task description are much more fine granular than in comparable forms in traditional work organization [8]. This small task granularity hold in particular for *micro-tasks*, which can be completed within a few seconds to a few minutes. These tasks are usually highly repetitive, e.g., adding textual descriptions to pictures, and are grouped in larger units, so called *campaigns*.

2.3 Related Work

There already exist a number of publications which study the structure of the YouTube CDN and its selection of video servers. A distributed active measurement platform is necessary for these evaluation, because the CDN mechanisms consider the client locations, both geographical as well as in terms of the connected access network. In [15] two university campus networks and three ISP networks were used to investigate the YouTube CDN from vantage points in three different countries. The results show that locality in terms of latency is not the only factor for video server selection.

While the view of five different ISPs on a global CDN is still narrow, the authors of [2] used PlanetLab to investigate the YouTube server selection strategies and load-balancing. They find that YouTube massively deploys caches in many different locations worldwide, placing them at the edge of the Google autonomous system or even at ISP networks. The work is enhanced in [1], where they uncover a detailed architecture of the YouTube CDN, showing a 3-tier physical video server hierarchy. Furthermore, they identify a layered logical structure in the video server namespace, allowing YouTube to leverage the existing DNS system and the HTTP protocol.

However, to assess the expansion of the whole YouTube CDN and its cache locations in access networks, the PlanetLab platform, which is located solely in NRENs, is not suitable, since it does not reflect the perspective of end users in ISP access networks. Therefore, a different distributed measurement platform is used in [14] which runs on end user equipment and thus implies a higher diversity of nodes and reflects the perspective of end user in access networks. However, the number of nodes that was available for the measurement is too small to obtain a global coverage of vantage points.

To achieve both, the view of access networks and a high global coverage with a large number of measurement points, the participation of a large number of end users in the measurement is necessary. Bischof et al. [3] implemented an approach to gather data form peer-to-peer networks to globally characterize the service quality of ISPs using volunteers.

In contrast to this we propose using a commercial crowdsourcing platform to recruit users running a specially designed measurement software and therewith act as measurement probes. In comparison to other approaches using volunteers, this approach offers better scalability and controllability, because the number and origin of the participants can be adjusted using the recruiting mechanism of the crowdsourcing platform. This is confirmed by Table 1 which compares a crowdsourcing study with a social network study quantitatively. The crowdsourcing study is described in [9]. The study is designed to assess the subjective QoE for multimedia applications, like video streaming. The same study was

Table 1. Quantitative Comparison: Crowdsourcing / Social Network Study

	Crowdsourcing (C)	Social network (S)
Implementation time	about 2 weeks; test implemented via dynamic web pages, application monitoring	same as for (C)
Time for acquiring people	5 minutes	2 hours, as users (groups) were asked individually
Campaign submission cost	16 Euro	0 Euro
Subjects reward	0.15 Euro	0 Euro
Number of test conditions	3	3
Advertised people	100	350
Campaign completion time	31 hours	26 days; strongly depends on advertised user groups however
Participating users	100	95
Reliable users (very strict filtering of users)	30	58
Number of different countries of subjects	30	3; strongly depends on users groups however

conducted additionally in a social network environment for recruiting test users. Table 1 shows that acquiring people in crowdsourcing platforms takes very short time compared to asking volunteers in a social network, which allows adding participants easily. Furthermore, the completion time of the campaign of 31 hours is much shorter compared to the 26 days for the social network campaign. Finally, in the crowdsourcing campaign workers can be selected according to their country, which allows distributing the campaign on many different countries. In the social network the coverage of countries depends on the network of user groups, which spread the campaign. Hence, it is easy to control the number and origin of subjects participating in a crowdsourcing campaign and the completion time is considerably fast, which makes the campaign scalable and controllable. The price you pay is the reward for the workers that summed up to a total of 16 Euro for that campaign.

To the best of our knowledge this is the first work which uses crowdsourcing for a distributed active measurement platform.

3   Measurement Description

To assess the capability of crowdsourcing for distributed active measurements we conduct measurements with both PlanetLab and the commercial Crowdsourcing platform Microworkers [18]. We measure the global expansion of the YouTube CDN by resolving physical server IP-addresses for clients in different locations.

3.1   Description of the PlanetLab Measurement

PlanetLab is a publicly available test bed, which currently consists of 1173 nodes at 561 sites. The sites are usually located at universities or research institutes. Hence, they are connected to the Internet via NRENs. To conduct a measurement in PlanetLab a slice has to be set up which consists of a set of virtual machines running on different nodes in the PlanetLab test bed. Researchers can then access these slides to install measurement scripts. In our case the measurement script implemented in Java extracted the server hostnames of the page of three predetermined YouTube videos and resolved the IP addresses of the physical video servers. The IP addresses of the PlanetLab clients and the resolved IP addresses of the physical video servers were stored in a database. To be able to investigate locality in the YouTube CDN, the geo-location of servers and clients is necessary. For that purpose the IP addresses were mapped to geographic coordinates with MaxMinds GeoIP database [12]. The measurement was conducted on 220 randomly chosen PlanetLab nodes in March 2012.

3.2   Description of the Crowdsourcing Measurement

To measure the topology of the YouTube CDN from an end users point of view who is connected by an ISP network we used the crowdsourcing platform Microworker [18]. The workers were asked to access a web page with an embedded Java application, which automatically conducts client side measurements. These include, among others, the extraction of the default and fallback server URLs from three predetermined YouTube video pages. The extracted URLs were resolved to the physical IP address of the video servers locally on the clients. The IP addresses of video servers and of the workers client were sent to a server which collected all measurements and stored them in a database.

In a first measurement run, in December 2011, 60 different users of Microworkers participated in the measurements. Previous evaluation have shown, that the majority of the platform users is located in Asia [6], and accordingly most of the participants of there first campaign were from Bangladesh. In order to obtain wide measurement coverage the number of Asian workers participating in a second measurement campaign, conducted in March 2012, was restricted. In total, 247 workers from 32 different countries, finished the measurements successfully identifying 1592 unique physical YouTube server IP addresses.

4   Results

In this section we show the results of the distributed measurement of the global CDN. The obtained results show the distribution of clients and servers over different countries. Furthermore, the mapping on autonomous systems gives insights to the coverage of the Internet.

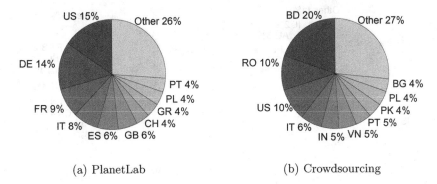

(a) PlanetLab   (b) Crowdsourcing

Fig. 1. Distribution of measurement points on countries in a) PlanetLab and b) Crowdsourcing platform

4.1   Distribution of Vantage Points on Countries

To investigate the coverage of measurement points we study the distribution of the PlanetLab nodes and Crowdsourcing workers. Figure 1(a) shows the distribution of PlanetLab nodes on countries over the world. The pie chart is denoted with the country codes and the percentage of PlanetLab nodes in the respective country. Most of the 220 clients are located in the US with 15% of all clients. However, more than 50% of the clients are located in West-Europe. Only few clients are located in different parts of the world. The tailored distribution towards Western countries is caused by the fact, that the majority of the PlanetLab nodes are located in the US or in western Europe.

Figure 1(b) shows the geo-location of workers on the crowdsourcing platform. In contrast to PlanetLab, most of the 247 measurement points are located in Asia-Pacific and East-Europe. The majority of the participating workers 20% are from Bangladesh followed by Romania and the US with 10%. This bias is caused by the overall worker distribution on the platform [6]. However, this can be influences to a certain extend by limiting the access to the tasks to certain geographical regions.

4.2   Distribution of Identified YouTube Servers on Countries

To investigate the expansion of the YouTube CDN we study the distribution of YouTube servers over the world. Figure 2(a) shows the location of the servers identified by the PlanetLab nodes. The requests are mainly directed to servers in the US. Only 20% of the requests were directed to servers not located in the US.

The servers identified by the crowdsourcing measurement are shown in Figure 2(b). The amount of requests being directed to servers located in the US is still high. 44% of clients were directed to the US. However, in this case the amount of requests resolved to servers outside the US is higher. In contrast to the PlanetLab measurement many requests are served locally in the countries

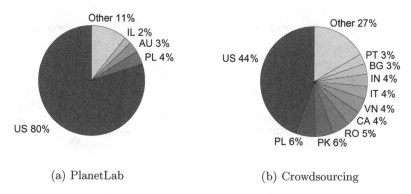

(a) PlanetLab   (b) Crowdsourcing

Fig. 2. Distribution of physical YouTube servers on countries accessed from a) PlanetLab nodes and b) workers of a crowdsourcing platform

of clients. Furthermore, the decrease of 80% to 44% of request being directed to the US shows a huge difference.

Hence, network probes being overrepresented in the US and Europe leads to a limited view of the content delivery network and the Internet. This shows the impact of different locations of measurement points on the view of the CDN. It also demands a careful choice of vantage points for a proper design of experiments in distributed network measurements. Although both sets of measurement points are globally distributed the fraction of the CDN which is discovered by the probes has very different characteristics.

The amount of servers which is located in the US almost doubles for the PlanetLab measurement. While 44% of the requests are resolved to US servers in the Crowdsourcing measurement, nearly all requests of PlanetLab nodes are served by YouTube servers located in the US. Although less than 15% of clients are in US, requests are frequently directed to servers in the US. That means that there is still potential to further distribute the content in the CDN.

4.3   Coverage of Autonomous Systems with YouTube Servers

To identify the distribution of clients on ISPs and to investigate the expansion of CDNs on autonomous systems we map the measurement points to the corresponding autonomous systems.

Figure 3(a) shows the autonomous systems of YouTube servers accessed by PlanetLab nodes. The autonomous systems were ranked by the number of YouTube servers located in the AS. The empirical probability $P(k)$ that a server belongs to AS with rank k is depicted against the AS rank. The number of autonomous systems hosting YouTube servers that are accessed by Planet-Lab nodes is limited to less than 30. The top three ranked ASes are AS15169, AS36040 and AS43515. AS15169 is the Google autonomous system which includes the Google backbone. The Google backbone is a global network that reaches to worldwide points of presence to offer peering agreements at peering points. AS36040 is the YouTube network connecting the main datacenter

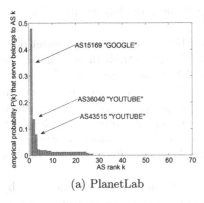
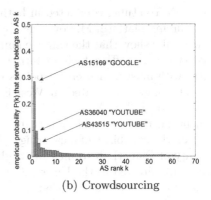

(a) PlanetLab   (b) Crowdsourcing

Fig. 3. Distribution of YouTube servers on autonomous systems from a) PlanetLab and b) Crowdsourcing perspective

in Mountain-View which is also managed by Google. AS43515 belongs to the YouTube site in Europe which is administrated in Ireland. Hence, two thirds of the servers are located in an autonomous systems which is managed by Google. Only few requests are served from datacenters not being located in a Google AS. The reason that request from PlanetLab are most frequently served by ASes owned by Google might be a good interconnection of the NRENs to the Google ASes.

Figure 3(b) depicts the autonomous systems where requests to YouTube videos from the crowdsourcing workers were directed. The empirical probability that a server belongs to an AS has been plotted dependent on the AS rank. The YouTube servers identified by the crowdsourcing probes are located in more than 60 autonomous systems. Hence, the YouTube CDN is expanded on a higher range of ASes from the crowdsourcing perspective compared to PlanetLab. Again the three autonomous systems serving most requests are the ASes managed by Google, respectively YouTube. But the total number of requests served by a Google managed AS is only 41%. Hence, in contrary to the PlanetLab measurement, requests are served most frequently from ASes not owned by Google. Here, caches at local ISPs managed by YouTube could be used to bring the content close to users without providing own infrastructure. This would also explain the large number of identified ASes providing a YouTube server. The results show that the PlanetLab platform is not capable to measure the structure of a global CDN, since large parts of the CDN are not accessed by clients in NRENs.

5   Conclusion

In this study we proposed the usage of crowdsourcing platforms for distributed network measurements to increase the coverage of vantage points. We evaluated the capability to discover global networks by comparing the coverage of video server detected using a crowdsourcing platform as opposed to using the PlanetLab platform. To this end, we used exemplary measurements of the global video CDN YouTube, conducted in both the PlanetLab platform as well as the crowdsourcing platform Microworkers.

Our results show that the vantage points of the concurring measurement platforms have very different characteristics. In the PlanetLab measurement the country with most measurement points is the US, while more than 50% of measurement points are located in West-Europe. In contrary most measurement points are located in Asia-Pacific and East-Europe in the crowdsourcing measurement. Further we could show that the distribution of vantage points has high impact on the capability of measuring a global content distribution network. The capability of PlanetLab to measure a global CDNs is rather low, since 80% of requests are directed to the United States.

Finally, our results confirm that the coverage of vantage points is increased by crowdsourcing. Using the crowdsourcing platform we obtain a diverse set of vantage points that reveals more than twice as many autonomous systems deploying video servers than the widely used PlanetLab platform. Part of future work is to determine if the coverage of vantage points can be even further increased by targeting workers from specific locations to get representative measurement points for all parts of the world.

Acknowledgement. The authors would like to thank Philipp Amrehn and Christian Moldovan for conducting the measurements and implementing the evaluation scripts.

This work was partly funded by Deutsche Forschungsgemeinschaft (DFG) under grants HO 4770/1-1 and TR257/31-1 and in the framework of the EU ICT Project SmartenIT (FP7-2012-ICT-317846). The authors alone are responsible for the content.

References

1. Adhikari, V., Jain, S., Chen, Y., Zhang, Z.: Vivisecting YouTube: An Active Measurement Study. In: Proceedings IEEE INFOCOM (2012)
2. Adhikari, V., Jain, S., Zhang, Z.: Where Do You "Tube"? Uncovering YouTube Server Selection Strategy. In: IEEE ICCCN (2011)
3. Bischof, Z.S., Otto, J.S., Sánchez, M.A., Rula, J.P., Choffnes, D.R., Bustamante, F.E.: Crowdsourcing isp characterization to the network edge. In: Proceedings of the First ACM SIGCOMM Workshop on Measurements Up the Stack (2011)
4. Cisco: Forecast and Methodology, 2012–2017. Cisco Visual Networking Index (2013)
5. Google: Peering & Content Delivery, https://peering.google.com/
6. Hirth, M., Hoßfeld, T., Tran-Gia, P.: Anatomy of a Crowdsourcing Platform - Using the Example of Microworkers.com. In: Workshop on Future Internet and Next Generation Networks (FINGNet), Seoul, Korea (2011)
7. Hoßfeld, T., Hausheer, D., Hecht, F., Lehrieder, F., Oechsner, S., Papafili, I., Racz, P., Soursos, S., Staehle, D., Stamoulis, G.D., Tran-Gia, P., Stiller, B.: An Economic Traffic Management Approach to Enable the TripleWin for Users, ISPs, and Overlay Providers. IOS Press Books Online, Towards the Future Internet - A European Research Perspective (2009)

8. Hoßfeld, T., Hirth, M., Tran-Gia, P.: Modeling of Crowdsourcing Platforms and Granularity of Work Organization in Future Internet. In: Proceedings of the International Teletraffic Congress, ITC (2011)
9. Hoßfeld, T., Schatz, R., Biersack, E., Plissonneau, L.: Internet Video Delivery in YouTube: From Traffic Measurements to Quality of Experience. In: Biersack, E., Callegari, C., Matijasevic, M. (eds.) Data Traffic Monitoring and Analysis. LNCS, vol. 7754, pp. 264–301. Springer, Heidelberg (2013)
10. InnoCentive, Inc.: Innocentive, http://www.innocentive.com/
11. Labovitz, C., Iekel-Johnson, S., McPherson, D., Oberheide, J., Jahanian, F.: Internet Inter-Domain Traffic. ACM SIGCOMM Computer Communication Review (2010)
12. MaxMind: GeoLite Databases, http://dev.maxmind.com/geoip/geolite/
13. PlanetLab: An open platform for developing, deploying, and accessing planetary-scale services, http://www.planet-lab.org/
14. Rafetseder, A., Metzger, F., Stezenbach, D., Tutschku, K.: Exploring youtube's content distribution network through distributed application-layer measurements: a first view. In: Proceedings of the 2011 International Workshop on Modeling, Analysis, and Control of Complex Networks (2011)
15. Torres, R., Finamore, A., Kim, J.R., Mellia, M., Munafo, M.M., Rao, S.: Dissecting Video Server Selection Strategies in the YouTube Cdn. In: 31st International Conference on Distributed Computing Systems, ICDCS (2011)
16. Tran-Gia, P., Hoßfeld, T., Hartmann, M., Hirth, M.: Crowdsourcing and its Impact on Future Internet Usage. it - Information Technology 55 (2013)
17. Von Ahn, L., Maurer, B., McMillen, C., Abraham, D., Blum, M.: recaptcha: Human-based character recognition via web security measures. Science (5895) (2008)
18. Weblabcenter, Inc.: Microworkers, http://microworkers.com/

The 15 Commandments of Market Entrance Pricing for Differentiated Network Services: An Antagonistic Analysis of Human vs. Market[*]

Patrick Zwickl[1], Peter Reichl[1,2], and Andreas Sackl[3]

[1] University of Vienna, Faculty of Computer Science,
Währingerstraße 29, 1090 Vienna, Austria
{Patrick.Zwickl,Peter.Reichl}@univie.ac.at
[2] Université Européenne de Bretagne/Télécom Bretagne,
2, rue de la Châtaigneraie, 35576 Cesson Sévigné, France
[3] FTW Telecommunications Research Center Vienna,
Donau-City-Straße 1/3rd floor, 1220 Vienna, Austria
sackl@ftw.at

Abstract. Confronted with soaring IP traffic demands and unsatisfying revenue prospects, charging and tariffing alternatives are about to regain significant attention in the telecommunications industry. While classical revenue optimization and customer perceptions, i.e., Quality of Experience (QoE), has been largely investigated by now, the understanding of customer valuations, i.e., willingness-to-pay, is still far from being sufficient. Hence, this paper revisits and extends the charging ecosystem by unifying empirically-backed demand and expenditure considerations with supply-side revenue optimization, and pays specific attention to the market introduction of new services, such as quality-differentiated network services. Finally, a series of (partially antagonistic) conclusions for Network Service Providers (NSPs) are derived and discussed.

Keywords: Quality of Experience, Willingness-to-Pay, Market Entrance, Profit, Optimization.

1 Introduction

Without any doubt, telecommunications has globalized the human communication, which strongly impacts the daily information exchange in business and in private. This all comes to the cost of high investments in network infrastructure, research and development, which have initially been justified by promising prospects (which, at least partially, have also turned to practice, i.e., $127 bill.

[*] The research leading to these results has received funding from the European Community's Seventh Framework Programme (FP7/2007-2013) under grant agreement n°248567 for the ETICS project. Additional support from the Austrian government and the City of Vienna in the context of the COMET program, the CELTIC project QUEEN, and from the EU Marie Curie program in the context of the RBUCE WEST International Research Chair NICE is gratefully acknowledged.

K. Fischbach and U.R. Krieger (Eds.): MMB & DFT 2014, LNCS 8376, pp. 162–176, 2014.

revenue by AT&T in 2012[1]. However, the entire telecommunications industry has been undergoing a drastic change during the course of time. Despite required continuous investments in infrastructure (e.g., LTE or fibre to the home), revenues and profits have been continuously falling[2]. Paired with soaring traffic demands mainly due to multimedia services [1], an economically challenging environment has been rendered for Network Service Providers (NSPs).

Looking for potential causes explaining the loss of prospect, charging practices may be regarded as primary tool for investigation. Historically, due to economies of scale, existing network infrastructure demanded for proper utilization, i.e., filling the "pipes". Irrespective of customer demands, flatrate prices [2] enticing high end user demands seemed to be the solution of choice, which substantially diminished unit prices). In turn, the revenue growth potential has been mainly limited to the axis of *increasing prices* (bundling) and enlarging the *customer base*. The latter axis seems to have reached its saturation, i.e., a cell phone subscription penetration of above 130% in European countries such as Austria or UK[3], especially if new usage paradigms, i.e., machine-to-machine communication, do not catch on. Corrections of end user bundle prices have been of debatable success—rather falling end user prices. In this light, different charging schemes and new revenue opportunities, e.g., quality differentiation, will rise in importance. Whereas price differentiation in the past was caused only by various volume limitations, current pricing schemes include volume limitations and bandwidth limitations, e.g. see [3], and may thus in the future be extended to finely tailored quality differentiation.

Although charging for Quality of Service (QoS) [2] and QoS-aware revenue optimization [4] have received considerable attention in academia, despite its limited success in practice, more advanced models and schemes which specifically target subjective user perceptions and thus lead to specific mechanisms for charging for Quality of Experience (QoE) [5], making use of QoS-differentiation capabilities have only been pursued by a few works [6]. This is especially problematic as network quality and transitively quality of over the top applications, e.g., video telephony, may best be classified as "experience products" requiring a posteriori perceptual evaluation [7], which exacerbates the initial product purchase and communication. Even beyond that, the notoriously difficult approximation of purchasing from product experiences (i.e., QoE)—as used e.g. in [8]—has again recently drawn the attentions towards holistic and empirical willingness-to-pay measurements for quality-differentiated service [9,10]—following the general discussion of customer satisfaction and purchasing decisions in [11]. However, those insights have not yet sufficiently been transferred to realistic market constellations or even practical market frameworks. This, on the one hand, includes a

---

[1] http://www.att.com/Investor/ATT_Annual/2012/downloads/ar2012_annual_report.pdf, last accessed: Oct 17, 2013.

[2] "Tellabs End of Profit": http://www.tellabs.com/markets/tlab_end-of-profit_study.pdf, last accessed: Oct 17, 2013.

[3] http://www.itu.int/en/ITU-D/Statistics/Documents/statistics/2012/Mobile_cellular_2000-2011.xls, last accessed: Oct 17, 2013.

requirement for studying revenue optimizations and on the other hand the need to systematically evolve from per-user perspectives of quality.

Even beyond that, the absence of an empirical understanding of raising human's willingness-to-pay may be regarded to be problematic, especially when being aligned to other market concepts like price dumping. We, thus, anticipate the existence of antagonisms between optimally serving user and market needs, which has insufficiently been targeted in literature so far.

In this context, the contribution of the present work is threefold: firstly, we will extend QoE charging models over [6] by supply-side revenue prospects, which will subsequently be instantiated with gathered empirical willingness-to-pay data for network video qualities. Secondly, on this basis market entrance pricing strategies and price changes receive an in-depth investigation, which thus significantly extends the somewhat preliminary discussion presented in [12]. Thirdly, a series of implications for pricing and service provisioning strategies are given.

The remainder of this work is structured as follows: after refining the QoE charging ecosystem in Section 2, Section 3 briefly continues with the proper market entrance pricing configuration. Building on a series of isolated but individually sound conclusions on optimal pricing strategies, Section 4 will address antagonisms between users and markets. Through a link to the supply-side revenue optimization, QoE charging prospects for NSPs are illustrated in Section 5. This work finally closes with a couple of concluding remarks and a related discussion on further work.

2   Ecosystem

While the testing for Quality of Experience (QoE) has been investigated for years, recently the relationship to charging has received new impetus [6]. As illustrated in Fig. 1 (red circle), charging for QoE faces the following fixed point problem [6]: due to capacity constraints, user demand is limiting QoS, which in turn directly impacts QoE. On the other hand, the charged prices are based on the delivered QoE, which at the same time may significantly influence the user expectations (and thus QoE perception) and thus future demand. Hence, this model leads to a sophisticated feedback behavior due to two intertwined feedback cycles, which has been shown to result in a non-trivial fixed point structure which has been analyzed and discussed in detail in [6].

In this paper, we propose to link this analytical understanding of QoE charging to empirical willingness-to-pay results, see Section 3.1. Such considerations allow a meaningful parametrization of demands and Average Revenues Per User (ARPU) as replacement for notoriously difficult approximations from QoE results. Linking these results with the underlying QoS input, supply-side optimization in terms of revenue can be applied. Thus, for a given population, revenue-optimal implications towards charging for QoS and QoE can be extracted, which will be iteratively constructed in this work.

On the basis of the model proposed in [6], we thus end up with unifying empirically obtainable demand data with optimal supply configurations in this

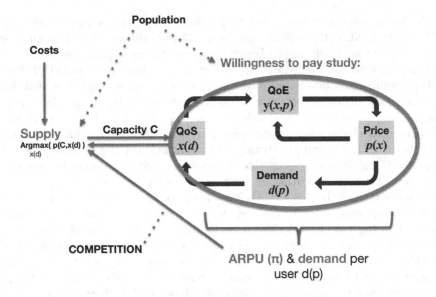

Fig. 1. The ecosystem of charging for QoE

work. However, the explicit quantification of the QoE function involved in the charging process is out of focus of the present work.

Instead, we focus on extending the problem scope from monopolistic service provisioning—as tested in our subsequently described study—to its competitive complement, and discuss a series of economic challenges arising from that. We will especially investigate the problem of revenue-optimal market entrance pricing strategies as antagonistic struggle between user preferences and market forces. Thus, this work especially focuses on the required balance between demand- and supply-side utility optimization, i.e., user- and usage-aware revenue optimization.

3   Market Entrance and Service Pricing

This section investigates market entrance pricing from a monopolistic, i.e., customers' willingness-to-pay for network services with a single provider, and market-based perspective in order to derive valuable conclusions on optimal market entrance configuration.

3.1   Willingness-to-Pay

We start with a comprehensive survey about recent study on users' willingness-to-pay for enhanced network services which has been conducted in order to derive valuable clues on market entrance demand and revenue levels under varying conditions. Note that this study has been designed in response to the shortfalls of a preceding study [10], which has not been able to reveal extrapolated purchasing behaviors and willingness-to-pay maxima.

The laboratory-based study has been conducted in the context of the EU FP7 project ETICS [13] in 2012, comprising 43 test subjects [12]. This number of participants is clearly large enough compared to the typical standard sizes for comparable user trials (e.g., 4 to 40 test user recommended in ITU_T Rec. P.910). Summarized briefly, we have been targeting the willingness-to-pay for network video advancements in a Video-on-Demand (VoD) setting. In particular, in the course of the trial each user has been watching three 20 minutes videos of their choice from an extensive HD video library, i.e., three measurement rounds $M1$, $M2$ and $M3$ strung together during each test session. By using a jog wheel[4], subjects have been able to purchase quality advancements without requiring neither an indication on their current quality level nor on the available quality bounds. In this way, their focus has been shifted towards price and quality perceptions, i.e., w.r.t *charging for QoE*. Each video started with a trial phase—allowing users to test video qualities during the first 5 minutes for free—after which the last selection has been taken as purchase for the remainder of the video. Thus, *active purchasing* decisions of users are tested. For obtaining realistic purchasing behaviors, test subjects have been provided with € 10, which they could use for in-experiment quality purchases or take home in cash after the completion of the experiments.

Table 1. Quality levels Q0 to Q19 in kBit/s

Q_0	Q_1	Q_2	Q_3	Q_4	Q_5	Q_6	Q_7
128	181	256	362	512	724	1024	1448
Q_8	Q_9	Q_{10}	Q_{11}	Q_{12}	Q_{13}	Q_{14}	Q_{15}
2048	2896	4096	5793	8192	11585	16384	23170

Q_{16}	Q_{17}	Q_{18}	Q_{19}	Quality class
32768	32768	32768	32768	in kBit/s

Our newly conducted study provides significant methodological advancements over works in literature, e.g., [10] and [9] (here, especially experiment 3 is relevant for our purposes). On the one hand, the usage simplicity is maintained from [10], while substantially increasing the number of quality levels, i.e., 17 H.264-encoded quality levels (from 128kbit to Blue-ray quality; cf. Table 1) and 20 quality classes (3 virtual quality classes only differing in price), introducing three tariffing options, i.e., maximum price p_{max} of € 2 (price plan A), € 3 (price plan B) and € 4 (price plan C), resp. (i.e., $p_i = \frac{i}{19} \cdot p_{max}$, $i = 0...19$). This fine-grained quality/price differentiation allows improving the interaction behavior, i.e., highly dynamic quality selection and application based on adaptive video streaming, as well as shifting towards High Definition (HD) resolution content—also see [12]. On the one hand, this is necessary in order to give the test subjects a sufficiently broad range of choices for matching their inner equilibrium, i.e., convergence to a price-quality fixed point [6], but on the other hand also to reveal and systematize tariffing-induced tradeoff considerations.

---

[4] http://retail.contourdesign.com/?/products/22, last accessed: Oct 17, 2013.

Special consideration has been paid to the empirical investigation of market entrance pricing, which requires the testing of different tariffing sequences: low prices and subsequent increases (*Group I*), the reverse sequence (*Group II*), as well as stable prices (*Control group*).

As main results from this study, the descriptive statistics firstly reveal a considerable willingness-to-pay for enhanced quality: € 1.42 (median) per 20 minutes movie at a medium quality level. By increasing the maximum price p_{max}[5] and thus the unit prices, the ARPU has been raised from € 0.74 at $p_{max} = 2$ to € 1.26 at $p_{max} = 4$. To our surprise, even virtual quality classes—providing no quality advancements over cheaper classes—have been purchased by customers seeking for the best quality, i.e., anticipating price discrimination. For more descriptive statics we refer to [12].

We have also observed that price reductions (Group II) do not attract impulse purchases, while price increases (Group I) immediately trigger equivalent quality reductions (cf. Fig. 2[6]). This will later be supported by a more detailed analysis in Sec. 4, but leads already here to a first conclusion.

Conclusion #1
*From a per-user perspective, NSPs are **not** recommended to offer unsustainable low teaser prices at market entrances that cannot be retained over time.*

The absence of behavioral adaption under price reductions may be purely subject to the human's desire to avoid dissatisfaction. Each active decision under contradictory cognitions (i.e., perceptible price and quality tradeoffs) may lead to cognitive dissonance (cf. [14]), which may be eliminated or mitigated by passivity.

3.2   Market Challenges

While the user trial described above addresses market entrance issues from the perspective of the individual user, the following paragraphs briefly review the standard market perspective, which prepares the subsequent discussion of the resulting antagonism between users and markets.

- *Lack of demand & two-sided market issues.* New services, esp. network qualities, may require a stimulation of the consumer demand. In analogy e.g. to UMTS in the past, stalemates may iteratively occur whenever non-iterative upgrades do not universally provide credible market perspectives. Thus, progressive pricing or intensive marketing provide an initial may motivate investments in quality-differentiated networks.

---

[5] Likewise linearly increasing the costs for each quality advancement.

[6] In absolute and normalized numbers, i.e., in the interval [0,1] where 1 equals Q_{16} and 0 is Q_0.

— *Market power.* When entering a new market, price dumping[7] (e.g., through unsustainable teaser prices) may be applied, if not against societal interest, in order to succeed on markets already settled around incumbent players.

— *Economies of scale.* Telecommunications immanently requires massive investments in infrastructure, e.g., macro-cells, in order to satisfy customer demands, i.e., network quality, and legal constraints (e.g., w.r.t. universal access). Thus, through a high infrastructure utilization unit price gains may boost the market share.

Thus, it follows that through the exploitation of unit price gains NSPs should seek for stimulating customer demands, e.g., teaser prices, and increasing their market share in order to attain a critical mass of customers. Hence, this yields the following conclusion on NSPs' pricing strategies:

Conclusion #2
Immature markets, i.e., market entrance with or without high competition, may be best served by progressively penetrating the market, e.g. through aggresive pricing, in order to decrease unit costs.

Note that conclusions #1 and #2 already lead to a first strategic antagonism for competitive and non-competitive (user-centric) market decision optima. In a competitive industry, approaching markets with low introductory prices may be necessary, despite simultaneously limiting the end user's willingness-to-pay. Without resolution, a strategic *dominance* to converge towards *low profitable* and *unsustainable* market entrance pricing may arise. This stands in analogy to debatable "filling the pipe" strategies in the past where long-term prospects have been traded for short-term yields—apparently reflected in declining revenues[8].

4   From Monopoly to Competition

Inferred by the empirical willingness-to-pay results above, implications on strategically optimizing the economic benefits of rolling out quality-differentiated services, i.e., market entrance, may be derived: in general, users seem to be reluctant to increase spending after reaching an initial convergence, e.g., avoiding new (impulse) choices, unless the stimulus is significantly huge, e.g., the 50% discount from tariff C to A. Contrary, small price increases have been immediately compensated by sensitive purchasing behaviors. Thus, high market entrance prices may be recommended in monopolies. This correlates to the theoretical concepts

---

[7] Definition by the European Commission: http://ec.europa.eu/trade/tackling-unfair-trade/trade-defence/anti-dumping/index_en.htm, last accessed: Dec 10, 2013.

[8] Wireless intelligence:https://wirelessintelligence.com/files/analysis/?file=2011-03-10-european-mobile-arpu-falls-20.pdf, last accessed: Oct 17, 2013.

of reference points—see [15,16]—which impact the decisioning bias. On the one hand, a status quo bias, e.g., a default offer or market entrance price, may facilitate passivity for future decisions and may, thus, essentially influence human decisions. We will, thus, empirically review such effects from a monopolistic perspective, which is aligned to market strategies in a second step.

4.1 Monopoly: A User Perspective

Leaving the control group of Section 3.1's results aside, which only provides two consistent measurements, we can characterize the purchasing behavior due to pricing over three measurements more clearly (see Fig. 2).

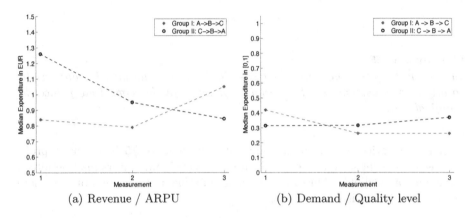

(a) Revenue / ARPU   (b) Demand / Quality level

Fig. 2. Revenue and qualiy level demand (normalized in $[0, 1]$ for measurements M_1, M_2, and M_3

This perspective reveals that the revenue tendency under price increases is reversed with growing price differences. Contrary, the revenue downturn is bottomed out when increasing from €3 to €4. Thus, subsequently a series of characteristics and conclusions can be derived for the case of price increases:

- Initially, demand curve is very price elastic, and flattens out later
- Small price increases lead to the purchasing of lower quality levels, with comparable or lower ARPU
- Bigger price increases are not (fully) compensated by behavioral adaption, thus revenue tends to increase

Hence, the subsequent conclusion can be derived:

Conclusion #3
Monopolistic price increases in large steps are more preferable for NSPs than small modifications[9].

Looking at price reductions, the following characteristics can be observed:

- Small price reductions do not stimulate demand
- Clearer price, e.g., +50%, incentives are recognized
- ARPU steeply decreases with small price reductions, but flattens out with magnitude of price reductions

Conclusion #4
In monopolistic markets, stable pricing[10] provides throughout the best revenue figures. However, if necessary, price reductions from high initial prices are preferred over price increases from low teaser prices.

Conclusion #5
In a competitive setting, larger but sustainable price cuts may be more useful to attract new customers (cf. Section 3.2), which at the same time reduce the marginal cost.

Whenever price reductions are applied according to #5 in order to profit from economies of scale and expenditure prospects, competitors may be forced to respond accordingly. This may culminate in a low-revenue equilibrium where demand sensitivity is (nearly) flat.

4.2   Unraveling Competitive Markets

Subsequently, market stimulation methods omitting debatable teaser prices are discussed in order to regain some control and prospects on future revenue: First of all, business partners and customers may be attracted by clear outlines of attractive service or market opportunities.

Conclusion #6
Increased marketing efforts (demand stimulation due to blandishing pricing effects as suggested by [17]) and ante-dated communication of investments (attracting interest of business partners) may be preferred over unsustainable introductory prices in the long run.

The degree of active user decisioning, i.e., reconsideration of purchases, may essentially influence optimal strategies:

---

[9] It may be tested whehther small price steps could recreate this effect.
[10] Prices that do not require modifications after their initial announcement.

Conclusion #7
Active decisions of users may be avoided when applying moderate price increases, e.g., through subtle price increase automatisms, in order to avoid active quality reductions—i.e., negative revenue effects s.t. active decisions (see Section 3.1 and 4.1) may be circumented to some extent[11].

Facing *low* and *high competition* under active purchasing decisions, the following conclusion applies:

Conclusion #8
*For **low competition**, significant price increases may be preferred to avoid revenue loss or stagnation. Small, but adequate, price reductions are advised (immediately revenue-effective), if necessary. In contrast, under **high competition**, more significant price cuts are advised due to market penetration effects and flattening revenue curves.*

Services may be tailored towards customer groups with varying price sensitivity of demand:

Conclusion #9
Price discrimination—e.g., through the functioning of virtual quality classes (see Section 3.1) and customer segments in [10]—is recommended. Teaser prices should be only applied to price-sensitive customers.

5   Supplier's Problem

Based on the gathered information on (non-)competitive demand patterns, the supplier's problem is to optimize profits based on the expected expenditure behavior.

We assume transferability of NSP's utility from obtained revenues—the NSP rationally valuates revenue growth. However, neither quality perceptions, i.e., QoE, nor the willingness-to-pay linearly increases with the invested resources—QoE often follows a concave, e.g., logarithmic [18], pattern. In order to avoid the difficulty of appropriately approximating the willingness-to-pay from QoE, we are constructing a supply model on the basis of the empirical data from Sections 3.

Due to economies of scale, investments (i.e., CAPEX) will pay off more quickly under a *full utilization of capacity*, i.e., a broad user base. We further assume that a more demanding customer requiring twice the resources of a discount customer (e.g., through higher quality demands), may require less than twice the costs in terms of customer support.

---

[11] Emprical parametrization is required for strategic optimality considerations.

We will subsequently construct a profit optimizer model p, which acts conversely to an auction where the best matching quality level x and its customers are served, while others are ignored (corresponding to an NSP offering a single revenue-optimal quality level). So, we foresee a system with strict access control, active QoS and thus QoE management centered around empirical revenue expectations (willingness-to-pay and demand). Classical QoS charging mechanism, as revisited in [2], often do not incorporate customer experiences influencing purchasing behaviors, while existing multi-class QoE charging approaches such as [8] only approximate willingness-to-pay from QoE. Despite the attractiveness of multi-class service offers, the lower technical complexity of access-controlled single-class systems may promote our straightforward design. For our case, p can be formalized by:

$$p(x, C, n) = \max_{x \in [0,16]} \pi(x, C) - CAPEX(C) - OPEX(C, n), \qquad (1)$$

where $OPEX(C, n)$ logarithmically flattens in n (the number of customers for the capacity C)[12] due to efficiency yields, x is the quality level, and $\pi(x, C)$ is the revenue generated from a capacity and provisioned x. In our case, the QoS $x(d)$ depends on the bandwidth demand d required for provisioning n video streams of a certain quality level—cf. the exponentially increasing bitrate demands in Table 1. This may be defined as follows:

$$q(d) = C/d \qquad (2)$$

where d is specified to be $d = \lfloor n \cdot r(x) \rfloor = C$ in order to fully, i.e., Pareto-efficiently, utilize the capacity C[13]. The term $r(x)$ is the resource demand (in kbit/s) for provisioning x, which is defind in correspondence to the quality levels Q_x of Table 1 for streaming a video to a single user:

$$r(x) = 128 \cdot 2^{\frac{x}{2}} \quad , \qquad (3)$$

with $x = 0, \ldots, 16$ as classes Q_{17}-Q_{19} have been introduced as virtual classes with requirements identical to class Q_{16}. Then, an upper limit (due to the convexity of $r(x)$ in (3) for the revenue π_i for user i (ARPU) follows by:

$$\pi_i(x) = p_{max} \cdot \frac{x}{19} \quad , \qquad (4)$$

with linear pricing steps as described in Section 3.1. This is linked to the empirical expenditure distribution data capturing the observed demand levels:

$$\pi(x, C) = \pi_i(x) \cdot min\Big(d(x), C/r(x)\Big) \quad , \qquad (5)$$

---

[12] Total costs, thus, have a form of $C \cdot a \cdot log(n) + C \cdot b$ with given a,b.

[13] Pareto-efficiency may also be achieved for $Q_{>16}$, which is explicitly excluded from the model.

where $d(x)$ is demand for x, which together with the capacity C and resource demands $r(x)$ limits the provisionable quantity. With this, the profit given in (1) can be calculated.

Due to the domination of π by demand growth, no interior extremum can be observed when optimizing π for x. On the other hand, the demand $d(x)$, according to the empirical results from Section 3 (cf. Fig. 3(a)) basically follows a beta distribution ϕ (cf. Fig. 3(b), which is characteristic for third degree price discrimination [19], e.g., s.t. quality attributes or heterogeneity in general [20].

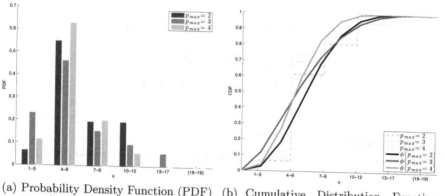

(a) Probability Density Function (PDF)   (b) Cumulative   Distribution   Functions (CDFs) and their approximation ϕ

Fig. 3. Demand for varying p_{max} and quality levels x

Observe from Fig. 3(a) that by increasing p_{max} the demand slightly shifts towards lower x values, i.e., a concentration on lower qualities. In any case, we find the demand maximum at $Q_{4 \geq x \geq 6}$.

Conclusion #10

π continuously increases in demand, thus converging to ∞. Hence, the provisioning of the x yielding the individually highest demand is preferable.

Conclusion #11

VoD services—under the given tariffing design and controlled conditions—should be provisioned with intermediate quality, i.e., Q_4 to Q_6.

For CAPEX and OPEX we can recognize directly increasing costs with capacity, thus converging to ∞ in C. Hence, a minimal C to satisfy rewarding demand is of course beneficial. Based on our definitions, costs logarithmically increase in n (while bargaining powers of individual users will decrease), thus marginal costs are decreasing in n.

Conclusion #12
Whenever no sufficient premium demand exists, i.e., very few customers utilizing C under acceptable bargaining powers, a substantial extension of the customer base may provide cost advantages over competitors.

When optimizing π over the empirical data gathered in Section 3 (43 participants) on a link with 10 Megabit/s, $x = 7, 6, 5$ for the respective p_{max} yield the respective maxima (see revenue details in Table 2)—detailing the claims of #11.

Table 2. Revenue optimal quality provisioning

	$p_{max} = 2$	$p_{max} = 3$	$p_{max} = 4$
Q_{x^*}	Q_7	Q_6	Q_5
π^*	5.2	8.52	8.42

Conclusion #13
Higher prices (p_{max} and price steps) yield higher or approximately equal profits.

Under a game-theoretic reasoning we assume that customers not being served their primary choice x may be most interested in slightly higher or lower x^* values (rendered optimal due to demand fluctuations and access control). Thus, we extend the model by accommodating for a linearly decreasing disposition to accept deviations $\delta = 1, 2, \ldots$ from their x,

$$d(x, \delta) = max\left(0, d(x + \delta) \cdot \left(1 - |\tfrac{\delta}{7}|\right)\right) \quad , \tag{6}$$

where $d(x, \delta)$ is the demand for the provisioned quality x, as linear relaxation around the original x.

Table 3. Revenue optimal quality provisioning with modified demand

	10 Mbit/s		Unconstrained	
	Q_{x^*}	π^*	Q_{x^*}	π^*
$p_{max} = 2$	Q_5	7.4	Q_9	17
$p_{max} = 3$	Q_4	12.6	Q_7	32
$p_{max} = 4$	Q_4	16.8	Q_8	28.6

Table 3 illustrates that a restriction of capacity C, e.g., 10 Mbit/s, becomes revenue effective under high demands—originating from the intake of customers interested in nearby quality-price matches. The revenue optimum at x^* using $d(x^*, \delta)$ first shifts towards lower x, but reverses when capacity constraints are loosened.

Conclusion #14
*High demands and low capacity shift the profitability towards **lower** x values, i.e., low quality services.*

Conclusion #15
Even under unconstrained capacity, any x > 9 is less profitable than optimal intermediate quality.

Linking Conclusions #12 and #15, we can state that an extensive customer base (i.e., highly demanded low/intermediate quality levels) is beneficial, which eventually represents another antagonism w.r.t. Conclusion #1.

6   Conclusions

The present work has extracted a series of conclusions, i.e., 15 commandments of quality-differentiated market entrance pricing, and aimed at conceptually integrating them in an overall QoE charging model. Amongst others, we have observed high demand sensitivity under price increases being opposed by stable demands for price reductions. While measures like teaser prices may serve the initial market stimulation, their effects may, thus, be counterproductive for NSPs' revenues in the long run—comparable to the debatable flat rate pricing. Beyond that, a series of strategic supply-side conclusions have been drawn from an empirically-fed optimization model.

While we recommend the concentration on low to intermediate quality levels, future work may extend the analysis towards enabling price discrimination. Beyond that, the acquired empirical input data requires further confirmation, and may especially profit from substantially lengthened measurement intervals—price changes e.g. rather per day, week etc.

References

1. Cisco: Cisco Visual Networking Index: Forecast and Methodology, 2011–2016. Whitepaper (2012)
2. Tuffin, B.: Charging the Internet Without Bandwidth Reservation: An Overview and Bibliography of Mathematical Approaches. Journal of Information Science and Engineering 19, 1–22 (2004)
3. Pradayrol, A., Levy, D.: European Telecom Operators: 4G – going faster, but where?, Arthur D. Little and Exane BNP Paribas (2013)
4. Keon, N.J., Anandalingam, G.: Optimal pricing for multiple services in telecommunications networks offering quality-of-service guarantees. IEEE/ACM Transactions on Networking (TON) 11(1) (February 2003)
5. Haddadi, H., Bonaventure, O. (eds.): Recent Advances in Networking. ACM SIGCOMM, vol. 1. ACM (2013)

6. Reichl, P., Maillé, P., Zwickl, P., Sackl, A.: A Fixed-Point Model for QoE-based Charging. In: ACM SIGCOMM 2013 Workshop on Future Human-Centric Multimedia Networking (2013)
7. Kirmani, A., Rao, A.R.: No Pain, No Gain: A Critical Review of the Literature on Signaling Unobservable Product Quality. The Journal of Marketing, 66–79 (2010)
8. Wahlmueller, S., Zwickl, P., Reichl, P.: Pricing and regulating Quality of Experience. In: 8th EURO-NGI Conference, pp. 57–64 (2012)
9. Hands, D. (ed.): FP5 Project M3I, IST199911429, Deliverable 15/2 – M3I user experiment results (2002)
10. Sackl, A., Egger, S., Zwickl, P., Reichl, P.: The QoE Alchemy: Turning Quality into Money. Experiences with a Refined Methodology for the Evaluation of Willingness-to-pay for Service Quality. In: Fourth International QoMEX Workshop (2012)
11. Homburg, C., Koschate, N., Hoyer, W.D.: Do satisfied customers really pay more? A study of the relationship between customer satisfaction and willingness to pay. Journal of Marketing, 84–96 (2005)
12. Zwickl, P., Sackl, A., Reichl, P.: Market Entrance, User Interaction and Willingness-to-Pay: Exploring Fundamentals of QoE-based Charging for VoD Services. In: IEEE Globecom 2013 (2013)
13. Le Sauze, N., Chiosi, A., Douville, R., et al.: ETICS: QoS-enabled Interconnection for Future Internet Services. Future Network and Mobile Summit (2010)
14. Festinger, L.: A theory of cognitive dissonance. Standford University Press (1957)
15. Kahneman, D., Tversky, A.: Prospect Theory: An Analysis of Decision under Risk. Econometrica 47(2), 263–292 (1979)
16. Oliver, A.: From Nudging to Budging: Using Behavioural Economics to Inform Public Sector Policy. Journal of Social Policy 42, 685–700 (2013)
17. Sackl, A., Zwickl, P., Egger, S., Reichl, P.: The Role of Cognitive Dissonance for QoE Evaluation of Multimedia Services. In: Workshop on Quality of Experience for Multimedia Communications (QoEMC), Globecom. IEEE (2012)
18. Reichl, P., Egger, S., Schatz, R., D'Alconzo, A.: The Logarithmic Nature of QoE and the Role of the Weber-Fechner Law in QoE Assessment. In: International Conference on Communications (ICC 2010). IEEE (2010)
19. Cowan, S.: The Welfare Effects of Third-degree Price Discrimination with Nonlinear Demand Functions. Technical report, Oxford University – Department of Economics (2007)
20. Ivaldi, M., Martimort, D.: Competition under nonlinear pricing. Annales d'Economie et de Statistique, 71–114 (1994)

A Framework for Establishing Performance Guarantees in Industrial Automation Networks

Sven Kerschbaum[1], Kai-Steffen Hielscher[2], Ulrich Klehmet[2] and Reinhard German[2]

[1] Industry Sector,
(Industry Automation Division)
Siemens AG, Gleiwitzer Straße 555
D-90475 Nürnberg, Germany
sven.kerschbaum@siemens.com
[2] Department of Computer Science 7
(Computer Networks and Communication Systems)
University of Erlangen-Nürnberg, Martensstraße 3
D-91058 Erlangen, Germany
{ksjh,klehmet,german}@informatik.uni-erlangen.de

Abstract. In this paper we investigate the application of Network Calculus for industrial automation networks to obtain performance bounds (latency, jitter and backlog). In our previous work we identified the modeling of industrial networks as the most challenging aspect since in industry most users do not have detailed knowledge about the traffic load caused by applications. However, exactly this knowledge is indispensable when it comes to modeling the corresponding arrival curves. Thus, we suggest the use of generalized traffic profiles, which are provided by the engineering tool. During the engineering process, the user has to specialize these profiles to meet the application configurations. The engineering tool derives the corresponding arrival curves from the specialized profiles and calculates the performance bounds using Network Calculus. To guarantee that the calculated performance bounds are kept during the runtime of the industrial automation, we must ensure that the real traffic flows do not exceed their engineered arrival curves. We therefore propose the use of shapers at the edge of the network domain. The shaper configurations can be automatically derived from the engineered arrival curves of the flows.

Keywords: Network Calculus, performance guarantees, quality of service (QoS), industrial automation networks.

1 Introduction

Historically, industrial automation networks were mainly based on specific networks called fieldbuses, e.g., PROFIBUS and Modbus. These fieldbuses interconnect programmable logic controllers (PLC), robot controllers, I/O devices, etc. to exchange data for monitoring, controlling and synchronizing industrial processes. The fieldbus protocols ensure that the end-to-end message delays remain within specific limits and meet the requirements of industrial processes. As a consequence, industrial automation networks are deterministic and allow their end-to-end delays to be determined.

K. Fischbach and U.R. Krieger (Eds.): MMB & DFT 2014, LNCS 8376, pp. 177–191, 2014.

In recent years, the office and automation world have increasingly merged. This is mainly due to company-wide information processing ("office meets factory"). Ethernet is a well-known, and widely implemented protocol. Its performance is continually increasing - especially the bandwidth. Hence, many of the present industrial Ethernet technologies, such as PROFINET, EtherCAT and POWERLINK, extend the standard Ethernet by adding new features and functionality to meet specific industrial requirements, in particular strict determinism and high reliability.

In this paper, we consider PROFINET RT networks which prioritize the real-time frames according to IEEE 802.1Q [1] to obtain a better QoS with regard to latency and jitter. However, real-time frames contend with best-effort frames for resources and are subject to queuing delays caused by best-effort frames which are already in transit. Thus, best-effort applications can have negative impact on the latency and the jitter of all real-time frames and their applications which require determinism. To guarantee worst-case latencies and maximal jitter for real-time flows, a formal method for the calculation of performance bounds during the engineering phase is needed. In our previous work [2] we identified the modeling of industrial networks as the most challenging aspect, since in industry most users do not have detailed knowledge about the traffic load caused by applications. This covers both industrial and best-effort traffic. But exactly this knowledge is indispensable when it comes to modeling the corresponding arrival curves. An approach which provides support to the user in modeling the arrival curves is therefore essential for the application of Network Calculus to industrial automation networks.

Industrial automation networks have been the subject of various studies concerning the timing aspects of data transmission. Formal verification techniques, such as model-checking, encounter the state-space explosion problem, which represents a serious issue. Several approaches, such as [3], have been proposed to alleviate the state-space explosion, but without success. Another approach to determining network performance is simulation. A multitude of simulation tools exist, e.g. OMNeT++ [4], OPNET [5], and ns-3 [6]. In [7] the authors modeled and analyzed heterogeneous industrial network architectures. The typical use case for simulation is to obtain mean values since the events during the simulation are stochastically scheduled. Nevertheless, one can model a worst-case scenario but due to multiplexing of flows within the network, this can be a very challenging task. In some cases it might not even be possible to identify the worst-case scheduling of messages analytically. Simulation is consequently not the best approach for the analysis of time-critical industrial automation networks.

The rest of this paper is organized as follows. Section 2 presents an overview of PROFINET and Network Calculus. In Section 3, we present our approach for the application of Network Calculus to industrial automation networks. In Section 4, we apply our approach to the Smart Automation, an industrial research facility created as a design laboratory and integration plant for the Industry Sector of Siemens AG in Nürnberg. Industrial communication within this plant is realized by PROFINET RT. Finally, Section 5 concludes this paper with a discussion of the obtained results and gives an outlook for future work.

2 Background

2.1 Industrial Automation

The term "automation" is mostly associated with factory floors where vehicles, printing equipment, etc. are produced. But automation is used in many more industries. The main fields of automation are factory and process automation [8].

Latency and Jitter Requirements. Each automation application requires different QoS in terms of communication quality with regard to latency and jitter. These requirements can be roughly divided into three classes, see Table 1, which are derived from experience with existing classes of applications in fieldbus technology [9].

Table 1. Quality of Service (QoS) Requirements in Field Communication

QoS Class	Application	Latency	Jitter
1	Controller-to-controller	100 ms	
2	Distributed I/O devices	10 ms	
3	Motion control	≤ 1 ms	≤ 1 μs

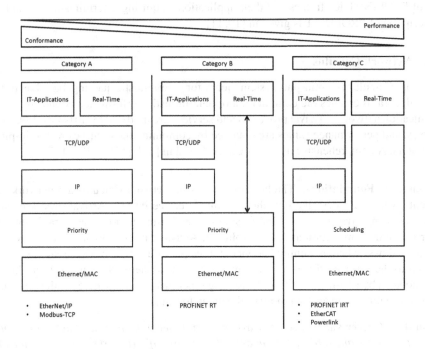

Fig. 1. Categorization of Real-Time Ethernet Systems

Implementation of Real-Time Ethernet. There are three main real-time categories, each offering a different QoS with regard to latency and jitter (see Figure 1).

Category A (e.g. EtherNet/IP and Modbus/TCP) uses standard, unmodified Ethernet hardware as well as the standard TCP/IP stack. Communication is not deterministic and mainly influenced by the TCP/IP protocol dynamics. All devices use IP-address based communication, thus supporting transmission of frames beyond a local network.

Category B (e.g. PROFINET RT) offers soft real-time by prioritizing the real-time frames according to IEEE 802.1Q and sending them directly to the Ethernet/MAC layer. This approach avoids TCP/IP protocol processing times, further reducing the latencies for real-time frames. Real-time communication is based on MAC addresses and is thus restricted to the local network.

Category C (e.g. PROFINET IRT, EtherCAT, POWERLINK) uses a TDMA approach to offer strict determinism for real-time frames. Standard Ethernet hardware can no longer be used. In the main, motion control applications require this kind of strict determinism. The main advantage of this approach is that the transmission times for the real-time frames can be calculated during the engineering phase, offering a guaranteed minimal latency and jitter.

In this paper, we focus on PROFINET RT which prioritizes real-time frames according to IEEE 802.1Q to obtain a better QoS with regard to latency and jitter. However, PROFINET RT frames contend with best-effort frames for network resources and are subject to queuing delay caused by best-effort frames which are already in transit. Thus, best-effort applications can have a negative impact on the latency and the jitter of PROFINET RT frames and their applications requiring determinism. A detailed description of PROFINET is given in [10, 11].

2.2   Network Calculus

Network Calculus is a min-plus system theory for deterministic queuing, based on min-plus algebra. It enables the computation of deterministic performance bounds in communication networks. Arrival processes and services are modeled by arrival and service curves, and performance values are obtained by combining those curves with min-plus operators. A comprehensive overview can be found in [12], [13], [14] or [15].

Theoretical Foundations. The building blocks of Network Calculus are network elements, which are described by their minimal service curves. Arrival processes are modeled using arrival curves. Models are evaluated using min-plus algebra, in particular min-plus convolution and deconvolution. Arrival curves provide an upper bound to input flows, whereas minimal service curves provide a way of expressing a lower bound to the service offered to the flows traversing the network element. Input flows are modeled by non-negative, non-decreasing functions $t \mapsto x(t)$ where t is the time and $x(t)$ is the cumulative amount of arrived data up to time t.

Definition 1 (Arrival Curve). *Let $\alpha(t)$ be a non-negative, non-decreasing function. Flow F is constrained by or has an arrival curve $\alpha(t)$ iff $x(t) - x(s) \leq \alpha(t - s)$ for all time points $t \geq s \geq 0$.*

A commonly used arrival curve is a rate-burst curve: $\alpha_{r,b}(t) = b + rt$ for $t > 0$ and 0 otherwise. The arrival curve reflects an upper limit for an input flow $x(t)$ with (average) rate r and instantaneous burst b. This means $x(t) - x(s) \leq \alpha_{r,b}(t - s) = b + r(t - s)$. The rate-bust curve is also named token bucket curve since a token bucket guarantees an arrival curve of rate-burst form.

An important Network Calculus operation is the following:

Definition 2 (Min-Plus Convolution). *Let $f(t)$ and $g(t)$ be non-negative, non-decreasing functions that are 0 for $t \leq 0$. The min-plus convolution is defined as*

$$(f \otimes g)(t) = \inf_{0 \leq s \leq t} \{f(s) + g(t - s)\}.$$

Definition 3 (Service Curve). *Consider a system S with input flow $x(t)$ and output flow $y(t)$. The system offers a (minimum) service curve $\beta(t)$ to the flow iff $\beta(t)$ is a non-negative, non-decreasing function with $\beta(0) = 0$ and $y(t)$ is lower bounded by the convolution of $x(t)$ and $\beta(t)$:*

$$y(t) \geq (x \otimes \beta)(t).$$

A commonly used service curve is the rate-latency function: $\beta(t) = \beta_{R,T}(t) = R \cdot [t - T]^+ := R \cdot \max\{0; t - T\}$. Rate-latency reflects a service element, which offers a minimum service of rate R after a worst-case latency of T.

A further important Network Calculus operation is the following:

Definition 4 (Min-Plus Deconvolution). *Let $f(t)$ and $g(t)$ be two non-negative, non-decreasing functions. The min-plus deconvolution of $f(t)$ by $g(t)$ is the function*

$$(f \oslash g)(t) = \sup_{s \geq 0} \{f(t + s) - g(s)\}.$$

Three Bounds. If the network element serves the incoming flow in FIFO order, the worst-case delay can be calculated using the following theorem:

Theorem 1 (Delay Bound [12]). *Assume a flow, constrained by arrival curve $\alpha(t)$, passing a system with service curve $\beta(t)$. The maximum delay d is given as the supremum of all possible data delays, i.e. is defined as the supremum of the horizontal deviation between the arrival and the service curve:*

$$d \leq \sup_{s \geq 0} \{\inf\{\tau : \alpha(s) \leq \beta(s + \tau)\}\}.$$

The following theorems are generally valid.

Theorem 2 (Backlog Bound [12]). *Assume a flow, constrained by arrival curve $\alpha(t)$, traverses a system that offers a service curve $\beta(t)$. The backlog $R(t) - R^*(t)$ for all t satisfies:*

$$R(t) - R^*(t) \leq \sup_{s \geq 0} \{\alpha(s) - \beta(s)\}.$$

Theorem 3 (Output Bound [12]). *Assume a flow, constrained by arrival curve $\alpha(t)$, traverses a system that offers a service curve $\beta(t)$. The output flow is constrained by the arrival curve $\alpha^*(t) = (\alpha \oslash \beta)(t)$.*

3   Approach for Guaranteeing Performance in Industrial Automation Networks

As described in Section 2.2, the Network Calculus model consists of the topology, i.e. the concatenation of nodes modeled by their service curves, and the traffic flows described by their arrival curves. Our approach is twofold and comprises both the engineering and the runtime of the industrial automation system. (1) The engineering tool provides generalized traffic profiles which can be specialized by the user to meet the application configurations. Next, the engineering tool derives the corresponding arrival curves from the specialized profiles and calculates the performance bounds using Network Calculus. (2) To guarantee that the calculated performance bounds are kept during the runtime of the industrial automation, shapers at the edge of the network domain are used to ensure that the real traffic flows do not exceed their engineered arrival curves. An overview of our approach is given in Figure 2.

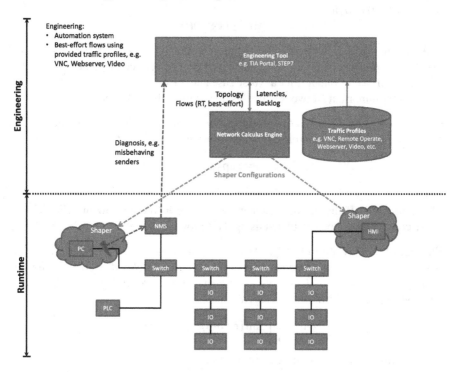

Fig. 2. Approach for Guaranteeing Performance in Industrial Automation Networks

3.1   Engineering

Usually, the user engineers the network topology within the engineering tool, e.g. SIEMENS TIA Portal [16]. This is also recommended by SIEMENS. Consequently, the network topology as well as the network components are known by the engineering tool, and their corresponding service curves can be easily derived since the engineering tool has detailed knowledge about the used industrial network components due to their general station description (GSD) which contains information like the maximum bridge delay and supported link speeds. When it comes to modeling the arrival curves for the flows, we have to distinguish between three types of traffic found in industrial automation networks: periodic and aperiodic real-time traffic as well as best-effort traffic.

Based on this model, Network Calculus can be applied to calculate the performance bounds and furthermore, the engineering tool derives the shaper configuration

Periodic Real-Time Flows. The periodic real-time flows (distributed I/O devices) depend on the industrial automation process engineered by the user. The periodic real-time flows are therefore known by the engineering tool. The corresponding arrival curves can be easily derived by the engineering tool without any user interaction since it knows all periodic control data frames and their transmission periods.

Aperiodic Real-Time Flows. The aperiodic real-time flows (controller-to-controller) are programmed by the user within the controller applications. The user therefore normally only knows the communication endpoints but not the traffic load. In [17] we reported a method to derive the arrival curves by performing a static code analysis of the controller programs. Here, we will only provide a short introduction to this topic.

The IEC61131-3 [18] standard defines different programming languages for programming programmable logic controllers (PLCs). Widely used are AWL, FUP, KOP and SCL. The engineering tool also comes with built-in libraries that support the user in programming the PLC, e.g. sending data (USEND, BSEND in AWL). Our proposed method analyzes these programs as shown in Figure 3 which is a semi-automated process since the program can contain statements that cannot automatically analyzed.

In the first step, the PLC hardware configuration must be analyzed. This includes the analysis of factors such as process and timer alarms, because these can lead to the execution of functions within the PLC program. The user can configure a minimum or a maximum cycle time for the PLC program.

In the next step, an abstract syntax tree (AST) is built from the original PLC program. ASTs are well-known from the field of compiler-techniques. All ongoing analysis are based on this AST.

- **Dead code analysis:** Code that is not reachable should be removed so that it will not be considered in the further analysis.
- **Alias analysis:** Determination of how storage locations are accessed by the program.
- **Data-flow analysis:** Analysis of data-flows for gathering information about the possible set of values calculated at various points in program.
- **BCET/WCET analysis:** Estimation of the best and worst-case execution times.
- **Flow analysis:** The flow analysis analyzes the program with regard to data transmission over the network. Both the amount of transmitted data as well as the execution times of the program will be taken into account. In this way, the arrival curves can be modeled.

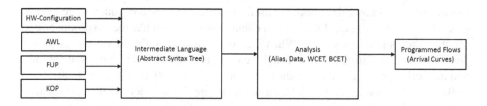

Fig. 3. PLC Program Analysis

Best-Effort Flows. Due to the growing trend towards merging automation and office networks, traffic caused by common IT applications, e.g. VNC for remote operation, video camera streaming and web servers, is increasingly transmitted over automation networks. The traffic caused by these applications depends on many factors such as the protocols used (HTTP, TCP/UDP) and of course the application itself. The user consequently has no knowledge about the traffic load, only the communication end points.

Our approach closes this gap by the use of generalized traffic profiles which are provided by the engineering tool. It is the user's responsibility to further specialize these generalized traffic profiles to obtain a more accurate model of the traffic load caused by applications within the automation network. Traffic profiles can be created either by analyzing the application and the protocols it uses or by taking measurements if the applications are "black-boxes".

We are aware that the arrival curves derived from the traffic profiles must not necessarily be upper bounds for the real traffic. We therefore require the use of shapers at the edge of the QoS domain to control the traffic that enters the automation network. The shapers are configured by the engineering tool in such a way that they match the assumed arrival curves. The calculated performance bounds are therefore valid independently of the real traffic caused by the best-effort applications.

Calculation of the Performance Bounds. After modeling both the network topology and all communication flows, Network Calculus can be applied to calculate latency bounds for both real-time and best-effort flows and backlog bounds for all network components. These results can then be used by the engineering tool to ensure that the latency bounds suit the application requirements (application cycle). Furthermore, the engineering tool can check for possible frame drops due to queue buffer overflows.

Various Network Calculus tools exist, such as the DISCO Network Calculator [19]. But due to SIEMENS requirements we had to implement our own Network Calculus Engine (NCE) [2] to perform the calculation within the engineering tool. It allows networks and especially industrial automation networks to be modeled. To date, the total and separated flow analysis methods have been employed.

The NCE is highly structured and consists of various modules. The most important modules are the network, curve and analysis module. The network module provides basic elements, e.g. nodes and links, that can be used to build up the entire network. The curve module provides the basic Network Calculus arrival and service curves, e.g. token bucket and rate-latency. It is worth mentioning that all elements, e.g. nodes, ports, curves, etc., can be parametrized as needed. For example, for a wired link, the length and the cable type can be specified, so that the link propagation delay is also taken into account. A complete overview of the architecture of NCE is provided in Figure 4.

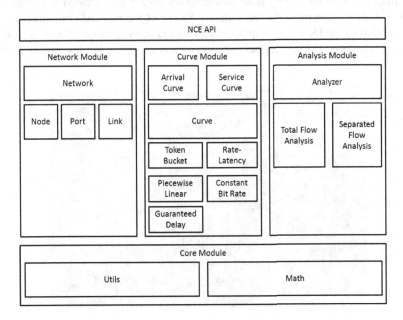

Fig. 4. Architecture of the Network Calculus Engine

3.2 Runtime

Our approach requires that shapers are placed at the entry of the QoS domain, e.g. where the best-effort traffic enters the automation network. These shapers ensure the traffic regulation in such a way that the traffic conforms to the corresponding arrival curves that have been assumed during the engineering phase. This guarantees that the calculated performance bounds are always valid.

The shaper configurations correspond to the arrival curves assumed during engineering. Traffic flows that significantly differ from their arrival curves can be easily detected by analyzing the backlog at the shaper. If a maximum level is exceeded, the shaper can immediately report it, e.g. sending an SNMP trap to a Network Management System, for instance the SIEMENS SINEMA Server [20]. This means that the requirement for shapers is not really a drawback, but instead additionally helps to improve the network diagnosis. The shaper must not necessarily be a separate device, it can also be either implemented directly on the end devices or at the ingress ports of the switches.

4   Application

In this section, we first introduce the Smart Automation (SmA) plant. Next, we provide a brief outline of how we modeled this plant using the presented approach. We then conclude this section by comparing the computed and measured end-to-end delays.

4.1   The Smart Automation Facility

The Smart Automation facility is an industrial research center created as design laboratory and integration plant for the Industry Sector of Siemens AG in Nürnberg. The SmA consists of the factory management system and several stations for filling, quality checking, transport, storing, capping/uncapping and emptying bottles. Figure 5 shows the SmA.

Fig. 5. Overview of the SmA

Functionality of the SmA. The SmA can be considered as a manufacturing system on a small scale. It consists of nine stations, all interconnected in order to operate together. According to the customer order, the system fills bottles with the selected solid pieces and if desired, using the bottle picker and the quality stations, the content of the bottles can be verified. In order to guarantee a continuous production cycle, a recycling process is executed, which dismantles the final product into its parts (caps, bottles, solid pieces). The factory management system (FMS), which is located at the process level, controls and monitors all stations. The FMS is also responsible for processing customer orders. The plant administrator can control the operation of SmA both at the control system (CS) and at the human-machine interface (HMI) located at the transport system station. As soon as the administrator operates at the HMI, the screen of the CS is shared with the HMI to remotely control the CS.

Network of the SmA. The SmA network topology is a ring, which consists of 5 industrial switches, namely SCALANCE X-208 and X-414. The ring interconnects all stations. A station is controlled and monitored by a PLC, e.g., SIMATIC S7-300. The ports of both the switches and PLCs are configured to offer their flows a FIFO service and a port rate of 100 Mbit/s. The simplified network topology is shown in Figure 6.

Communication in the SmA. Stations can only communicate with the FMS and vice versa. If stations need to communicate between one another, communication is handled by the FMS. All process data is sent using PROFINET RT.

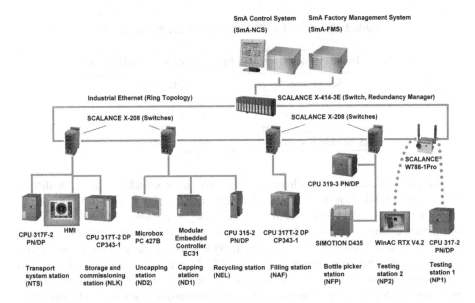

Fig. 6. SmA Network Topology

In general, communication in the SmA can be split between periodic, aperiodic and best-effort traffic. Each station sends information about its state to the FMS periodically once every second. The FMS also sends information about its state periodically once every second to each station. Aperiodic traffic occurs, for example, if the FMS requests specific operations from a station, e.g. to transport a bottle from NLK to NAF. The aperiodic traffic needed for processing a customer order comprises filling one bottle with one solid piece.

Remote operation of the SmA at the HMI uses the VNC protocol, which is based on the Remote Framebuffer Protocol [21]. All frames sent by the VNC server and its client are therefore sent as best-effort frames. To model the traffic caused for remote operation, we both analyzed the protocol and performed various measurements. The result of our measurements was a generalized traffic profile for remote operation via VNC, which depends on a few parameters that must be specified by the user. These parameters are the screen size, the color depth, the compression and the fraction of the screen that changes with a certain frequency. The specific values with regard to the SmA are given in Table 2. These are used to derive the corresponding arrival curves (CS-HMI), which are given in 3. The formulas for calculation of the burst and the rate are out of scope and are thus not specified in this paper.

Modeling the SmA. The SmA has been modeled according to its topology, which consists of an industrial PC, several PLCs, the HMI and switches. The physical ring is split by the SCALANCE X-414 which acts as the ring manager. Thus, we have two resulting feed-forward networks that are modeled and analyzed by the engineering tool. The worst-case results of both analyses is then presented as the global worst-case.

Table 2. Generalized VNC Traffic Profile and Parametrization

VNC Traffic Profile Parameters	Parametrized SmA VNC Profile
Screen size	1024x768 pixel
Color depth	24 bit
Compression	no compression (raw)
Screen change fraction	20 %
Screen change frequency	1 Hz

The performance of a switch mainly depends on its switching fabric. A distinction must be made here between blocking and non-blocking of data flows with no output contention, store-and-forward and cut-through of frames, and half-duplex and full-duplex communication mode. The design of the internal switching fabric is therefore critical to the performance of a switch. Widely used switching fabrics are shared memory, shared bus and crosspoint matrix [22]. In general, industrial switches have a non-blocking switching fabric in full-duplex mode to avoid collisions and the application of CSMA/CD. Furthermore, store-and-forward is often used. The maximum bridge delay of the used switches is 5 μs due to their GSD files. The port rates used in the SmA are 100 Mbit/s. Considering the non-preemptive scheduling mechanism of data sending, the following applies: Assuming the worst-case, a frame always has to wait until a frame, possibly of lower priority, has been completely sent including the necessary Ethernet interframe gap (IFG), which is 96 bit times. Since the maximum frame size is 1538 Byte, the worst-case sending time including IFG is $T =$ (1538 Byte + 12 Byte) / 100 Mbit/s + 5 μs = 129 μs. We therefore modeled the service of each switch port using rate-latency service curves with a rate of 100 Mbit/s and a latency of 129 μs: $\beta(t) = 100$ Mbit/s $\cdot (t - 129\,\mu s)$. Similarly, industrial PCs and PLCs offer equal services to their flows.

The arrival curves of the different communications have been modeled using upper token bucket curves. We have modeled the periodic, aperiodic and best-effort traffic as well as the acknowledgment traffic of the different communications. We have provided a brief excerpt in Table 3.

Results: Performance Bounds and Shaper Configurations. In this section, we present the calculated delays using NCE. In addition, we performed multiple measurements to determine the "real" worst-case delays in the SmA. During all measurements, there was no remote operation at the HMI, thus, we have no measurements containing VNC traffic. Additionally, remote operation does not require hard-real time guarantees.

The results of the calculation and the measurements are compared in Table 4. Summarizing, the results are as follows: Firstly, the calculated delay bounds are actually upper bounds, and therefore the Network Calculus is an appropriate application in industrial networks. Secondly, it is obvious that in worst-case, some state information frames will not reach their destination within the application cycle of 1 s, e.g. FMS $\rightarrow$ NLK. This is mainly due to possible remote operation via VNC.

Table 3. Excerpt of the Modeled Traffic

Traffic	Src	Dest	Arrival curve
		periodic traffic	
State info	Station X	FMS	$\alpha(t) = 0.000904$ Mbit/s $\cdot t + 113$ Byte
State info	FMS	Station X	$\alpha(t) = 0.000968$ Mbit/s $\cdot t + 121$ Byte
		aperiodic traffic	
Request empty bottle	FMS	NLK	$\alpha(t) = 0.000208$ Mbit/s $\cdot t + 204$ Byte
Request order picking	FMS	NLK	$\alpha(t) = 0.00022$ Mbit/s $\cdot t + 1500$ Byte
Bottle tracking	NTS	FMS	$\alpha(t) = 0.0847$ Mbit/s $\cdot t + 847$ Byte
Request bottling	FMS	NAF	$\alpha(t) = 0.000404$ Mbit/s $\cdot t + 581$ Byte
Request encapsulation	FMS	ND1	$\alpha(t) = 0.000349$ Mbit/s $\cdot t + 282$ Byte
		best-effort traffic	
Remote Operate: HMI-CS	HMI	CS	$\alpha(t) = 0.219070$ Mbit/s $\cdot t + 167$ KByte
Remote Operate: CS-HMI	CS	HMI	$\alpha(t) = 10.037200$ Mbit/s $\cdot t + 7708$ KByte

Table 4. Comparison of the NCE Delay Bounds and the Measurements

Flow	Source	Destination	NCE Delay Bound	Measurement
State info	NTS	FMS	57 ms	0.31 ms
State info	FMS	NTS	2 s 472 ms	0.25 ms
Bottle tracking	NTS	FMS	56 ms	0.26 ms
State info	NAF	FMS	3 ms	0.22 ms
State info	FMS	NAF	2 ms	0.22 ms
Request bottling	FMS	NAF	2 ms	0.37 ms
State info	NLK	FMS	57 ms	0.28 ms
State info	FMS	NLK	2 s 472 ms	0.43 ms
Request empty bottle	FMS	NLK	57 ms	0.17 ms
Request order picking	FMS	NLK	2 s 471 ms	0.29 ms
State info	ND1	FMS	57 ms	0.29 ms
State info	FMS	ND1	2 s 472 ms	0.31 ms
Request capping	FMS	ND1	2 s 472 ms	0.23 ms
Remote Operation via VNC	CS	HMI	3 s 12 ms	n/a
Remote Operation via VNC	HMI	CS	0 s 67 ms	n/a

To guarantee safe operation of the SmA, i.e. meet the required application cycle of 1 s, we have two options: We could either not support remote operation and thus remove the HMI from the automation plant or we could smooth the burst created by remote operation. Smoothing the burst means reducing the burst of its arrival curve as appropriate. Thus, two shapers are required to ensure that the real bursts are smoothed with regard to the assumed burst during the calculation: the first for shaping the traffic sent from the HMI to CS, and the second for the opposite direction.

During our measurements the SmA was operating normally, what means that the traffic load was not the worst-case, e.g. no interference with VNC traffic. Thus, the measured latencies are much smaller then the calculated bounds. Nevertheless, our proposed approach provides tight bounds. Just like in simulation it is also almost impossible to obtain worst-case measurements due to the challenging tasks of identifying the worst-case scenario and operating the automation facility accordingly.

5 Conclusion

In our previous work [2] we identified that the most challenging aspect of the application of Network Calculus to industrial automation networks concerns the modeling of arrival curves of both industrial and best-effort applications during the engineering phase. We have therefore proposed an approach to support the user in modeling the application flows within the network by specializing generalized traffic profiles provided by the engineering tool.

We must ensure that the actual flows do not exceed the engineered arrival curves during industrial automation runtime. Our approach therefore also includes the use of shapers at the edge of the QoS domain. In addition, this approach enables the diagnosis of misbehaving traffic flows which is essential in industrial automation networks.

We have focused in our study on industrial automation networks. Nevertheless, our approach could also be applied to standard Ethernet networks as well as other Ethernet technologies such as IEEE 802.1 AVB Gen. 1 and IEEE 802.1 AVB Gen. 2 (Time-Sensitive Networks) assuming that the service curves for the used schedulers, e.g. credit-based shaper in IEEE 802.1 AVB Gen. 1, exists. In upcoming work, we will apply our approach to IEEE 802.1 AVB Gen. 2 (Time Sensitive Networks). The main study will therefore focus on analysis of the proposed schedulers, e.g. time-aware shaper and bandwidth limiter [23], and the creation of appropriate service curves, so that Network Calculus can be applied to obtain performance guarantees.

References

1. IEEE: Media Access Control (MAC) Bridges and Virtual Bridged Local Area Networks. IEEE 802.1Q (2011)
2. Kerschbaum, S., Hielscher, K.-S.J., Klehmet, U., German, R.: Network Calculus: Application to an Industrial Automation Network. In: MMB & DFT Workshop Proceedings, WoNeCa (March 2012)
3. Witsch, D., Vogel-Heuser, B., Faure, J.-M., Marsal, G.: Performance analysis of industrial Ethernet networks by means of timed model-checking. In: 12th IFAC Symposium on Information Control Problems in Manufacturing (2006)

4. OMNeT++, http://www.omnetpp.org

5. The OPNET Modeler, http://www.opnet.com/products/modeler/home.html

6. ns-3, http://www.nsnam.org

7. Fummi, F., Martini, S., Monguzzi, M., Perbellini, G., Poncino, M.: Modeling and analysis of heterogeneous industrial networks architectures. In: DATE, pp. 342–344. IEEE Computer Society (2004)

8. PROFIBUS Nutzerorganisation e. V. (PNO): PROFINET and IT. Technical report, PROFIBUS Nutzerorganisation e. V. (PNO) (2008)

9. Jasperneite, J., Neumann, P.: How to guarantee realtime behavior using Ethernet. In: 11th IFAC Symposium on Information Control Problems in Manufacturing (INCOM 2004), Salvador-Bahia, Brazil (April 2004)

10. IEC: Digital data communication for measurement and control - Fieldbus for use in industrial control systems. IEC61158 (1999)

11. IEC: Digital data communication for measurement and control - Fieldbus for use in industrial control systems. IEC61784 (1999)

12. Le Boudec, J.-Y., Thiran, P.: Network Calculus. LNCS, vol. 2050. Springer, Heidelberg (2001)

13. Chang, C.S.: Performance Guarantees in Communication Networks. Springer, London (2000)

14. Cruz, R.L.: A calculus for network delay, Part I: Network elements in isolation. IEEE Transactions on Information Theory 37(1), 114–131 (1991)

15. Cruz, R.L.: A calculus for network delay, Part II: Network analysis. IEEE Transactions on Information Theory 37(1), 132–141 (1991)

16. SIEMENS: TIA Portal, http://www.industry.siemens.com/topics/global/en/tia-portal/tia-portal-framework/pages/default.aspx

17. Kerschbaum, S., Hielscher, K.-S.J., German, R.: Automatische Generierung des Network Calculus-Modells aus einem Simatic STEP7-Projekt. In: 3. Jahreskolloquium "Kommunikation in der Automation (KommA 2012)", Lemgo, Jürgen Jasperneite and Ulrich Jumar (November 2012)

18. IEC: Programming languages for programmable logic controllers. IEC61131-3 (2013)

19. Schmitt, J.B., Zdarsky, F.A.: The DISCO network calculator: a toolbox for worst case analysis. In: Lenzini, L., Cruz, R.L. (eds.) VALUETOOLS. ACM International Conference Proceeding Series, vol. 180, p. 8. ACM (2006)

20. SIEMENS: SINEMA Server, http://www.automation.siemens.com/mcms/industrial-communication/en/ie/network-management/sinema-server/Pages/sinema-server.aspx

21. Richardson, T., Levine, J.: The Remote Framebuffer Protocol. RFC 6143 (March 2011)

22. Seifert, R.: The Switch Book: The Complete Guide to LAN Switching Technology, 1st edn. John Wiley & Sons, Inc., New York (2000)

23. Götz, F.-J.: Guaranteed Latency for Control-Data-Traffic in Time Sensitive Networks. In: IEEE 802.1 Time-Sensitive Networks (Interim Meeting in York, England). IEEE Computer Society (September 2013)

Target-Specific Adaptations
of Coupling-Based
Software Reliability Testing

Matthias Meitner and Francesca Saglietti

Informatik 11 - Software Engineering
University of Erlangen-Nuremberg
Erlangen, Germany
{matthias.meitner,saglietti}@informatik.uni-erlangen.de

Abstract. This article presents some approaches to software reliability testing supporting high coverage of component or (sub-)system interactions while enabling the selection of test cases according to target and scenario-specific criteria. On the one hand, in order to allow for reliability assessment, automatic test generation approaches must support the provision of stochastically independent and operationally representative test data. On the other hand, crucial sub-system interactions must be tested as intensely as possible, with particular concern for the even distribution of testing effort or for the prioritization of domain-critical data. Depending on such application-specific peculiarities, different multi-objective optimization problems are approached by novel genetic algorithms, successively applied to an interaction-intensive example in order to illustrate their practicality.

Keywords: Software reliability, interaction coverage, statistical sampling theory, coupling-based testing, multi-objective optimization, genetic algorithm.

1   Introduction

Modern information society increasingly tends to rely on service provision offered by interacting systems. Typically, such systems originate from completely independent environments concerning a.o. their functional context or their dependability and performance demands. In order to cooperate towards a common super-ordinate task, decentralized, autonomous systems growingly tend to interact, giving rise to so-called systems-of-systems.

The growing multiplicity of potential interplay of such applications induces crucial fault sources at interaction level. In particular, classical unit and integration testing strategies of monolithic and component-based systems may no longer suffice to ensure a sufficient degree of dependability [5] in case of inherently correct sub-systems sporadically interplaying in inadequate ways.

Therefore, today's software engineering community requires novel systematic and measurable approaches to detect emergent behavior [8] by unforeseeable interplay effects.

K. Fischbach and U.R. Krieger (Eds.): MMB & DFT 2014, LNCS 8376, pp. 192–206, 2014.

Especially in case of dependable applications requiring conservative reliability estimation, software tests must capture the variety of sub-system interactions as much as reasonably possible, while reflecting software behavior under realistic operative conditions.

A technically sound approach addressing both criteria was developed in [10]. While providing a helpful technique for combining statistical and structural testing strategies, its major draw-back concerns its incapability to distinguish between interaction entities in terms of the evenness of their occurrence or of their domain-specific importance.

For this reason, new approaches were developed, capable of optimizing test case selection also in the light of balancing or prioritizing interaction tests.

The article is organized as follows:

- section 2 and section 3 provide a brief overview of an existing automatic test generation approach [10] to reliability and integration testing by summarizing the underlying criteria for statistical and coupling-based testing and by deriving a multi-objective optimization procedure pursuing their fulfillment;
- section 4 proposes three adaptations of this approach addressing different application-specific targets and scenarios;
- section 5 reports on the successful application of the three adapted approaches to an interaction-intensive example;
- finally, section 6 comments on the investigations reported by some concluding remarks.

2   Requirements for Reliability and Integration Testing

2.1   Test Data Selection

The application of statistical sampling theory requires the following constraints on the test data selection:

- test data must be selected independently for each test case;
- test data must be selected at the same probability of occurrence as during operation.

On the other hand, the process of test execution must fulfill the following conditions:

- the execution of a test case (in the following denoted as a test run) does not influence the outcome of other test runs;
- no or only few failures occur during testing;
- any software failure occurrence is detected.

In case of a low number of failure occurrences, statistical sampling theory is still applicable at the cost, however, of a lower reliability estimate. In case of a significant number of failure occurrences, the responsible faults are assumed to be removed before a new data sample is generated and tested.

Since this article addresses late testing of highly dependable software, in the following it is assumed that no failure occurs.

Moreover, we consider software systems reacting to discrete demands, e.g. the driver's command to a software-based gear-box controller [16], or the detection of an anomalous state requiring the initiation of a protection function. For such applications, unreliability is measured in terms of the probability of failure on demand. In principle, the theory is also applicable to failure rates related to continuous operation [2].

If none of the above mentioned conditions is violated, statistical testing theory [2, 7, 12, 13] allows to derive a conservative software reliability estimation by bounding the failure probability p at any given confidence level β [2, 18], assuming a sufficiently high number n > 100 of correctly executed test cases:

$$p \leq 1 - \sqrt[n]{1-\beta}$$

Though not always easily practicable, this theory was successfully applied a.o. to an industrial software-based gear-box controller [16].

The present article focuses on the conditions concerning test data selection, while the conditions concerning test execution and test evaluation must be ensured by constructive measures like reset mechanisms and test oracles.

Since statistical sampling theory requires test data to be independent, input values must not be correlated. Input parameter, however, may be semantically correlated e.g. by dependencies related to

- logical patterns (e.g. checksums), or
- physical laws (e.g. kinetic energy, mass and speed).

These correlations are evidently application-inherent (i.e. they cannot be eliminated during test case selection) and have to be captured by the operational profile. On the other hand, correlations arising during instantiation of functionally independent parameters have to be avoided or removed by filters based on adequate correlation measures (see section 3).

2.2   Coverage of Data Flow across Components

While offering a sound approach to conservative reliability assessment, statistical sampling theory admittedly relies on one single experiment related to the random generation of one large set of representative and independent test cases.

Evidently, this one-time generation process cannot be expected to cover all relevant interaction scenarios [10]. In fact, a considerable number of crucial interaction scenarios may be missed. In order to prevent this from occurring, the approach was extended such as to cover a certain amount of interactions though maintaining the original targets concerning operational representativeness and test case independence.

Among the existing model- and code-based interaction coverage concepts [1, 4, 14, 15, 17] coupling-based coverage [4] aims at capturing interactions between components by transferring classical data flow testing concepts from an intra-module to an inter-module perspective. Essentially, it considers the effects of a method (the *caller*) in one component invoking another method (the *callee*) in another component distinguishing between three types of so-called '*coupling definitions*', i.e. of definitions of variables whose value is successively used in a different component, like

- the last definition of a formal parameter before a call ('*last-def-before call*'),
- the last definition of a formal parameter before a return ('*last-def-before-return*'),
- the definition of a global variable ('*shared-data-def*'),

as well as between three types of so-called *'coupling uses'*, i.e. of uses of variable values defined in a coupling definition located in a different component, like

- the first use of a formal parameter in a caller after the callee execution (*'first-use-after-call'*),
- the first use of a formal parameter in a callee (*'first-use-in-callee'*),
- the use of a global variable (*'shared-data-use'*).

Figure 1 illustrates the main concepts of coupling-based testing by means of an example.

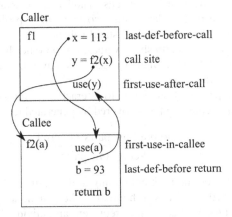

Fig. 1. Coupling-based interactions between two components

[4] introduces a number of different testing criteria based on the coverage of coupling pairs, i.e. of pairs consisting of a coupling definition and a corresponding coupling use. For example, the testing criterion *'all-coupling-uses'* was defined to require the coverage of all existing coupling pairs.

3   Test Case Generation by Multi-objective Optimization

The automatic test generation approach presented in [10] simultaneously pursues three objectives: while the first two are required in order to allow for reliability assessment by statistical testing, the third objective refers to interaction coverage to be maximized without violating, however, any of the other two criteria previously mentioned (in the following denoted as *knock-out* criteria).

The first objective O_1 concerns the generation of test cases according to an operationally representative data profile expected to be available on the basis of a preliminary estimation of the frequency of occurrence of the underlying input parameter values. With respect to this target, data fitness may be evaluated by means of goodness-of-fit tests like the χ^2-, the *Kolmogorov-Smirnov* or the *Anderson-Darling* test [6]. The conformity of the data observed to the target distribution can be evaluated by analyzing whether the underlying test statistic S_1 does not exceed a critical value T_1.

The second objective O_2 regards statistical independence of test data concerning uncorrelated parameters. Statistical correlation can be evaluated by *auto-correlation* measures addressing the dependency of a specific parameter value within a test case on other values of the same parameter in further test cases as well as by *cross-correlation* measures addressing the dependencies between different parameter values within the same test case. Classical cross-correlation measures are *Pearson's* product moment correlation coefficient [3], *Spearman's* rank correlation coefficient, *Kendall's* τ and *Cramer's V* [19]. In order to assess stochastic independence, the absolute value S_2 of a correlation measure is compared with a maximum threshold value T_2, where parameters with values S_2 lower than T_2 can be considered to be acceptably independent.

As already mentioned, the threshold values T_1 and T_2 are essential for the purpose of assessing the acceptance of test data with respect to their profile conformance and stochastic independence: the lower the threshold values, the more accurately reliability testing can be carried out. Low threshold values, on the other hand, evidently restrict the space of admissible data; in particular cases, this may limit the chances of achieving high interaction coverage.

Finally, the third objective O_3 is related to interaction coverage and is measured as the relative amount S_3 of coupling pairs covered by generated test cases:

$$S_3 = \frac{\#\text{coupling pairs covered}}{\#\text{coupling pairs}}$$

Due to its high complexity, the problem aiming at the optimization of all three objectives must be approached by means of heuristics like genetic algorithms. In more detail, each potential test case set is taken to represent an individual within a population. The fitness of each individual reflects the degree to which it fulfills the objectives.

Populations are successively generated by selecting and manipulating existing individuals [20]: cross-over operators exchange test cases among individuals or input values among test cases, while mutation operators replace single test cases or single input values. Finally, in order to avoid fitness decay, elitism operators are applied to maintain the best individuals for the successive generation.

With respect to each objective O_i, $i \in \{1,2,3\}$, the fitness of each individual is evaluated by means of the corresponding metric S_i. While the coupling measure S_3 already lies within the normalization interval $[0;1]$ by definition, the goodness-of-fit metric S_1 and the correlation metric S_2 have to be normalized by the following normalization function N:

$$N(S_i) = \begin{cases} 1 & \text{for} \quad S_i \in [0, T_i] \\ -\dfrac{0.9}{\max_i - T_i} \cdot S_i + \dfrac{0.9 \cdot \max_i}{\max_i - T_i} & \text{for} \quad S_i \in (T_i, \max_i] \end{cases} \quad i \in \{1,2\}$$

where $\max_i$ denotes the highest value taken by S_i within a test case population. The normalization function is illustrated in figure 2.

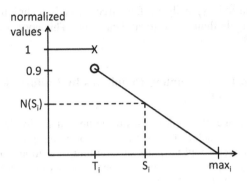

Fig. 2. Normalization function for measures S_i, $i \in \{1,2\}$

For any test case set TS, the fitness of TS is determined as the weighted sum of its three normalized objectives:

$$F(TS) = 1.0 \cdot N(S_1) + 1.0 \cdot N(S_2) + 0.1 \cdot S_3$$

The non-steady normalization function and the weight factor 0.1 for S_3 were chosen such that test sets violating at least one knock-out criterion (i.e. $N(S_1) < 0.9$ or $N(S_2) < 0.9$) have a fitness value $F(TS) < 2$, while test sets fulfilling both knock-out criteria (i.e. $N(S_1) = N(S_2) = 1$) have a fitness value $F(TS) \geq 2$. This holds regardless of the size of the interaction coverage achieved.

4   Optimal Distribution of Testing Effort

The all-coupling-uses coverage measure S_3 considered so far merely counts the relative amount of coupling pairs covered; hereby, every coupling pair covered has the same impact on the overall coverage measured. This approach, however, may not be fully appropriate in the following situations.

As test cases are generated according to an underlying operational profile, the probability of covering specific pairs may be very low in case of extremely non-uniform distributions. In such cases, it may be unrealistic to target 100% coupling pair coverage; it may be reasonable instead to cover at least all coupling definitions, while aiming at distributing the test cases as evenly as possible among them. Evidently, this more modest testing strategy may skip coupling pairs representing relevant scenarios; therefore, its usage is not recommended in case of critical applications. Details will be introduced in section 4.1.

On the other hand, even in case of highly reliable software requiring full coverage of coupling pairs, the distribution of test cases among coupling pairs should be kept as uniform as possible, in order to balance their chances of being accurately checked for correctness. This strategy will be elaborated in section 4.2.

Finally, it may be unrealistic to consider all variables as equally relevant, as done so far. On the contrary, software reliability may be particularly sensitive to the correctness of specific variables. In particular, safety of software-based applications may especially depend on a number of particularly critical process variables. These must be preliminarily identified, typically by fault tree analysis techniques, and require to be tested more thoroughly than non-critical data flows. This approach [9] will be summarized in section 4.3.

4.1 Adaptation 1: All Coupling Definitions by Uniform Relative Coverage of Their Coupling Pairs

Assuming full coverage of coupling uses to be unrealistically demanding, test generation should be targeted such as to cover each coupling definition at least once; in addition, tests should cover coupling pairs of coupling definitions in comparable relative amounts. By doing so, however, the all-coupling-uses coverage originally achieved should not be diminished.

For this purpose, the original fitness factor S_3 is scaled to a new factor S_3' by:

$$S_3' = S_3 \cdot \frac{\sum\limits_{i=1}^{n}\left(1 - \frac{|c_i - \bar{c}|}{\max(c_i, \bar{c})}\right)}{n}$$

where

- n denotes the total number of coupling definitions,
- for $i \in \{1,...,n\}$, c_i denotes the relative amount of coupling pairs of coupling definition i already covered,
- $\bar{c}$ denotes the average of such relative amounts over all coupling definitions, i.e.

$$\bar{c} = \frac{1}{n} \cdot \sum_{i=1}^{n} c_i$$

For arbitrary i, the weighting term $1 - \dfrac{|c_i - \bar{c}|}{\max(c_i, \bar{c})}$ is shown in figure 3 as a function of c_i.

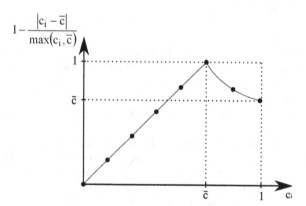

Fig. 3. Weighting term as function of c_i

This term evaluates to

- 0, if $c_i = 0$, i.e. if no coupling pair was yet covered for coupling definition i (worst situation),
- 1, if $c_i = \bar{c}$, i.e. if the percentage amount of coupling pairs covered for coupling definition i coincides with the average of such percentage amounts (best situation).

In other words, in the first case test case sets are penalized if they miss to cover coupling definition i, while in the second case test case sets are especially rewarded as they succeed in covering coupling definition i as much as the average of all coupling definitions.

Therefore, the optimization procedure making use of the adapted fitness factor S_3' consequently favors the coverage of yet uncovered coupling definitions and pursues their uniform coverage, while maintaining a high coverage of coupling pairs.

4.2   Adaptation 2: Uniform Coverage of Coupling Pairs

Even in case of full coupling pair coverage, the number of times each coupling pair was triggered may be extremely fluctuating. In such cases it may be reasonable either to minimize the overall number of test cases necessary to reach full coverage (as successfully done in [11]) or to adapt the optimization procedure towards uniformity of coupling pair coverage.

This can be achieved by scaling the original factor S_3 to a new fitness value S_3'' :

$$S_3'' = S_3 \cdot \frac{\sum_{i=1}^{m}\left(1 - \frac{|n_i - \bar{n}|}{\max(n_i, \bar{n})}\right)}{m}$$

where

- m denotes the number of coupling pairs,
- for $i \in \{1,\dots,m\}$ n_i denotes the number of test runs covering coupling pair i,
- $\bar{n}$ denotes the average number of such runs over all pairs, i.e.

$$\bar{n} = \frac{1}{m} \cdot \sum_{i=1}^{m} n_i$$

For arbitrary i the weighting term $1 - \frac{|n_i - \bar{n}|}{\max(n_i, \bar{n})}$ is shown in figure 4 as a function of n_i.

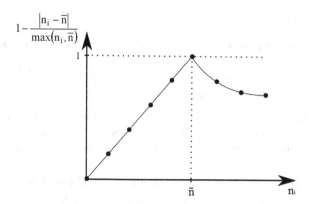

Fig. 4. Weighting term as function of n_i

This term evaluates to

- 0, if $n_i = 0$, i.e. if coupling pair i was not yet covered at all,
- 1, if $n_i = \bar{n}$, i.e. if coupling pair i was covered exactly an average number of times.

In other words, in the first case test case sets are penalized as they miss to cover coupling pair i, while in the second case test case sets are especially rewarded as they succeed in covering coupling pair i exactly an average number of times.

On the whole, this optimization procedure favors the testing of those coupling pairs whose number of executions still is below average. On the other hand, test cases executing coupling pairs more than average are penalized, thereby supporting uniformity over all pairs.

This approach also works for the purpose of uniformity over coupling definitions by defining m to represent the number of coupling definitions and n_i to represent the number of executions of coupling definition i.

4.3   Adaptation 3: Different Relevance of Coupling Pairs

When dealing with critical software, as in case of safety-relevant applications, some variables may influence system reliability more intensely than others. This may imply different testing demands for different process variables, an aspect not yet taken into account so far in sections 4.1 and 4.2. For this purpose, an additional adaptation of coupling-based testing [9] aims at strengthening the testing of critical variables by favoring test data covering relevant coupling pairs. For each coupling pair i it takes into account the following parameters:

- a weight w_i reflecting the priority in testing coupling pair i and rewarding the generation of corresponding test cases; priorities may be determined on the basis of a preliminary fault tree analysis determining the criticality of certain variables;
- a target number t_i of executions for coupling pair i; target numbers t_i inhibit the rewards w_i induced by priorities as soon as the target number of test cases is reached; on the one hand, target numbers should grow with the relevance of the corresponding coupling pair; on the other hand, the target number must take into

account the frequency of occurrence of that coupling pair during operation. Preliminary feedback on the expected operational profile can be obtained on the basis of a random initial population. Such a feedback can be successively corrected by increasing the target number of relevant coupling pairs and lowering the target number of less relevant coupling pairs. For rarely occurring coupling pairs, appropriate minimum values are to be determined;

- a decrease factor d_i lowering the impact of weight w_i, the more the corresponding coupling pair is already covered; decrease factors d_i are used for balancing the testing of coupling pairs with identical weight w_i by favoring those coupling pairs so far only covered below reasonable expectation.

The original fitness factor S_3 is replaced by a new normalized metric S_3''' taking into account the original criterion S_3 as well as the parameters described above:

$$S_3''' = S_3 \cdot \frac{\sum\limits_{i=1}^{m} \sum\limits_{j=1}^{\min(n_i,t_i)} \dfrac{w_i}{d_i^{j-1}}}{\sum\limits_{i=1}^{m} \sum\limits_{j=1}^{t_i} \dfrac{w_i}{d_i^{j-1}}}$$

where

- m denotes the total number of coupling pairs,
- n_i denotes the number of test cases covering coupling pair i, $1 \leq i \leq m$.

4.4   Summary and Additional Remarks

Table 1 summarizes the different test targets and scenarios under which the three adaptation approaches proposed are particularly recommended.

Table 1. Recommended adaptations for different test targets

Expected coverage of coupling pairs	Test target	Recommended adaptation
below 100%	all coupling definitions by uniform relative coverage of their coupling pairs	adaptation 1 based on fitness factor S_3'
100%	uniform coverage of all coupling pairs	adaptation 2 based on fitness factor S_3''
100%	multiple coverage of coupling pairs according to their different relevance	adaptation 3 based on fitness factor S_3'''

It is also possible to use both fitness factors S_3' and S_3'' sequentially in a common, dynamically adaptive approach. In case domain experts cannot preliminarily estimate whether optimized test cases will achieve full coverage, the underlying genetic algorithm starts by measuring interaction coverage via factor S_3'. As soon as full coverage is reached, S_3' (just evaluated to 1) is replaced by S_3'', thus supporting a more uniform coverage of coupling pairs, as described in section 4.2.

5   Application and Evaluation of Adaptive Approaches

The approach developed was applied to a software-based system consisting of five components:

- one central component denoted as Controller,
- four further components denoted as Service 1, Service 2, Service 3 and Service 4 providing cooperating tasks.

The application processes three independent input parameters of type integer or double. Depending on these inputs, the Controller invokes components Service 1 and Service 2 which may imply further calls to components Service 3 and Service 4. Between two and six parameters are exchanged during method calls. Figure 5 offers a graphical representation of the invocation hierarchy.

In terms of coupling-based testing, the system contains 12 coupling definitions and 44 coupling pairs. Though relatively small in dimension, the system is characterized by a relatively high intensity of component interaction.

In the following, the three adaptive approaches are applied to this example; each application assumes a different operational profile which is defined by the distribution functions of each of the three independent input parameters.

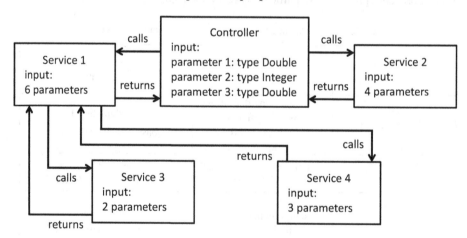

Fig. 5. Application example with interacting components

Concerning distribution conformance, for each goodness-of-fit test a corresponding threshold value was derived at significance level 0.1; concerning stochastic independence, the threshold value was defined as 0.1.

5.1   Application and Evaluation of Adaptation 1

All experiments reported in this sub-section were conducted with test sets comprising 1000 test cases and a skewed operational profile rendering full coverage unrealistic. At first, a test case set was randomly generated without making use of optimizing procedures. As shown in figure 6 (a) the corresponding coverage achieved is relatively low, in particular completely missing some coupling definitions. On the other hand, the classical, non-adapted optimization approach described in section 3 allows for a significant increase in coupling definition coverage, as shown in figure 6 (b), while missing to address specific problems concerning either coupling definitions remained uncovered or coupling pairs not uniformly covered for different coupling definitions.

The results of the improved optimization procedure based on adaptation 1 are finally shown in figure 6 (c): while the new average coverage $\bar{c}$ is close to the previous one, the relative coverage of coupling pairs per coupling definition is well balanced, as illustrated by the graphical region delimited by the values c_i, which is nearly congruent to the regular polygon delimited by their average $\bar{c}$.

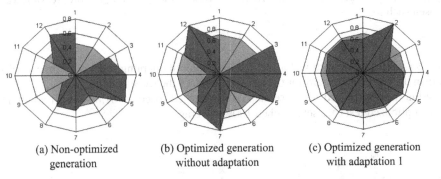

| (a) Non-optimized generation | (b) Optimized generation without adaptation | (c) Optimized generation with adaptation 1 |

Fig. 6. Optimization results for adaptation 1 (light grey: $\bar{c}$, dark grey: c_i, $i \in \{1,...,12\}$)

In order to ensure experimental comparability, the original non-optimized test case sets from 6 (a) were used as starting population for the optimizations illustrated in 6 (b) and 6 (c). The same holds for the evaluations presented in sections 5.2 and 5.3.

5.2   Application and Evaluation of Adaptation 2

The average deviation of coupling pair executions from their average number

$$\bar{d} = \frac{1}{m} \cdot \sum_{i=1}^{m} |n_i - \bar{n}|$$

was evaluated for the classical approach and for adaptation 2, each applied for the generation of 1000 test cases. Both the classical approach and its adaptation 2 could achieve 100% coverage, while a non-optimized test case set only reached 75% coverage, leaving 11 coupling pairs uncovered. The adapted approach could achieve a reduction of the average deviation from 134.5 to 91.9.

As expected, the test case set resulting from the revised approach could achieve a higher uniformity in covering the coupling pairs.

5.3   Application and Evaluation of Adaptation 3

Finally, the application of the third adapted approach [9] is reported in the following, where the test case sets generated by the underlying genetic algorithm consisted of 5000 test cases each.

According to its criticality, each coupling pair was classified as highly relevant, moderately relevant or lowly relevant; corresponding weights w_i were assigned. For the purpose of an experimental estimation of realistic frequencies of occurrence of coupling pairs, a random initial population was generated and for each coupling pair the maximum number of its executions determined. These numbers were successively weighted according to the criticality of each coupling pair i, yielding target parameters t_i. To exclude exceedingly low values for coupling pairs with rare occurrences, minimum targets were defined. Additional factors d_i balance the number of test cases for coupling pairs of identical relevance by correcting the original reward induced by weights w_i via a decreasing geometric progression. In more detail, the progression was chosen such that

$$d_i^{t_i-1} = 10$$

In other words, the reward w_i for the first execution of coupling pair i is 10 times higher than the corrected reward for the t_i-th execution of the same coupling pair.

While non-optimized test case sets only managed to cover 81.8% of all coupling pairs, optimized test case sets reached 100% coverage.

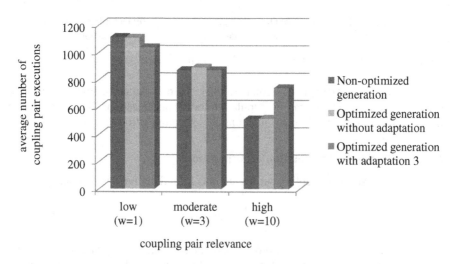

Fig. 7. Results obtained by application of adaptation 3

Figure 7 illustrates the benefits of this approach by comparing non-optimized test case sets, test case sets optimized without adaptation and test case sets optimized using adaptation 3: the adaptive approach succeeded in increasing the number of executions of highly relevant coupling pairs by ca. 44% at the price of reducing the test amount concerning the less relevant coupling entities by ca. 7%, while the number of executions of moderately relevant coupling pairs did not vary considerably.

6   Conclusion

In this article, an existing test generation procedure based on multi-objective optimization was adapted for the purpose of increasing uniformity over tested interactions as well as test intensity concerning domain-specific relevant interactions.

The practicality of the three resulting approaches was evaluated by means of an example showing that interaction testing can be systematically tailored to application-specific constraints, while supporting the applicability of statistical testing.

Acknowledgment. The authors gratefully acknowledge that the work presented was partly funded by Siemens Corporate Technology.

References

1. Alexander, R.T., Offutt, A.J.: Coupling-based Testing of O-O Programs. Journal of Universal Computer Science 10(4), 391–427 (2004)
2. Ehrenberger, W.: Software-Verifikation. Hanser (2002)
3. Hartung, J.: Statistik. Oldenbourg (1995)
4. Jin, Z., Offutt, A.J.: Coupling-based criteria for integration testing. Journal of Software Testing, Verification and Reliability 8(3), 133–154 (1998)
5. Jung, M., Saglietti, F.: Supporting Component and Architectural Re-usage by Detection and Tolerance of Integration Faults. In: 9th IEEE International Symposium on High Assurance Systems Engineering, pp. 47–55. IEEE Computer Society (2005)
6. Law, A.M., Kelton, W.D.: Simulation Modeling and Analysis. McGraw-Hill (2000)
7. Littlewood, B., Wright, D.: Some conservative stopping rules for the operational testing of safety critical software. IEEE Transactions on Software Engineering 23(11), 673–683 (1997)
8. Maier, M.W.: Architecting principles for systems-of-systems. Systems Engineering 1(4), 267–284 (1998)
9. Meitner, M., Saglietti, F.: Adaptation of Coupling-Based Reliability Testing for Safety-Relevant Software. In: Berekovic, M., Danek, M. (eds.) 26th International Conference on Architecture of Computing Systems. Workshop Proceedings. VDE (2013)
10. Meitner, M., Saglietti, F.: Software Reliability Testing Covering Subsystem Interactions. In: Schmitt, J.B. (ed.) MMB & DFT 2012. LNCS, vol. 7201, pp. 46–60. Springer, Heidelberg (2012)
11. Oster, N., Saglietti, F.: Automatic Test Data Generation by Multi-objective Optimisation. In: Górski, J. (ed.) SAFECOMP 2006. LNCS, vol. 4166, pp. 426–438. Springer, Heidelberg (2006)

12. Parnas, D., van Schouwen, J., Kwan, S.: Evaluation of Safety-Critical Software. Communications of the ACM 33(6), 636–648 (1990)
13. Quirk, W.J. (ed.): Verification and Validation of Real-time Software. Springer (1985)
14. Rehman, M., Jabeen, F., Bertolino, A., Polini, A.: Testing software components for integration: a survey of issues and techniques. Journal of Software Testing, Verification, and Reliability 17(2), 95–133 (2007)
15. Saglietti, F., Oster, N., Pinte, F.: Interface Coverage Criteria Supporting Model-Based Integration Testing. In: Platzner, M., Großpietsch, K.-E., Hochberger, C., Koch, A. (eds.) 20th International Conference on Architecture of Computing Systems. Workshop Proceedings, pp. 85–93, VDE (2007)
16. Söhnlein, S., Saglietti, F., Bitzer, F., Meitner, M., Baryschew, S.: Software Reliability Assessment based on the Evaluation of Operational Experience. In: Müller-Clostermann, B., Echtle, K., Rathgeb, E.P. (eds.) MMB & DFT 2010. LNCS, vol. 5987, pp. 24–38. Springer, Heidelberg (2010)
17. Spillner, A.: Test Criteria and Coverage Measures for Software Integration Testing. Software Quality Journal 4(4), 275–286 (1995)
18. Störmer, H.: Mathematische Theorie der Zuverlässigkeit. Oldenbourg (1970)
19. Storm, R.: Wahrscheinlichkeitsrechnung, mathematische Statistik und Qualitätskontrolle. Hanser (2007)
20. Weicker, K.: Evolutionäre Algorithmen. Vieweg+Teubner (2002)

Simulating the Energy Management on Smartphones Using Hybrid Modeling Techniques

Ibrahim Alagöz, Christoffer Löffler, Vitali Schneider, and Reinhard German

Department of Computer Science 7,
University of Erlangen-Nuremberg, Germany
{german,vitali.schneider}@cs.fau.de,
ibrahim.alagoez@eei.stud.uni-erlangen.de,
christoffer.loeffler@informatik.stud.uni-erlangen.de
http://www7.cs.fau.de

Abstract. With the global growth of the market for smartphones new business ideas and applications are developed continuously. These often utilize the resources of a mobile device to a considerable extent and reach the limits of these. In this work we focus on the simulation of an on-demand music service on a modern smartphone. Our simulation model includes higher level descriptions of the necessary hardware components' behavior and their energy consumption. Thereby, the detailed simulation of battery plays a key role in the project. With this simulation study we find optimal parameters for the users of the examined application to maximize playback time, improve its battery life and reduce costly data transmissions.

Keywords: smartphone, energy management, streaming music on-demand, battery lifetime, kinetic battery model, simulation study.

1   Introduction

With the global growth of the market for smartphones new business ideas and applications are continuously developed. These often exhaustively utilize the potential capabilities and resources of the devices. The users of these services often face the problem that some apps deplete the battery life too much. Regarding the complex relations between different apps, their settings, system software and hardware in such a device, it is hardly possible to make exact statements about the resource utilization and the resulting lifetime in advance. Nevertheless, using simulation approaches it is feasible to predict the expected system behaviour and to test various scenarios.

In this paper we focus on simulating a music streaming application on a smartphone with the deeper analysis of the battery performance and power consumption of the involved hardware modules. Our simulation model enables us to detect the bottlenecks of the application as well as of the mobile device and lets us predict the system's behavior for different parameter configurations. Thereby, we optimize the parameters of a music streaming app that the user can set in order to maximize the playback time.

K. Fischbach and U.R. Krieger (Eds.): MMB & DFT 2014, LNCS 8376, pp. 207–224, 2014.

The system we simulate consists of an Android smartphone *HTC Incredible S* and the music streaming app *Ubuntu One Music*. It enables the user to stream music over the smartphone's data connection, which in our scenario can be either the WiFi or the 3G network. The smartphone is set to continuously play music and is exclusively used for that task. While a data connection is active the device pre-fetches music to a local storage. The device plays the stored music continuously until either the storage or the battery is empty.

The simulated system consists of software and hardware components like chipsets and battery. Accordingly, our smartphone model consists of three parts, each describing an aspect of the smartphone. We model the app's behavior, which controls the hardware. The hardware model implements the device's different chipsets, which determine the system's performance and power consumption. Finally, the battery model simulates the performance of the smartphone's battery. Thereby, the integration of power consumption as an input unit into the non-linear kinetic battery model (*KiBaM*) [1] and the modeling of correlated WiFi data rates using a linear time invariant system are key methods presented in this paper.

Due to overall complexity of the system as well as of the user's interaction with the smartphone we had to simplify certain aspects of the system. Thus, in our scenarios the user does not skip tracks and never activates the screen. Furthermore the granularity of the simulation model of certain hardware modules is limited and focuses strictly on the behavior for the use-case which can be validated.

The parameters for the optimization are limited to the controls provided to the user by the music streaming client and by the usage scenario. A scenario is defined by the time the user spends in WiFi and 3G networks. If the user switches off the data connection, the battery lasts much longer. Another important parameter is the size of the device-local storage to buffer music files. We show that the difference between 100MB and 5GB is significant in terms of power efficiency.

The rest of the paper is organized as follows. Section 2 illustrates some related work. In section 3 we describe the simulation model which consists of software, hardware and battery components. There we explain the integration of power consumption into the kinetic battery model. In section 4 we present techniques used for input modeling. The sampling of correlated random variates for the WiFi bitrate is a key topic. In section 5 we present the validation of the simulation model. We show our optimization results in section 6 and our conclusions in section 7.

2   Related Work

In this section we provide a brief summary on some of the related work on battery modeling, power estimation and signal processing.

The existing battery models have been classified by Jongerden in [2] into four categories: electrochemical, analytical, stochastic, and electrical circuit models.

The author evaluates these different battery models and concludes the analytical *KiBaM* model, which was proposed in [1], to be most suitable for battery performance modeling. The authors of [3], [4], and [5] describe hybrid approaches based on the *KiBaM* model and extended by an electrical circuit model in order to predict the dynamic circuit characteristics of the battery additionally to its non-linear capacity effects and runtime.

In [6] the authors describe a modeling technique to monitor the power consumption of hardware modules of a smartphone using the power estimation and logging tool *PowerTutor* [7].

The basics of the signal processing and filtering algorithms applied in this work can be found in [8] and [9].

3   Simulation Model

Our simulation model consists of three layers: software, hardware and battery. Thereby, we employed a hybrid modeling approach with combined discrete-event and continuous simulation techniques. Thus, the software and the hardware layers are modeled following the discrete event simulation paradigm [10] with the use of finite state machines (FSMs), which interact by message passing. Furthermore, to represent the continuous performance of the battery, which is based on the *KiBaM* model, we are using system dynamics (SD) approach. The simulation model is completely realized in the simulation framework AnyLogic [11] that is capable of hybrid simulations.

Figure 1 shows the main view of the simulation model in AnyLogic. The software layer models the behavior of the *Ubuntu One Music* streaming client. The hardware layer implements relevant physical components of the smartphone like CPU, sound, memory, and network modules. In our work we focus strictly on the necessary parts for our scenario. Components like the screen, which are not involved for music playback and which usage patterns cannot be correctly validated, are excluded. The modules of software and hardware components communicate with connected components by exchanging messages over ports. Furthermore, the hardware components consume power continuously and need, therefore, to be connected to the battery model via so-called auxiliary variables from the system dynamics package of AnyLogic. The battery layer simulates the discharge of battery and causes stopping of the simulation if its state-of-charge reaches 0%.

3.1   Application / Software Module

We simplify the *Ubuntu One Music* app on the smartphone to two central functionalities. The first one is downloading music from the cloud servers to memory. The second is playing music from memory. As shown in Figure 2 we modeled the behavior of the app as two concurrent FSMs.

The *DownloadFSM* controls the downloading task and initiates the network module to download a music track by sending a message to it. Thereby, it switches to the downloading state where it waits for a message from the network module. Such messages indicate either a finished download, upon which

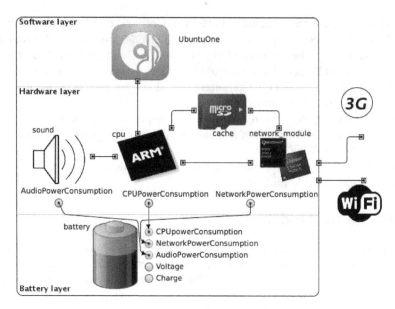

Fig. 1. Main view of the simulation model

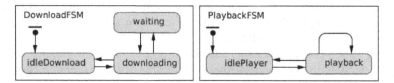

Fig. 2. Parallel state machines of the application module

the FSM returns to *idleDownload*, or an interruption caused by a full memory or a network failure. In case of interruption the FSM switches to waiting state. Then, after a timeout, it sends a restart message and returns to the downloading state.

The *PlaybackFSM* controls the playback of downloaded music. It starts in *idlePlayer* and takes the transition to *playback* when there is enough data available in the app's local buffer, which is refilled with the data from the memory module in every simulated second. During the playback this buffer is decremented by the amount of data which equals to 1s of music depending on the specified music bit rate. When that local buffer is drained the FSM returns to *idlePlayer*. During the simulation we measure the total playback time which is central to the optimization of parameters.

3.2 Hardware Modules

Like in the real scenario, our hardware model is controlled by the software model. Thus the current state of both app FSMs has influence on several hardware modules and finally on their power consumption.

CPU. In our simulation model the CPU is primarily used to forward control messages between the app and hardware components, since the application logic is simulated at the software layer. Additionally, the CPU module also provides the power consumption for the different application steps that are triggered by messages from other components. As shown in Figure 3 the FSM of the CPU consists of a four distinct states which represent tuples of two overall system states: downloading and playback. Each state consumes thereby power at a different scale. In the section on input modeling we will explain this in more detail.

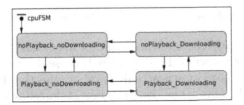

Fig. 3. State machine of the CPU module

Network Module. The network module implements the downloading of data over the available network connections: WiFi or 3G. In this module we measure the accumulated times spent in WiFi or 3G, and the downloaded data for each connection type.

The module consists of two state machines (see Figure 4), the *DataFSM* for downloading and the *EnergyFSM* for power consumption. The *DataFSM* contains only two states: *idle* and *downloading*. A download starts when a message with the file size arrives. Every second downloaded data is saved to the memory by sending a message to the memory module. The sizes of these data depend on the current bitrate of the available network, which can vary and needs to be sampled according to distributions shown in section 4.2. The downloading state is left either on the event of a finished or an interrupted download. The download can be interrupted due to full memory or if the current network becomes unavailable. In all cases the *DataFSM* switches back to idle and sends the corresponding message to the app component.

The *EnergyFSM* models the power consumption of the WiFi and the 3G network interfaces. Thereby, only one network is active at the same time, e.g., if WiFi is used, 3G is completely shut down and consumes no power. Our measurements were conducted with this simplification in mind. When the simulation starts, the *EnergyFSM* is in the *off* state. It switches to one of the sub FSM, either to WiFi or to 3G, depending on which network is available at the time. The implementation of both sub FSMs is based on the work presented in [6] and [12].

If the WiFi network is active, the state *low* is entered first. When the download is started, the real-world chipset switches into the state *high*, which consumes more power but provides higher bandwidth for downloads. When the number of transferred packages drops below a certain threshold, the chipset switches to the power

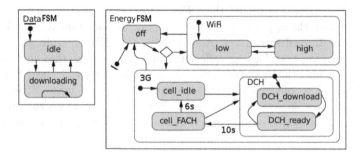

Fig. 4. Network module's finite state machines

conserving low state. We simplified this behavior in our model by switching from *high* to *low* only after a download task finishes, because the bit rates we have measured during the download were nearly always above this threshold.

If the 3G network is available, the low power state *cell_idle* is entered. Upon the start of a download, the chipset switches to the DCH-mode, in which it consumes most power. After the download is finished it returns to *cell_idle*, with a short stopover in the state *cell_FACH*. In the FACH mode the power consumption is in between that of DCH and idle.

Memory. The file storage memory, represented by a SDCard in Figure 1, is used to store the downloaded music. It serves as an adapter between the software layer and the network and does not consume power. We can parameterize the phone's local storage by limiting the memory size, which affects the playback time, as can be seen in section 6.

Audio. Our simulation model features the sound module as a separate hardware component with its own power consumption. Its FSM consists of the states *idle* and *playback*. Its transitions are triggered by messages from the software layer.

3.3 Battery Module

The battery, as shown in the Figure 5, is modeled according to the *KiBaM* model with the use of SD. As mentioned in [2] *KiBaM* is able to accurately simulate the non-linear behavior of a battery with regard to the recovery effect. Other models, e.g., the electrochemical model, were considered but excluded, because they offer marginal improvements to the precision at very high effort [2]. The modeling is based on a black-box view at real battery parameters which are deduced by testing of the battery's discharge behavior.

The capacity model of *KiBaM* consists of two charge wells, y1 and y2 representing the available energy and the chemically bound energy, as shown in Figure 5. These two wells are designed for modeling both the recovery and the rate-capacity effect of a battery in order to define its usable capacity. The discharge is the time-discrete value i(t) depicted as *load* in Figure 5. It draws on y1 until its capacity is drained. The second well, y2, refills the first one continuously with the recovery rate k.

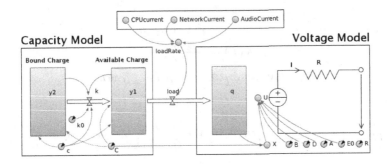

Fig. 5. SD model of battery

Since the *KiBaM* model requires a discharge current, but only power consumption of a hardware module can be accessed from the smartphone, we created an adapter to transform the overall power consumption from the discrete event model of the hardware layer into a discharge current. The adapter function is based on the voltage model (see Figure 5), which is taken from [5] and is required for the calculation of the instantaneous open circuit voltage U. In Equation 1 the expression for U is given, which depends on the variable $X(t)$ and is parametrized by E_0, A, B, and D. Thereby, the variable X stands for the normalized charge at the time t. The calculation of it according to [5] is given in Equation 2. The estimation of parameters will be discussed later in the input modeling part.

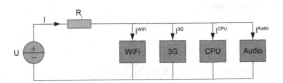

Fig. 6. Conceptual circuit design of hardware modules

For computing the overall discharge current we designed the circuit given in Figure 6, which consists of hardware modules with an internal battery resistance. We used the assumption in [6] that the overall power consumption of all hardware components can be calculated by summing up the individual power consumptions: $P = P^{WiFi} + P^{3G} + P^{CPU} + P^{Audio}$. Thus, we decided to place the components in parallel order to achieve parallel branches in which each component is served by its individual current, whereby the same voltage is applied to each of them as shown in Equation 3.

For the conversion of the power consumption to current we first observed a relation between the branch currents depending on the individual power consumptions (see Equation 4) and then we used *Kirchhoff's circuit law* for the computations in Equation 5. We solve the unknown I^{WiFi} of this quadratic equation and compute the overall current I with Equations 3 and 4.

$$U(t) = E_0 + A \cdot X(t) + \frac{B \cdot X(t)}{D - X(t)} \tag{1}$$

$$X(T) = \frac{C - \int_0^T i(t)dt}{C} \tag{2}$$

$$\begin{aligned} I &= I^{WiFi} + I^{3G} &&+ I^{CPU} + I^{Audio} \\ U^{WiFi} &= U^{3G} &&= U^{CPU} = U^{Audio} \end{aligned} \tag{3}$$

$$\Rightarrow I^{3G} = I^{WiFi}\frac{P^{3G}}{P^{WiFi}}; \quad I^{CPU} = I^{WiFi}\frac{P^{CPU}}{P^{WiFi}}; \quad I^{Audio} = I^{WiFi}\frac{P^{Audio}}{P^{WiFi}} \tag{4}$$

$$U = I \cdot R_i + U^{WiFi}$$

$$\Leftrightarrow U = [I^{WiFi} + I^{3G} + I^{CPU} + I^{Audio}] \cdot R_i + \frac{P^{WiFi}}{I^{WiFi}} \tag{5}$$

$$\Leftrightarrow 0 = [I^{WiFi}]^2 \cdot [1 + \frac{P^{3G}}{P^{WiFi}} + \frac{P^{CPU}}{P^{WiFi}} + \frac{P^{Audio}}{P^{WiFi}}] \cdot R_i - I^{WiFi} \cdot U + P^{WiFi}$$

4   Input Modeling

This section is segmented into the three different abstraction layers of the model: software, hardware, and battery.

4.1   Software

The only input parameters required for the software module are delays for timed transitions in *DownloadFSM*, which take impact on the average download rate and the recovery of the battery. The first parameter relates to the delay between downloads. For downloading of music tracks the app creates Java threads that are successively dispatched. But in between, different other threads of other applications and of the operating system are scheduled, which cause a delay between downloads. We measured these time delays with our device while downloading an amount of music files and modeled them in our model with the fixed mean delay of 3s. Another point is that downloads can be interrupted because of connection loss or full cache. Restarting downloading occurs after a fixed duration of 4s that can be extracted from the source code of the *Ubuntu One Music* application.

4.2   Hardware

The input modeling for the hardware layer consists of two major areas: the power consumption of hardware modules and the download data rates of 3G and WiFi networks.

For measuring the required parameters we logged the information from the smartphone with the tool *PowerTutor* [7]. Among others, it measures the data rates of network modules and approximates the power consumption of each hardware component of the smartphone within a configurable time step and saves it to log files. Furthermore, we used the distribution fitting tool *ExpertFit* [13] to analyze these logs and to look for suitable distribution functions.

CPU. The instantaneous power consumption of the CPU module depends on the tasks which are executed. For instance the download and the playback task have a main impact on the power consumption, next to the background tasks scheduled by other applications and also by the operating system.

So we decided to define 4 states depicted in Figure 3 whereby transitions between these states are triggered if enabling respectively disabling of the download and playback task occurs. In contrast to the remaining hardware modules we decided to model the power consumption of the CPU as a stochastic process because we had to deal with random background tasks.

For each state we conducted an independent experiment in which we logged every second the power consumption and estimated for that a distribution with the *ExpertFit* tool. For each state we obtained different *beta* distributions with the parameters listed in Table 1.

Table 1. Parameters of *beta* distributions for power consumption of the CPU's states

	p (lower shape)	q (upper shape)	min	max
¬download ∧ ¬playback	1.71	5.77	3	430
download ∧ ¬playback	1.53	3.82	20	430
¬download ∧ playback	2.01	6.14	36	414
download ∧ playback	1.72	1.93	20	417

Power Consumption of Network Modules. The *PowerTutor* application estimates the power consumptions of the defined states in Figure 4 which is summarized in the following table:

Table 2. Power consumption of the network states

WiFi		3G		
Low	High	IDLE	FACH	DCH
20mW	710mW	10 mW	401 mW	570 mW

WiFi Data Rates. We measured the download data rates achieved by WiFi network module with the help of the tool *PowerTutor*. The measurements were conducted with $1m$ proximity from a *WiFi 802.11n* router while downloading the music tracks using the *Ubuntu One Music* app.

In Figure 7a) we present the histogram and the lag correlation plot of the download data rates. We can observe that the data rates are correlated, which is primarily caused by bursts during the downloads. For our use-case it is important to model these bursts, because the use of fixed data rates leads to high

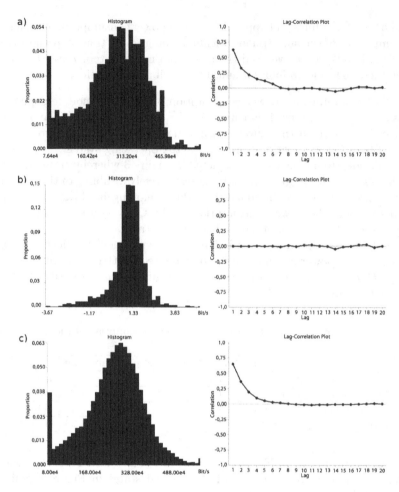

Fig. 7. Histogram and lag correlation plot of the a) measured, b) differential, and c) simulated WiFi download data rates

inaccuracy, which we could state in validating the simulation's download, playback and battery discharge times (see section 4). If the download bit rates are much higher than the playback rate, then the cache can overflow so that the energy used for downloading the music file packets is wasted. As a consequence less energy remains in the battery for playback. The correlation of download data rates is also important to determine the peak size of stored data when the cache size is assumed unlimited.

In order to generate the correlated data rates we use statistical methods for correlating and decorrelating of random variates. These methods are employed in the field of digital communications to reduce the transmission power for antennas [9]. Based on this, our approach is firstly decorrelating the download data rates with a pre-filter such that distribution fitting with *expertFit* can be processed. The fitted distribution is needed to generate random variates on runtime in *AnyLogic*. Using an inverse post-filter the correlation properties can be added to the generated random variates again in order to obtain similar correlated data rates during the simulation. In Figure 7 the histogram and the lag correlation plots after pre-filtering (b) and post-filtering (c) are also shown.

For decorrelating random variates, which are identically distributed but also correlated, a prediction filter has been designed. The output of this filter gives predictions of subsequent random variates. For further explanations the following definitions are needed:

– b[k]: download data rates $\hat{=}$ identically distributed, correlated random variates
– $\hat{b}[k]$: predictions of download data rates

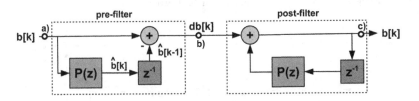

Fig. 8. Signal flow graph with relations between $b[k]$, $\hat{b}[k]$ and $db[k]$

The Figure 8 shows the signal flow graph of the prediction filter $P(z)$ which depicts the relations between $b[k]$, $\hat{b}[k]$ and $db[k]$. The mathematical relation between $b[k]$ and $\hat{b}[k]$ is given in Equation 6, where N is the degree of the finite prediction filter $P(z)$ and '*' stands for a convolution operation. The prediction filter $P(z)$ uses the statistical properties of the random variates $b[k]$ in order to generate $\hat{b}[k]$ in such a way that $\hat{b}[k-1]$ predicts $b[k]$. For achieving decorrelated random variates we use the operation in Equation 7.

$$\hat{b}[k] = \sum_{n=0}^{N} p[n] \cdot b[k-n] = p[k] * b[k] \qquad (6)$$

$$db[k] = b[k] - \hat{b}[k-1] \qquad (7)$$

In the following $db[k]$ is called *differential download data rates*. It can be observed in the Figure 7b) that the *random variates* $db[k]$ are decorrelated but are differently distributed than the random variates $b[k]$. It is possible to generate these (i.i.d) random variates $db[k]$ with AnyLogic. After $db[k]$ is generated a post-filter is implemented, which transforms the random variates $db[k]$ to the original random variates $b[k]$ (see Figure 8). With the knowledge of the lag correlation coefficients of $b[k]$ the prediction filter $P(z)$ can be constructed by solving the *Yule-Walker-Equations*. A matrix Φ_{bb} and a vector φ_{bb} are constructed as shown in Equation 8, where $\phi_{bb}[k]$ denotes the k-lag-correlation coefficient and N the filter degree of the prediction filter, which is calculated by Equation 9.

$$\Phi_{bb} = \begin{pmatrix} \phi_{bb}[0] & \phi_{bb}[1] & \cdots & \phi_{bb}[N] \\ \phi_{bb}[1] & \phi_{bb}[0] & \cdots & \phi_{bb}[N-1] \\ \vdots & \vdots & \ddots & \vdots \\ \phi_{bb}[N] & \phi_{bb}[N-1] & \cdots & \phi_{bb}[0] \end{pmatrix}$$

$$\varphi_{bb} = \big(\phi_{bb}[1] \; \phi_{bb}[2] \; \cdots \; \phi_{bb}[N+1] \big)$$

(8)

$$P = \Phi_{bb}^{-1} \cdot \varphi_{bb}, \text{ with } P = \big(p[0] \; p[1] \cdots p[N] \big)$$

(9)

In Figure 7a) it can be seen that the first 7 lag correlation coefficients are almost non-zero and would have the most impact in the solution of the *Yule-Walker-Equations*. So we set the filter degree N to 6 and get the filter shown in Figure 9 for generating $db[k]$. Overall, we achieve during our simulation data rates with the statistical properties given in Figure 7c).

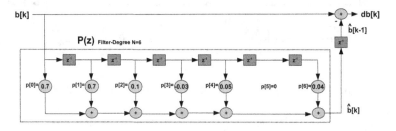

Fig. 9. Filter design to generate $db[k]$

3G Data Rates. For 3G we were not able to get a distribution of the data rates. There are numerous effects which influence the rate, many cannot be affected or are not known to the authors. One such impact is for example the number of users in the same 3G cell. Therefore we chose a triangular distribution with a minimum zero, a mean 800KBit/s and a maximum 3.6MBit/s. These values were measured by a research group at chip.de [14].

Audio Interface. The power consumption for the audio interface is logged by the tool *PowerTutor*, but the accuracy is limited. The tool approximates it with the fixed value of 384mW. Since we have no other means to access the value, we are forced to use this data. The validation of the complete model shows no disadvantage which we can trace back to this value.

Memory. The internal storage of the phone is not modeled as a consumer of power, but as a logical entity setting parameters of the device and scenario. The storage size is crucial for the different finite state machines.

4.3 Battery

We calculated the parameters necessary for our capacity model based on three independent experiments. Each experiment discharged the battery at a different

Table 3. Parameters of the capacity model

k0	c
0.0005 1/s	0.91

rate until the battery was empty. With the least-squares-algorithm we approximated the following parameters:

For estimating the parameters of the voltage model logs were recorded during discharging the battery in equidistant timestamps Δt. Among others, the current $i(\Delta t \cdot k)$ and the open circuit voltage $U(\Delta t \cdot k)$ have been recorded, where k is a scalar. Using these values we could calculate the short circuit voltage $V(\Delta t \cdot k) = U(\Delta t \cdot k) - i(\Delta t \cdot k) \cdot R_i$ as well as the normalized charge X according to Equation 2. To find the required parameters for the voltage model the constraint 10 has been derived from Equation 1. The resulting estimated parameters of the measurements are given in Table 4.

$$\min_{E_0, A, B, D, R_i} \sum_k \left[V(\Delta t \cdot k) - E_0 + A \cdot X(\Delta t \cdot k) + \frac{B \cdot X(\Delta t \cdot k)}{D - X(\Delta t \cdot k)} + i(\Delta t \cdot k) \cdot R_i \right]^2$$

(10)

Table 4. Parameters of the voltage model

E_0	B	R_i	A	D
3.64V	0.09V	0.122 Ω	0.25V	1.29

5 Validation

In this section we present the validation of hardware and battery components and of the whole system.

5.1 Hardware

We validated the generation of the correlated WiFi bitrates. For this we downloaded about 425MB of data with our test device and logged the download bitrates. We calculated the mean and standard deviation of the measured bitrates and compared them with those generated during the simulation runs. As it is shown in Table 5 the relative error for the mean bitrate is about 1.1%.

Furthermore, we also calculated the squared error of 0.14 for the achieved correlation coefficients according to the expression given in Equation 11, where AKF stands for auto correlation function with a coefficient k.

$$\sum_k \left[AKF^{REAL}(k) - AKF^{SIMULATED}(k) \right]^2 = 0.14$$

(11)

Table 5. Validation results of the simulated WiFI download rate

	Real	Simulated	Relative error
Mean	2,688,717 bit/s	2,658,050 bit/s	1.1%
Deviation	1,167,606 bit/s	1,238,357 bit/s	6.0%

5.2   Battery

For the validation of the battery we conducted three experiments with different load levels for the battery. We set the smartphone's discharge current to a fixed discharge rate and logged the battery lifetime. Table 6 shows that our battery model has a relative error of only 2% for high discharge currents. For lower load levels the error grows. This is due to the difficulty of maintaining a constant discharge rate in the real system. Since we used no external discharge devices the Android OS' background tasks introduced noise into the power consumption.

Table 6. Comparison and relative error of the simulated and the real batteries' lifetimes

Mean current	Lifetime real	Lifetime simulated	Relative error
148.72 mA	10h 2min 10s	9h 13min 1s	8 %
297.72 mA	3h 59min 18s	4h 19min 53s	9 %
484.54 mA	2h 29min 55s	2h 27min 13s	2 %

Furthermore, we validated the short circuit voltage $V(t) = U(t) - i(t) \cdot R_i$ by computing the relative error as follows:

$$\Phi(t) = \frac{\left| V^{REAL}(t) - V^{SIMULATED}(t) \right|}{V^{REAL}(t)} \tag{12}$$

The resulting relative error $\Phi(t)$ given in percent for three different discharge currents $i_1(t)$, $i_2(t)$ and $i_3(t)$ is presented in Table 7.

Table 7. Validation results of the short circuit voltage

Mean current	Min$\{\Phi(t)\}$ in %	Max$\{\Phi(t)\}$ in %	Mean$\{\Phi(t)\}$ in %
mean$\{i_1(t)\}$=148.72 mA	0.009 %	1.2 %	0.4 %
mean$\{i_2(t)\}$=297.72 mA	0.5 %	6.2 %	2.6 %
mean$\{i_3(t)\}$=484.54 mA	0.6 %	4.5 %	3 %

5.3   System Wide

We use the system wide validation to validate the power consumption of the different hardware components as well as the software's correct modeling. We measure the system's data rate and power consumption for a test scenario, in which we download 425MB and compare the results with our simulation model.

The first experiment uses only the WiFi network interface and does not play music. The box plots in Figure 10 show how exact the WiFi interface is simulated based on 100 replications. The comparison shows a deviation of the battery discharge value of just 2%, while the relative error of download time is 5%. These relative errors would become much higher if we neglect the correlation of the WiFi download data rates. For instance, we obtained the relative errors of 54% for the battery discharge value and 53% for the download time, if just using an uncorrelated distribution of download rates shown in Figure 7a).

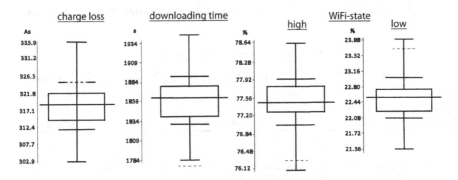

Fig. 10. Boxplots for charge loss, downloading time and proportion of state allocation for WiFi; dashed lines show measurement from real device

Because of the difficulties in simulating the 3G network module as described in the previous sections, the validation of this module is much more complicated. Although, our simulation model produces good results for download bitrates that match the observations made in [14], the values only represent approximations of the very fluctuating rates in the real world. Due to the simplified modeling approach the overall power consumption of the simulated network module in 3G state was not more then 10% beyond the values we could measure on our hardware with a stable connection.

6   Results

The simulation study's goal is to provide users and developers with possible default parameters to maximize the user's playback time. For this we evaluated several practical scenarios and present the results in Table 8. The scenarios differ by the time the smartphone spends in WiFi, 3G or offline mode. The same cache size of 10GB was set for each use case.

For the first scenario we let the user stay in a WiFi network for 2 hours and in a 3G network for the rest of the simulation. The results in the first line of Table 8 show that on average 3110MB of music were uselessly downloaded and could not be played back because of a lack of energy. The battery was drained on average after already 6.57h.

Based on these results we limited the time for downloads to 2 hours, since 3110 MB of wasted downloads show space for improvement. In the second scenario the user stood in a WiFi network for 30m and in a 3G network for 90m. Our simulation shows an extremely extended battery life and playback time on average, 22.26h and 17.98h respectively.

The difference in the battery lifetime and the actual playback time hinted to a drained storage due to a slow 3G connection. Therefore we set the time in the WiFi and 3G network to 60m each in the third scenario. The playback time increased on average to 20.6h and the wasted data accounted just to 56.4MB on average. This configuration yields the best results for continuous music playback.

Table 8. Results for different scenarios

n	Time in WiFi	Time in 3G	Network off	Wasted Downl.	Battery lifetime	Playback
1	2h	Rest	Never	3110MB	6.57h	6.57h
2	30M	90M	2h	0MB	22.26h	17.98h
3	60M	60M	2h	56.4MB	20.60h	20.6h

Table 9 shows the confidence interval half-length for mean values calculated for the confidence level fixed to 95%. The quite small confidence intervals after 100 replications indicate that the results seem to be accurate.

Table 9. The mean confidence interval half-length for the mean values from table 8

n	Wasted Downloads	Battery Lifetime	Playback
1	3.38MB	0.003h	0.003h
2	0.0MB	0.024h	0.032h
3	1.9MB	0.01h	0.01h

During the simulation the storage never reached values over 3.11GB. The results furthermore show that users should set the storage space on the device to that value in order to maximize their battery lifetime. This enables them to just switch off the data transmission and saves valuable power for an extended playback time.

Developers of music on demand services are well advised to analyze users' listening pattern and pre-fetch the most listened music tracks. Our simulations show that services which operate purely on demand have a high potential of frustrating customers by draining their smartphone's battery.

Our results show that a default storage size of 100MB is not fitted for power users who listen to more than 6 hours of music at a time. This results in a behavior very similar to ongoing streaming instead of power conserving pre-fetching.

7 Conclusions

We conducted a simulation study in which we analyze the optimal parameters for the use-case of on demand music streaming for modern smartphones. For the simulation we modeled a smartphone consisting of three layers, the software, hardware and battery layer. The paradigm for the software and hardware layer is discrete-event simulation using finite state machines and for the kinetic battery model is system dynamics.

For the input modeling we analyzed log files and used fitted distributions or analyzed source code of the application in order to deduce input parameters. We implemented a linear time invariant system to generate correlated random variates for WiFi download rates.

We conducted several experiments with the implemented model. Our primary interest was the optimization of the music application's playback time. The results show that the user can expect significant differences in playback times with certain settings and scenarios. On the other hand several improvements of the music application are conceivable. Pre-fetching of data for music added to the user's playlists should be automatically done in WiFi networks and preferably while the device is recharging in order to extend the devices battery's lifetime.

Possible improvements are a more exact modeling of the 3G module's power consumption and the use of external measurement hardware for the device's battery. It may improve the battery model's parameters for lower discharge currents. Future work will include the use of a next-generation smartphone with more detailed logging capability and extended use-cases for better optimization results.

We created a flexible simulation model which executes in few minutes and which can be used to investigate other scenarios with different system configurations. With modifications to the software component the simulation model could possibly simulate other applications than music streaming.

References

1. Manwell, J.F., McGowan, J.G.: Lead Acid Battery Storage Model for Hybrid Energy Systems. Solar Energy 50(5), 399–405 (1993)
2. Jongerden, M.R.: Model-based Energy Analysis of Battery Powered Systems. PhD thesis, Enschede (December 2010)
3. Chen, M., Rincón-mora, G.A.: Accurate Electrical Battery Model Capable of Predicting Runtime and I-V Performance. IEEE Transactions on Energy Conversion, 504–511 (2006)
4. Kim, T., Qiao, W.: A Hybrid Battery Model Capable of Capturing Dynamic Circuit Characteristics and Nonlinear Capacity Effects. IEEE Transactions on Energy Conversion 26(4) (2011)
5. Manwell, J., et al.: Improvements to the Hybrid2 Battery Model. In: American Wind Energy Association. Windpower 2005 Conference
6. Zhang, L.: et al: Accurate Online Power Estimation and Automatic Battery Behavior Based Power Model Generation for Smartphones. In: Proc. 8th IEEE/ACM/IFIP Int'l Conf. on Hardware/Software Codesign and System Synthesis. ACM (2010)

7. PowerTutor: Version 1.5, UMich, Northern University, Google Inc. (2013), http://www.powertutor.org
8. Prandoni, P., Vetterli, M.: Signal Processing for Communications. CRC Press (2008)
9. Kammeyer, K.D.: Nachrichtenübertragung, 15th edn. Vieweg+Teubner, Reihe Informations-/Kommunikationstechnik, Wiesbaden, Germany (August 2011)
10. Law, A.M.: Simulation Modeling and Analysis, 4th edn. Mcgraw-Hill Professional (August 2006)
11. AnyLogic: Version 6 (2013), The AnyLogic Company, http://www.anylogic.com
12. Balasubramanian, N., Balasubramanian, A., Venkataramani, A.: Energy Consumption in Mobile Phones: A Measurement Study and Implications for Network Applications. In: Proc. 9th ACM SIGCOMM on Internet Measurement Conference, IMC 2009, pp. 280–293. ACM, New York (2009)
13. ExpertFit: Version 6.0.2 Flexsim Software Products, Inc. (2012), http://www.averill-law.com/distribution-fitting
14. Pauler, W., Heinfling, B.: Das beste Netz aller Zeiten! Website Available online at http://www.chip.de/netztest (visited on September 3, 2013)

Performance of LTE for Smart Grid Communications

Georgios Karagiannis[1], Giang T. Pham[1], A. Dung Nguyen[1],
Geert J. Heijenk[1], Boudewijn R. Haverkort[1], and Frans Campfens[2]

[1] University of Twente, The Netherlands
[2] Alliander, The Netherlands
{g.karagiannis,b.r.h.m.haverkort,g.j.heijenk}@utwente.nl,
{t.g.pham,a.d.nguyen}@student.utwente.nl,
frans.campfens@alliander.com

Abstract. The next generation power grid (the "Smart Grid") aims to minimize environmental impact, enhance markets, improve reliability and service, and reduce costs and improve efficiency of electricity distribution. One of the main protocol frameworks used in Smart Grids is IEC 61850. Together with the Manufacturing Message Specification (MMS) protocol, IEC 61850 ensures interoperability within the Smart Grid by standardizing the data models and services to support Smart Grid communications, most notably, smart metering and remote control. Long Term Evolution (LTE) is a fourth-generation (4G) cellular communications standard that provides high-capacity, low-latency, secure and reliable data-packet switching. This paper investigates whether LTE can be used in combination with IEC 61850 and MMS to support smart metering and remote control communications at a desirable quality of service level. Using ns-3 simulation models, it is shown that LTE can indeed satisfy the main IEC 61850 and MMS performance requirements for these two applications.

Keywords: Smart grid communications, IEC 61850, LTE, simulation models, ns-3, quality-of-service.

1 Introduction

The current power grid is evolving towards a so-called "Smart Grid", which promises to efficiently deliver electricity in a sustainable, economic and secure way. The current power grid infrastructure has existed for several decades, but cannot cope anymore with the emerging challenges. For example, the European 20-20-20 targets [1] aim to (1) reduce green house gas emission by 20% in 2020 (80% in 2050), (2) increase share of renewables in EU energy consumption to 20%, and (3) achieve an energy-efficiency target of 20%. In order to meet these targets, more use of Distributed Energy Resources (DERs) that run on renewable energy, such as solar or wind has to be integrated, which does impose new challenges for the grid. These challenges together with factors, such as the need for higher resiliency against failures, better security and protection, etc., drive the grid towards a modernized infrastructure and bring new benefits to both utilities and customers. In order to realize this objective,

K. Fischbach and U.R. Krieger (Eds.): MMB & DFT 2014, LNCS 8376, pp. 225–239, 2014.
© Springer International Publishing Switzerland 2014

Smart Grid requires bidirectional communication between the components within the grid, such as power plants, substations and control centres.

In this paper we explore the requirements for smart grid communications, and investigate the potential of integrating two already standardized communication systems to fulfil these requirements. For the lower communication layers we propose to use LTE (Long-Term Evolution) [2] for 4G cellular communications. As application-level protocol we consider IEC 61850, which has been defined for interoperability among intelligent electronic devices (IED's) in smart grids. We investigate how LTE and IEC 61850 [3] can be integrated to support two key applications in smart grids, i.e., smart metering and remote control. The main contributions of this paper lie in (1) a clear specification of the performance requirements, (2) the establishment of a new architecture, that integrates IEC 61850 and LTE, and (3) a simulation-based performance evaluation.

This paper is organized as follows. Section 2 addresses background information on LTE, IEC 61850 and MMS. Section 3 then discusses the performance requirements, whereas Section 4 proposes a new overall integrated architecture. A detailed performance evaluation is reported in Section 5. Section 6 concludes the paper and provides recommendations for future work.

2   IEC 61850, MMS and LTE

The **International Electrotechnical Commission (IEC) 61850** protocol [3] is an open standardized, extensible protocol that can be applied for the support of smart metering services. It has originally been defined to solve the interoperability problem among different Intelligent Electronic Devices (IEDs) from different manufacturers within a substation. In addition to that, IEC 61850 also defines a set of abstract remote control communication services for exchanging information among components of a Power Utility Automation System. These services are denoted as Abstract Communication Service Interface (ACSI) services and are described in [4]. Examples of such services are, e.g., retrieving the self-description of a device, the fast and reliable peer-to-peer exchange of status information, the reporting of any set of data (attributes) and/or sequences of events, the logging and retrieving of any set of data, the transmission of sampled values from sensors, time synchronization, file transfer, and online (re)configuration.

Within IEC 61850, IED functions are decomposed into core logical functions called Logical Nodes (LNs). Several LNs can be grouped into a Logical Device (LD), which provides the communication access point for IEDs. The LDs are hosted by a single IED. By standardizing the common information model for each LN and for their associated services, IEC 61850 is able to provide the interoperability among IEDs of different manufacturers in the substation automation systems.

By specifying a set of abstract services and objects, IEC 61850 allows the user to design different applications without relying on the specific protocols. As a consequence, the data models defined in IEC 61850 can be used for a diverse set of communication solutions. IEC 61850 has been extended outside the scope of substation automation systems to cover Remote Terminal Units (RTUs), Distributed Energy Resources (DERs), electric vehicles (EVs), and the communication to the control centre. Therefore, it can potentially be applied to support (smart) metering and remote control communication services within the distribution network.

At application level, the **Manufacturing Message Specification** (MMS) [5] (and IEC 61850-8-1) has been chosen, since after some small modifications, it does provide (1) smart metering and remote control communication services, and (2) the required complex information models that support the mapping of IEC 61850 abstract objects. Another advantage of using MMS is that it provides high flexibility by supporting both TCP/IP and OSI communication profiles.

Long Term Evolution (LTE) [2] is a fourth generation (4G) communication technology standardized by the 3rd Generation Partnership Project (3GPP). It is capable of providing high data rates as well as support of high-speed mobility. It has a completely packet-switched core network architecture. Compared to UMTS, the LTE system uses new access schemes on the air interface: Orthogonal Frequency Division Multiple Access (OFDMA) in the downlink and Single Carrier Frequency Division Multiple Access (SC-FDMA) in the uplink, which brings flexibility in scheduling as well as power efficiency. LTE features low latency in both the control plane and user plane. The success and rapid roll-out of LTE in many countries have led to an increased interest to use this networking technology for, among others, smart metering, distribution automation, fault location, etc., within electricity distribution networks. Therefore, LTE is a promising choice as the Wide Area Network (WAN) communication technology to support IEC 61850 MMS-based smart metering and remote control services.

Few research studies focussed on the performance of LTE when applied in Smart Grids, cf. [6]. However, to the best of our knowledge, there has been **no previous work** that specifies how IEC 61850 MMS, in combination with LTE, can be used for smart metering and remote control communication services. There are a number of logical nodes defined in IEC 61850 that represent different functions of an IED within the substation domain, however, there is no specification on how the logical nodes can be used for smart metering and remote control applications. In addition, there has been no previous work that discusses how the IEC 61850 MMS used for smart metering and remote control communications can be integrated with an LTE system.

In this paper we propose a solution to integrate the IEC 61850 MMS used for smart metering and remote control application with the LTE communication system. The performance of the integrated solution is evaluated using extensive simulations, performed with the ns-3 simulation environment [7], [8]. The following questions are addressed:

1. What are the performance requirements of IEC 61850 MMS on the LTE system when used to support smart metering and remote control communication services for the smart grid?
2. Can LTE be used and integrated with IEC 61850 MMS to support smart metering and remote control communication services in smart grids (functionally and performance-wise)?

3   Functional and Performance Requirements

Smart metering is the first application that utilizes a two-way communication channel to provide reliability, robustness and efficiency to the smart grid; it lays a foundation for future applications to be built. Utility companies are moving towards advanced metering infrastructure (AMI) with the widespread roll-out of smart meters, which features two-way communication that does not only allow utilities to perform auto-mated readout functions (like its predecessor Automatic Meter Reading (AMR)) but also allows the control of smart meters, cf. [9].

IEC 61850 was specified to provide interoperability inside the Substation Automa-tion System (SAS) by providing abstract definitions of the data items and services that are not depending on any underlying protocol. The abstract data and object models of IEC 61850 allow all IEDs to present data using identical structures that are directly related to their power system functions, cf. IEC 62351-4. However, while the abstract models are critical to achieve a high level of interoperability, these models need to be operated upon by a set protocols that are practically relevant for the power industry. Therefore, one of the main requirements on an underlying communication system, like LTE, is the capability of supporting IEC 61850 abstract objects and services mapping. The requirements that need to be satisfied by the integrated solution are listed below.

Architecture. The architecture that specifies how the IC 61850 communication system can be integrated with LTE is not available and therefore it needs to be specified.

Integration of IEC 61850 MMS and LTE communication protocol stacks. The integration of these two communication protocol stacks is not available and therefore it needs to be specified.

IEC 61850 LN information objects for smart metering and remote control communication services. The IEC 61850 LNs that can be used for smart metering and remote control communications are not available and therefore they need to be specified.

Scalability. This challenge applies more to smart metering services, since it is ex-pected that over 200 million smart meters will be deployed in Europe between 2011 and 2020, which will have a massive demand for the network. The large number of smart meters also affects the performance of the used communication systems.

Latency (delay). For a smart metering service it is preferable to collect meter data in real-time, because utilities can correctly predict the load profile, perform load fore-casting, dynamic balancing between generation and consumption, support real-time pricing and demand response, etc. In general, with the meter data collected in real-time, the stability and intelligence of the grid are greatly improved.

Moreover, latency is the most important requirement for remote control communi-cation since receiving a late control command may seriously affect the safe operation of the electricity grid. According to IEC 61850-5 [10], the most important perfor-mance requirement that was mentioned is transfer time. Transfer time is specified as the complete transmission time of a message including the handling at both ends (sender, receiver). For smart metering services the end-to-end delay requirement ranges from 500ms to 1000ms, while for remote control communication services it ranges from 100ms to 1000ms, cf. [10]. In this research, we concentrate on the 100ms transfer time requirement for remote control communication services and on the 500ms requirement for the smart metering communication services.

Quality of Service (QoS). This challenge applies more to remote control communication services. Since such services are considered very critical, it might be needed to prioritize these services. In a public, shared LTE network, many different background traffic types are supported. Therefore, the remote control communication should be distinguished and assigned higher priority in order to guarantee its performance requirements.

Reliability. The communication system needs to be reliable such that all the IEC 61850 related information is exchanged successfully.

Security. The communicated IEC 61850 related information needs to be protected from security attacks. Therefore security services, such as authentication, confidentiality and integrity are needed.

4   Integration of LTE with IEC 61850 Communication System

We concisely present the integration of LTE and the IEC 61850 communication system such that the requirements discussed in Section 3 are fulfilled. For conciseness, not all requirements will be used. In particular, we focus on: (1) defining an architecture, (2) integrating the IEC 61850 MMS and LTE communication protocol stacks, (3) defining the IEC 61850 LN information objects used for smart metering and remote control communications, (4) the verification of the latency requirements, and (5) the verification of the prioritization requirement assuming that the QoS related performance bottleneck is the LTE eNodeB used on the downlink communication path (eNodeB towards the mobile devices). The two performance requirements ((4) and (5)) will be addressed in Section 5.

Although important, scalability, reliability and security requirements are not further considered in this paper, for two reasons: (1) the LTE system is designed in such a way that it is considered to be scalable and reliable when used to support services like smart metering and remote control communications, (2) IEC 61850 can be used in combination with IEC 62351 for security support [11].

4.1   Overall Architecture

The architecture that can be used for the integration of the LTE and the IEC 61850 communication systems applied to support smart metering and remote control communication services is visualized in Fig. 1 (more details can be found in [12] and [13]). The key entities in this architecture are as follows:

The **MMS server** represents the IED's located in the smart grid distribution network that need to be controlled. The MMS server can represent an individual Distributed Energy Resource, a micro-grid or a home-grid. A micro-grid is composed of home-grids, individual DERs and a Regional Control and Management Centre

(RCMC) that is controlling and managing these home-grids and individual DERs. The home-grid is composed of in-home private DERs, smart household appliances, and a Home Control and Management (HCMC) that is controlling and managing these devices. The MMS server supports in addition to the MMS server functionality also the following communication protocol stacks: IEC 61850, IEC 62351 and LTE.

The **MMS client** and **MDMS (Meter Data Management System) Host** represents the control centre. Between the MMS client and MMS server there is always an application association. For one application association, the MMS entity that sends an initiation-request to establish the association will be the MMS client and the other one is the MMS server. One MMS client can establish multiple application associations with different MMS servers. After an application association has been established, the MMS client can send requests to read, write or delete variables at the MMS servers. The MDMS Host functionality is used by the smart meter service and represents the meter data management system. The MDMS Host, similar to the MMS client, can establish multiple application associations with different Smart Meters or DC Smart Meters. In addition to the MMS client and MDMS Host functionalities, the control centre supports also the communication protocol stacks for IEC 61850, IEC 62351, LTE.

The **Smart Meter** represents either an individual Smart Meter functionality, i.e., a Smart Meter associated with one apartment, or a Data Concentrator Smart Meter that aggregates the Smart Meter related information associated with all the apartments located in a building.

4.2   Integrating IEC 61850 MMS and LTE Communication Protocol Stacks

The IEC 61850-based smart metering and remote control communication services have to meet several communication requirements defined in IEC 61850-5, cf. [10].

Most importantly, the core ACSI services, like smart metering and remote control communication services are mapped to the MMS protocol, which supports both the TCP/IP and the OSI communication profiles. Therefore, it is required that the underlying integrated communication system supports at least one of these two communication profiles. This means that each of the entities specified in Fig. 1 that support the IEC 61850 MMS module, i.e., Smart Meter, DC Smart Meter, MMS Client and MMDS Host, needs to support at least the TCP/IP communication protocol stack. In addition, these entities will also need to support the adaptation protocol layers required when MMS is mapped over the TCP/IP communication profiles, cf. Fig. 2.

4.3   IEC 61850 LN Information Objects

In smart metering and remote control communication services used in Smart Grid distribution networks, there are four types of equipment that need to be modelled:

— Distributed energy resources (DER): such as PV panels and energy stores.
— Smart household appliances: such as TV sets, electric heaters, or a refrigerator.
— Home Control and Management Centre (HCMC): that can reside in a MMS server.

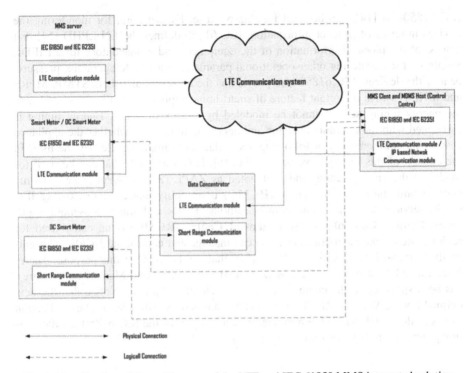

Fig. 1. Visualization of the architecture of the LTE and IEC 61850 MMS integrated solution

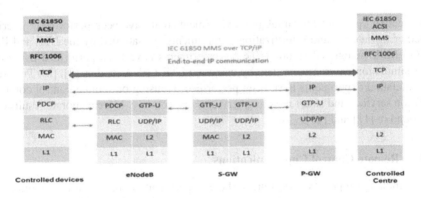

Fig. 2. Integrated LTE and IEC 61850 MMS communication protocol stacks

— Remote Control and Management Centre (RCMC): that can reside in a MMS server.

DERs can be modeled using the existing LNs defined in IEC 61850-7-420 and in IEC 61850-90-7 and IEC 61850-90-8. **Smart household appliances** are new devices that need to be modeled according to IEC 61850. Therefore, in addition to existing LNs also new LNs need to be specified. Two of the existing LNs, i.e., MMXN, MMTN, cf.

IEC 61850-7-4 [14], can be used for this purpose. Furthermore, for monitoring the devices in terms of product information, IEC 61850 defines the LN LPHD [14] that consist of the physical information of the equipment and is mandatory for all IEDs. Similarly, for monitoring other operational parameters such as temperature, pressure, heat of the devices, IEC 61850 also provisions the corresponding LNs STMP, MPRS and MHE [15]. An important feature of smart home appliances that is associated with the energy tuning needs cannot be modeled by any existing LN. Energy tuning is associated with the operational status and operating mode, i.e., whether the appliance is working autonomously or following a schedule or being controlled by the user. In the context of this research we defined in [16], [17] a new LN that can be used for modeling the energy tuning and is denoted as ZAPL (Z type APpLiances). **Home control and management centre (HCMC)** is an entity that can use existing IEC 61850 services to manage and control in-home DERs and smart household appliances. **Remote Control and Management Centre (RCMC)** is an entity used for regional areas, like neighborhoods, that can manage and control the HCMC. Currently, there are no LNs specified in IEC 61850 that can be used for this purpose. Therefore, a new LN, denoted as ZHCM (Z type Home Control and Management centre), has been specified in the context of this research, cf. [16], [17]. Notice that the new defined LNs, ZAPL and ZHCM, have been submitted by Alliander as standardization inputs to the Dutch NEC57 committee, which is a part of the IEC 61850 standardization group, where they are currently being discussed.

5   Performance Evaluation

This section describes the simulation experiments that have been performed to verify whether the latency and prioritization requirements are satisfied by the LTE and IEC 61850 MMS integrated solution. These experiments have been performed using the ns-3 simulation environment, thereby using the LTE LENA models [7], [8]. Two sets of simulation experiments have been performed, focusing on remote control communication services and smart metering services, respectively. More elaborate results can be found in [12] and [13].

5.1   Remote Control Communications

The simulation topology used during these experiments is based on the architecture shown in Fig. 1. However, of all the entities in Fig. 1, only the MMS client, MMS server and the LTE communication system are used in the simulations. Furthermore, the LTE communication system uses only one eNodeB (i.e., base station) and EPC (Evolved Packet Core) uses only one S-GW/P-GW (Serving Gateway/Packet Data Network Gateway) entity. In addition to these entities, the simulation topology includes typical UE (User Equipment) nodes and servers that are able to generate and use traffic that is non IEC 61850-based; we denote this as background traffic.

The system parameters, as used in the simulations, are summarized in Table 1. All the parameters are typical for LTE release 8, which is implemented in the ns-3 LENA

M5 simulation environment, cf. [8]. An important functionality that needs to be mentioned is the MAC (Medium Access Control) scheduling mechanism, which can be used to implement the prioritization of IEC 61850-based traffic over background traffic. In particular, two types of MAC (Medium Access Control) scheduling mechanisms are supported: Round Robin (RR) and Priority-aware Round Robin (PrioRR). The RR scheduler, cf. [13], divides the network resources among the active flows, i.e., the logical channels with non-empty queue. The PrioRR scheduler is specified in detail in [13] and is based on the RR scheduling mechanism, however in such a way that available resource blocks are assigned to flows with a higher priority first.

The used model for the MMS protocol stack is based on [5] (and IEC 61850-8-1) and its implementation in ns-3 is described in [12]. The LTE background traffic is generated using the traffic mix models specified in [18], [19], as given in Table 2.

Table 1. System parameters as used in all simulation studies

Parameters	Values
Uplink bandwidth	5MHz (25 RBs)
Downlink bandwidth	5MHz (25 RBs)
Uplink EARFCN	21100 band 7 (2535MHz),
Downlink EARFCN	3100 band 7 (2655MHz),
CQI generation period	10ms
Transmission mode	MIMO 2x2
UE transmission power	26dBm
UE noise figure	5dB
eNB transmission power	49dBm
eNB noise figure	5dB
Cell radius	2000m (typical sub-urban case)

The following performance metrics are evaluated. The **average delays** specify the averages of the MMS traffic delays. There are two types of MMS traffic delays:

— Initiation delay: time from the start of the connection setup until the Initiate-Response is received at the client;
— Request (polling) delay: time from the start of the polling request until a response is received at the client.

The **Cumulative Distribution Function** of the request delay is used in order to observe the maximum delay value measured during the simulation experiments and to compute delay variance (jitter). The **throughput** (bits/second) shows how much data is successfully transmitted over the LTE network. It is calculated as the total data received in the downlink over the simulation time. The **downlink packet loss ratio** (**PLR**) shows the reliability of the communication link and is calculated as:

$$PLR(DL) = \frac{packets\_sent\_by\_eNB - packets\_received\_by\_UE}{packets\_sent\_by\_eNB}.$$

Throughput and packet loss ratio are measured at the PDCP (Packet Data Convergence Protocol) layer, while delay is measured at the application layer, see [12], [13]. In order to evaluate the impact of integrating IEC 61850 MMS remote control communication traffic in a public LTE network, **different traffic mixes** will be used with the percentage of background traffic over remote control communication traffic, such as 80/20, 60/40. In each experiment with a specific traffic mix, the number of MMS nodes and background nodes will be increased but the traffic mix (percentages) is maintained. For the MMS traffic, we assume that the control centre (MMS client) sends a control request to the MMS nodes (MMS servers) and waits for the response. If the response is positive then the control centre sends a new control request. For the background traffic, the traffic mix follows the mix of 5 different traffic types with the percentage of nodes defined in Table 2. The ns-3 implementation of the models used to generate background and MMS traffic is described in [12].

Table 2. Background traffic mix

Application	Traffic category	Percentage
VoIP	Real-time	30%
FTP	Best effort	10%
HTTP	Interactive	20%
Video streaming	Streaming	20%
Gaming	Interactive real-time	20%

For each traffic mix experiment type, two different sets of experiments will be conducted, one using the RR and the other using the PrioRR MAC scheduler. In the normal (non-overloaded) experiments the total traffic load is increased up to 80% of the maximum cell capacity in the downlink direction. The maximum cell capacity in the downlink direction is defined as the capacity where the downlink throughput is not anymore increasing when the traffic load is constantly increasing. In all the performed simulations, 95% confidence intervals are computed (and shown) using on average 20 simulation runs.

For the 80/20 traffic mix, we start with the number of background nodes of 10. Subsequently, we calculated the number of MMS nodes (MMS servers) such that the MMS traffic load is equal to approximately 20% of the total traffic load generated by both MMS nodes and background (UE) nodes. Then we increase the number of background nodes in steps of 10. The number of MMS nodes will be increased to meet the condition such that the traffic mix is always 80/20.

Since we only focus on the downlink path from the control centre to the MMS server nodes, only the results associated with downlink communication path are collected and analyzed. It is important to notice that in case the total traffic load on the downlink direction is lower than 80% of the maximum cell capacity in the downlink direction, all active flows can be served within 1 (or very few) TTI (Transmission Time Intervals; 1 TTI = 1ms), regardless of what scheduler is used.

Throughput. Fig. 3 shows the average throughput results that include the overall average throughput, background average throughput and MMS (i.e., remote Control

Communications) throughput, when the RR and the PriorRR MAC schedulers are used. Since the total traffic load on the downlink direction is lower than 80% of the maximum cell capacity in the downlink direction, it is to be expected that most of the packets are delivered successfully. Therefore, approximately equal throughput results are obtained for the scenarios that use the RR or PrioRR MAC schedulers.

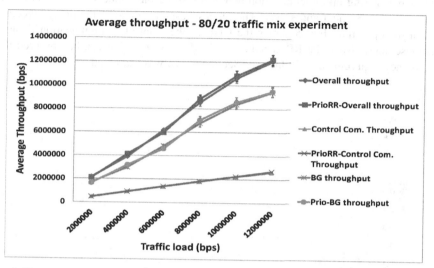

Fig. 3. Throughput performance in 80/20 traffic mix experiment with both Round Robin and Priority-aware Round Robin schedulers

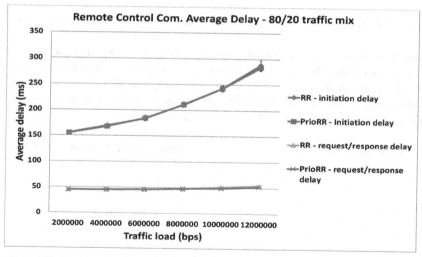

Fig. 4. Remote control communication average delays in 80/20 traffic mix experiment

Average Delay. Fig. 4 illustrates the average delay when the RR and PrioRR schedulers are used. Due to the fact that the total traffic load on the downlink direction is lower than 80% of the maximum cell capacity in the downlink direction, all active flows can be served within 1 (or very few) TTI, regardless of what scheduler is used. This also means that approximately equal average delay results are obtained for the scenarios that use the RR or PrioRR MAC schedulers. In Fig. 4, two types of average delays are shown: the initiation delay and the request delay. The initiation delay is seen when setting up the connection and establishing the application association between the MMS client and server. The request-response delay is the delay perceived in normal operation. Fig. 5 shows the CDF of the Control communication request-response delay, when the RR scheduler is used. From Fig. 5 it can be observed that the latency requirement of 100ms, see Section 3, is always satisfied.

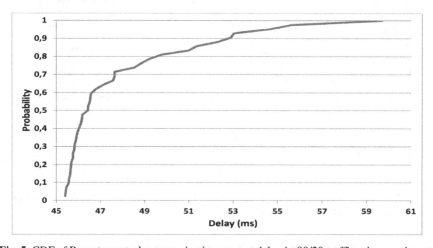

Fig. 5. CDF of Remote control communication request delay in 80/20 traffic mix experiment

Packet Loss Ratio. Fig. 6 illustrates the packet loss ratio (PLR) when the total traffic load increases. Since the total traffic load on the downlink direction is lower than the 80% of the maximum cell capacity in the downlink direction, the PLR results are approximately equal for the RR and PrioRR. When the traffic load increases, due to limited available radio resources, the PLR increases as expected.

Discussion. In this section only a subset of the remote control communication experiments have been presented. The complete set of experiments can be found in [13]. All the experiments show that the integration of IEC 61850 MMS and LTE is not only possible, it also provides a good performance in terms of delay, throughput and packet loss. When the traffic load generated does not exceed the maximum cell capacity in the downlink direction, the request/response delay is only 50% (50 ms) of the delay requirement specified by IEC 61850 for the medium-speed automatic control interactions. Furthermore, the traffic overload simulation experiments, which due to paper size limitations, are not presented in this paper but can be found in [13], show that when the generated traffic load exceeds the cell capacity in the downlink direction, the PrioRR MAC scheduler does provide a much better delay and throughput performance for the remote control communication traffic. However, the trade-off is that the performance of other less-important background traffic is reduced. Moreover, in overload situations, independently of which MAC scheduler is used, the request/response delay is lower than the delay requirement specified by IEC 61850.

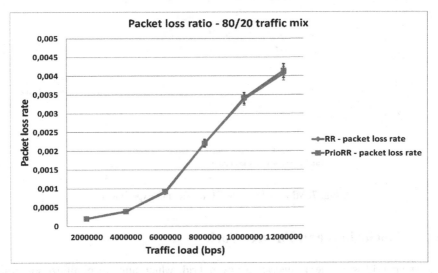

Fig. 6. Packet loss ratio in 80/20 traffic mix experiment

5.2   Smart Metering Experiments

The simulation topology is chosen as before, with the main difference that instead of using the MMS server, the Smart Meter entity is used, and instead of using the MMS client, the MDMS Host entity is used, cf. Fig. 1. Furthermore, in this set of experiments only the RR MAC scheduler is used. The simulation parameters and performance measures, including the background traffic, are similar to those used in Section 5.1, with the main difference that the cell radius is 800m, instead of the 2000m used previously (due to the smaller radio coverage cell area used for this MMS service). The traffic mix used in this set of experiments are the same as the ones used in Section 5.1. We only show simulation results on the MMS average delays for the 80/20 traffic mix. The complete set of experiments can be found in [12].

The delay performances of the smart meter initiation process and smart meter request (polling) process are illustrated in Fig. 7. From this figure, it can be observed that, as expected, both the average delays (initiation and polling) increase when the total traffic load increases. Furthermore, it can be observed that the average delay for the initiation process is much higher than the average polling delay. This is due to the fact that in the initiation process more MMS messages need to be exchanged in order to set up the connection and to establish the application association between the MMS client and server (initiate-request and initiate-response messages).

An important conclusion is that the obtained MMS average delay results, cf. Fig. 7, are below the latency (MMS transfer time) requirement of 500ms as specified in Section 3.

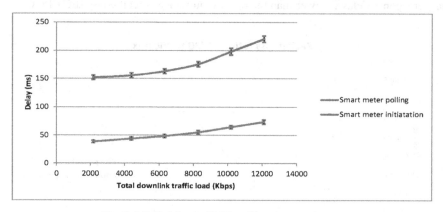

Fig. 7. MMS delay in 80/20 traffic mix experiment

6   Conclusions and Future Work

The smart grid is the next generation power grid, which aims to minimize environmental impact, enhance electricity markets, improve reliability and service, and reduce costs and improve efficiency. The most deployed communication protocol framework that can be used for the communication support in smart grids is the IEC 61850 MMS protocol framework. This paper proposes how LTE can be used and can be integrated with IEC 61850 MMS to support smart metering and remote control communications in smart grid distribution networks. In particular, this paper provides an overall architecture, the integration of the IEC 61850 MMS and LTE communication protocol stacks, the definition of IEC 61850 LN information objects used for smart metering and remote control communications, as well as a simulation-based validation of the performance requirements. Using ns-3 simulation experiments we have shown that LTE can satisfy these performance requirements on smart metering for remote control communication services.

Regarding recommendations for future work, additional simulation experiments could be done to verify the performance of IEC 61850 MMS over LTE when different types of background traffic mix are used, different LTE-based configuration parameters are used, or other IEC 61850 time-critical services are used.

References

1. Böhringer, C., Rutherford, T.F., Tol, R.S.J.: The EU 20/20/2020 targets: An overview of the EMF22 assessment. J. Energy Economics 31, 268–273 (2009)
2. 3GPP Technical Specification 36.300: Evolved Universal Terrestrial Radio Access (E-UTRA) and Evolved Universal Terrestrial Radio Access Network (E-UTRAN); Overall description; Stage 2 (Release 8). 3GPP (2008)

3. IEC 61850-1 specification: Communication networks and systems for power utility automation – Part 1: Introduction and Overview. IEC 61850-1 TR Ed.2. IEC (2012)
4. IEC 61850-7-2 specification: Communication networks and systems for power utility automation – Part 7-2: Basic information and communication structure – Abstract communication service interface (ACSI). IEC 61850-7-2 Ed.2. IEC (2008)
5. ISO 9506-1: 2003 specification: Industrial automation systems, Manufacturing Message Specification. Part 1. ISO 9506-1-2003(E). ISO (2003)
6. Cheng, P., Wang, L., Zhen, B., Wang, S.: Feasibility study of applying LTE to Smart Grid. In: 1st IEEE International Workshop on Smart Grid Modeling and Simulation (SGMS), pp. 108–113. IEEE press (2011)
7. NS-3 official website, http://www.nsnam.org/ (visited in October 2013)
8. LENA Design Documentation, http://lena.cttc.es/manual/lte-design.htm (visited in October 2013)
9. De Craemer, K., Deconinck, G.: Analysis of State-of-the-art Smart Metering Communication Standard. In: 5th Young Researchers Symposium, ESAT - ELECTA, Electrical Energy Computer Architectures, pp. 1–6. KU Leuven (2010)
10. IEC 61850-5 specification: Communication networks and systems for power utility automation – Part 5: Communication requirements for functions and device models. IEC 61850-5. IEC (2003)
11. IEC 62351-1 specification: Power systems management and associated information exchange - Data and communication security - Part 1: Communication network and system security - Introduction to security issues. IEC 62351 v. 1.0. IEC (2007)
12. Pham, T.G.: Integration of IEC 61850 MMS and LTE to support smart metering communications. M.Sc. thesis. University of Twente (2013), http://www.utwente.nl/ewi/dacs/assignments/completed/master/reports/report-Giang.pdf (visited in October 2013)
13. Nguyen, A.D.: Integration of IEC 61850 MMS and LTE to support remote control communications in electricity distribution grid. M.Sc. thesis. University of Twente (2013), http://www.utwente.nl/ewi/dacs/assignments/completed/master/reports/report-Dung-Nguyen.pdf (visited in October 2013)
14. IEC 61850-7-4 specification: Communication networks and systems for power utility automation – Part 7-4: Basic communication structure – Compatible Logical Node classes and data classes. IEC 61850-7-4. IEC (2008)
15. IEC 61850-7-420 specification: Communication networks and systems for power utility automation – Part 7-420: Basic communication structure – Distributed energy resources Logical Nodes. IEC 61850-7-420 Final Draft International Standard (FDIS). IEC (2008)
16. Nguyen, A.D.: Use of IEC 61850 for low voltage microgrids power control. Internship report. University of Twente (2013), http://www.utwente.nl/ewi/dacs/assignments/completed/internship/reports/2013-nguyen.pdf (visited in October 2013)
17. Pham, T.G.: Use of IEC 61850 for asset management in low voltage microgrids. Internship report. University of Twente (2013), http://www.utwente.nl/ewi/dacs/assignments/completed/internship/reports/2013-pham.pdf (visited on October 2013)
18. NGMN White Paper: NGMN Radio Access Performance Evaluation Methodology. NGMN white paper, Version 1.3. NGMN Alliance (2008), http://www.ngmn.org/uploads/media/NGMN_Radio_Access_Performance_Evaluation_Methodology.pdf (visited in October 2013)
19. Kwan, R., Leung, C., Zhang, J.: Multiuser scheduling on the downlink of an LTE cellular system. J. Research Letters on Communications 3, 1–4 (2008)

An IDE for the LARES Toolset

Alexander Gouberman[1], Christophe Grand[2],
Martin Riedl[1], and Markus Siegle[1]

[1] Institut für Technische Informatik,
Universität der Bundeswehr München,
Werner-Heisenberg-Weg 39, 85579 Neubiberg, Germany
firstname.lastname@unibw.de
[2] Pôle SPID,
ENSTA-Bretagne,
2 rue François Verny, 29200 Brest, France
christophe.grand@ensta-bretagne.fr

Abstract. In order to support the editing, validation and analysis of
LARES dependability model specifications, a textual editor and a graphical user interface for performing experiments have been developed. In
collaboration with the LARES toolset library they serve as an Integrated
Development Environment (IDE) based on the Eclipse framework. The
paper first introduces the features of the LARES language by means of a
hysteresis model taken from the literature. It then describes the textual
Editor Plugin. Beyond standard features such as syntax highlighting and
code completion, it emphasises syntactical and semantic validation capabilities. Subsequently, the View Plugin component is presented, that
is used to perform the experiments and to gather the analysis results
from the solvers. The current state of development of a graphical Editor
Plugin and other features of the LARES IDE are also addressed.

1 Introduction

LARES (LAnguage for REconfigurable Systems) is a language and toolset for
modelling the dynamic behaviour of systems, with a focus on dependability,
fault-tolerance and reconfigurability. Previous papers about LARES focussed on
the expressiveness of the modelling language [13,14], its semantics [23,14] and
its transformation to evaluation formalisms such as Stochastic Process Algebra
(SPA) or Stochastic Petri Nets (SPN) [12].

The present paper is the first one in which the LARES toolset is described
from the user's point of view. We present an Integrated Development Environment (IDE), consisting of a sophisticated textual Editor Plugin as well as a View
Plugin which serve as a comfortable user interface during all phases of model
specification, validation, quantitative analysis and result presentation. Fig. 1
gives an overview of the LARES IDE, comprising the editor and the analysis
view component, both Eclipse-based plugins, and the LARES library. When the
active page inside the Eclipse instance is a LARES specification (indicated by
the filename extension *lrs*), the textual Editor Plugin becomes active and performs a validation of the model w.r.t. the LARES metamodel. The View Plugin

K. Fischbach and U.R. Krieger (Eds.): MMB & DFT 2014, LNCS 8376, pp. 240–254, 2014.

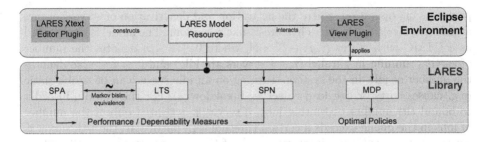

Fig. 1. The Eclipse-based LARES IDE

parses the model, extracts the defined measures and constructs and visualises the instance graph (which depicts the model's structure in terms of submodel instances). The View Plugin also allows the user to perform additional checks (e.g. for the presence of deadlocks or unsafe states), to investigate the state space and to visualize analysis results. For interacting with the specified model, e.g. to initiate an analysis, the LARES library is applied. That library implements all aspects related to the language and its transformation to the target formalisms where the actual analysis is carried out. Beside the already mentioned SPA and SPN target formalisms we also support flat Labelled Transition Systems (LTS) and Markov Decision Processes (MDP). The library also interfaces with the solvers, thereby abstracting from their specific interfaces. The LARES toolset is available from [11]. Among related approaches we mention the COMPASS project with the hierarchic language SLIM [9] that applies the powerful nuSMV solver [10], MoDeST [17] as a very concise language to describe non-hierarchic systems applying numerous tools for analysis, and the very mature AltaRica language [21] that lately also includes some extensions to enable non-functional analysis. Compared to these approaches, LARES focusses on hierarchic systems with complex interaction patterns. Beyond triggering reactions based on the current state, LARES offers flexible types of synchronisation by means of reactive expressions which take the combinatorics of subsequent behaviours of each component into account.

The paper is structured as follows: Sec. 2 introduces the LARES language by means of a non-trivial example taken from the recent literature. It presents two approaches, representing different degrees of modularity of how to model the system in a more or less modular fashion. Sec. 3 details the textual Editor Plugin which – beyond syntax highlighting and code-completion – offers advanced syntactical validation, and also partial semantic validation. Sec. 4 presents the analysis environment and its capabilities to perform calculations and visualise the analysis results. Sec. 5 briefly sketches our current efforts in developing a graphical Editor Plugin and the View Plugin, after which the paper concludes with Sec. 6.

2   Compositional Modelling with LARES by Example

For describing the modelling capabilities of LARES, we consider the "multiple parallel hysteresis" queueing model from [20]. It is a model for load-dependent power-saving operation, where the activation and deactivation of servers occurs at different levels, leading to a hysteresis-like behaviour. The model is represented as a CTMC with states $(i, j) \in \mathbb{N} \times \mathbb{N}$, where $0 \le i \le n$ denotes the number of servers running in parallel ($n - i$ servers are idle) and $0 \le j \le size$ denotes the number of jobs in the system. Turning on an idle server can be problematic (e.g. causes costs or can lead to server breakdowns). For this reason, in order to bound the number of waiting jobs, a server is activated only if the number of jobs in the queue exceeds a certain threshold. In particular, the i-th server is activated if $j = w^{(i)}$ and deactivated only if the queue is empty ($j = 0$), which leads to a hysteresis (see Fig. 11(b)).

In order to specify this model in LARES, we first briefly outline the LARES language. A LARES model consists of Behavior and Module definitions. A Behavior represents (one dimension of) the state space of a system component, in which transitions can be guarded by a guard label and either delayed by an exponential distribution or triggered immediately by a weighted discrete distribution. A Module can instantiate Behaviors or other Modules, thus providing a hierarchy of instantiations (instance tree), in which the Module representing the root instance is specified by a System definition. Furthermore, in a Module definition, the guarded transitions of instantiated Behaviors can be triggered by a guards statement, dependent on assertions over states. This triggering can be either direct or by interaction with other guard labels in form of synchronisation or choice. LARES supports three types of synchronous interactions: sync (all addressed guard labels have to be provided to perform a synchronized transition), maxsync (all transitions which offer the guard labels will take place) and choose (if only a single guard label is offered then the transition will take place). Moreover, inside a Module definition one can specify further Behavior and Module definitions, Instance statements for instantiating Modules, and Condition statements representing logical expressions over states (or other Conditions). forward statements are like guards statements, but comprise additionally a forward label which may be triggered externally (producing an information flow towards all Behavior instances). Initial statements define an initial state configuration and Probability statements specify desired transient or steady state measures. Note that due to the instance hierarchy there are visibility constraints on states/conditions and guard/forward labels. Thus, Condition statements can be used in order to lift state assertions from Behavior instances towards a Module, and forward statements to propagate triggering events from a Module towards Behaviors. For increasing the modelling flexibility, Behaviors and Modules can be parametrised and expand statements can be defined, which define a shortcut for symmetric statements.

Due to the described expressiveness, there are several ways how to specify the hysteresis model with LARES. For the purpose of this paper, we present two LARES specifications given in Fig. 2 and 3. Fig. 2 describes the whole hysteresis model in a planar way by defining a single Behavior Composed with parameters for the number n of servers (with default value 1), the width w (s.t. the hysteresis widths are given by $w^{(i)} = i \cdot$ w), the size of the queue (set by default to n*w),

```
 1  Behavior  Composed ( size=n*w,n=1,w=1,lambda ,mu) {
        expand(i in {0 .. n − 1}, j in {0 .. i*w}) {  State s[i,j] }
        expand(j in {0 .. size}) { State s[n, j] }
        // case (1): not all servers are busy
        expand(i in {0 .. n − 1}) {
 6        expand(j in {0 .. i*w − 1}) {
            Transitions from s[i,j] → s[i,j+1], delay exponential lambda
            Transitions from s[i,j+1] → s[i,j], delay exponential i * mu
          }
          Transitions from s[i,i*w] → s[i+1,i*w], delay exponential lambda
11        Transitions from s[i+1,0] → s[i,0], delay exponential (i+1) * mu
        }
        // case (2): all servers are busy
        expand(j in {0 .. size − 1}) {
          Transitions from s[n,j] → s[n,j+1], delay exponential lambda
16        Transitions from s[n,j+1] → s[n,j], delay exponential n * mu
        }
    }

    System Hysteresis ( size=n*w + 5 ,n=3,w=4) :
21      Composed ( size=size , n=n ,w=w,lambda =4.0,mu=2.0) {
        Initial init = Composed.s[0,0]
        expand(i in {0 .. n − 1}) {
          Condition serverBusy[i] = OR(j in {0 .. i*w}) { Composed.s[i, j] }
        }
26      Condition serverBusy[n] = OR(j in {0 .. size}) { Composed.s[n, j] }

        Probability queueFull = Transient(Composed.s[n, size], 10.0)
        expand(i in {0 .. n}) {
          Probability serverBusy[i] = Transient(serverBusy[i], 10.0)
31      }
        Probability allServersBusy = SteadyState(serverBusy[n])
    }
```

Fig. 2. Planar LARES specification of a multiple parallel hysteresis model with queue length size, n servers and equidistant hysteresis widths $w^{(i)} = i \cdot w$

and rates lambda and mu for the arrival and service processes (without default values). The first two expand statements (lines 2 .. 3) define the running indices i and j in order to declare all the states s[i,j]. The ranges for the indices are dependent on the values of other parameters. The expand statements (lines 5 .. 17) define all the necessary exponential transitions dependent on the two cases as specified in the comments. Note that expand statements can also be nested. The Behavior definition is instantiated in the System definition Hysteresis which defines its own parameters and sets (resp. overwrites) the parameters of the Behavior (line 21). Since the whole hysteresis model is specified in a single Behavior, there is no need to define any guard labels for the transitions. In the System we first set the initial state to s[0,0] and define the measure queueFull which computes the transient probability at $t = 10$ for the state s[n,size] of the Behavior instance Composed (line 28). Furthermore, in order to analyze the number of running servers, we specify the conditions serverBusy[i] which represent all states in which exactly i servers are active (lines 23 .. 26). For this reason, we abstract of the number of jobs in the queue by disjunction.

```
     Behavior Queue(size=1, lambda) {
 2     expand(i in {0 .. size}) { State s[i] }
       expand(i in {0 .. size-1}) {
         Transitions from s[i] → s[i+1], delay exponential lambda
       }
       expand(i in {1 .. size}) {
 7       Transitions from s[i]    if ⟨deq⟩    → s[i-1]
       }
     }

     Behavior Service(n=1, mu) {
12     expand(i in {0 .. n}) { State active[i] }
       expand(i in {0 .. n-1}) {
         Transitions from active[i]   if ⟨activateNext⟩ → active[i+1]
       }
       expand(i in {1 .. n}) {
17       Transitions from active[i]
             if ⟨deactivate⟩ → active[i-1], delay exponential i * mu
             if ⟨process⟩    → active[i], delay exponential i * mu
       }
     }
22
     System Hysteresis(size=n*w + 5, n=3, w=4) :
               Q ← Queue(size=size , lambda=4.0) ,
               S ← Service(n=n, mu=2.0) {
       Initial init = Q.s[0], S.active[0]
27     expand(i in {0 .. n-1}) {
         Condition switch[i] = Q.s[1 + i * w]
         switch[i] & S.active[i] guards sync { S.⟨activateNext⟩, Q.⟨deq⟩ }
       }
       !S.active[0] guards sync { S.⟨process⟩, Q.⟨deq⟩ }
32     Q.s[0] guards S.⟨deactive⟩

       Probability queueFull = Transient(Q.s[size], 10.0)
       expand(i in {0 .. n}) {
         Probability serverBusy[i] = Transient(S.active[i], 10.0)
37     }
       Probability allServersBusy = SteadyState(S.active[n])
     }
```

Fig. 3. Towards greater modularity: Splitting the arrival and service process into different Behaviors

As one can see, the planar representation of the whole hysteresis model can be difficult to understand and may be prone to errors (e.g. consistency regarding the index values and ranges). For this reason, Fig. 3 shows an alternative LARES specification of the same system by splitting the model into several parts: a Behavior for the Queue and a Behavior for the Service process. The queue is responsible for the arrival process (line 4) and provides for interaction a guard label <deq> in order to dequeue a job (line 7). Note that these guarded transitions do not provide any distribution type. This means that they act passively if a synchronisation is desired. The service process defines the states active[i] in order to denote i running servers. An additional server can be immediately activated if the guard label <activateNext> is triggered (line 14). Furthermore, a server can be deactivated, which takes some time in order to complete the job first (line 18). By triggering the <process> guard label, the server remains active after service completion (line 19).

The System definition instantiates both behaviours with the names Q resp. S (lines 24 .. 25). The Condition switch[i] (line 28) provides information about states when an activation of a further server can take place, i.e. if a job enters the queue s.t. the hysteresis width $w^{(i)}$ is exceeded. In this case the guards statement (line 29) synchronously activates a further server and dequeues a job from the queue, but only if there are not enough servers running (S.active[i] additionally satisfied). Since the transitions for both guard labels do not provide any distribution type (both are passive), we model an immediate synchronous transition. If there is at least one server running a guards statement (line 31) allows to synchronously process a job and dequeue the next job. Here the <process> transitions in the Service behavior provide the exponential distribution type, which is also the composed synchronous distribution, since the Q.<deq> transitions are passive. The third guards statement (line 32) is responsible for the deactivation of servers, if the queue is empty. Finally, the Probability statements (lines 34 .. 38) specify the same measures as in Fig. 2.

In order to emphasise the modularity aspects of LARES we propose a third LARES specification for the same model on the LARES website [11]. There, the service process (from Fig. 3) is split into distinct server instances (represented by a Module definition), which yields a non-trivial instance tree with intermediately instantiated Modules. Surely the reachable state space gets enlarged since symmetries in the service process are unfolded. However, these symmetrical states can be aggregated by lumping.

3   Textual Editor Plugin

In order to support the LARES modeller we implemented an editor environment for the LARES DSL (domain specific language) which runs in Eclipse. For this purpose we use the Xtext framework [8] which generates default implementations for both the DSL and the editor components. Xtext needs two models: a DSL grammar model and a DSL object model (see Fig. 4). The *LARES Grammar* model is textually specified within the Xtext editor and conforms to the *Xtext Grammar* meta-model. Here all parser rules for the grammar of the LARES language are specified in an EBNF-like style. A *textual LARES* model (conforming to the LARES Grammar model) is parsed by the XText framework and transformed into an instance of the DSL object model. In our case the object model is provided by the *LaresDsl* model which in turn conforms to the *Ecore* meta-model. Concretely, the LaresDsl model corresponds to the textual notation and provides types which represent the entities of the LARES language.

In order to be able to parse a textual LARES model into the LaresDsl object model, a connection between both is specified inside the LARES Grammar model. As an example consider Fig. 5. Here a parser rule named TransitionStatement parses a character string starting with "Transitions from" and transforms to a *TransitionDefinition* object in the object model. The *TransitionDefinition* object is fed with the following information: a cross-reference to an existing source state of type *State* created when an ID is parsed, an optional list of indices for the source

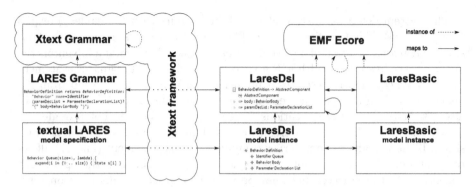

Fig. 4. Interrelations between the LARES models and their model instantiations

state by delegating to the `IndexList` parser rule and a non-empty list of transitions which delegate to the `Transition` parser rule.

```
TransitionStatement returns TransitionDefinition:
   "Transitions" "from"
   sourceState = [State | ID] (sourceStateIndexList = IndexList)?
   (transitions += Transition)+;
```

Fig. 5. Specification of `TransitionStatement` parser rule in the LARES Grammar model. Italic text denotes the connection to the LaresDsl object model.

As mentioned, LaresDsl corresponds to the textual notation of LARES, which also allows to represent "dynamic" LARES constructs such as parameters, arithmetic expressions and expand statements. These dynamic parts of LaresDsl can be made "static" by an in-place transformation to a resolved LaresDsl model (cf. Sec. 3.2). We further define the *LaresBasic* model, which abstracts Lares-Dsl from these dynamic constructs and textual pecularities such that a graphical editor can be directly supported (cf. Sec. 5). The transformations between Lares-Dsl and LaresBasic are implemented in a rule-based fashion by applying ETL (Epsilon Transformation Language [18,2]).

3.1 Editor Features

In addition to the mentioned parsing functionality, Xtext also generates a minimal default implementation for the infrastructure of the LARES editor, which is briefly outlined in the following. We also show how some of these features were modified and new features added in order to be able to specify valid LARES models and assist the modeller while editing. For this reason Fig. 6 shall serve as an example of a parametrised `Behavior` definition named B.

Xtext comes with a default *scoping* functionality, which allows to restrict the view on objects which can be cross-referenced. Since LARES follows the object-oriented paradigm, e.g. allows to build models in a modular and hierarchical way,

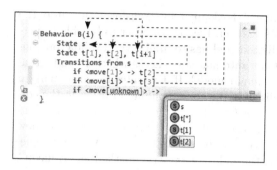

Fig. 6. Behavior definition with cross-references (dashed arrows), error markers and content assist

information can be encapsulated. For this reason we modified the default scoping feature by restricting the visibility of objects that can be cross-referenced. As an example, Behavior B in Fig. 6 defines four states, which are cross-referenced in the transition statement as source or target states. Note that the t states are indexed with arithmetic expressions. The parameter i is cross-referenced in the index expression of state t[i+1]. All defined parameters and states are only visible inside the Behavior, i.e. they cannot be referenced from the outside.

The cross-references can be visualised to the modeller by the *hyperlinking* feature, which allows to jump in the editor from a textual region representing a cross-reference to the textual element representing the referenced object. In order to establish a cross-reference, Xtext comes with a default *linking* feature. As already mentioned, LARES models are parametrizable and allow to model arithmetic expressions and set expressions. These expressions belong to the LaresDsl object model and are not evaluated on-the-fly while editing. For this reason, we made the linking smarter by matching the index list in patterns in order to create a cross-reference which is either correct or a provisional suggestion to the first matched appropriate object. As an example, the target state t[3] references to the suggested state definition t[i+1], since all other state definitions starting with t do not match the pattern '3' of the index list. Note that without evaluating the arithmetic expressions, it is not guaranteed to find the semantically correct cross-reference.

Consider for this Fig. 7: The source states t[1,1] and t[i,i] could match all of the state definitions, since the parameter i is not known and the expression 1+1 is not evaluated. Therefore they are referenced to the first found match t[1,i]. In the same way the target state t[2,1] is refer-

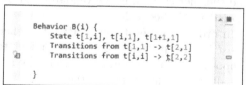

Fig. 7. Linking feature: The cross-reference t[2,2] cannot be matched to any state

enced to t[i,1]. However, for the target state t[2,2] no defined state can be surely matched, regardless of which value the parameter i takes. Therefore no cross-reference is created and the LARES model is considered as invalid.

The semantics of a LARES model is defined by transformation into the Stochastic Process Algebra CASPA [22] (cf. Fig. 1). In order to be able to perform this transformation, the LARES model has to fulfil several validation constraints. The default *syntax validator* automatically checks whether the textual model conforms to the LARES Grammar model. If it violates the grammar, an error marker is created and visualised at the corresponding location in the editor. Furthermore, an Ecore *reference validator* also checks if all cross-references in the model have been established. Remember that Xtext restricts the view on objects that can be cross-referenced by the scoping feature. As an example, Fig. 6 shows two violations. First, the index `unknown` is marked as erroneous, since there is no defined parameter named `unknown` in the scope of the reference. Second, the target state in a transition is compulsory (by the grammar) and has to be specified. In order to be able to check the LARES model for additional semantical validation constraints, Xtext provides a *validator* feature. We describe in the following only a few of the implemented constraints checked during validation. First of all, names of objects of specific types have to be unique in scope. Second, the ranges for numerical values are restricted, e.g. rates of an exponentially delayed transition have to be positive. Last but not least, definitions which induce cyclic dependencies cannot be evaluated and have to be checked.

As an example, in Fig. 8 the `Condition` statements b and c are cyclic and same also holds for `d[1]`. In the `expand` statement for each value of i in the range between 2 and 10 a `Condition` named `d[i]` is defined, which also induces cycles, if this statement were expanded into nine separate `Condition` statements. However, since arithmetic and set expressions are not evaluated the cyclic dependency can not be assured

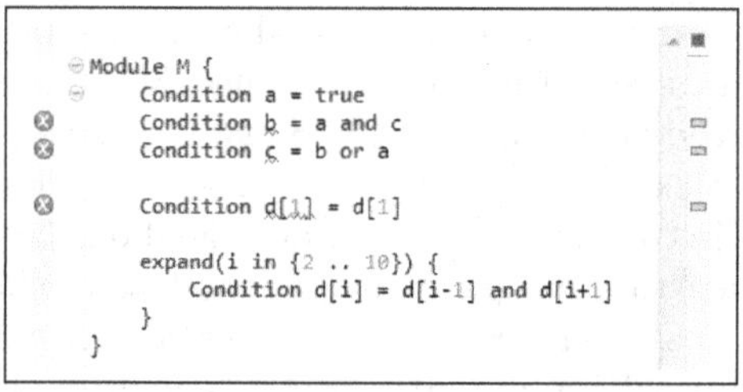

Fig. 8. Validation feature: Elements can be checked for cyclic dependencies

and thus not checked in the validator feature. We will deal with this problem in more detail in Sec. 3.2.

In order to support the LARES modeller in the user interface, the *content assist* feature provides context-dependent textual proposals. By default these proposals contain all grammar elements and cross-referencable objects which are allowed in the context of the cursor. As an example, Fig. 6 shows proposals for states in the scope of the target state reference. Since LARES statements do not employ separators, many parser rules from different semantical contexts might be applicable, s.t. the plethora of default proposals might rather confuse LARES newcomers. For this reason we modified the content assist by a context-dependent filtering of the default proposals. Moreover, we added some typical templates and comments to the proposals [16].

As already mentioned, the parsing process transforms a textual model to the LaresDsl object model. This transformation can be reverted by the *serializer* feature which plays an important role in Sec. 3.2. Note that the LARES language is descriptive, which means that the order of the statements does not matter. For this reason different textual representations might yield the same LaresDsl object model when parsed. Therefore the serializer transforms into one of the possible textual representations. In order to make the serialised textual representation more readable (following some textual modelling conventions), a *formatter* feature has been implemented, which is responsible for the pretty printing functionality [16].

3.2 Deep Validation

LARES models are analyzed by performing several sequential transformation steps, which all together resolve parameters and references to conditions and labels (forward resp. guard labels), thereby ending up in an intermediate model. This resolved model can then be either transformed to a SPA specification [22] or by performing a reachability analysis into an LTS [15] (cf. Fig. 1) upon which state-based computations are performed in order to return the desired measure values. Each of these transformations can only be performed correctly if some assumptions or necessary restrictions are met in the source model of the corresponding transformation. In order to further assist the modeller, these assumptions can be validated before executing the transformation. If a constraint has proven to be invalid, the modeller can be notified with additional information about the error type and its origin in the source model.

The first transformation step performed on a LARES model is the parameter resolution phase. Here arithmetic expressions and set expressions are evaluated and looping and recursive constructs are expanded (e.g. the **expand** statements). As an example Fig. 9 shows a LARES specification with parameters and an equivalent specification without parameters.

```
Behavior B(N=0, w) {                          Behavior B {
    expand(i in {1 .. N}) {                       State s[1], s[2], s[3]
        State s[i]                                Transitions from s[1] -> s[2], weight 1.0
        Transitions from s[i]                     Transitions from s[2] -> s[3], weight 2.0
            -> s[i % N + 1], weight i*w           Transitions from s[3] -> s[1], weight 3.0
    }                                         }
}

System main : B(w=1.0, N=3) {                 System main : B {
    Initial init = B.s[1]                         Initial init = B.s[1]
}                                             }
```

Fig. 9. Parameter resolution: Two equivalent LARES specifications. Left: parametric dependencies and **expand** statement. Right: all parameters are resolved.

We implemented this transformation with EPL (Epsilon Pattern Language [2]) as an in-place transformation, i.e. an arbitrary LaresDsl model is transformed into a resolved LaresDsl model. The EPL transformation is defined in a descriptive pattern-based way, which allows to split the rather complex recursive

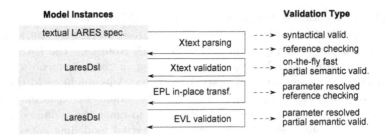

Fig. 10. Validation process

and iterative transformation into several independent parts, thus improving the maintenance and correctness of the transformation. In Fig. 9 the Behavior B is instantiated in the System main and defines the values w and N which can be substituted in the Behavior definition. Now all arithmetic expressions which refer to these parameters can be evaluated to numbers. Therefore the set expression in the expand construct can be resolved s.t. in turn all arithmetic expressions which refer to i can be resolved and finally evaluated.

If a necessary cross-reference to some object cannot be established in the parameter resolution phase, it is considered as invalid and the modeller is informed with an error marker on the appropriate cross-referencing element in the editor. For instance, if the EPL transformation is performed on the model in Fig. 8 the resolution of the expand statement produces such a cross-reference error, since after resolution there is no Condition definition named d[11]. In order to be able to create these error markers in the editor, we accompany the EPL transformation with a *Trace* model, which maps a resolved LaresDsl element to the element from which it originated by transformation. Once all cross-references are established, the resolved LaresDsl model can be serialised to its textual representation which can be viewed or edited with the LARES editor and manually investigated and validated by the modeller. Finally, the resolved LaresDsl model is further validated by constraints defined in EVL (Epsilon Validation Language [19,2]), which roughly speaking perform (among others) once more the fast on-the-fly validations from the Xtext validator but now for all resolved LaresDsl elements [16]. The whole validation workflow is summarised in Fig. 10. Note that the validation process for the analysis presented here is not complete, since further transformations in the LARES workflow are not pre-validated. The reason is that for some model constraints an expensive reachability analysis on the composed state space has to be performed.

4   View Plugin

In order to extend the graphical user interface (GUI), the LARES View Plugin has been developed to carry out the analysis in a comfortable way. It aims to support the experiments by steering the analysis process, the visualisation of results and their management. It has been developed as an Eclipse View

Plugin component, which reacts on specific editor events to synchronise to modifications applied to the model. Whenever the current model has changed, the instance tree is internally reconstructed, then converted to a DOT graph [5] and drawn on an SWT composite [7] using the ZEST library [3]. Fig. 11(a) shows the GUI of the View Plugin: the instance graph of a LARES model is instantaneously visualised on the GUI (cf. ⑥). A more elaborated version (including the provided Condition and forward identifiers of all instances as well as the associated Behavior definitions) can be serialised in the DOT format if required (cf. ①). In order to check whether the intended semantics is met for some specific construct inside a LARES model, if e.g. a modeller is not certain about the transformation semantics, the plugin allows to dump the generated SPA specification (cf. ④). For smaller models, also a reachability analysis to generate a DOT graph of the composed state space might help for model validation (cf. ② and Fig. 11(b)). Moreover, the ability of the CASPA tool to determine the k-most probable paths into a set of target states [24], for instance deadlock states, is accessible using the GUI and can be directly visualised (cf. ③ and ⑥). The Probability measure statements specified in a LARES model are extracted (cf. ⑦): the transient measures are grouped following the associated analysis timepoint, while the steady-state measures are within a single group since their timepoint is implicitly considered infinity. For all transient measures, a dialogue is opened when performing their analysis to ask for additional equidistant intermediate timepoint analysis. Then the transformation workflow as implemented by the LARES library is performed to construct the SPA specification which is accepted and analysed by the CASPA process algebra solver. The obtained results are collected in a list (cf. ⑨) for which a copy&paste feature has been implemented to allow a transfer to external tools such as spreadsheet packages. Simultaneously, the results are visualised (cf. ⑩) in terms of an xy-plot drawn by the JFree chart library [6]. Since each timepoint requires its own independent analysis run, parallel execution following the number of logical CPU cores is supported. There is also a progress monitor for the analysis (cf. ⑧). Finally, output information and errors occurring while parsing, transformation or analysis are reported (cf. ⑪) to give feedback to the user in the case of issues that have not already been detected by the semantic validation features included in the textual Editor Plugin. These outputs can help the user to fix his model or to obtain further knowledge about the intermediate steps of the transformation or analysis of a model. It is planned to connect to a database to save and manage the experiments performed (cf. ⑤). There the results obtained from the solvers are stored together with the version of the specification used for analysis, e.g. to compare different model parametrisations.

Internally, the View Plugin is a mixed Scala/Java project that uses the AKKA actor library [1] for decoupling the internal components via message passing and assuring smooth usability of the GUI, since each component is realised as an actor which itself is a lightweight process. In consequence, the GUI does not block the whole IDE, despite performing an analysis burdening the CPU.

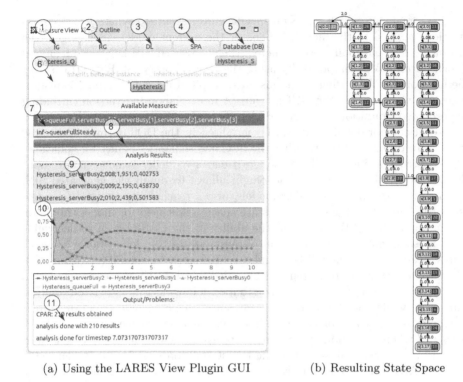

(a) Using the LARES View Plugin GUI   (b) Resulting State Space

Fig. 11. Analysis of the multiple parallel hysteresis model from Fig. 2

5 Ongoing Development

Currently a *graphical* LARES editor is also in development, using the Eclipse Graphiti framework [4] and plain Java. Beyond the application of graphical layout algorithms, Graphiti directly supports EMF models. To facilitate the interchange of model information, we specified the LaresBasic model (cf. Sec. 3). Two diagram types, one for a Module definition and another one for the Behavior definition have been developed. The class structure generated from the LaresBasic model is used to deal with a graphical LARES representation. The Graphiti classes have been extended to realise the graphical notation and tooling. Thus standard features such as *delete, resize* or wizards to construct diagrams were inherited and could be used out-of-the-box. Furthermore, the layout information of a LARES model had to be separated from the content, and the *drill-down* functionality (i.e. construct/open new diagrams inside another via double-click) needed to be implemented to enable a smooth navigation among the different diagram entities. As a medium term goal, we aim to complete the graphical editor to ease the LARES modelling for new users not yet familiar with the textual syntax. As a long term goal, we aim for a hybrid graphical/textual editor that integrates both approaches, in order to experience the best from both worlds.

As already indicated, it is foreseen for the LARES View Plugin to establish a database binding to save and manage experiments. For that purpose, a simple database query language will be applied to store current experiments or to gather results of older ones for further processing or comparison.

6   Conclusion/Outlook

We have presented an informative overview on the LARES IDE with a focus on the textual Editor Plugin. This plugin was created in a model-driven way by employing the Xtext and Epsilon frameworks. The editor is enhanced beyond the semantically correct scoping mechanism with several assisting features, like a smart content assist, cross-reference linking and a fast partial model validation facility. These extended editor features support the user by a facilitated access to the modelling world of LARES. Furthermore, it allows to perform a deep validation by transforming parametrised LARES models into parameter-free LARES models. The LARES View Plugin has also been detailed in this paper. This user interface enables a modeller to analyse LARES specifications and calculate the measures of interest. Intermediate representations, such as the reachability graph or the generated process algebra model, can be used to validate the model beyond the syntactical and semantic aspects captured by the grammar and the transformations applied, thus ensuring that the model indeed has the desired behaviour. The graph representations (instance graph or reachability graph) and the xy-plots can easily be serialised in the SVG file format for further use e.g. in publications.

We have also already extended the LARES language with the capability to specify Markov reward models and Markov decision processes [14,15], such that measures regarding the performability of a LARES model can be specified and an optimal policy w.r.t. to such a measure can be computed. In the future, in addition to the issues discussed in Sec. 5, we plan to provide the necessary tooling for these extensions on the LARES website [11].

Acknowledgments. We thank Dominik Schwindling for his work on the graphical Editor Plugin, and Deutsche Forschungsgemeinschaft (DFG) who supported this work under grants SI 710/7-1 and by DFG/NWO Bilateral Research Programme ROCKS.

References

1. Akka toolkit (2013), http://akka.io/
2. Epsilon (2013), http://www.eclipse.org/epsilon/
3. Graphical Editing Framework, GEF (2013), http://www.eclipse.org/gef/
4. Graphiti (2013), http://www.eclipse.org/graphiti/
5. Graphviz - Graph Visualization Software (2013), http://www.graphviz.org/
6. Jfree (2013), http://www.jfree.org/
7. Standard widget toolkit (2013), http://www.eclipse.org/swt/
8. Xtext (2013), http://www.eclipse.org/Xtext/

9. Bozzano, M., Cimatti, A., Roveri, M., Katoen, J.P., Nguyen, V., Noll, T.: Codesign of dependable systems: a component-based modeling language. In: Proc. of the 7th IEEE/ACM Int. Conf. on Formal Methods and Models for Codesign, MEMOCODE 2009, pp. 121–130. IEEE Press, Piscataway (2009)
10. Cimatti, A., Clarke, E., Giunchiglia, E., Giunchiglia, F., Pistore, M., Roveri, M., Sebastiani, R., Tacchella, A.: NuSMV 2: An openSource tool for symbolic model checking. In: Brinksma, E., Larsen, K.G. (eds.) CAV 2002. LNCS, vol. 2404, pp. 359–364. Springer, Heidelberg (2002)
11. Design of Computer and Communication Systems Group (Inf 3) UniBw: LARES website (2013), http://lares.w3.rz.unibw-muenchen.de/
12. Gouberman, A., Riedl, M., Schuster, J., Siegle, M.: A Modelling and Analysis Environment for *LARES*. In: Schmitt, J.B. (ed.) MMB & DFT 2012. LNCS, vol. 7201, pp. 244–248. Springer, Heidelberg (2012)
13. Gouberman, A., Riedl, M., Schuster, J., Siegle, M., Walter, M.: LARES - A Novel Approach for Describing System Reconfigurability in Dependability Models of Fault-Tolerant Systems. In: ESREL 2009: Proceedings of the European Safety and Reliability Conference, pp. 153–160. Taylor & Francis Ltd. (2009)
14. Gouberman, A., Riedl, M., Siegle, M.: A Modular and Hierarchical Modelling Approach for Stochastic Control. In: MIC 2013: Proc. of the 32nd IASTED Int. Conf. on Modelling, Identification and Control. ACTA Press (2013)
15. Gouberman, A., Riedl, M., Siegle, M.: Transformation of LARES performability models to continuous-time Markov reward models. In: Proc. 7th Int. Workshop on Verification and Evaluation of Computer and Communication Systems (VECOS 2013). eWiC, British Computer Society (2013)
16. Grand, C.: Extension of a textual editor for the specification language LARES - Model transformation, validation and feature development. Master's thesis, Bundeswehr University Munich (2013)
17. Hartmanns, A.: MODEST - A unified language for quantitative models. In: FDL, pp. 44–51. IEEE (2012)
18. Kolovos, D.S., Paige, R.F., Polack, F.A.C.: The Epsilon Transformation Language. In: Vallecillo, A., Gray, J., Pierantonio, A. (eds.) ICMT 2008. LNCS, vol. 5063, pp. 46–60. Springer, Heidelberg (2008)
19. Kolovos, D.S., Paige, R.F., Polack, F.A.C.: On the evolution of OCL for capturing structural constraints in modelling languages. In: Abrial, J.-R., Glässer, U. (eds.) Rigorous Methods for Software Construction and Analysis. LNCS, vol. 5115, pp. 204–218. Springer, Heidelberg (2009)
20. Kühn, P.J., Mashaly, M.: Performance of self-adapting power-saving algorithms for ICT systems. In: IFIP/IEEE International Symposium on Integrated Network Management (IM 2013), pp. 720–723 (2013)
21. Point, G.: AltaRica: Contribution à l'unification des méthodes formelles et de la sûreté de fonctionnement. Thèse de doctorat, Université Bordeaux I (2000)
22. Riedl, M., Schuster, J., Siegle, M.: Recent extensions to the stochastic process algebra tool CASPA. In: Fifth International Conference on Quantitative Evaluation of Systems, QEST 2008, pp. 113–114 (2008)
23. Riedl, M., Siegle, M.: A LAnguage for REconfigurable dependable Systems: Semantics & Dependability Model Transformation. In: Proc. 6th Int. Workshop on Verification and Evaluation of Computer and Communication Systems (VECOS 2012), pp. 78–89. eWiC, British Computer Society (2012)
24. Schuster, J., Siegle, M.: Path-based calculation of MTTFF, MTTFR, and asymptotic unavailability with the stochastic process algebra tool CASPA. Journal of Risk and Reliability 225(4), 399–406 (2012)

Fluid Survival Tool: A Model Checker for Hybrid Petri Nets

Björn F. Postema, Anne Remke,
Boudewijn R. Haverkort, and Hamed Ghasemieh

Centre for Telematics and Information Technology
Design and Analysis of Communication Systems
University of Twente, The Netherlands
{b.f.postema,a.k.i.remke,b.r.h.m.haverkort,h.ghasemieh}@utwente.nl

Abstract. Recently, algorithms for model checking Stochastic Time Logic (STL) on Hybrid Petri nets with a single general one-shot transition (HPNG) have been introduced. This paper presents a tool for model checking HPNG models against STL formulas. A graphical user interface (GUI) not only helps to demonstrate and validate existing algorithms, it also eases use. From the output of the model checker, 2D and 3D plots can be generated. The extendable object-oriented tool has been developed using the Model-View-Controller and Facade patterns, DOXYGEN for documentation and QT for GUI development written in C++.

1 Introduction

HPNGs allow to model continuous and discrete variables of a system with a single stochastic event. Therefore, HPNGs can be used to model fluid critical infrastructures [2] like water, gas and oil networks. Since critical infrastructures may fail and their continuous operation is of utmost importance for both industry and society, survivability is an important property for these systems.

The logic STL [6] has recently been introduced to easily formulate measures of interest for HPNG models, such as survivability measures. To automate the evaluation of STL formula for HPNGs, we developed the FLUID SURVIVAL TOOL (FST) [9] for model checking HPNG models against an STL specification.

FST has an extendable software design based on the software engineering principles of the Model-View-Controller and Facade patterns, and uses DOXYGEN for documentation. The GUI has been implemented with QT and the tool has been written in C++. It implements the region-based algorithm for the transient analysis of HPNGs [5] and for model checking HPNGs against STL [6].

The paper is organised as follows. First, the HPNG modelling formalism and STL specification are discussed in Section 2. Section 3 describes the tool functionality and design, as well as the Graphical User Interface (GUI) and presents results for a running example.

K. Fischbach and U.R. Krieger (Eds.): MMB & DFT 2014, LNCS 8376, pp. 255–259, 2014.

2   Hybrid Petri Nets and Stochastic Time Logic

An HPNG is formally defined as a tuple $\langle \mathcal{P}, \mathcal{T}, \mathcal{A}, m_0, x_0, \Phi \rangle$, which consist of a set of places $\mathcal{P}$, a set of transitions $\mathcal{T}$, a set of arcs $\mathcal{A}$, the initial marking vectors m_0 and x_0, and a tuple of functions Φ that define additional parameters. The discrete and continuous dynamics of HPNGs are formally defined in [7]. Figure 1 presents an HPNG model of a water tower that

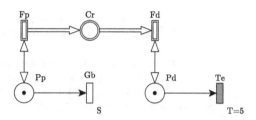

Fig. 1. Water tower HPNG model

consists of a reservoir, represented by continuous place Cr (a circle with a double border), with an input and an output pump, represented by the continuous transitions Fp and Fd (rectangles with double border), that are connected to the reservoir using continuous arcs (white arrows). The remaining part of the HPNG describes how the inflow stops when the input pump breaks after a random amount of time, modelled by a general transition (a rectangle with a single border) and how the outflow stops deterministically after 5 hours, modelled by a deterministic transition (a grey rectangle). Discrete arcs (black arrows) connect discrete places (a single circle) to deterministic and to general transitions and vice versa. When transition Gb fires, a token is removed from the discrete place Pp. This disables the continuous transition Fp, since it is connected to place Pp with a test arc (arc with two arrowheads). Similarly, the outflow stops when transition Fd becomes disabled due to the removal of the token in place Pd.

Measures of interests for HPNGs can be described using the logic STL [6]:

$$\Psi := tt \mid x_\mathcal{P} \leq c \mid m_\mathcal{P} = a \mid \neg\Psi \mid \Psi_1 \wedge \Psi_2 \mid \Psi_1 \, \mathcal{U}^{[T_1,T_2]} \, \Psi_2,$$

where $T_1, T_2, c \in \mathbb{R}^{\geq 0}$; $a \in \mathbb{N}^{\geq 0}$. Atomic formulas $x_\mathcal{P} \leq c$ and $m_\mathcal{P} = a$ compare continuous and discrete markings with a predefined constant. STL formulas can be negated ($\neg\Psi$) and combined with conjunction ($\Psi_1 \wedge \Psi_2$). The until operator $\Psi_1 \, \mathcal{U}^{[T_1,T_2]} \, \Psi_2$ describes that during the evolution of the system, property Ψ_1 should hold, until in the time interval $[T_1, T_2]$ property Ψ_2 becomes true. In [7] the formal semantics for STL on HPNGs is given.

Using algorithms from [6] and [9], so-called satisfaction intervals are computed for all but nested until formula. These represent all intervals from the support of the random variable that defines the firing time of the general one-shot transition for which the resulting evolution of the HPNG fulfils the STL property (at a certain time τ). Then, by integrating the probability density function of the random variable over the satisfaction intervals the probability that the STL property holds at a given time τ is computed.

Table 1. In- and output with corresponding functionalities

Functionality	Input	Output/Button
Model checking [6] [9]	HPNG model STL formula Time to check t	✓ ✗
Stochastic time diagram [5]	HPNG model	
Transient probabilities [5]	HPNG model Time range Continuous atomic property A constant/constant range	

3   Fluid Survival Tool Overview

Table 1 summarizes the functionality of FST. HPNG models (textually specified) can be model checked against an STL specification for a specific time (t), in order to generate a model checking verdict. FST provides insight in the time-based evolution by generating graphical stochastic time diagrams from the HPNG models and transient probabilities can be computed. Also 2D and 3D plots can be automatically generated.

The model checking tool FST has an extendable object-oriented design with a GUI. This has been achieved through the composition of a Software Development Kit (SDK) consisting of the C++ compiler GCC, the GUI library QT and the Integrated Development Environment (IDE) QT CREATOR [3]. Additionally, the SDK contains DOXYGEN [8] for documentation, SVN [1] for version control and a project page for information, releases and bug tracking [4]. Moreover, the Model-View-Controller and Facade software patterns are added for designing extendable GUI. So, to run a functionality with these software patterns, the user interacts with the view class that evokes the controller to pass a request to the Facade class that evokes the model checking algorithms. Then, feedback is provided to the controller class such that the view can be updated. Figure 2 shows a screenshot of the tool FST where the HPNG model of the water tower from Figure 1 is loaded as (textual) input. The tool consists of a menu bar (**1**), a button for each functionality (**2**), a textual HPNG model editor (**3**) and a logger to provide textual feedback (**4**). When the functionality buttons are clicked a configuration dialog pops up where all the input variables from Table 1 are requested and the output is provided, accordingly.

The 2D plot in Figure 3 shows the probabilities that the amount of fluid in the reservoir is smaller or equal to 0.4 m^3 for the example model over a range of time, where the input pump breaks according to an exponential distribution (with mean 10). Time in hours is on the x-axis and the probability is on the y-axis. This probability is calculated for the time range $[0, 100]$ with a time step of 1. The 3D plot in Figure 3 additionally parametrises the maximum amount

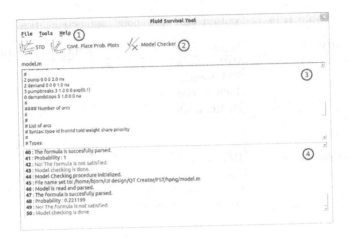

Fig. 2. FST main screen

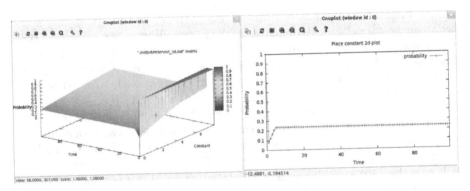

Fig. 3. 3D and 2D output of FST

of fluid in the reservoir, i.e., the amount of fluid that should not be exceeded, over the range 0.0 to 8.0 m^3 with a step size of 0.2 m^3.

References

1. Apache Software Foundation: Subversion (2000), http://subversion.apache.org/
2. Conrad, S.H., LeClaire, R.J., O'Reilly, G.P., Uzunalioglu, H.: Critical national infrastructure reliability modeling and analysis. Bell Labs Technical Journal 11(3), 57–71 (2006)
3. Digia: Qt and Qt Creator (2009), http://qt-project.org/
4. FST Projectpage (2013), https://code.google.com/p/fluid-survival-tool/
5. Ghasemieh, H., Remke, A., Haverkort, B., Gribaudo, M.: Region-based analysis of hybrid petri nets with a single general one-shot transition. In: Jurdziński, M., Ničković, D. (eds.) FORMATS 2012. LNCS, vol. 7595, pp. 139–154. Springer, Heidelberg (2012)

6. Ghasemieh, H., Remke, A., Haverkort, B.R.: Survivability evaluation of fluid critical infrastructure using hybrid Petri nets. In: 19th IEEE Int'l. Symposium PRDC (2013)
7. Gribaudo, M., Remke, A.: Hybrid Petri nets with general one-shot transitions: model evolution. Technical report, University of Twente (2012), http://130.89.10.12/~anne/pub/tecrep.pdf
8. van Heesch, D.: Doxygen (2001), http://www.stack.nl/~dimitri/doxygen/
9. Postema, B.F.: Fluid Survival Tool: A model checker for Hybrid Petri nets. MSc thesis, Department of Computer Science, University of Twente (2013)

DelayLyzer: A Tool for Analyzing Delay Bounds in Industrial Ethernet Networks[*]

Mark Schmidt[1], Sebastian Veith[1], Michael Menth[1], and Stephan Kehrer[2]

[1] University of Tuebingen, Chair of Communication Networks, Tuebingen, Germany
[2] Hirschmann Automation and Control GmbH, Neckartenzlingen, Germany

Abstract. In this paper, we present the DelayLyzer which is a tool for the calculation of delay bounds using network calculus. It respects the specifics of Industrial Ethernet by implementing not only STP and RSTP but also MRP as forwarding mechanism. The tool allows to specify failure scenarios and alternate forwarding protocols for which delay bounds can also be computed.

1 Introduction

Industrial Ethernet is used for factory automation and other mission critical applications. It excels through the robustness and durability of its devices, as well as the implementation of special protocols, e.g. for failure protection. While conventional Ethernet implements the Spanning Tree Protocol (STP) or Rapid STP (RSTP) as forwarding and rerouting mechanism [6], Industrial Ethernet frequently relies on ring structures and the Media Redundancy Protocol (MRP) to protect failures [5]. Since Industrial Ethernet is often deployed for real-time applications, it is important to show a priori that maximum delay bounds will not be exceeded when the network is fed with a certain traffic pattern.

This paper describes the DelayLyzer, which is a tool for the calculation of delay bounds in Industrial Ethernet networks based on network calculus. It supports forwarding mechanisms that are specific to Industrial Ethernet like MRP. In addition, the tool allows to specify failure scenarios, calculates backup paths according to the implemented forwarding and protection protocols, and recomputes the delay bounds for these failure cases. Likewise, alternative forwarding protocols can be easily investigated. Thus, the DelayLyzer supports planning of Industrial Ethernet networks for challenging conditions.

Section 2 gives a brief overview of network calculus which is the theoretical base of the tool. Section 3 describes the graphical user interface of the tool, the internal data and its visualization, how use cases may be analyzed, and how results are displayed.

2 Network Calculus

We first explain basics about how network calculus computes performance metrics for a single link, and then we clarify how this method can be applied to an entire network.

---

[*] This work was funded by Hirschmann Automation and Control GmbH. The authors alone are responsible for the content of the paper.

K. Fischbach and U.R. Krieger (Eds.): MMB & DFT 2014, LNCS 8376, pp. 260–263, 2014.

Network Calculus Applied to a Single Link. Network calculus is a mathematical framework developed by Cruz [3, 4], Chang [2] and Le Boudec [7] to determine delay bounds in networks. Network calculus models the maximum amount of data delivered by a flow to a link or a node by a rate-burst curve. This is essentially a token-bucket limited description of a flow's traffic. The general case of such an arrival curve is a piece-wise linear function of time. In a similar way, the delay added by the processing in links and nodes can be expressed by a rate-latency curve, the so-called service curve. Network calculus provides operations on curves that eventually facilitate the computation of maximum delay and backlog on a link. In addition, an output bound can be calculated to characterize the timely behavior of the flow after having passed the considered network element. The approach is scientifically backed by an algebraic theory.

Network Calculus Applied to a Network. To extend network calculus from a single link to a network, essentially the output bound of a flow from a predecessor link is taken as arrival curve for the next link. Schmitt and Zdarsky developed algorithms to calculate the maximum delay for a flow when traversing a series of nodes and links in a feed-forward network [10, 12]. They proposed two simple variants: Total Flow Analysis (TFA) and Separated Flow Analysis (SFA). In addition, other authors proposed more complex algorithms leading to tighter delay bounds [8, 9, 11, 1].

Forwarding and protection mechanisms in Ethernet networks are simple and lead to feed-forward networks so that network calculus can be used for the computation of delay bounds in that context. We developed variants of TFA and SFA as well as a combination thereof (mTFA) and implemented them in our tool.

3   Tool Description

The DelayLyzer calculates upper bounds for flow delays in specified use cases. To that end, a description of the network, of the flows, and of the path layout of the flows are required. The path layout is determined by the network, the set of failed network elements, and the applied forwarding protocols. In the following we explain the graphical user interface of the DelayLyzer, the components of a use case, how failures may be specified and how the path layout of flows are computed, how a delay analysis can be performed, and how results are provided.

Graphical User Interface. Figure 1 illustrates a screenshot of the DelayLyzer for the use case "Substation". The menu bar of the main window allows to load existing use cases from file (Load), to create new use cases from scratch (New), and to exit the application (Exit). Several use cases may be open simultaneously which can be chosen from the drop-down menu "Use Cases". Each use case has its own internal window. The drop-down menu "File" in the menu bar of the use case window allows storing and closing a use case.

Specification of Use Cases. A use case comprises a network consisting of nodes, links, subnetworks, and flows. Details about them are available in the tabs in the

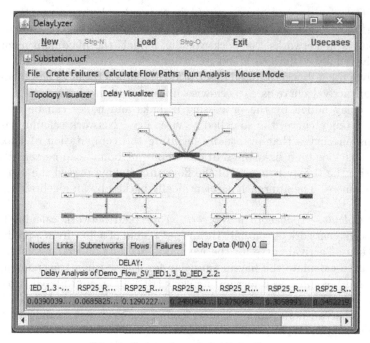

Fig. 1. Screenshot of the DelayLyzer

lower part of a use case window. They indicate, e.g., performance and configuration data of links and nodes, the set of nodes and links belonging to subnetworks together with the applied forwarding protocols, and the source and destination node for each flow as well as its maximum burst size and rate.

The tool provides features to specify use cases and to store them in the "use case format" (ucf). It is also able to read the data from ucf-files and from the format of Hirschmann's HiVision tool. Although HiVision data contain only a subset of the ucf information, they are useful to import basic data of existing use cases.

The upper part of the use case window holds the "Topology Visualizer" tab which displays the network topology based on the use case information. When nodes, links, and flows are selected in the respective tabs, they are highlighted in the "Topology Visualizer". The path of a flow can be shown only after the calculation of its layout.

Specification of Failures and Computation of Path Layout of Flows. The tab "Failures" provides a choice of failure scenarios and allows selection. The choice contains by default only the failure-free scenario but may be enlarged by the drop-down menu "Create Failures". The "Topology Visualizer" tab shows the topology for the selected failure scenario and also the delay analysis will performed only for the selected failure scenario.

The delay analysis requires the path layout of all flows. The drop-down menu "Compute Path Layout" allows to compute this path layout, which is done based on the use case information. Other entries in the drop-down menu "Compute

Path layout" support changing the forwarding protocols in subnetworks. After a successful change, the path layout needs to be recomputed.

Delay Analysis and Results. The drop-down menu "Run Analysis" provides a choice of different algorithms (TFA, SFA, mTFA) for delay analysis which may be performed upon selection. As soon as an analysis is completed, a "Delay Visualizer" tab and a "Delay Data" tab appear in the upper and lower part of the use case window. The "Delay Data" tab indicates the maximum delay for each flow after each hop as well as its maximum overall delay. A flow in the "Delay Data" tab may be selected; then the "Delay Visualizer" highlights the path of that flow within the topology. Each flow is associated with an allowed delay budget. Appropriate colors from green to red indicate in the "Delay Data" and the "Delay Visualizer" how much of that budget is already spent from the source of a flow up to each intermediate hop and its destination. This feature facilitates the interpretation of the numerical results.

Investigations have shown that the upper bound for the delay of a flow, that is not affected by a failure, may be longer or shorter in failure scenarios compared to the failure-free scenario. It is longer if additional flows share the paths of that flow, but it may be shorter if fewer flows share its path since some network elements have failed. Likewise, flows redirected to other paths may have shorter or longer delay bounds.

References

1. Bouillard, A., Jouhet, L., Thierry, E.: Tight Performance Bounds in the Worst-Case Analysis of Feed-Forward Networks. In: IEEE Infocom (March 2010)
2. Chang, C.S.: Performance Guarantees in Communications Networks. Springer
3. Cruz, R.L.: A Calculus for Network Delay, Part I: Network Elements in Isolation. IEEE Transactions on Information Theory 37(1), 114–131 (1991)
4. Cruz, R.L.: A Calculus for Network Delay, Part II: Network Analysis. IEEE Transactions on Information Theory 37(1), 132–141 (1991)
5. IEC: IEC 62439-2: Industrial communication networks - High availability automation networks - Part 2: Media Redundancy Protocol (MRP) (2010)
6. IEEE: IEEE 802.1D: IEEE Standard for Local and metropolitan area networks: Media Access Control (MAC) Bridges (2004)
7. Le Boudec, J.Y., Thiran, P.: Network Calculus. Springer (2004)
8. Lenzini, L., Martorini, L., Stea, G.: Tight End-to-End per-Flow Delay Bounds in FIFO Multiplexing Sink-Tree Networks. Performance Evaluation 63(9) (October 2006)
9. Lenzini, L., Mingozzi, E., Stea, G.: A Methodology for Computing End-to-End Delay Bounds in FIFO-Multiplexing Tandems. Performance Evaluation 65(11-12)
10. Schmitt, J.B., Zdarsky, F.A.: The DISCO Network Calculator – A Toolbox for Worst Case Analysis. In: VALUETOOLS (2006)
11. Schmitt, J.B., Zdarsky, F.A., Fidler, M.: Delay Bounds under Arbitrary Multiplexing: When Network Calculus Leaves You in the Lurch... In: IEEE Infocom
12. Schmitt, J.B., Zdarsky, F.A., Martinovic, I.: Performance Bounds in Feed-Forward Networks under Blind Multiplexing. Tech. rep., University of Kaiserslautern

Author Index

Printed in the United States
By Bookmasters